The voices in this book are prophetic and paramount in making a clarion call to the global Christian church to be ambassadors of Christ's reconciliation and to boldly act justly, love mercy, and walk humbly in serving people to the end of the earth.

Mary Alice Trent, PhD
Professor of English,
Indiana Wesleyan University, Marion, Indiana, USA

In view of the worldwide events in our turbulent time, this book offers readers invaluable insight and understanding of resilience in integral mission of the global church. These multiple voices provide refreshing and compelling ways, in both theory and praxis, to embrace and embody the transforming power of the whole gospel for the whole creation.

Xiaoli Yang, PhD
Research Scholar, University of Divinity,
Charles Sturt University, Bathurst, Australia

This book is an exceptional resource in the way it brings to light under-represented issues in the academy and the church today. In the Middle East the implications of issues around poverty, injustice and conflict are often underestimated or overlooked. The global perspectives in this resource are like "a cry in the wilderness" to every listening ear. Every page throbs with resilience. It is sweeping, challenging, inspiring and applicable!

Grace Al-Zoughbi
Lecturer in Biblical Studies,
Bethlehem Bible College, Palestine

This book is about resilient communities, and resilience may be a word that is more *en vogue* lately, but it is as old as humanity's first couple and God's care for them after disaster struck. Resilience is not external to who we are as God's people but is part of the fabric of our being and acting in the world as Christians are enabled by the Spirit to be light and salt even in the most tragic contexts. This extensive volume looks at the multifaceted ways communities have reflected upon their engagement with the world and the biblical-theological bases that frame the church's mission. This is a book that will engage seminary students, pastors, community leaders and activists alike, with thought-provoking essays and challenging questions for how best we are to live as followers of Christ in our many different ways and places.

C. Rosalee Velloso Ewell, PhD
Principal,
Redcliffe College, Gloucester, UK
Executive Director,
Theological Commission, World Evangelical Alliance

Relentless Love may be the clearest indication to date that a revolution in Christian mission is already underway. Through a diverse collection of voices, this compelling volume reveals new ways of being church that are emerging from the Majority World and are fueled by a shalomic imagination for the common good. This book is a vital guide for operationalizing the love of God as the love of neighbor, while equipping us to appreciate that love of neighbor always invites love of neighborhood.

Dwight J. Friesen, DMin
Associate Professor of Practical Theology,
The Seattle School of Theology and Psychology, Washington, USA

The 7th Micah Global Consultation called for a renewal of faith and energy in the face of global scandals – poverty, injustice, and conflict. The authors in this volume meet that challenge resoundingly. In these chapters you will find the biblical, theological, and spiritual reimagining that defines personal and collective resilience in the face of these contemporary realities. With heavy hearts, yet renewed energy and continued resolve, this book encourages us to say "No!" to injustice and "Yes!" to God's shalom!

Rev Darrell Jackson, DTh
Associate Professor and Director of Research,
Whitley College, University of Divinity, Melbourne, Australia

As the contributors to this volume point out, integral mission is intuitively practiced in Africa, Asia, Latin America, and Oceania, where 67 percent of all Christians now live. Compared to what has been a largely Western enterprise, these community-based cultures offer solutions to human problems from a fundamentally different perspective. This book presents a starting point for a new global Christian approach; as opposed to a Western theoretical framework that artificially separates evangelism and social justice, this new approach coheres the whole message and story of the Bible, fostering community resilience and redressing injustice at its roots. And, as a bonus, some contributors wisely contend for greater representation for women in every level of leadership – after all, women do most of the work.

Todd M. Johnson, PhD
Eva B. and Paul E. Toms Distinguished Professor of
Mission and Global Christianity,
Gordon-Conwell Theological Seminary, Hamilton, Massachusetts, USA

This book is a rich distillation of twenty-first-century practitioner-wisdom; contextually relevant and laced with enduring biblical and theological insight. A recommended read for those thirsty for transformation.

Carol Kingston-Smith
MA Tutor,
ForMission College, Birmingham, UK
Co-founder, "the jusTice initiative"

The biggest challenge which evangelical mission theology faces today is the augmentation of the integral mission concept. This is an inevitable missional request, and the COVID-19 situation will accelerate this request. I highly recommend this book as the most appropriate resource to respond to these current needs.

Hyun Mo (Tim) Lee, PhD
Professor of Missions,
Korea Baptist Theological University and Seminary, Daejeon, South Korea
Chair, Missions and Evangelism Committee,
Asia Pacific Baptist Federation

It is incredibly exciting to see a book on integral mission from authors around the world, reflecting on mission and resilience in their various contexts! I know of no book comparable to this, and I particularly appreciate the contributions from Africa, because evangelical reflections on mission by leaders here are much needed.

Stephanie A. Lowery, PhD
Lecturer in Theology,
Africa International University, Nairobi, Kenya

This book presents distinctive theological and biblical features of contextual development. Each study is based on a specific theme close to the social and cultural context of the contributor. The list of the contributors reveal a heavy emphasis on Majority World scholars and on the diversity of church traditions. The authors make a remarkable connection between the theology process and the real-life experience of God's people. This collective contextual theology, however, is also pertinent to the global church. Furthermore, the book succeeds in being both biblically truthful and culturally applicable, emphasizing that the word of God is for the whole of humanity throughout its entire history and various cultures. Each author represents contemporary rationale among an extensive selection of traditional academics. The book will inspire and challenge local and global church leaders and theologians.

Julie C. Ma, PhD
Professor of Missions and Intercultural Studies,
Oral Roberts University, Tulsa, Oklahoma, USA

Graham Joseph Hill is a foremost leader in bringing critical conversations and theological reflection from the Majority World to the forefront for the edification of the church worldwide. In this great work, Hill brings leading global voices together around the essential topic of resilience and compassionate Christian witness. The depth and timeliness of this book and its importance in integral mission cannot be overstated.

Lisa Rodriguez-Watson
National Director, Missio Alliance

Relentless Love provides holistic hope in these challenging days. This collection brings together a wide range of profound reflective practitioners whose combined voice helps us better understand how to present the face of Christ with resilience, spirituality, compassion, and reconciliation. Thank you to Micah Global for its rich biblical challenge to act justly, love mercy, and to walk humbly with our God.

Perry Shaw, EdD
Former Professor of Christian Education,
Arab Baptist Theological Seminary, Beirut, Lebanon

Let's just admit it: bearing witness to the whole gospel among the last, the least, and the lost in the world is exhausting. How do we counter the onset of what can be called integral mission fatigue? Many of us have come to rely on Micah Global to inspire, encourage, and buoy us in the work. This volume, which brings together select voices from the last consultation held in the Philippines, calls us with one voice to resilience in the Spirit, not only to sustain ourselves, but to flourish in our service to the world's most vulnerable.

Al Tizon, PhD
Executive Minister, Serve Globally, Evangelical Covenant Church
Affiliate Associate Professor, Missional and Global Leadership,
North Park Theological Seminary, Chicago, Illinois, USA

Relentless Love

Relentless Love

Living Out Integral Mission to Combat Poverty, Injustice, and Conflict

Edited by

Graham Joseph Hill

© 2020 Micah Global

Published 2020 by Langham Global Library
An imprint of Langham Publishing
www.langhampublishing.org

Langham Publishing and its imprints are a ministry of Langham Partnership

Langham Partnership
PO Box 296, Carlisle, Cumbria, CA3 9WZ, UK
www.langham.org

Published in partnership with Micah Global

Micah Global
www.micahglobal.org

ISBNs:
978-1-83973-037-5 Print
978-1-83973-038-2 ePub
978-1-83973-039-9 Mobi
978-1-83973-040-5 PDF

Graham Joseph Hill hereby asserts his moral right to be identified as the Author of the General Editor's part in the Work in accordance with sections 77 and 78 of the Copyright, Designs and Patents Act 1988.

All rights reserved. No part of this publication may be reproduced, stored in a retrieval system or transmitted, in any form or by any means, electronic, mechanical, photocopying, recording or otherwise, without the prior written permission of the publisher or the Copyright Licensing Agency.

Requests to reuse content from Langham Publishing are processed through PLSclear. Please visit www.plsclear.com to complete your request.

Unless otherwise indicated, Scriptures taken from the Holy Bible, New International Version®, NIV®. Copyright © 1973, 1978, 1984, 2011 by Biblica, Inc.™ Used by permission of Zondervan.

Scripture quotations marked (NRSV) are from the New Revised Standard Version Bible, copyright © 1989 National Council of the Churches of Christ in the United States of America. Used by permission. All rights reserved.

Scripture quotations marked (ESV) are from The Holy Bible, English Standard Version® (ESV®), copyright © 2001 by Crossway, a publishing ministry of Good News Publishers. Used by permission. All rights reserved.

Scripture quotations marked (NLT) are taken from the Holy Bible, New Living Translation, copyright © 1996, 2004, 2007, 2013, 2015 by Tyndale House Foundation. Used by permission of Tyndale House Publishers, Inc., Carol Stream, Illinois 60188. All rights reserved.

British Library Cataloguing-in-Publication Data
A catalogue record for this book is available from the British Library

ISBN: 978-1-83973-037-5

Cover & Book Design: projectluz.com

Langham Partnership actively supports theological dialogue and an author's right to publish but does not necessarily endorse the views and opinions set forth here or in works referenced within this publication, nor can we guarantee technical and grammatical correctness. Langham Partnership does not accept any responsibility or liability to persons or property as a consequence of the reading, use or interpretation of its published content.

For C. René Padilla

Contents

Foreword xvii
    Melba Padilla Maggay

Preface: Micah Global 7th Triennial Consultation xxv
    Integral Mission and Resilient Communities Addressing
    Poverty, Injustice, and Conflict
    Sheryl Haw

1 *Misión Integral*.. 1
    The Challenge of World Christianity
    Graham Joseph Hill

Part 1: Resilience, the Church, and Integral Mission

2 Resilience and Integral Mission 19
    David Boan

3 Righteousness, Suffering and Participation in Philippians 3:7–11 ... 29
    Integral Mission and Paul's Gospel
    Andrew Steere

4 Dangerous Resilience? 41
    The Institutional Church and Its Systemic Resistance to Change
    Thandi Gamedze

5 Poorology.. 51
    Getting the Seminary into the Slum
    Viv Grigg

6 How Do Missionaries Become Resilient? 65
    Preliminary Findings from the Resilient Missionary Study
    *Geoff Whiteman, Emily Edwards, Anna Savelle, and
    Kristina Whiteman*

7 The Gospel and the Future of Cities. 77
    A Call to Action
    Participants of the Gospel and Future of Cities Summit

Part 2: Resilience, Peace, and Justice

8   Biblical Teachings on Social Justice 93
      Manavala Reuben

9   Addressing Gender and Leadership Gaps in Development-Oriented Organizations 101
      Amy Reynolds and Nikki Toyama-Szeto

10   Deeper Understanding for More Resilience in the Work for Peace and Justice 115
      Vilma "Nina" Balmaceda

11   God's Preference for the Poor 125
      The Bible and Social Justice in Ireland
      Patrick Mitchel

12   Worship and Justice 143
      Spirituality that Embodies and Mobilizes for Justice
      Sandra Maria Van Opstal

13   Proclamation and Demonstration 157
      CB Samuel

14   What Is Required? 167
      Florence Muindi

15   Beyond Compassion to Solidarity 175
      Peter McVerry

Part 3: Resilience, Spirituality, and Compassion

16   "My God, My God, Why Have You Forsaken Me?" 189
      The Necessity of Lament for Spiritual Resilience in Contexts of Poverty and Injustice
      Clinton Bergsma

17   Building Resilient Communities 203
      The Importance of Integrating Mental Health and Well-Being in Effective Development Thinking and Practice
      Becca Allchin, Stephanie Cantrill, and Helen Fernandes

18   Indigenous Voices 219
      The Spiritual Strength of the Peoples of Abya Yala
      Jocabed Reina Solano Miselis

19 The Gospel and Resilience in the Pursuit of the Common Good . . . 223
    D. Zac Niringiye

20 Against All Odds – and Ends 231
    Ruth Padilla DeBorst

21 Resilience and Disaster and the Church's Response 239
    Johannes Reimer

Part 4: Resilience, Mobilization, and Partnerships

22 Building Resilience with Local Churches and Communities 245
    Jané Mackenzie, Chris McDonald, Stanley Enock, and Mari Williams

23 Church and Community Mobilization in Cooperation to Build
    Resilient Communities in South East Asia 261
    *Fennelien Stal, Debora Suparni, Arshinta Soemarsono, and
    Norman Franklin C. Agustin*

24 Lessons from the Frontline of Global Movement-Building 277
    Reflections from Three Years of Tearfund's Restorative
    Economy Approach
    Naomi Foxwood, Richard Gower, Helen Heather, and Sue Willsher

25 North and South 293
    Boureima Diallo

Part 5: Summaries from the Six Consultation Tracks

26 "Church and Community Resilience" Consultation Track 301
    The Church at the Heart of the Resilient Community
    David Boan

27 "Church and Corruption" Consultation Track 305
    Martin Allaby

28 "Formation for Integral Mission (Discipleship)"
    Consultation Track 307
    Tori Greaves and Ruth Padilla DeBorst, INFEMIT

29 "Urban Shalom" Consultation Track 313
    Joel Kelling and Fiona Kelling

30 "Reconciliation as the Mission of the Church"
    Consultation Track 319
    Johannes Reimer

31 "Integral Mission and Community Health" Consultation Track....323
   James Pender, Jim Oehrig, and Sara Kandiah

32 Final Remarks...333
   Integral Mission and Community Resilience
   Sheryl Haw

Bibliography 337
About Micah Global..351
List of Contributors 353

Foreword

Almost half a century ago, a seismic change in evangelicalism's theological paradigms began. It was articulated in its incipient form in the 1974 Lausanne Covenant and encapsulated more comprehensively in the term "integral mission" as defined by the Micah Network Declaration in 2001. Since then, the borders of the theology and practice of integral mission (IM) have been stretched and expanded by practitioners out in the trenches, theologizing on their feet from out of the dust and heat of battles waged in the streets, in slum communities, in marketplaces, in moribund seminaries, and in corridors of power.

This book is in a way a marker in the journey towards a more holistic understanding of the gospel and what societies can be like when we take more seriously the fact that the *missio Dei* – what God is doing in the world – is nothing less than the making of "a new heaven and a new earth."

The focus on "resilience" – the theme of the seventh world assembly of Micah Global held in the Philippines – suggests that we have come to a juncture in this movement where fatigue is setting in and we need to return to the spiritual resources of our faith, even as we explore new paths of social and missional engagement and being "church" in the doing of it.

The first three parts of the book – resilience as it relates to the church and IM, peace and justice, and spirituality and compassion – are efforts to make theological sense of the concerns and issues that have surfaced in the course of our praxis in "proclaiming and demonstrating" the whole gospel. The rest of the book is distillations of research on mass mobilization and practical approaches to partnerships with churches and local communities. The closing part of the book reports the insights of various group consultations on such topics as building resilient communities, bringing shalom in the city, the church and corruption, reconciliation and healing the trauma of conflict, and community health.

Let me zero in and comment on the theological significance of this book as it reflects on our work of being "the church among the poor."

The first part tries to connect the institution we know as "church" to the task of increasing resilience.

This section has two chapters reporting research that shows that at the heart of resilience is healthy relationships, both in the recovery of communities in disaster situations and in sustaining missionaries in the field. The good news is that the church is uniquely positioned to heal the walking wounded among us because of its relationship networks – its social capital, if you like – that enable it to pull together resources and succour immediately and compassionately the communities that surround it.

There is a bit of bad news in this, however. Thandiwe Sarah Gamedze raises the phenomenon of churches having a kind of "dangerous resilience," perpetuating rigid leadership and governance structures and a "received Christology" that holds Christians in Africa and elsewhere captive and unable to "name Christ for themselves."

Adding to this note of dissonance is the hermeneutical challenge to the way the gospel and its salvific meaning has been reduced to merely securing a ticket to heaven. Andrew Steere makes the case that Pauline letters such as Galatians have been misread as a conflict between the law and grace. Quoting J. D. G. Dunn, he argues that the Second Temple Jews – Jesus's contemporaries – viewed the giving of the law "not as a means to gain righteousness, but as a means of living righteously."

The chapter is a theological corrective to evangelicalism's undue fixation on "assurance of salvation." It is good to be reminded that the Reformers' theme of "*sola fide, sola gratia*" is actually a sixteenth-century reading, a contextual appropriation driven by the "introspective conscience of the West" as previously articulated by Krister Stendahl. What originally was Paul's response to the Jew–Gentile social crisis was read by the likes of the monk Martin Luther as an assurance that he was saved apart from "works of the law." Earnestly desiring certainty and freedom from the burdens of penance, Luther located his sense of the good news in "justification by faith," a theme that was to shape Protestantism in the face of excessive accretions to the law and church tradition as defined by medieval Catholicism.

The second part groups together peace and justice concerns, and underscores the need for resilience in seeking shalom and the righting of wrongs.

The authors Amy Reynolds and Nikki Toyama-Szeto point out the irony of faith-based development organizations attending to the cause of women and girls in their educational or anti-violence programmes, yet neglecting to address gender dynamics and gaps in their leadership as organizations.

The chapters on justice by Manavala Reuben and Vilma Balmaceda put forward the biblical teaching that justice and shalom, the "righting of wrongs" and "right relationships," must go together. Balmaceda observes that the Old Testament "shalom," often understood as merely a personal "separate peace," also means "restitution" or "reparation"; it has the effect of "fulfilling a contract," which leads to relationships restored.

The nineteenth-century religious conflicts in Ireland form the historical backdrop to Patrick Mitchel's analysis of the theology that frames the social engagement of the Catholic Trócaire and of Tearfund Ireland. Trócaire's praxis has for its motive force Vatican II and Catholic Social Teaching on such themes as human dignity, option for the poor, and the common good. These are backgrounded, however, by the secular narrative of "rights-based" development, perhaps as a reaction to the "Bible wars of the 1820s." Tearfund sources its foundational beliefs more directly from the Bible and fairly recent theologizing on what is now known as "integral mission." Both agencies share a similar concern for the poor and depart from the "souperism" of an earlier era, which tended to use charity as a means to an end – the end being to disseminate and safeguard the faith and not really to combat social inequality or reform society. We still find traces of this pragmatism in current evangelical efforts to serve the poor.

The Irish context of immense wealth, and even social compassion, side by side with massive homelessness also serves as a disturbing backdrop to Peter McVerry's moving stories of accompanying homeless people with horrific childhoods. Mostly young people, they usually turn to drugs or alcohol in the effort to forget the trauma of abuse. We must, he says, move beyond compassion to solidarity. In compassion you get to pick and choose who to help and how: "people might give big cheques to a homeless charity at Christmas, but if there is any attempt to open a shelter for homeless people in their neighbourhood, they could be the first out picketing to prevent it." "In *solidarity* I do not decide who I will be compassionate towards . . . I don't decide that this person is deserving and that person not deserving – it is their pain that causes me to reach out to them."

This "solidarity in suffering" is a necessary rite of passage for those of us who are called to bear the marks of what it took Jesus to sacrifice for others. Some of us may have romantic notions about living in the slums or forsaking careers to battle evil forces in high places. Florence Muindi holds up the cost of this kind of self-emptying, and the need for readiness to get battle-scarred as we soldier on: "The kingdom of God is taken by violence," she warns, "and we have to seek it by addressing that warfare."

It is perhaps in worship, the kind that truly brings us face to face with a compassionate and holy God, that we find the collective strength to stand up to the powers. Sandra Maria Van Opstal makes a case for worship leaders to become not merely musicians, but "pastors, prophets, or guides who lead people where they need to go instead of where they want to go."

The third part explores the relationship of spirituality and compassion to resilience.

What do we do when we are face to face with situations where God seems to be inexplicably absent? Clinton Bergsma restores to our radar screen a resource that the psalmists relied on in ancient times when utter darkness descended: lamentation. "Poverty naturally raises questions of theodicy, and lament offers itself as a powerful and appropriate process for maintaining spiritual resilience in situations of injustice and poverty." He quotes the Old Testament scholar Walter Brueggemann thus: "A community of faith that negates lament soon concludes that the hard issues of justice are improper questions to pose at the throne [of God], because the throne seems to be only a place of praise . . . [and they] are left with only grim obedience and eventually despair. The point of access for serious change has been forfeited when the propriety of this speech form is denied."

Communities that suffer devastating disasters, or individuals exposed to prolonged grief and suffering, usually go through what sociologists call "disabling perplexities." They are unable to move forward from out of their emotional and psychological trauma, rendered powerless by mental discomposure. I have seen this happen in Tacloban, Leyte, hard hit by Typhoon Haiyan, the biggest in history to make landfall. Survivors walked around like zombies, as with the story of a woman in a white bridal gown salvaged from among relief goods, who trudged around shoeless, scrounging for food from out of the ruins.

Becca Allchin, Stephanie Cantrill, and Helen Fernandes provide evidence, based on research and community-building experiences, that integrating mental health in development processes is critical to building resilient communities.

Similarly, it is possible that the loneliness of atomized individuals in modern or postmodern societies may be healed by going back to the communal life that now survives mostly among indigenous peoples. Jocabed Reina Solano Miselis tells us that listening to indigenous voices offers an integral vision of community, for it is a sensibility that is acutely aware of the interrelatedness and interdependence of all living beings in the social and cosmic environment. It makes the encounter with different cultures a place not of strangeness, but of conviviality, coexistence, and a sense of plurality.

Zac Niringiye pointedly asks the question, "Why don't we Christians pursue the common good?" He notes how preoccupied we are with self-protection, with preserving our wealth and well-being. "So, when we enter public space, we are contesting for our space, our views, and not the views of the other." In place of the abstractions of systematic theology, he enjoins a return to Story, to the oral narratives of his people where one could find traces of grace, and to the story of the gospel itself: "there is no doubt that not only is the gospel story the common good, but in the gospel there is the common good. We can boldly enter the public square to commend what the gospel teaches about the common good."

And so, like Jesus of Nazareth, we go about doing good like all earnest disciples. But as Ruth Padilla DeBorst reminds us, it is easy to turn our do-gooding into a messianic task, as if we bear the weight of the world upon our shoulders. Overwhelmed by the immensity of the needs around us, we grow tired and lose sight of the big picture, the fact that what God is doing is so much bigger than the success or failure of our mission enterprises. Drawing insights from the example of Mother Teresa and Bishop Óscar Romero, she holds up three things that will renew our work: expanding our sense of identity from the limited "us" to a communal identity that includes even "them"; enlarging our vision of what can be done even with our "five loaves and two fish," seeing the unseen potential of what is small, personal, and local; and knowing that while we live within limits, as creatures of time and circumstance, the drama of God's purposes and activity in the world is beyond us and will last and outlive us.

There is, within the Micah fellowship itself, an undercurrent of debate on the role of the institution we call "church." Brothers and sisters in the Majority World have raised concerns about transplanted churches whose organizational and theological ethos is mostly made in the image of churches from the "imperial West." Against this critique of the church is Johannes Reimer's ringing declaration: "Without the church, the world turns dark, because the light is gone. The world without a church is less fruitful, because salt is not available, and, as a result, God the Father is not praised (Matt 5:13–16)."[1]

From where I sit, when the church is truly church it serves as the social context in which the saving power and love of God are made visible. Historically, it has been the institution used by God to save the lost and serve the community in which it is located. But to insist that the church is the only agent of God's kingdom work is to truncate the gospel and is sociologically naïve.

The church is primarily tasked with the preaching of the Word and the equipping of God's people for the work of ministry out in the world. This is its institutional mandate; it is not primarily to "serve tables," as Peter put it, lest,

---

1. See chapter 21 of this book.

like liberal churches, we neglect the spiritual needs of our people and simply become a social welfare agency.

Inevitably, as churches grow and societies get more complex, we will need to invent new structures – new wineskins, if you like, which will contain the new wine that God is growing. Part of the paradox of our faith is that the gospel is always new wine; it is always doing new things, for that is what Jesus is doing: "Behold, I make all things new." But the wineskins are always getting old and soon become obsolete. There is a time for reinventing, even retiring, things we have always associated with "the things of God" – be it the Anglican Prayer Book, the King James Bible, or the usual charity institutions that have arisen since the social crisis over the neglect of Hellenistic widows in Acts 6. In our time, in the effort to find new ways of being "church" in the contemporary world, faith-based NGOs have mushroomed, bearing witness that Jesus is "good news for the poor."

The kingdom – the reign of God – is to be made visible not just in the church but in all other structures of society. The kingdom is bigger than the church, and "church" as an institution does not exhaust the meaning of the visible church.

The *ecclesia visibilis* is not just the church at worship, but the church in the marketplace, in media and the arts, in academe, or in politics. This is the church *scattered*, as distinct from the church *gathered*, in the language of the late John R. W. Stott.

The chapters of this book are explorations from a variety of starting points – moving pictures and narratives mostly coming out of contexts glossed over and unlistened to, at least by dominant theological traditions. It is in this way that Micah serves as a significant catalyst to the growth of the global church: it is a space where the tired soldiers of Christ can rest and have their wounds tended, and their doubts and theological perplexities not so much resolved as attended to and corporately lamented.

Ruth Padilla DeBorst, at the close of her chapter, ferrets out from the treasure trove of Latin America's struggles these words attributed to Bishop Romero:

> The kingdom is not only beyond our efforts – it is even beyond our vision.
> We accomplish in our lifetime only a tiny fraction of the magnificent enterprise that is God's work.
> Nothing we do is complete, which is a way of saying that the kingdom always lies beyond us . . .

We may never see the end results,
but that is the difference between the master builder and the worker.
We are workers, not master builders;
ministers, not messiahs.
We are prophets of a future not our own.

May this prayer renew our faith and make our hearts sufficiently strong and resilient as together we work for God's vision of a just and gentle world as a global community.

Melba Padilla Maggay, PhD
President, Micah Global

Preface

Micah Global 7th Triennial Consultation

Integral Mission and Resilient Communities Addressing Poverty, Injustice, and Conflict

Sheryl Haw

Every three years Micah facilitates a Global Consultation, inviting Christian ministries to come together and work through the issues and concerns currently being faced around the world under an overarching theme that resonates with our vision and mission. It is an inspiring week that demonstrates the oneness we have in Christ that bridges geographical, cultural, language, and denominational divides, uniting us around our shared passion for integral mission. We learn together, and challenge one another on how to:

- Effectively respond to the scandal of poverty, injustice, and conflict in such a way that God's shalom is evident in word, deed, and signs.
- Discern theologically and practically together to speak and act with prophetic authority so as to disciple our nations and hold leaders to account for their responsibilities for the flourishing of humanity and all of creation.
- Walk together in humility, serving one another, as we seek to enable the local church to be an agent of change in each community.

The theme for our September 2018 triennial built on the previous triennial themes (see table), as we explored our understanding of integral mission and community resilience.

Micah Triennials

No.	Global Consultation	Location
1st	Integral Mission September 2001	Oxford, UK
2nd	Globalization and the Poor September 2003	Queretaro, Mexico
3rd	Integral Mission in a World of Conflict September 2006	Chiang Mai, Thailand
4th	Creation Stewardship and Climate Change July 2009	Limuru, Kenya
5th	Integral Mission and the Community: Local Church, Local Change, Global Impact September 2012	Thun, Switzerland
6th	Integral Mission and Shalom: Justice, Peace, and Joy September 2015	Lima, Peru
7th	Integral Mission and Resilient Communities: Addressing Poverty, Injustice, and Conflict September 2018	Manila, Philippines

Integral Mission

The word "integral" means "wholeness," signifying complete and essential components that are necessary for the functioning of the whole.

This term "wholeness" was expressed in the Lausanne Covenant back in 1974: "Evangelisation requires the whole church to take the whole gospel to the whole world." Why did the writers insist on using the word "whole"? Perhaps they did not want *anything* or *anyone* to be left out. In other words:

Whole church: This includes every single believer – all are called, and all are sent. If we don't have a clear biblical understanding of what the church is, and what is meant by "church," we will start to compartmentalize. Our understanding of church is therefore critical: we need an integral or whole understanding. Our M Series booklet *Rethinking Church* seeks to address this important question. Church is not simply a mechanism commissioned to a task (God's mission), but it is also the fruit, the impact, and the outcome of the gospel. If we are unhappy with what we see as church today (what it looks like, acts like, and speaks like), then we have to acknowledge that the gospel message that birthed the church has not been whole! This is an outrageous statement. We often say in Micah that the biggest hurdle we face in sharing the gospel today is that people calling themselves Christians are not living it out, hence the world gets a wrong impression about Christianity. Similarly, when the church does not reflect Christ, we get the wrong impression of what the church is meant to be.

Whole gospel: This means the whole Bible (Old and New Testament), the whole revelation of God, and we cannot talk of the gospel without recognizing the centrality of Christ and the cross. Indeed, the gospel, the good news, is the power to bring justice, healing, redemption, reconciliation, restoration, and transformation – life in all its fullness (everything that we long for and work for in Micah). We therefore say that integral mission has to flow from our being in Christ.

We have found that one of the concerning weaknesses in practitioners today is that they are biblically illiterate. We "cherry pick" verses from the Bible but don't engage with the whole story of God's mission. This limits our capacity to respond to all the questions, hurts, and challenges of the world today. Our M Series booklet entitled *Living in God's Story* shows that an understanding of our identity and purpose in God's overarching story is critical to fulfilling our calling. The scope of God's mission and hence our mission is revealed and summed up well in Colossians 1:20: "to reconcile to [God] *all things*, whether things on earth or things in heaven, by making peace through [Jesus's] blood shed on the cross" (emphasis added).

Whole world (creation): This includes every aspect of God's creation – geographical, chronological, humanity, and all living things, all things visible and invisible, in heaven and on earth. Everything is included in God's redemptive mission. We need to see God's mission in much broader terms than that which we sometimes narrowly focus on, which has tended to be a human-centric mission. God's mission includes redeeming political, economic, social, and religious ideologies, beliefs, and practices. There is no place, no entity, no structure, no aspect of life that God's mission is excluded from: the public square, the family home, the prison cell, the battlefield – all are included. Our book *Missio Politica* addresses God's mission in politics. Indeed, the Greek term for "church" used in Matthew 16:18 is *ecclesia*, which is a political term meaning "a people called out to take responsibility." Responsibility for what? For God's creation and God's mission.

Second Corinthians 5:17–20 says:

> Therefore, if anyone is in Christ, the new creation has come: the old has gone, the new is here! All this is from God, who

> reconciled us to himself through Christ and gave us the ministry of reconciliation: that God was reconciling the world to himself in Christ, not counting people's sins against them. And he has committed to us the message of reconciliation. We are therefore Christ's ambassadors, as though God were making his appeal through us. We implore you on Christ's behalf: be reconciled to God.

We are the fruit, the new humanity, the expression of all that is to come – and we demonstrate this in and through all we do and say. And we are sent as Christ was sent to preach the good news to the poor, to proclaim freedom for the prisoners and recovery of sight for the blind, to release the oppressed, and proclaim the year of God's favour (Luke 4:18–19).

If we feel overwhelmed by this task, we can be encouraged that we are not alone. The power to bring transformation is drawn from our being in Christ and his good news which we are called to proclaim and demonstrate. The Holy Spirit gives us the words, teaches us his ways, and touches people's lives in and through all we do and say. And God has called a diverse group of people together, bringing gifts, expertise, skills, languages, capacities, and personalities, so that together we can impact every aspect of God's world.

The Micah Global Consultations give us a taste of this exciting and inspiring diversity and unity in action. From every nation, tribe, and tongue we gather to discern together how we can be more effective for God's mission in God's world!

Integral mission is therefore an expression of the whole church, living out the whole gospel in the whole world. Our M Series booklet entitled *Five Marks of Mission* captures the theology and practice of this well.

To read more about integral mission, see our M Series book *Integral Mission: Biblical Foundations*.

Resilient Communities

What do we mean by each of these words?

Resilience is the ability to recover quickly from difficulties, and to cope with life's shocks and challenges.

Resilient communities describes the sustained ability of a community to draw on available resources to withstand, respond to, and recover from adverse situations.

Of course, some resilience can be construed as stubbornness and the resistance to change and adapt. We are focusing on the positive interpretation.

Jesus knew what lay ahead of him in Jerusalem. Luke 9:51 says, "As the time approached for him to be taken up to heaven, Jesus resolutely set out for Jerusalem." "Resolutely" means he was determined, decided, and unwavering in his commitment to see this through. The journey had many challenges, as even his closest friends deserted him; yet even as he hung painfully on the cross, he interceded for us to be forgiven.

What was key in Jesus's resilience to move towards the cross? It was that he knew who he was and what God's calling for him was, and he was fully informed by God's Word – he was obedient to God and his Word.

If we were to define success indicators and impact measurement approaches for Jesus's missional approach, what would they look like?

- Number of people healed
- Number of people fed (on two separate days)
- Number of people trained and sent out
- Number of people attending the conference on the hillside!
- Amount of funds raised
- Number of people deciding to follow Jesus
- Number of people who stood with him after his arrest and spoke out for him at his trial

Two thousand years later, we may recognize the magnitude of his impact. I wonder what our impact will be?

Since our first triennial back in 2001 we have seen an increasing understanding and application of integral mission. We recognize that we have much to do and we ourselves need to be resilient in our commitment to live out God's mission together.

I would like to thank everyone who contributed to this book, a collation of the sessions and papers shared. Thank you to the Micah Board, who give up their time to oversee Micah. Thank you to our hosting members in the Philippines, who went the extra mile to enable us all to meet in their wonderful country. I especially note the Centre for Community Transformation (CCT) and Micah Philippines, who helped make this a special time together. Finally, a special thanks to Graham Joseph Hill, for his servant-hearted approach to collecting and editing the material.

Micah is currently formed by over eight hundred members from more than ninety-five countries around the world. Each member walks with Micah, inspired by our shared vision to see communities living life in all its fullness, free from poverty, injustice, and conflict. It is our hope that, as you get a taste of the discussions expressed in this book, you also will be inspired, and we look forward to welcoming you to our next gathering.[1]

---

1. Every three years the region hosting the global consultation is rotated to encourage access from people in different parts of the world and across Micah Global's membership.

1

Misión Integral

The Challenge of World Christianity

Graham Joseph Hill

In September 2018, hundreds of Christian leaders from all over the world gathered in the Philippines for the Micah Global 7th Triennial Consultation on "Integral Mission and Resilient Communities: Addressing Poverty, Injustice, and Conflict." The focus on integral mission and resilient communities covered a range of areas such as resilience and God's mission, resilience in the pursuit of justice, resilience and persistent compassion, resilience and disasters response, and resilience and partnerships.

The challenge is to help churches and Christian organizations grasp a vision of *misión integral* that contributes to building resilient communities. To do this, we need to listen and learn from the many and diverse voices of world Christianity. This learning posture is crucial for integral mission and resilient communities.

Misión Integral: The Resilience of World Christianity

It's common for the media to focus on large natural disasters: earthquakes, fires, tsunamis, famines, and the like. These disasters have devastating effects on communities. Yet the persistent local ongoing causes of death, poverty, disease, conflict, and corruption often go unreported by the media. These affect poor and often marginalized communities in profound and ongoing ways. When international agencies and governments respond to large disasters, they rarely focus on ways to build long-term capacity for future community resilience in the face of shocks or ongoing challenges. Corrupt, unjust, broken systems and institutions perpetuate poverty, death, and conflict. Resilience is one of the great challenges facing communities all over the world today.

Micah Global defines resilience and integral mission carefully. "Resilience [is] the ability to recover quickly from difficulties, the ability to cope with life shocks and challenges." "Resilient communities [are communities that have] the sustained ability . . . to draw on available resources to withstand, respond to, and recover from adverse situations." Why does Micah Global focus on integral mission as a key part of building community resilience? "Recognising that a reconciled community has the greatest capacity to work together for the healing and restoration of its people, we centre our mission in Christ, so that all we do and say has a transforming impact, enabling communities to live life in all its fullness, free from poverty, injustice, and conflict."[1]

As I listened to the speakers during the Micah Global 7th Triennial Consultation, many themes stood out to me. (These speakers came from all over the globe, and reflected the diverse and multi-voiced nature of world Christianity.) I was impressed by the consistent message that God calls his people to preserve and proclaim the gospel through an integral mission. This integral (or holistic) mission thoroughly integrates social justice, community development, church health, and evangelism. Our focus on integral mission and community resilience honours Jesus Christ when our convictions are life-giving and life-affirming – rooted in Scripture, and committed to a biblical way of affirming and integrating social justice, community resilience, gospel faithfulness, the whole message of the Bible, and passion for Jesus Christ and his kingdom.

During the Consultation, I came to the personal conviction that we nurture integral mission and resilient communities – and address poverty, injustice, and conflict in Christ-honouring ways – when we do the following nine things:

1. *Honour the whole Bible:* Prioritize and reflect the whole message and story of the Bible, and submit to the authority of Scripture in belief and practice (2 Tim 3:16–17).

2. *Honour mission as God intended:* Completely integrate social justice and evangelism. Move towards a holistic mission (sometimes called integral mission) – one that fully integrates gospel proclamation,

---

1. From the description of the Micah Global 7th Triennial Consultation, accessed October 2020, 2, https://live-micah-global.pantheonsite.io/wp-content/uploads/2020/10/Micah-Global-Consultation-Flyer-English.pdf.

evangelism, church planting, social justice, peacemaking, reconciliation, care for the poor, welcoming the stranger and undocumented immigrant, and more (Matt 22:34–40; Luke 4:18–19; Matt 25:34–36).

3. *Honour the local church:* Regard the role of the local church as the primary locus of God's redemptive activity, while also joining with God in society (with his people and with secular institutions) to bring justice, peace, and reconciliation to a broken world. The relationship between our redemptive work through the church, and then through society's institutions, is a first–then and not an either–or (2 Cor 5:11–21).

4. *Honour God's just will:* Acknowledge how often the Law and Prophets combine God's will (*mishpat* etc.) with righteousness/justice (*zedek*), and how wide ranging that *zedek* is. God's will, justice, and love are inseparable (Deut 16:20; Matt 22:37–40).

5. *Honour the witness of Jesus Christ:* Reflect Jesus's own care for the poor, marginalized, and exploited (Matt 11:4–6; Luke 14:16–24).

6. *Honour our grace-given obligations:* Respond to the obligation we have because of the grace of God in Christ to be generous to the poorer saints throughout the world, so there might be equality. Do good to all and especially to the household of faith (2 Cor 8:12–13; Gal 6:10).

7. *Honour the gospel and the liberation offered in Christ:* Recognize that it is Christ who brings redemption and freedom, not governments. Christians are called to influence governments and speak to power; but it is the gospel and person of Jesus Christ that truly liberates and gives life to the full (Rom 1:16–17).

8. *Honour the whole church:* Listen to and learn from all God's people, especially those who have been historically ignored or silenced. These help us grasp social justice and Christian faith more fully. The first will be last, and the last will be first (Mark 10).

9. *Honour belief and practice:* All Christian convictions must be expressed in our habits and practices (Jas 2:17).

There is an ongoing danger in the church that any one group will think that because of their race, gender, or theological tradition, they know and understand the full counsel of God. With that in mind, the theology and practice of integral mission is always a work in progress. It is always provisional and open to change through the collective wisdom offered by all of God's people from all over the global church. The whole global church must have the freedom to discern together the whole will of Christ on the relationship between social justice, integral mission, and the gospel.

Jesus's church can offer hope for resilient communities, and help address poverty, injustice, and conflict, when it adopts the same mind as Christ Jesus: one of self-sacrifice, humility, and service.

> Therefore if you have any encouragement from being united with Christ, if any comfort from his love, if any common sharing in the Spirit, if any tenderness and compassion, then make my joy complete by being like-minded, having the same love, being one in spirit and of one mind. Do nothing out of selfish ambition or vain conceit. Rather, in humility value others above yourselves, not looking to your own interests but each of you to the interests of the others.
>
> In your relationships with one another, have the same mindset as Christ Jesus:
>
> who, being in very nature God,
>   did not consider equality with God something to be used to
>   his own advantage;
> rather, he made himself nothing
>   by taking the very nature of a servant,
>   being made in human likeness.
> And being found in appearance as a man,
>   he humbled himself
>   by becoming obedient to death –
>   even death on a cross! (Phil 2:1–8)

When we follow Christ's example of humility and service, our efforts towards integral mission and resilient communities will bear fruit that will last. Abiding in the Vine bears such fruit (John 15:1–17). Do all things for the sake of Christ, his church, his justice, his gospel, and his world.

Misión Integral: The Shifts of World Christianity

The church has shifted away from Western contexts and towards Majority World contexts (African, Asia-Pacific, Latin American, Eastern European, etc.). By 2025, two-thirds of Christians will live in Asia, Africa, Oceania, the Middle East, the Caribbean, and Latin America.² Philip Jenkins concludes,

> We are currently living through one of the transforming moments in the history of religion worldwide. Over the last five centuries, the story of Christianity has been inextricably bound up with that of Europe and European-derived civilizations overseas, above all in North America. Until recently, the overwhelming majority of Christians have lived in white nations . . . Over the last century, however, the centre of gravity in the Christian world has shifted inexorably away from Europe, southward, to Africa and Latin America, and eastward, toward Asia. Today, the largest Christian communities on the planet are to be found in those regions.³

There are, in fact, two shifts happening simultaneously. The *first shift* is the move of world Christianity from being predominantly a Western church to mainly a church of the Majority World (the developing world or the Global South). The *second shift* is the move away from a view that social justice and gospel proclamation are at odds, and towards the conviction that these are completely complementary, integrated, and inseparable in an "integral mission" and a fuller vision of the gospel of Jesus Christ.

These two shifts are interwoven. The rise of the churches of the Majority World has seen the rise of conviction about the power and truth of integral mission. Majority World Christians call the worldwide church to integral mission. In my book *Global Church*, I wrote the following:

> There has been a recent flood of books on missional theology and practice in the West. This is a welcome development. But much of the missional growth of the church has been in Asia, Africa, and Latin America. Conversion rates in those contexts have been astounding. Missional passion in those settings is thrilling and humbling. And while mission in those settings has not always been contextual or integral – especially because of the influence of colonialism, globalization, and Western culture – many in those settings are demonstrating what integral mission looks like.

---

2. S. B. Bevans, R. Schroeder, and L. J. Luzbetak, "Missiology after Bosch: Reverencing a Classic by Moving Beyond," *International Bulletin of Missionary Research* 29, no. 2 (2005): 69.

3. P. Jenkins, *The Next Christendom: The Coming of Global Christianity*, 3rd ed. (Oxford: Oxford University Press, 2011), 1.

> [Those of us in the West] can learn much from the integral mission among the churches of Indigenous settings and the Majority World. We can especially learn from their focus on the kingdom of God. Their commitment to bring healing and justice and freedom and transformation to whole persons and whole communities is instructive. We can also learn from their focus on incarnational immersion among the poor and exploited and marginalized. And we can learn from their missional integrity.[4]

God is calling his church to embrace integral mission. This is about joining with Jesus as he establishes his kingdom of love and peace and justice. C. René Padilla says,

> When the church is committed to an integral mission and to communicating the gospel through everything it is, does, and says, it understands that its goal is not to become large numerically, nor to be rich materially, nor powerful politically. Its purpose is to incarnate the values of the Kingdom of God and to witness to the love and the justice revealed in Jesus Christ, by the power of the Spirit, for the transformation of human life in all its dimensions, both on the individual level and on the community level.[5]

Misión Integral: The Mission of World Christianity

Our mission must be transformational and integral. This is what the voices of world Christianity teach us.

In my role as Director of the Global Church Project, I've had the privilege of listening to hundreds of often unheard voices from around the world as they enter into a powerful conversation about the shape of church and mission in the twenty-first century.[6] I have filmed interviews with many hundreds of Majority World Christians (Christians in Africa, Asia, the Middle East, Eastern Europe, Latin America, Oceania, the Caribbean, First Nations, aboriginal and indigenous peoples, and immigrant [diaspora] communities). My goal is to

---

4. From G. J. Hill, *Global Church: Reshaping Our Conversations, Renewing Our Mission, Revitalizing Our Churches* (Downers Grove, IL: IVP Academic, 2016), 60. Copyright © 2016 by Graham Joseph Hill. Used by permission of InterVarsity Press, www.ivpress.com.

5. C. R. Padilla, "What Is Integral Mission?," http://www.dmr.org/images/pdf%20dokumenter/C._René_Padilla_-_What_is_integral_mission.pdf.

6. See the Global Church Project at https://theglobalchurchproject.com.

amplify their voices and what they say about justice, discipleship, witness, and mission.

If you asked me to summarize what Christians in these Majority World contexts say about mission, I would tell you that *they call the global church to integral mission (*misión integral*)*. In other words, *misión integral is* the form of mission presented and pursued throughout world Christianity. It may not always be called that, but most Christians outside the West intuitively practise and advocate forms of integral mission. Such mission has the power to renew the church and the world, and to invest our local and global mission, worship, and discipleship with new vibrancy.

What is this *misión integral* that world Christianity calls us to embrace? What does it mean to say that mission must be *integral*? What does integral mission look like, and how is it practised?[7]

Integral mission isn't just about what the church does; it is, more importantly, about the nature of the church. Integral mission is about the church's being and not just its doing. Vinoth Ramachandra says that integral mission "has to do with the church's integrity." The church has integrity when it aligns its social justice and proclamation, its peacemaking and teaching, its compassion and advocacy, its public and private practices, its actions and preaching, and its passion for humility, mercy, love, truth, compassion, and justice.[8] Ramachandra says, "Integral mission is then a way of calling the church to keep together, in her theology as well as in her practice, what the Triune God of the Biblical narrative always brings together: 'being' and 'doing,' the 'spiritual' and the 'physical,' the 'individual' and the 'social,' the 'sacred' and the 'secular,' 'justice' and 'mercy,' 'witness' and 'unity,' 'preaching truth' and 'practicing the truth,' and so on."[9]

The "Micah Declaration on Integral Mission" defines *integral mission* (*misión integral*) and prioritizes the role of the local church in such mission. Christian leaders, activists, and theologians from all over the world gathered together to draw up this declaration. Here is some of what it says:

---

7. The rest of this section of this chapter is adapted from my book *Global Church*, where I show how mission must be both transformational and integral. Here I explore the *nature* and *practices* of integral mission by listening to and learning from *the many voices of world Christianity*. Adapted from Hill, *Global Church*, 55–60. Copyright © 2016 by Graham Joseph Hill. Used by permission of InterVarsity Press, www.ivpress.com.

8. Hill, *Global Church*, 66–67.

9. V. Ramachandra, "Integral Mission: Exploring a Concept," in *Integral Mission: The Way Forward*, ed. C. V. Mathew (Kerala: Christava Sahitya Samithy, 2006), 45–46.

> Integral mission or holistic transformation is the proclamation and demonstration of the gospel. It is not simply that evangelism and social involvement are to be done alongside each other. Rather, in integral mission our proclamation has social consequences as we call people to love and repentance in all areas of life. And our social involvement has evangelistic consequences as we bear witness to the transforming grace of Jesus Christ.
>
> If we ignore the world we betray the word of God, which sends us out to serve the world. If we ignore the word of God we have nothing to bring to the world. Justice and justification by faith, worship and political action, the spiritual and the material, personal change and structural change, belong together. As in the life of Jesus, being, doing and saying are at the heart of our integral task . . .
>
> The grace of God is the heartbeat of integral mission . . .
>
> God by his grace has given local churches the task of integral mission. The future of integral mission is in planting and enabling local churches to transform the communities of which they are part. Churches as caring and inclusive communities are at the heart of what it means to do integral mission.[10]

Integral mission invites the church to join with Jesus Christ in his being, doing, and saying. Such mission brings "justice and justification by faith, worship and political action, the spiritual and the material, personal change and structural change" together. As the church pursues Jesus's integral mission it reflects the values and spirit of Micah 6:8:[11] "He has shown [all you people] what is good. And what does the LORD require of you? To act justly and to love mercy, and to walk humbly with your God."

Integral mission means that the church's mission is to whole persons in whole bodies and whole communities, through the whole church. God redeems, renews, and restores our entire persons and communities. Jesus is concerned for every part of our life – our mind, body, family, employment, community, neighbourhood, sexuality, well-being, and spirit. So God calls his church to serve individuals, people groups, and whole cultures. Integral

---

10. Micah Network, "Micah Network Declaration on Integral Mission," accessed October 2020, 1–2, https://live-micah-global.pantheonsite.io/wp-content/uploads/2020/10/integral_mission_declaration_en.pdf.

11. Hill, *Global Church*, 66–67.

mission is transformational because it involves the transformation of all of creation – of whole persons, families, and communities.[12]

This is the way Jesus and the early churches understood the mission of God. Integral mission isn't just about what the church *does*, it is also about the church's *nature* and *being*. Our God is a missionary God who cares deeply about the well-being of whole persons, whole communities, the whole world. Integral mission arises out of this missional nature of the triune God. Since God is missional – and cares about the renewal of all people and all creation – his church is also missional, and must care about the same things.

The church's integral mission is not primarily a task, operation, action, programme, or strategy. It is a response to Jesus and his gospel and kingdom. God gives his church a missional nature and vocation, and calls the church to serve Jesus and his world.

When the church ignores issues of justice, peacemaking, poverty, and reconciliation, it denies the call of God and refuses to reflect the image of Christ. We can never allow our gospel to become so compromised and disfigured that it becomes about "a conscience-soothing Jesus, with an unscandalous cross, an other-worldly kingdom, a private, inwardly limited spirit, a pocket God, a spiritualized Bible, and an escapist church [whose] goal is a happy, comfortable, and successful life, obtainable through the forgiveness of an abstract sinfulness by faith in an unhistorical Christ."[13]

It is easy to fall into this trap, and to abandon God's call to integral mission. Jamie Wright puts it this way:

> I often fail to address the most pressing needs because my heart and mind are set too intently on the future . . . Sometimes I see the Church doing this, too. I've seen folks who are so hell bent on figuring out where a poor soul is going to spend eternity that they either don't see or don't care about what that person needs *today*. And I see a lot of sad, hurting, broken people walking away from this Church that seems to care so much about whether or not they're "saved" but doesn't bother to find out that they're *lonely*. Or sick. Or starving to death. Or that they're overwhelmed by raising

---

12. S. Escobar, *A Time for Mission: The Challenge for Global Christianity* (Leicester: Inter-Varsity Press, 2003), 142–154. Note that *A Time for Mission* and *The New Global Mission* are the same book. The first is the Inter-Varsity Press (UK) edition, and the second is the InterVarsity Press (US) edition.

13. O. E. Costas, *Christ outside the Gate: Mission beyond Christendom* (Maryknoll, NY: Orbis, 1982), 80.

children, or financial burden, or porn addiction, or whatever. The people around us are navigating landmines that could take them down at any moment. And some in the Church want to hand them a Bible tract and say, "It will all be okay, if only you make it into Heaven someday" . . .

Live alongside people, and be keenly aware of their needs. Feed them if they're hungry and look out for the crap in their way, so that if possible you can help them through it, or even better, around it. Because if you really care about any one person's future, eternal or otherwise, you'll be heavily invested in their today.[14]

Only mission that is *integral* has *integrity*. This is because the gospel has integrity (the integrity of the heart and person of Jesus Christ), and integral mission reflects and embodies the integrity of the gospel. Vinoth Ramachandra says,

Integral mission has to do with the Church's *integrity*. Integral mission flows out of an integral gospel and an integrated people. There is a great danger that we transform the mission of the church into a set of special "projects" and "programs," whether we call them "evangelism" or "socio-political action," and then look for ways to integrate them methodologically . . . The primary way the church acts upon the world is through the actions of its members in their daily work and their daily relationships with people of other faiths . . . "Integral mission" has to do with the basic issue of the integrity of the church's life, the consistency between what the church is and what it proclaims.[15]

Integral mission is gospel mission. In other words, all gospel-shaped mission is integral mission. The gospel should never be reduced to a privatized, individualistic gospel that is only about God dealing with personal sin and pain. God redeems us from the power of sin and death. Through Jesus's death and resurrection our personal sins are forgiven and we are set free *from* sin and death *to* a new life of fullness, hope, faith, love, and glory. But the full gospel of Jesus is much more expansive and cosmic than mere personal or individual forgiveness of sin. The gospel story extends from creation to new creation, from Genesis to Revelation. The gospel tells us that in Jesus Christ,

---

14. J. Wright, "Dog Piles," 10 February 2011, accessed 8 November 2019, https://theveryworstmissionary.com/2011/02/dog-piles/.

15. Ramachandra, "Integral Mission," 57.

God restores all things, all people and all creation, to his originally intended shalom – his perfection, glory, justice, harmony, peace, flourishing, goodness, and wholeness.

The world is fed up with false and inadequate forms of the gospel. Christians are too. When people hear a gospel that is about personal forgiveness and salvation *and* also about God forming a people who join with him in restoring all creation to God's perfect justice, peace, love, and freedom, they hear the gospel as *good news*. Simon Leigh-Jones puts it strongly: "I'm bored of a gospel that's only about me, my soul, and I. I'm bored of a gospel seemingly offering no good news about a dying planet. I'm bored of a gospel almost silent on issues like racism, gender inequality, and global injustice."[16] The gospel Leigh-Jones describes is common in the West, but it is not the gospel of Jesus Christ. What is the true and full gospel? Michael Frost puts it this way: "The gospel is the good news that God himself has come to rescue and renew all of creation through the work of Jesus Christ on our behalf."[17] Or, in the words of Scot McKnight, "The gospel is the work of God to restore humans to union with God and communion with others, in the context of a community, for the good of others and the world."[18]

Integral mission is attractive to people who are poor, suffering, and oppressed precisely because it's transformational. Integral mission is focused on human flourishing, freedom from oppression, and the renewal of all creation. Mission that is truly *integral* is always *transformational*. Orlando Costas says that transformational mission always includes proclaiming, discipling, mobilizing, growing, liberating, and celebrating. These "make up the church's mission-in-life."[19] And these things are always expressed in the local, messy, everyday realities of people and their churches, families, and neighbourhoods.

Transformation, in the words of Vinay Samuel, "is to enable God's vision of society to be actualized in all relationships, social, economic, and spiritual, so that God's will may be reflected in human society and his love be experienced

---

16. Quoted by Michael Frost in a Facebook conversation on 7 November 2019, accessed 8 November 2019, https://www.facebook.com/michaelfrost6.

17. Michael Frost in a Facebook conversation on 7 November 2019, accessed 8 November 2019, https://www.facebook.com/michaelfrost6.

18. S. McKnight, *Embracing Grace: A Gospel for All of Us* (Brewster, MA: Paraclete, 2005), xii.

19. O. E. Costas, *The Integrity of Mission: The Inner Life and Outreach of the Church*, 1st ed. (San Francisco: Harper & Row, 1979), xiii.

by all communities, especially the poor."[20] *Mission as transformation* (another way of talking about integral mission) combines evangelism and social action, secular and sacred, theory and practice, personal and communal, and more. By bringing all these things together, integral mission honours local communities and their specific concerns, frees people from oppressive use of power, enlivens people's spiritual and social lives, and inspires people to strive for God's kingdom of peace, reconciliation, love, justice, and solidarity.

Integral mission is a long-term process, achieved only through the kinds of integral commitments expressed in the "Micah Declaration on Integral Mission." Transformation is impossible without commitment to local people, in specific communities and families, in particular settings. Vinay Samuel reminds us that integral mission involves a long-term "commitment to community building" and demands "the unity of the whole body of Christ."[21] As I say elsewhere, integral mission

> recognizes the person in community and appreciates the centrality of social units. It discerns where God is present and at work in the community. It invites people to take part in what God is already doing. Integral mission invests in contexts. It builds social bonds, social reconciliation, social community, and social transformation. Integral mission discerns where God is at work in the world. It notices where the values of the kingdom are flourishing – integrity, service, humility, peace, and freedom. Transformational mission seeks to develop these values. It does this through mission, discipleship, community building, and social action.[22]

Vinay Samuel challenges the church to respond to human need. He says the values of the kingdom of God that shape integral mission are clear. And these values become practices. The first value is human dignity. The second is freedom of conscience without threat or control. The third is participation in decisions that affect one's life and community. The fourth is struggle against evil

---

20. V. Samuel and C. Sugden, eds., *Mission as Transformation: A Theology of the Whole Gospel* (Oxford: Regnum, 1999), ii.

21. Samuel and Sugden, *Mission as Transformation*, 227–235; V. Samuel and A. Hauser, *Proclaiming Christ in Christ's Way: Studies in Integral Evangelism* (Oxford: Regnum, 1989), 10–12.

22. Hill, *Global Church*, 57.

and injustice. And, finally, the fifth is the cultivation of hope, respect, dignity, humility, faith, love, equity, and mutuality.[23]

Jesus calls his people to declare the whole gospel to the whole world, in word, sign, and deed. The Spirit inspires us to seek "justice and reconciliation throughout human society" and the liberation of all people "from every kind of oppression."[24] René Padilla says that to achieve this goal we need to ensure that our mission is "truly *evangelical* – rooted in the gospel and consequently bringing about transformation in society."[25]

Similarly, Orlando Costas affirms the emphasis placed on the *whole gospel* in the phrase "the whole gospel for the whole world." He challenges us to explore what we mean by the *whole world*: "a vision of 'the whole world' is essential for a faithful and relevant proclamation of the whole gospel."[26] According to Costas, the whole world is both the object and the context of the whole gospel. Jesus gives his gospel to the world. "Hence, the whole world, the world of humans and the world of things, is the object of the gospel." The world is also the context of the gospel. "It is the context in which the good news of salvation was first given and received and is today proclaimed and heard. Outside the world there is no gospel and certainly no Christian mission."[27]

Integral mission leads us to care for (to include and to be led by) the poor, marginalized, outsider, broken, and those on the periphery. Costas says we share in Christ's suffering "by serving . . . the poor, the powerless, and the oppressed."[28] Outside the gate, we "become apostolic agents in the mobilization of a servant church toward its crucified Lord, outside the gate of a comfortable and secure ecclesiastical compound."[29]

The voices of the global church call us to a particular kind of mission: to *misión integral*.

---

23. V. Samuel and C. Sugden, eds., *The Church in Response to Human Need* (Grand Rapids, MI: Eerdmans, 1987), 149–150.

24. C. R. Padilla, *Mission between the Times: Essays on the Kingdom* (Grand Rapids, MI: Eerdmans, 1985), 186–199.

25. C. R. Padilla and T. Yamamori, eds., *The Local Church, Agent of Transformation: An Ecclesiology for Integral Mission* (Buenos Aires: Ediciones Kairos, 2004), 19–20.

26. Costas, *Christ outside the Gate*, 163.

27. Costas, 163. This paragraph is copied directly from Hill, *Global Church*, 58–59.

28. Costas, *Christ outside the Gate*, 172.

29. Costas, 194.

Misión Integral: The Challenge of World Christianity

Misión integral is indispensable for building community resilience. And *misión integral* is the challenge (and possibility!) presented by Majority World Christians to the worldwide church. This is illustrated in the themes of *integral mission and community resilience* covered in the chapters of this book.

Part 1 is on "Resilience, the Church, and Integral Mission." David Boan outlines the relationship between integral mission and community resilience, and the role the church plays in building resilience (chapter 2). Andrew Steere shows how "recovering Paul's emphasis on Christ's cruciform life and death as the paradigmatic example of God's righteousness may assist us in looking through a more critical theological lens at our missional efforts" (chapter 3). Thandi Gamedze considers the church's call to change, but resistance to do so. "It is time to shake off all chains that keep us in stagnation. We were not made for control but for liberation, and if God's dream is for our collective, unbridled freedom, then we need to learn to embrace it too" (chapter 4). Viv Grigg discusses how the church might build resilient learning networks, by getting the seminary into slums and by building institutes for city transformation (chapter 5). Geoff Whiteman, Emily Edwards, Anna Savelle, and Kristina Whiteman examine how missionaries become resilient (chapter 6). The participants of the Gospel and Future of Cities Summit issue a call to action for Christians to engage with urban challenges and opportunities, including UN-Habitat's "New Urban Agenda" (chapter 7).

Part 2 is on "Resilience, Peace, and Justice." Manavala Reuben unpacks the biblical teachings on social justice and shows how "justice is at the very heart of the Christian faith, even though this fact is yet to be understood by many Christians" (chapter 8). Amy Reynolds and Nikki Toyama-Szeto call the church to address gender and leadership gaps in development-oriented organizations (chapter 9). Vilma "Nina" Balmaceda leads us to "a deeper understanding of the biblical teachings on peace and justice, with the desire to encourage resilience among Christians working with the most vulnerable communities" (chapter 10). Patrick Mitchel describes God's preference for the poor, and how this is illustrated in social justice movements in Ireland (chapter 11). "God is not indifferent to the plight of the poor, the hungry, the illiterate, the victims of war and prejudice, and those oppressed by military, political, and economic tyranny. The church has no choice but to dive in and help those whose worldly address lies within one of the many suburbs of hell. It has no choice but to accept the partnership with God in the creation of a better world."[30] Sandra Maria Van Opstal outlines how worship and justice are inseparable, and how we need a spirituality that embodies and mobilizes for justice (chapter 12). CB Samuel reminds us, "*The gospel is integral in character. You can't present a spiritual gospel and separate all the actions out as something else. The proclaimed gospel is integral in character. And the more integral our gospel is, the more integral our mission will be*" (chapter 13). Florence Muindi offers five essentials for taking part in what God is doing, and for becoming a part of the transformation process. These are salvation, surrender, seeking a life of prayer, sacrifice, and strategy (chapter 14). Peter McVerry calls the church to move beyond compassion to solidarity (chapter 15).

Part 3 is on "Resilience, Spirituality, and Compassion." Clinton Bergsma delves deep into Scripture to show the necessity of lament for spiritual resilience in contexts of poverty and injustice (chapter 16). Becca Allchin, Stephanie Cantrill, and Helen Fernandes show how building resilient communities is enhanced by integrating mental health and well-being in effective development thinking and practice (chapter 17). Jocabed Reina Solano Miselis invites us to listen and learn from indigenous voices, including the spiritual strength of the peoples of Abya Yala (chapter 18). D. Zac Niringiye challenges the church to see that the gospel compels believers to pursue the common good, the well-being of others in the world (chapter 19). Ruth Padilla DeBorst suggests we are called to renew three things: our sense of identity, our sense of sight, and our sense of time, all in light of God's identity, God's vision, and God's timing (chapter 20). "May God's Spirit continue granting us all renewed identity, new sight, and a new sense of time so that we may stand against all odds and even against all ends in full confidence that there is not death but abundant life at the end of God's story." Johannes Reimer says, "The promise of Jesus is unprecedented: the recovery of the church will push hell out of the gates of the world, and communities will become more and more resilient to disasters" (chapter 21).

Part 4 is on "Resilience, Mobilization, and Partnerships." Jané Mackenzie, Chris McDonald, Stanley Enock, and Mari Williams describe how we can build resilience within local churches and communities (chapter 22). Fennelien Stal, Debora Suparni, Arshinta Soemarsono, and Norman Franklin C. Agustin examine how churches and community groups can cooperate to build resilient communities, and illustrate this through examples in South East Asia (chapter 23). Tearfund have spent the last three years innovating around a model designed to help create the political space needed to challenge the broken governance systems, vested interests, and ultimately prevailing social values

---

30. D. S. Ferguson, *Biblical Hermeneutics: An Introduction* (Atlanta: John Knox, 1986), 194.

that are preventing the bold actions necessary for change. Naomi Foxwood, Richard Gower, Helen Heather, and Sue Willsher outline Tearfund's approach, including their focus on three key components of movement-building (mobilizing, organizing, and connecting), and then offer key lessons from Tearfund's work (chapter 24). Boureima Diallo challenges the churches of the North and South (the West and the Majority World) to cooperate together for the sake of the gospel, integral mission, and resilient communities (chapter 25).

Part 5 consists of "Summaries from the Six Consultation Tracks" of the Micah Global 7th Triennial Consultation. These tracks were "Church and Community Resilience" (chapter 26), "Church and Corruption" (chapter 27), "Formation for Integral Mission" (chapter 28), "Urban Shalom" (chapter 29), "Reconciliation as the Mission of the Church" (chapter 30), and "Integral Mission and Community Health" (chapter 31). Finally, Sheryl Haw offers final reflections on integral mission and community resilience, and next steps for our Micah worldwide community (chapter 32).

In this book, over thirty Christians involved in integral mission, development organizations, and local churches wrestle with how Christians can contribute to community resilience through involvement in integral mission, peacemaking, justice, and more. The contributors to this book come from almost every continent of the world. Their insights into mission, discipleship, peacemaking, resilience, and more have the potential to transform the church's faith and witness today.

The church is capable of building resilience and helping to address poverty, injustice, and conflict. *Misión integral* focuses on holistic justice and compassion. This grounds the church in a biblical passion to integrate justice and proclamation, witness and social concern, and evangelism and community transformation. The body of Christ needs biblical frameworks and practical tools for engagement which help support and build community resilience. In this book, Christians from all over the globe explore how integral mission builds community resilience. Today, more than ever, *misión integral* is the challenge of world Christianity, and the hope for community resilience.

Part 1

Resilience, the Church, and Integral Mission

2

Resilience and Integral Mission

David Boan

Resilience has garnered much attention the past decade due to the potential to help people and communities to better withstand destructive impacts, such as from natural or human-made disasters. A great deal of work has gone into developing a body of evidence on resilience, both to clearly describe resilience and to clarify important components. For faith-based development organizations and local faith communities there is the additional question of whether there is a role for faith and church in developing resilience that is consistent with the theology and mission of the church. In this chapter, we provide an overview of the issues of evidence and theology. We then pose a third issue, the utility of the resilience model. What we mean by utility is that evidence and theological alignment matter only if the resilience model helps us to do something. If we understand all the evidence and theology but are no better prepared to act, it is all an intellectual exercise with little or no practical value.

The discussion begins with some of the critical evidence for resilience, including whether it is more of a theoretical model or if there is evidence of application. The discussion is limited to recent research and provides a sense of where this evolving topic is heading.

One group of studies focuses on resilience and its effect on disaster recovery and trauma. If resilience means resisting and recovering from harm, such as from a disaster, and if disaster preparedness can be assumed to help a community better resist harm, then several studies show the factors underlying preparedness, and hence resilience.

For example, Hoffman and Muttarak show that high social capital, in addition to education and disaster experiences, motivates people to prepare for a disaster.[1] What is meant by social capital in these studies varies, but it generally means active participation in the life of the community, including developing connections or relationships across the community. Similarly, Cui and Han looked at which people maintained their preparedness after a disaster.[2] They found that people with strong community bonds maintained their preparedness following a disaster, while people with low community bonds showed a significant decline in preparedness. Their way of measuring bonds emphasized social cooperation and engagement, which is a type of social capital.

Researchers such as Ögtem-Young demonstrate a different approach to understanding resilience.[3] They have questioned the approach of linking resilience to disasters and trauma. His view is in the tradition of many social scientists who argue that a disaster-oriented approach leaves out the many cultural and local community elements essential to understanding resilience. He describes how resilience develops from everyday experiences, and particularly how everyday faith plays a vital role in resilience. Using in-depth interviews, he showed how people encounter loss, discrimination, crime, and other hardships in their daily lives apart from a disaster. Their ability to cope with these events is an essential aspect of resilience not addressed in disaster-focused studies. Further, religion was a critical resilience factor for many but not all subjects. The role of religion depended on other factors, such as education, culture, and economic status.

The importance of these studies is that they show how research is clarifying the underlying constructs that lead to resilience. They show that resilience is not a single or homogeneous trait, but rather a collection of actions (ongoing social interactions) and traits (bonds, awareness, strategies) that broadly lead to a variety of conditions that we associate with healthiness, including the ability to respond to harm. Importantly, several authors are describing how those actions and traits are not just those associated with disasters but are part of the fabric of everyday life. This view is essential for many reasons: it expands the range of conditions that we consider when examining resilience; it shows how communities never at risk of disasters still develop, and need to

---

1. R. Hoffmann and R. Muttarak, "Learn from the Past, Prepare for the Future: Impacts of Education and Experience on Disaster Preparedness in the Philippines and Thailand," *World Development* 96 (2017): 32–51.

2. K. Cui and Z. Han, "Resilience of an Earthquake-Stricken Rural Community in Southwest China: Correlation with Disaster Risk Reduction Efforts," *International Journal of Emergency Response and Public Health* 15, no. 3 (2018): 407.

3. O. Ögtem-Young, "Faith Resilience: Everyday Experiences," *Societies* 8, no. 1 (2018): 10.

develop, resilience; and it expands our opportunities to promote and facilitate the development of resilience.

Finally, this work is essential for the connection to faith and church, both of which often appear in discussions of resilience. Boan and Ayers describe how local faith communities provide a range of resources and activities that build resilience.[4] These include equipping people to become more active members of the community (thus building social capital), reducing the barriers between community groups that isolate people and increase vulnerability, and providing a faith-centred source of support. These many and various functions of the faith community are described as forming a shared resilience, meaning a community-level resilience that results from cooperative action to build acceptance, shared resources, and justice.

Given the above evidence, does it follow that integral mission advances resilience? To answer this question, we will summarize the elements of integral mission. We then present a sample of the research that suggests resilient communities also demonstrate elements of integral mission.

What are the actions that are associated with integral mission? If we look at the "Cape Town Commitment" (CTC) we will find the following:[5]

> We urge church leaders and pastors to equip all believers with the courage and the tools to relate the truth with prophetic relevance to everyday public conversation, and so to engage every aspect of the culture we live in.

Believers are to be equipped to engage in society and culture, to be active participants in community life (public conversation) and engage in the culture.

> We encourage Christ-followers to be actively engaged in these spheres [government, business, and academia], both in public service or private enterprise, in order to shape societal values and influence public debate.

Believers not only engage in discussion, but they also shape the public debate.

> Corruption is condemned in the Bible. It undermines economic development, distorts fair decision-making and destroys social cohesion. No nation is free of corruption. We invite Christians in

---

4. D. Boan and J. Ayers, *Faith and Community: Creating Shared Resilience* (Carlisle: Langham Global Library, 2020).

5. Selected excerpts from the Lausanne Movement, "The Cape Town Commitment: A Confession of Faith and a Call to Action," 2010, accessed 19 September 2019, https://www.lausanne.org/content/ctcommitment.

> the workplace, especially young entrepreneurs, to think creatively about how they can best stand against this scourge.

This is a call to exercise a prophetic voice. To speak prophetically is to speak out publicly on God's behalf when the community, government, or organization is violating God's plan. Here, it is specifically a call to confront corruption.

> We urge church pastors and leaders to teach biblical truth on ethnic diversity. We must positively affirm the ethnic identity of all church members.

Here the Commitment calls for welcoming diversity and speaking out against racism and other forms of oppression and prejudice.

> For the sake of the gospel, we lament, and call for repentance where Christians have participated in ethnic violence, injustice or oppression.

Continuing the theme of diversity, the CTC recognizes that Christians have also participated in racism, and calls for repentance and correction.

> We commit ourselves to . . . Expose, resist, and take action against all abuse of children, including violence, exploitation, slavery, trafficking, prostitution, gender and ethnic discrimination, commercial targeting, and wilful neglect.

Our final example is related to violence against children in all its forms.

These are not the sum of the commitments, but they are examples of specific actions that are part of integral mission, actions that include confronting violence, child abuse, and corruption, as well as valuing ethnic diversity and becoming active participants in the public sphere. We can now ask if there is evidence of a connection between these actions and resilience.

Starting with the example of engaging in the public sphere, we do not attempt to address the question of what the church should do but focus only on the narrow question of effect. That is, what is the effect when a church engages in the community to build resilience, and is that effect consistent with the aims of integral mission?

Our first example comes from Pieterse, who looked at ten church community projects in South Africa.[6] Using in-depth interviews, he asked how these projects impacted the well-being of the poor. He noted numerous benefits, from economic support to health to well-being, but central to them all

---

6. H. Pieterse, "A Grounded Theory Approach to the Analysis of Sermons on Poverty: Congregational Projects as Social Capital," *Verbum et Ecclesia* 33, no. 1 (2012): 1–7.

was the sense among the recipients that these were provisions from God, which led to a sense of spiritual well-being. Pieterse summarized his findings from his interviews: "The category of spiritual well-being of the poor now forms the central concept in this conceptual framework of the effects of congregational projects on the well-being of the poor. All the other categories [of church service] are related to this central concept . . . God's love in action in the experience of the well-being of the poor [emphasis added]."[7]

Churches create social capital by bringing together people who share a common faith and values and building relationships among them. In the process, the people are informed about the content of their faith identity and how that identity relates to the larger world. This results in their being equipped to become active in their communities and reach out beyond the walls of their church. Engaging with people across social boundaries and barriers is a critical element of resilience.

Several studies look at the impact of reducing boundaries between people, such as the integration of minorities and immigrants into society, and the resilience of the community. Lester and Ngyuen asked if US communities that assist immigrants to integrate across all sectors of the community (as opposed to relegating them to ethnic enclaves) fare better compared with those that do not.[8] This study measured resilience as changes in unemployment and income over ten years that included the Great Recession. Employment diversity was a proxy for community support for immigrants and refugees. After studying twenty matched communities, they found evidence that communities that more broadly integrated immigrants across the economy fared better during the Great Recession than communities that marginalized immigrants. They see the difference as rooted in reducing social and economic barriers to the inclusion of immigrants and minorities, which leads to functional diversity.

There is a well-established connection between poverty and resilience, but what about the ability of churches to reduce the number of people in poverty? This is not a simple yes/no question. Eliminating poverty is about more than providing resources. It requires more complex attention to policy, economic factors, and a host of factors that create opportunity for the poor. Kretzschmar provides an informative analysis from comparing the

---

7. Pieterse, "Grounded Theory," 7.

8. W. Lester and M. Nguyen, "The Economic Integration of Immigrants and Regional Resilience," *Journal of Urban Affairs* 38, no. 1 (2016): 42–60.

experience in Chile with that in South Africa.⁹ In Chile the Catholic Church was consistent in its support for the poor and standing against the corruption and flawed policies of the government, all of which was an essential factor in the reduction of poverty and economic disparity in Chile. In contrast, the role of the church in South Africa was more mixed, in some cases complicit with the apartheid government. Likewise, progress on poverty and disparity was mixed. Kretzschmar concludes, "In the future, the impact of the church on the government's policies and practices with respect to poverty alleviation will depend on its credibility within civil society. Such credibility will derive from the church's own intellectual and practical involvement in social protection and poverty reduction, and its freedom from the materialism of our time."[10]

Finally, can the church reduce violence against children? The current campaign to end violence against children rests in part on the assumption that engaging faith communities is necessary for success. However, is there evidence to support this assumption? This is another complex issue. Child abuse is often associated with certain church groups. For example, churches and individuals that see God as punitive and condemning are more likely to engage in abusive practices towards children. What these churches and communities with high rates of child abuse have in common is social isolation. When churches engage with their communities, including working with agencies such as social services, they become factors in the reduction of child maltreatment. We argue that community engagement is fundamental to integral mission and that such engagement has broad community impact, including reduction of violence.

These are not conclusive reviews of the evidence, but the evidence shown does suggest a pattern. Our sample of evidence provides support for the argument that at least some of the elements of integral mission, as described in the "Cape Town Commitment," are shown to be related to community resilience. It should also be evident that not all faith groups embrace these actions. There are unfortunate examples of faith groups contributing to ethnic violence, corruption, and division within their communities. Thus, we cannot say that these actions occur automatically among people of faith. Hence the call for trained leaders who properly teach and equip believers.

---

9. L. Kretzschmar, "An Ethical Analysis of the Implementation of Poverty Reduction Policies in South Africa and Chile and Their Implications for the Church," *HTS Theological Studies* 70, no. 1 (2014): 1–11, accessed 10 September 2019, http://www.scielo.org.za/scielo.php?script=sci_arttext&pid=S0259-94222014000100044&lng=en&tlng=es.

10. Kretzschmar, "Ethical Analysis," 11.

This leads us to the third and final question for our discussion: Is there anything unique about the church's contribution to resilience? Alternatively, does the church as the church (that is, not as an NGO) live in the community in a way that results in greater resilience in the community?

Based on the above discussion, we can suggest five ways in which the church promotes resilience. This does not mean other organizations would not act in similar ways, but these ways are either unique to the church or carried out in a way that is distinctive of the church. Recognizing these unique contributions is essential in order for the church to maintain its identity as a church when working in the community. The concern over this issue is a significant barrier to church and community engagement. Some church leaders express concern that if they work with the community, they risk losing their identity as a church. Others express concern that community engagement is the domain of government and NGOs, and that, while church members may serve, it is not part of the mission of the church. If the church sees a unique and vital community contribution that is an expression of the mission of the church, it may be a step towards overcoming these concerns.

We selected five activities that illustrate how the church contributes to community resilience. Describing them one at a time risks implying that they are separate activities. However, it is essential to see them as part of a whole community approach where these activities are each a part of a broad strategy to demonstrate the power of the church to transform the local community. These activities are building social capital, healing spiritual injury, building trust, serving as a voice for the vulnerable, and correcting the roots of injustice.

Many organizations build social capital. When international NGOs go into a community, they will typically recruit local people to staff their programmes. While this builds skills, it is also criticized as removing talent from the local community to serve NGO purposes. Churches build social capital in ways that differ in a few key respects. First, churches can create opportunities for people to participate in education, small groups, speaking, and service programmes, all of which build a variety of skills and the confidence to take these skills outside the church. These opportunities may be ongoing, or people may participate in temporary or intermittent ways, all of which expands participation across the faith community. Churches integrate engagement with faith, values, and local community membership. Just as people join a church because they see in it the opportunity to act on their faith and values, so the church then helps them to see where engaging with the community is a further expression of their faith and values.

Faith communities can be a source of healing and resilience when they care for the suffering with a compassion grounded in their faith. Disasters are often a spiritual and moral crisis. It is usual for people to ask, "Where is God in this crisis?" Connecting with people who have a shared faith is especially valuable when facing a spiritual crisis as it can be a demonstration of God's compassion and caring. Further, people may explore their spiritual crisis more openly when they are with someone who shares their faith.

Faith institutions can connect the local community to external resources by leveraging trust. Consider the example of the Ebola outbreak in Liberia, and now in DRC. The local community does not easily trust Westerners nor accept Western-based interventions. In the case of DRC, Westerners are suspected of bringing Ebola into the community. Faith leaders helped change this behaviour in Liberia by serving as a trusted bridge between the local community and Western health workers. The same strategy is now underway in DRC.

Through relationships with the vulnerable, churches can act as a voice for those who lack their own voice. This is especially important when considering how vulnerable groups are marginalized and have complex needs for assistance. For example, people living in extreme poverty often face prejudice and discrimination that complicates and undermines change efforts. Confronting extreme poverty requires much more than sharing resources. It requires recognizing the multiple ways people remain in poverty, and coming alongside to help speak out for change.

The example of extreme poverty also illustrates how behind vulnerability, mistrust, and marginalization lies injustice. Integral mission calls the church to confront injustice and care for the victims of injustice. Many organizations confront injustice, but the church brings several additional elements. First, the church is the community and thus lives with the injustice and understands it at an intimate level. It may even contribute to the injustice since the local culture that allows injustice is also the cultural context for the church. If we start with the view that culture develops through conversations among people who have trusting relationships, then we can see that the church has a role in maintaining and spreading the local justice, even where that culture has aspects of injustice. When the church speaks out against injustice, it can be a potent force for cultural change. This is especially the case when the church faces its role in injustice, repents, and calls for change. In this way, the church has a potential role unlike any other organization to change the root causes of injustice, and, by changing them, to build a more resilient community.

Finally, these different elements of church engagement are dynamic activities (dynamic in that they are continually evolving) that work together.

They are similar to the whole community model of development where different groups and community elements (government, NGOs, ethnic groups, etc.) are brought together to create a more inclusive approach to development. The label "whole community mission" might be used to describe the way a church views the community when it considers all of the elements described above. That means building a clear theological foundation, recognizing vulnerability and injustice that exists within the church, equipping people for mission, serving the most vulnerable and the victims of injustice, and more. Each of these efforts builds upon the others in a complete approach that is an expression of integral mission and a complete approach to community resilience.

Conclusion

This brings us to several conclusions.

The church is capable of building resilience but can potentially act in ways that undermine resilience. While the church is called to engage prophetically in the community, some groups emphasize being apart from the community. The church apart from community creates barriers and separateness and teaches non-engagement, all of which weaken community resilience.

Integral mission's focus on justice and compassion, grounding the church community theologically and equipping the church body with the tools for engagement, is the fundamental approach to community that builds the community characteristics needed to build community resilience.

Further, integral mission calls us to recognize when we fail, lament that failure, learn, and go forward. This openness to the truth about us and our church makes growth possible and guards against the risks of destructive engagement.

3

Righteousness, Suffering and Participation in Philippians 3:7–11

Integral Mission and Paul's Gospel

Andrew Steere

On a rainy night in 2011, a flatbed truck rumbled down a potholed road to Kijabe Hospital, perched high on the edge of the East African Rift Valley escarpment. The bed of the truck was littered with victims of a major road accident, some of whom had experienced traumatic amputations. This not being an uncommon occurrence at the 102-year-old mission hospital, the "major disaster" code was sounded and off- and on-duty doctors and nurses poured into the hospital to treat the living.

I spoke with one of the doctors on duty a few hours later. Exhausted and de-adrenalizing after hours in Emergency, she shared that this was the first time in her decades-long career that she didn't have to ask where to go when she arrived at the hospital: she had followed the splashes of blood on the floor to the right surgical theatre. Wanting to encourage her, I asked, "What keeps you going when you have days like this?" After a lengthy pause, she replied that she understood that the primary "gospel importance" of her work was that by treating the sick, she extended their lives so that they might have a greater chance of hearing the gospel and making a decision for Christ. This was what she drew encouragement from.

I was startled. I was prepared to hear that this faithful physician drew strength from Jesus's encouragement "I was sick and you took care of me . . . just as you did it to one of the least of these . . . you did it to me" (Matt 25:36–40 NRSV), or perhaps from the exhortation of the Jerusalem apostles to Paul to "remember the poor" (Gal 2:10). I was not prepared to hear that she saw her primary value in transactional terms: how many people she had told about Christ, or who were treated and converted as a result.

Following this conversation and many like it later, I became interested in how different theological perspectives on the gospel mobilize and influence our praxis in mission. For example, when some of the victims of trauma in 2011 died in the Emergency Department before committing their lives to Christ, did the physicians with a transactional/salvific paradigm see their medical efforts as wasted energy? What gospel value did they see in their compassionate medical care *itself*? Not being a physician (but married to one), I have profound empathy and appreciation for these workers and others like them who labour amid constant death and suffering often sixty-plus hours per week.

Does It Matter?

In one sense, who cares? Do theological perspectives really *matter* when under-five mortality rates in East Africa are an order of magnitude higher than in the West[1] and there is only one surgeon for every two hundred thousand people?[2] Jesus told us to "Go . . . and make disciples" (Matt 28:19), so shouldn't we just get on with it? In my field of long-term medical mission, cross-cultural workers are a self-selecting group of passionate, driven people. All of my colleagues are measurably fruitful in their participation with God in God's mission of restoration and reconciliation, so *does it really matter* whether they have a "transactional/salvific" or an "integral mission" paradigm? It is beyond the scope of this chapter to explore this question fully. God's power is made perfect in our weakness (2 Cor 12:9), and it is my experience that God can move powerfully through those who wrestle with theological questions as well as through those who do not.

However, it is also true that thinking well and deeply about God is not opposed to the Spirit. Christians have understood for millennia that we are

---

1. The World Bank, "Mortality Rate, under-5 (per 1,000 Live Births)," 2016, accessed 29 May 2018, https://data.worldbank.org/indicator/SH.DYN.MORT.

2. "Global Surgery Map," College of Surgeons of East, Central and Southern Africa, 2018, accessed 29 May 2018, http://www.cosecsa.org/global-surgery-map.

to love God not just with our hearts and souls, but also with our minds (Luke 10:27). My entering thesis for this chapter is that for most of the workers and churches with whom I interact, strategic and operational planning regarding how to best place resources in mission (church planting? justice? economic empowerment?) *may be, at its core, influenced less by missional perspectives than by theological interpretations of the gospel.*

I have observed that the local church leaders and cross-cultural workers alongside whom I labour have diverse and divergent views regarding the gospel. In some cases, they understand it primarily in terms of individual salvation, in which the primary hope of humanity is being saved "from" the world so that they can "go to heaven when they die."[3] In others, the gospel proclaimed by Jesus and the apostles of the early church has been wholly reframed by post-Enlightenment European problems such as the Protestant Reformation.[4] For still others, there is little theological contextualization of their work, and their efforts have a largely humanistic emphasis.

So is clear thinking about God and the gospel important? I suggest yes, for a few reasons. First, because none of the three views discussed in the previous paragraph were held by followers of Christ in the first few centuries after Jesus's crucifixion. Each of these different perspectives originated in the West relatively recently in modern history. Second, because I suspect that some conflict and burnout in cross-cultural workers and church leaders is influenced at least as much by their picture of God and what God is doing in the world (saving us "from" it? redeeming and restoring? hovering wrathfully nearby?) as by mental/emotional factors. Finally, because I have seen relationships between cross-cultural workers and local church leaders deteriorate not simply because of cultural differences, but because of an underlying (and unspoken) "the ends justify the means" approach of a transactional/salvific theological paradigm.

In this chapter it is my hope to contribute to the conversations of Micah members globally by inviting you to spend some time reflecting on the nature of the gospel in conversation with one Pauline text in particular: Philippians 3:7–11. I invite you to ask, "What insights do Paul's themes of righteousness,

---

3. While there is support for this view in Scripture, scholars point out that it has roots in the pre-Christian philosophies of Plato and ancient Gnosticism.

4. One example: the dichotomy between "faith" and "works" which arose during the Reformation period of the sixteenth century and which has dominated Protestant theology regarding salvation and justification since. Many scholars have pointed out that the insights of sixteenth-century Protestants regarding "justification by faith alone," while prophetic for the sixteenth century, are also anachronistic, as they forced a sixteenth-century framework of the excesses of the Catholic Church onto Paul's immediate problem of whether Gentile converts to Christianity should adhere to Torah law.

suffering, and participation in this passage give us about the good news of Jesus and the missional efforts of those who declare allegiance to Christ as Lord?"

Finally, acknowledging that the work of a vocational Christ-follower is often filled with suffering and loss, I hope to provide encouragement to those who are in a season of lament. I pray that the Spirit will give life and peace, and that you might experience "the same mind . . . that was in Christ Jesus" (Phil 2:5).

Summary

In this chapter, I explore Paul's theology behind his self-reflections in Philippians 3:7–11:

> Yet whatever gains I had, these I have come to regard as loss because of Christ. More than that, I regard everything as loss because of the surpassing value of knowing Christ Jesus my Lord. For his sake I have suffered the loss of all things, and I regard them as rubbish, in order that I may gain Christ and be found in him, not having a righteousness of my own that comes from the law, but one that comes through faith in Christ, the righteousness from God based on faith. I want to know Christ and the power of his resurrection and the sharing of his sufferings by becoming like him in his death, if somehow I may attain the resurrection from the dead.

I argue that in commending the model of his own life in this passage, Paul is not simply encouraging the Philippians to have a hope in the midst of suffering which is based in a "belief in" Christ. Rather, Paul is describing how things *actually work* in the "new age" inaugurated by Christ: it is a reality defined by participation in and transformation through Christ's cruciform life and death. Employing words linked grammatically and rhetorically to the Christ hymn of 2:6–11, Paul describes how he (and the Philippians, by extension) should live in light of the present reality of God's righteousness and power: participating in Christ and conforming to Christ's sacrificial, self-emptying death.

Context within and behind the Letter: Paul's Usage of *Dikaio-* Words

Before proceeding to analysis of the text, it is helpful to make a single contextual observation. Paul uses the Greek word *dikaiosyne* twice in the text of Philippians 3:7–11: "not having a righteousness [*dikaiosyne*] of my own" (3:9a); and "the righteousness [*dikaiosyne*] from God based on faith" (3:9b). *Dikaiosyne* and other related words (which share the *dikaio-* root) are used by Paul frequently, more than 120 times in his letters. They are translated variously in context as "justly," "righteousness," "justice," "justified," "acquitted," "declared righteous," "righteous judgement," or "justification" in the NIV, NRSV, and ESV. One form of particular relevance to our analysis of Philippians 3:7–11 is *dikaiosyne theou* ("God's righteousness," or "righteousness from God"), used by Paul in 3:9b. In his other writings, Paul refers specifically to *dikaiosyne theou* six times in Romans (1:17; 3:5, 21, 22; 10:3; 14:17) and once each in 1 (1:30) and 2 (5:21) Corinthians.

There is significant discussion and debate among biblical scholars regarding Paul's theological intent behind these words in each of their contexts. Given the importance of the themes of righteousness/justification for our understanding of the gospel and God's mission, it is helpful to briefly summarize this scholarship into three major interpretative streams so that we might keep their unique insights in the backs of our minds as we analyse the passage. Why? Any student of Scripture learns that among the sixty-six books of the (Protestant) Bible are found ancient forms of poetry, diatribe, persuasion, narrative, and lament – and that these different forms of writing should accordingly be read with different interpretative lenses appropriate to their particular form. Just as we do not read the Song of Solomon in the same way that we read the book of Acts, it is helpful to approach the weighty themes of justification and righteousness with similar intentionality and intellectual humility.

A first stream of interpretation among biblical scholars is known as the traditional Protestant perspective, which tends to interpret Paul's theological orientation regarding *dikaiosyne* as being related to "works righteousness": the potential or futility of earning salvation by one's own efforts. This view derives most recently from Luther in the sixteenth century: the primary problem they understand Paul to be writing about is that by relying on the works required by the law, one is working to secure salvation by one's own efforts. Accordingly, an emphasis within this first stream is on the antithesis between faith and law as well as between Christianity and Judaism.[5] According to this perspective, God's *dikaiosyne* is primarily understood in forensic or transactional terms – God's gift through Christ's death and resurrection which gives believers a right

---

5. See, for example, J. M. G. Barclay, *Paul and the Gift* (Grand Rapids, MI: Eerdmans, 2015), 137.

standing or right relationship with him which they were unable to "earn" on their own.[6]

The second stream of interpretation is the New Perspective on Paul. Relevant particularly to Paul's gain/loss terminology within Philippians 3:7–11, this stream argues that Paul is referring to casting aside not his *personal shortcomings*, but rather his *significant achievements* as a righteous Pharisee – in favour of a new *dikaiosyne*.[7] A key argument of this grouping of biblical scholars is that there is little evidence within "Second Temple Judaism" (the Jews of Jesus's and Paul's day) that most Jews believed one could (or desired to) attempt to *gain* a right covenantal relationship with God by obeying the law. They point to the first-century Jewish religious commentaries on the Hebrew scriptures (the Pseudepigrapha and Palestinian Targums), in which they find evidence that Jews of the Second Temple period believed "the law was given not as a means to *gain* righteousness, but as a means of *living* righteously" (emphasis added).[8]

Finally, a third interpretative stream views Paul's usage of *dikaiosyne* in light of the unexpected in-breaking of the triumph of God in the Christ event, seeing an "apocalyptic" theme (in which a new age has broken in upon and superseded the old) as the coherent thread within Paul's gospel.[9] This apocalyptic or "post-New Perspective" stream of biblical studies prioritizes the unexpected disruption of the in-breaking of God in Christ, Paul's own experiences of vision and revelation, the present and future liberation of humanity and the world, and the cosmic nature of the powers of sin and death.[10]

Relevant to Philippians 3:7–11 is one of the key differences regarding *dikaiosyne* between the third stream and the first two: the third stream has

---

6. G. Tomlin, *Philippians, Colossians*, Reformation Commentary on Scripture, New Testament (Downers Grove, IL: InterVarsity Press, 2013); M. Luther, *Luther's Works*, vol. 4, American ed. (St. Louis, MO: Concordia, 1955), 156–157; J. Calvin, *Commentaries* (Bellingham, WA: Logos Bible Software, 2010), 92.

7. K. Stendahl, "The Apostle Paul and the Introspective Conscience of the West," *Harvard Theological Review* 56, no. 3 (1963): 199.

8. J. D. G. Dunn, *The Theology of Paul's Letter to the Galatians*, New Testament Theology (Cambridge: Cambridge University Press, 1993), 77.

9. "Apocalyptic" is a term used often in biblical scholarship, in the biblical context of the Greek term *apokalypsis*, "unveiling, to make fully known." Usages of the word "apocalyptic" in this chapter should be read with this definition in mind, not the modern definition which refers to destruction, devastation, or the "end times."

10. E. Käsemann, *Primitive Christian Apocalyptic* (London: SCM, 1969), 131–137; J. C. Beker, *Paul the Apostle: The Triumph of God in Life and Thought* (Philadelphia: Fortress, 1980); D. A. Campbell, *The Deliverance of God: An Apocalyptic Rereading of Justification in Paul* (Grand Rapids, MI: Eerdmans, 2009).

more of an emphasis on participation in and transformation by the believer in the new age inaugurated by Christ. Believers have received the action of God in Christ as an "apocalyptic event marking the end of the old age and thus the religious structures that defined the old age."[11] However, they also receive and live in light of its reality through participation.

In conclusion, these different interpretative streams allow us scope for reflection regarding what exactly Paul is on about when he speaks of "the righteousness from God based on faith" (3:9). Space limitations do not allow me to engage with their debates in detail, but all three interpretative streams have important insights for our consideration of Paul's theology and the gospel. However, in Philippians 3:7–11 Paul's emphasis is on participation and transformation, and the contributions of the apocalyptic stream are particularly helpful. Gorman has it right when he notes that in Philippians "Paul calls the Philippian believers . . . to perform in their common life the story of the crucified and exalted Messiah Jesus, the Lord in whom they live."[12]

Theological Reflections
Analysis

In Philippians 3:7–11 we find three important themes for Paul – righteousness, suffering, and participation – combined together concisely. To consider what might have been Paul's big-picture understanding of God and the gospel (his "theology") behind these themes, it helps to recall the source of Paul's profound shift from persecutor of Christ-followers to zealous apostle. Paul received a new understanding of God and Christ through direct revelation (*apokalypsis*) from God (Gal 1:12, 16; 3:23), and his encounter with the risen Christ in Acts 9:3–7 was likely the event that initiated this. It was not by careful study or persuasive argument that Paul changed his views; God "apocalypsed" to Paul that God was fully present in Christ, a truth that God was also revealing through the work of the Holy Spirit to Paul and others (1 Cor 2:10–16). This revelatory source of Paul's changed understanding permanently altered his awareness of God's self-revelation in Christ and *dikaiosyne*.

Having experienced such profound change, Paul now has a new understanding of what is of most value: "knowing Christ Jesus my Lord" (3:8). The thematic emphasis in this passage is on participation in God's

---

11. J. Bassler, "The Theology of Romans 1:18 – 4:25," Theology of Paul's Letter Group at the Society of Biblical Literature (SBL) Annual Meeting, Washington, DC, 1993.

12. M. J. Gorman, *Apostle of the Crucified Lord* (Grand Rapids, MI: Eerdmans, 2017), 412.

righteousness which comes through faith in Christ (3:9b), and he speaks of "knowing Christ" as "[knowing] the power of his resurrection," "sharing [in] his sufferings," and "becoming like him in his death" (3:10). Framed within an "already–not yet" eschatological (study of the final things, the ultimate destiny of the created order) orientation, Paul understands that he lives in a new age inaugurated by Christ.

What does this mean? Present among many Jews of Paul's day was the concept of two epochs of world history: the present age, when evil and death are rampant, and the age to come, when evil and death will be destroyed and justice and peace will triumph.[13] In Philippians 3:7–11 and some of Paul's other writings (Rom 16:25; Gal 1:3–5; 6:15; Eph 1:21; 2:7; 3:9; 1 Cor 2:7–8; 10:11), we find evidence that Paul shared this paradigm, believing that the "coming age" had been inaugurated by Christ (it is "already" here), but that it is *not yet fully here* in completion – awaiting the return of the Messiah. Paul speaks from this convergence, where being "found in Christ" in the future is linked with being "found in Christ" in the present. Thus, while the Philippians are directed to a future hope later in the sentence ("somehow . . . attain the resurrection," 3:11), in these earlier verses Paul says it is an experience which is also present in orientation, entered into now.

Because the new age is already here, in the *present* Paul aligns his participation with the pattern of Christ described in the Christ hymn of Philippians 2:6–11. This participation includes a knowledge of "the power of his resurrection" and transformation ("becoming like him," 3:10) in the present. His present participation is founded in a *future* hope of physical resurrection when the new age which has not yet completely arrived comes in fullness. Paul encourages the Philippians that as they too participate in God's righteousness and act with believing allegiance in Christ as Lord, they will inevitably experience suffering resulting from conformity to Christ's kenotic (self-emptying) and cruciform pattern. In this passage we find evidence of a theological perspective in which imitation of Christ's cruciformity is ultimately participation in God's self-giving nature and mission: the loving mission of God to the world in Christ and through the Spirit.

So what are some implications for workers in integral mission? I shall apply a missional hermeneutic proposed by Darrell Guder, asking, "How did

---

13. N. T. Wright, *Paul and the Faithfulness of God*, Christian Origins and the Question of God (London: SPCK, 2013), 476–477; B. R. Gaventa, ed., *Apocalyptic Paul: Cosmos and Anthropos in Romans 5–8* (Waco: Baylor University Press, 2013), 21.

this particular text continue the formation of witnessing communities then, and how does it do that today?"[14]

Reflection 1: Righteousness – God's "Right-Wising Activity" – Is Both Received and Entered into through Believing Allegiance

In Paul's two usages of *dikaiosyne* in these verses, there is overlap between and support for each of the three main streams of interpretation described earlier. However, unique among his writings, in Philippians 3:7–11 Paul explicitly links God's righteousness with participation in Christ's death and resurrection on the one hand, and with transformation in the life of the believer on the other. In so doing, he describes a righteousness from God which is inseparable from transformative participation in Christ's death and resurrection – the implication being that it is *both* received *and* participated in.

This view is supported by the views of the New Perspective and the apocalyptic interpretative streams' understanding of God's righteousness as "God's right-wising activity" among humanity and all creation, which requires participation by the believer and is inherently transformative.[15] In contrast to that which "comes from the law" (3:9a), Paul says it now comes "through faith in Christ" (3:9b). But what does Paul mean by "faith"? Paul's description of the faith of the believer as the means by which God's right-wising activity is entered into contains several theological and missional insights. The Philippians would likely have heard "faith" as "believing allegiance"[16] (in contrast to an understanding of faith as a kind of "mental assent") to Christ as Lord. This would have been crucial in their formation as a witnessing community, due to its subversion of their Roman context – where allegiance was demonstrated in public to Caesar and other gods in daily life through cultic ritual and social activities. In my own context of East Africa, applying an understanding of faith as "believing allegiance" alongside Paul's linking of participation and transformation to God's righteousness provides similarly important insights.

A single example relates to the "faith" terminology in East Africa. Most cross-cultural workers and African Protestant churches are heavily weighted towards evangelicalism,[17] and salvation and conversion are often framed in the

---

14. D. L. Guder, "Missional Hermeneutics," *Mission Focus: Annual Review* 15 (2007): 108.

15. M. J. Gorman, *Becoming the Gospel* (Grand Rapids, MI: Eerdmans, 2015), 152.

16. Gorman, *Becoming the Gospel*, 69.

17. J. Nkansah-Obrempong, "Evangelical Theology in Africa," *Evangelical Review of Theology* 34, no. 4 (2010): 294.

context of "believing in Jesus" or "putting your faith in Christ." This is linked with an understanding that the primary orientation of the gospel is towards the *future* and explained primarily in terms of a *future* experience ("Do you want to go to heaven when you die?").

An underlying assumption of this paradigm is a largely forensic understanding of God's righteousness, and the traditional Protestant interpretative stream described earlier. The transactional aspect to righteousness as a declaration of right standing before God in Paul's writings is a regular staple in evangelistic preaching. Kenyan theologian Jesse Mugambi suggests that this inclination towards the forensic (future-oriented) and away from the participatory (present-oriented) has had a negative impact on the formation of witnessing communities in East Africa:

> The numerical strength of African Christianity does not match its social engagement in any African country. Generally, Christianity has been introduced to the continent as a religion whose aim is to secure eternal life for believers after their death. Anything that the believers do now is not for the purpose of ensuring better livelihood on earth, but insurance for the life to come. The predominance of this other-worldly teaching has led to abdication of social responsibility on the part of clergy and laity, especially with regard to political and economic affairs.[18]

A recovery of Paul's emphases on the present aspects (the transformative and participatory) of a righteousness from God which is *both* received *and* entered into through faith has practical implications for the East African church and integral mission. It may help us to understand that participation in God's ongoing transformative and redemptive work in Christ is an embodiment of the faith of a witnessing community. A focus on both receiving as well as participating in and being transformed by God's righteousness through believing allegiance to Christ may begin to address the inverse relationship between size and "influence for good" within the African church that Mugambi has noted. Additionally, this "both–and" perspective provides support for the concept of integral mission and formation of resilient communities which are an embodiment of the kind of faith to which Paul is referring.

---

18. J. Mugambi, "Christianity in Africa, 1910–2010," in *Atlas of Global Christianity, 1910–2010*, ed. T. M. Johnson and K. R. Ross (Edinburgh: Edinburgh University Press, 2009), 110.

Reflection 2: Knowing Christ by Participation in the Suffering Inherent in a Life Lived for the Sake of Others

Paul's language of "knowing Christ" provided a theological basis for the Philippians' own suffering: as they participated in God's righteousness with believing allegiance in Christ as Lord, it was inevitable that they would experience similar sufferings to those of Christ through their own kenotic and cross-shaped behaviour. In our own contexts of integral mission globally, how are we to locate our own suffering in the context of a "right-wising" God?

A theological understanding of the kind of suffering Paul describes in 3:7–11 as being that which is naturally experienced in a cruciform life lived for the sake of others (as modelled by Christ) is helpful. It provides a hope founded not only in the eschatological – one day, the Lord will return and restore and redeem all of the suffering creation – but also in the present. Paul encourages the Philippians and us today that power and "knowing Christ" are found in the present *by participating in the same kinds of sufferings that Christ did: those which are for the sake of others*. An understanding that being willing to subject yourself to this kind of suffering is participation in God's "right-wising activity" and God's nature provides encouragement and hope when children continue to die of preventable illnesses, we face corruption or opposition, and exhaustion sets in. This, at the core, suggests Wright, is an embodiment of the gospel: "The 'present age' and the 'age to come' are grinding against one another, like upper and lower millstones, as God's new world is brought to birth. Those who find themselves seized by the message of Jesus will be caught in the middle and *will thereby provide in themselves further evidence of the message*, the news that the crucified Messiah is now the Lord of the whole world."[19]

Reflection 3: Participation – the Pauline Inseparability of the Proclamation and Demonstration of the Gospel and Its Implication for Integral Mission

Paul's self-reflections in 3:7–11 linking knowing Christ, righteousness, faith, suffering, and participation imply active rather than passive participation in Christ. "This is how things actually work in God's righteousness," he may be understood to be saying: "as we receive and enter into it, we will partner with Christ and conform to Christ's sacrificial, self-emptying life and death by taking on the burden of loving others at cost to ourselves. In so doing, we will experience the power of the Spirit both in the present and in the future."

---

19. N. T. Wright, *Paul: A Biography* (San Francisco: HarperOne, 2018), 123.

Paul's emphasis on participation in these verses has implications for integral mission and our understanding of the gospel, particularly in regards to how a witnessing community might participate in the *missio Dei*.[20] Paul *tells* the Philippians to bear witness to God's divine mission (2:12–18), and then in 3:7–11 he *shows* them that bearing witness involves Spirit-enabled participation in the divine mission as described in 2:1–4 and as revealed in the incarnate, crucified, and exalted Christ (2:6–11).

What can practitioners of integral mission learn from this? Do we place priority on evangelism and proclamation of the gospel, or are participatory and demonstrative efforts such as compassionate health care in resource-poor contexts, social justice, and peacemaking initiatives to be given equal weighting in the strategic and operational plans of churches and mission organizations? While important ecumenical declarations, including the Lausanne Covenant of 2010,[21] note that proclamation and demonstration of the gospel must go hand in hand, a quick glance at the mission statements of a few of the larger mission organizations shows a continued emphasis on proclamation to the "unreached" or "least reached" instead of embodying God's righteousness in the form of ongoing redemptive and transformative efforts.[22] Recovering Paul's emphasis on Christ's cruciform life and death as the paradigmatic example of God's righteousness may assist us in looking through a more critical theological lens at our missional efforts.

---

20. I use the term *missio Dei* alongside the concept of Christian "mission" here with the understanding that Christian "mission is not primarily a human work but the work of the triune God." K. Daugherty, "*Missio Dei*: The Trinity and Christian Missions," *Evangelical Review of Theology* 31, no. 2 (2007): 163.

21. Lausanne Movement, "The Cape Town Commitment," 2010, accessed 30 August 2019, https://www.lausanne.org/content/ctcommitment.

22. Serving in Mission, "What We Do," last modified 2016, accessed 29 May 2018, https://www.sim.org/what-we-do; Africa Inland Mission, "Reaching Africa's Unreached," last modified 2017, accessed 29 May 2018, https://aimint.org/; International Mission Board, "Vision and Mission," last modified 2018, accessed 29 May 2018, https://www.imb.org/vision-and-mission/.

4

Dangerous Resilience?

The Institutional Church and Its Systemic Resistance to Change

Thandi Gamedze

The church as an institution is highly resilient. Over the ages, it has weathered all kinds of conditions, and, to all intents and purposes, emerged on the other side unscathed. For those within its indestructible walls, this is generally held up as a thing to be celebrated. It is made biblical, using for justification Isaiah 9's "Of the increase of his government and of peace there will be no end." It is attributed to "Jesus building his church." I believe, however, that there is room (and indeed necessity) to critique this notion when applied universally. The oft-prized "resilience" of the church (or maybe of the Western church – although in a globalized and "post"-colonial world, such distinctions are not so easy to draw, so perhaps we are talking about the institutional church) is often little more than the careful employ of tactics of empire to maintain control, resist change, and uphold the status quo.

Jesus, in his relentless advocacy of the liberation of all, exposed and resisted such tactics at every turn, completely willing for the temple as it existed then (and perhaps all that it had come to symbolize) to quite literally be destroyed to this end. As the church today, we must continually be careful that our desire to facilitate the infiltration of the kingdom into every area of society and the earth is not co-opted by a desire to maintain control and preserve the status quo. In fact, we must begin by interrogating the former desire itself and unpacking what really lies behind it. After all, history holds countless volumes in which the desire for domination has been hidden under the guise of kingdom infiltration. Often we are welcomed (and subsequently colonized) into the church by the *institution* rather than by Jesus himself, and, as a result, end up adopting institutional values that at times do not correlate with those of Jesus.

Sometimes, the fervour to stand up for the kingdom at all costs is unknowingly a fervour to stand up for the preservation of the church as an institution at all costs – an action that requires heavy doses of control. We are unaware that this choice to opt for control is essentially a choice to opt out of freedom. We are unaware that such choices are actually bringing death to the kingdom, and, by extension, to ourselves. The institution that we give our lives to strategically preserve becomes salt to the kingdom's yeast, killing it upon contact, ensuring that it cannot spread as it was designed to.

If we are truly Jesus-followers, freedom for all (the antithesis of control and domination) has to be a pillar that we keep constantly in our sights. If we are truly Jesus-followers, we must follow him into walking out the kingdom in such a way that if the temple becomes problematic, we do not resist its destruction, whatever that needs to look like.

Jesus showed that the temple existed to serve the kingdom, and not the other way around. If it ceased to perform this task, its destruction was necessary. Perhaps the "resilience" of today's temple should not be unthinkingly celebrated. Perhaps it too is in need of a demolition of sorts, that we might be transformed into a vessel that does not limit what can flow through us. Our starting point needs to be the recognition and naming of the tactics that the institutional church employs (consciously or unconsciously) that make us resistant to change, including the change that we desperately need.

Pedagogy

History shows us that education has been used both to control and oppress, and to empower and liberate. This is no different in the history of the church as a people. In many cases the pedagogy of the institutional church has not led to freedom. It has been one-sided, elite-driven, and largely disempowering. From early on, we are told what to believe. Questioning and doubt are inextricably linked to shame, and we quickly learn to sweep them under the carpet. The concept of "holiness" is utilized to render certain things "un-critique-able." And unfaltering faith (or at least the guise of it) is celebrated.

This is cemented in the church's methods of teaching (in which I am including the curation of the "classroom"). The construction of Sunday services is generally as follows. Chairs, facing the front of the room, are set up for occupation by the "learners." Generally, after a few songs of worship, it is time for the sermon. The "teacher" stands at the front with a microphone and shares what he or she has to say, with no space for other input. At the end of this, the service usually finishes without anyone else getting to agree, disagree, or simply share their views.

A key feature in this is what I like to think of as "blank-slate ideology," and I believe that as a concept it undergirds much of the control that has been, and is being, imposed upon various groups in the society's trajectory.

John Locke wrote of this concept in reference to the minds of human beings, saying that we are born as blank slates – each a *tabula rasa* – that become filled upon exposure to various teachings and experiences.[1] Freire problematizes this notion of the mind being a blank slate in his *Pedagogy of the Oppressed*. He refers to the type of education that such a narrative produces as "the 'banking' notion of education," where learners are viewed merely as "receptacles to be filled" – or blank slates to be written on – disempowered from developing the critical consciousness necessary to engage in transformation of the status quo.[2]

Naomi Klein, in her book *The Shock Doctrine*, connects the dots between two occurrences which also are founded on this blank-slate ideology.[3] She first references the ways in which various forms of torture are used for the purpose of wiping a person's consciousness clean, as it were, leaving that person open to being controlled and manipulated towards various agendas. Second (and this is the major thrust of the book), Klein compares this "blank-slate-ness" to that of countries that have undergone some kind of chaos or shock (natural disaster, war, etc.), leaving them vulnerable to the external vulture-like imposition of various neo-liberal agendas.

I would argue that colonialism was also rooted in a blank-slate ideology, as the colonization of land was justified in terms of the land's "uninhabited" nature: the perfect blank slate waiting to be filled with stories of a brave new world (penned, of course, by the colonizer). Even slavery and the ways in which enslaved people were separated from their families, homes, and heritages seems an intentional disorientation of whole peoples – the mass wiping clean of slates in order that a story of the slave master's choosing might be written.

---

1. J. Locke, *An Essay concerning Human Understanding* (Oxford: Clarendon, 1894).

2. P. Freire, *Pedagogy of the Oppressed* (New York: Herder & Herder, 1968).

3. N. Klein, *The Shock Doctrine: The Rise of Disaster Capitalism*, 1st ed. (New York: Metropolitan, 2007).

Freire says that "the oppressor consciousness tends to transform everything surrounding it into an object of its domination."[4] Such domination is made far more possible when the objects are blank slates.

Whether thinking is founded upon a *belief* in pre-existing "blank slates" (John Locke's theories about the newborn mind, colonization) or an intentional *creation* of blank slates (slavery, torture), I believe red flags must always go up. Consciously or otherwise, inherent in this thinking is always a desire to control, in the best-case scenarios coinciding with a belief that such control is necessary and beneficial. Ultimately, blank-slate ideology makes colonization possible, whether it is of land, minds, or economies.

I think that the church, often perhaps in well-meaning ways, is guilty of this ideology. And this belief system continues to inform the ways in which we practise faith. Generally, the most "mature" person (this maturity often being informed by societal biases and intersectional inequalities), the person who is seen to have the tightest grasp on this concept of Truth (which we love to portray as being so black or white), is the one who gets to "fill the receptacles" of the so-called "less mature" ones. And the less mature must sit quietly and listen, unquestioningly allowing their receptacles to be filled up, swallowing whole what is being handed out to their outstretched arms.

On the rare occasion that space is made for interaction, this generally looks like questions from the listeners being directed at the speaker, who is positioned even further by this as the Holder of All Truth. Even the way that the room is set up solidifies this notion. All the chairs look towards the Holder of All Truth. To see the faces of others in the room, we must uncomfortably strain our necks. Whether this is intentional or not, the curation of a space matters, and in the way that the Sunday gathering space is set up we are subconsciously instructed that our opinion, or that of anyone else who happens to be sitting in this sea of forward-facing chairs, is unimportant unless it comes from or has at least been verified by the Holder of All Truth.

Yet the times that have been for me the most challenging and shaping have been when my scriptural input has come, not from one person at the front of a church building but from a discussion with a group of people at various points in their different journeys who see the world differently from me. To hear a person's views on a scripture, before the church has had a chance to condition that person into seeing it exactly as it does, is life-giving and illuminating. Yet such people are rarely given the microphone in a church service. They must wait until their beliefs align perfectly with the beliefs of those in charge;

---

4. Freire, *Pedagogy of the Oppressed*, 58.

only when they can show this *might* they be given a voice. The words of the writer of Hebrews have been weaponized, scripturally maintaining the silence and control of those still classified as "milk-drinkers" – the power to classify assumed by the self-proclaimed "meat-eaters." And in so doing, we are cut off from even the possibility of change.

Musa Dube pushes against this notion by speaking about the need for those who have been marginalized within the church to "name Christ for themselves," as opposed to simply retaining and using "the received Christology."[5]

I think this speaks to the concept of humans being image-bearers of God, a concept that is key in this conversation because it shatters any possibility of blank-slate ideology. It means that we have never been, and never will be, blank slates; that each individual *always* brings something worthy of stopping in wonder for; that knowledge is always made more valuable as it interacts with the holy image borne within.

Building upon this, I believe the indwelling of the Holy Spirit in each of us who follow Jesus is also important. I am somewhat encouraged that the statement "There is no junior Holy Spirit," apparently coined by a revivalist called David Walters, is gaining traction in parts of the church. It makes the point that the Holy Spirit does not adjust his power or significance depending on who he is inhabiting (the fact that we must even make such a statement shows up our problematic beliefs). The intention behind this is to empower the church to take children seriously, as carriers of God with important contributions to make inside and outside the church. This is such an important message; if we truly believe it (not just for children but for all Jesus-followers at all points in their faith), the ways in which we practise "church," and the ways in which we teach and learn when it comes to faith, will become radically different.

When we classify some as teachers and others as learners, we prohibit ourselves from being transformed by the gospel shared by a Samaritan woman. We *must* skill ourselves in the ability to learn from any source. We must become empowered in listening to and following the Holy Spirit both ourselves and with others. We must learn to actively engage, believing that we ourselves have something to bring, as much as others have something to bring. We must learn to "name Christ for ourselves."[6] We must revolutionize the pedagogy that seeks (even unintentionally) to control and oppress, and actively believe that Truth does not simply abide within those at the front with the microphone,

---

5. M. W. Dube, "Who Do You Say That I Am?," *Feminist Theology: The Journal of the Britain & Ireland School of Feminist Theology* 15, no. 3 (2007): 347.

6. Dube, "Who Do You Say That I Am?," 347.

but in us all, waiting to be refined and expanded through authentic interaction and engagement.

Governance

I think this belief that each person has something important to offer needs to be applied to the institutional church's governance structures, too. Obviously these structures differ greatly among churches, thus critique cannot be universally applied. However, in much of my experience and observation, I have noticed recurrent themes which act to make the church resilient against disruption of the status quo. Any change that occurs is almost always incremental (tinkering with service times, changing the gathering space, adding some new songs to the worship repertoire, etc.), with core practices going mostly untouched.

Ultimately, governance is about who gets to make decisions, and how these decisions are made. When we think about these questions within the set-up of the institutional church, we generally see a pyramid shape: a clear hierarchy where the top position is occupied by the church leader, the next layer might be the elders, and the bottom layer is the church congregants (likely there are multiple layers within this group – men, married women, single women, and children). Decisions about theology, about worship practices, about who gets to speak and who doesn't, about how the church's money is used, and so on, are determined at the top and are experienced by those at the bottom. I could say much about this kind of governance structure, but here I will restrict this commentary to the topic of making the church resistant to change.

Making it to the top of the hierarchy is a process. In many cases, it is a male-only club, which already removes half of the population from the running. Often, proof of theological education will be necessary, and as the majority of theology schools teach a majority of Western evangelical theology, it is likely that candidates' beliefs will differ little from those of their peers. Candidates will also most likely be required to have been members of the church for a significant period of time, having gone through membership/foundation courses or the like, and will thus be schooled in the theology and practices of that particular church expression. Each of these qualifiers for leadership prevents anyone with a radically different outlook from getting into a position of being able to make decisions. Thus, the make-up of decision-makers remains consistent, and the decisions made keep things largely as they have always been.

It is telling to ask who is excluded from decision-making. Women are often at the top of this list. Whether due to inherent differences, socialization according to gender roles, experiences of life within a patriarchal society, or a combination of these, often there are differences in the ways in which women view certain things about the world compared with men (obviously this is not generalizable). When women are excluded from leadership roles, the church cuts itself off from change that might come about from these different views being expressed within a decision-making capacity. Similarly excluded from spaces of decision-making are new Christians. Unless these individuals have a history within the church, often their sole picture of the church is captured within their experience of Jesus and their salvation, as well as perhaps some impressions from Scripture that they have read since. Thus, it is likely that their image of the church is radically different from that of the institution itself. However, as these individuals are seen as "spiritually immature," their image of the church does not get to see the light of day within any spaces of decision-making, and thus has little impact on the direction of the church. Many others whose positions afford them views in conflict with the status quo are similarly excluded from decision-making, ensuring the continuation of church as usual.

As an aside – because this is a case in which things play out slightly differently – I also mention the influence of the "invisible hand of the market" that often also plays a significant role in church governance acting to maintain the status quo. As churches are generally funded by congregational tithes, money talks, and often loudly. In the reversal-of-the-pyramid facade so often touted by free-market ideology, power is devolved to congregants – or at least to their money. The church "product" is commodified, and congregants are painted, or paint themselves, as consumers. When something happens in the church that they do not like (the preaching of theology that is too radical, a black person being put into leadership, etc.), they weaponize their money, holding leadership to ransom until they fix their "mistakes" or else suffer the consequences. Consumer rights prevail, and if the consumers are not satisfied with the "product," they remove their capital. Any leader desiring change who, against all the odds, has made it into leadership is cut off at the knees. And while proponents of free-market ideology love to portray it as democratic, giving the power to the people, in reality, in such a scenario, money simply assumes the position of dictator, and those without it are further excluded from decision-making.

For the institutional church to have hope of change, efforts must be made to flatten governance structures, at least to a degree, and leadership must be opened up to include a diverse range of voices that can hear God from different contexts and see the world from different perspectives.

A-Contextualization and Compartmentalization

I think one of the most dangerous things happening in society today is our collective and progressive loss of ability to see how things fit into a bigger picture. Things are so often viewed in an a-contextualized, "snapshot" form. In many ways, a few of which I will explore here, the institutional church seems to be both an expression and a perpetuator of this.

I see this compartmentalization expressed in the Sunday service in a number of ways. While many feel that the church at large has moved on from the idea of wearing your "Sunday best" (although this is definitely not the case throughout), nevertheless this idea seems to remain. It has simply evolved from being expressed physically to being expressed emotionally. Largely, churchgoers continue to feel social pressure to portray their "best," most "spiritual" selves at church. Similarly, the church itself is often "dressed up," creating a separation between it and the context in which it resides. This a-contextualization and compartmentalization also happens in our messaging. Theology that makes little sense when held up to the light of its context is preached unquestioned.

Additionally, such sacred/secular differentiation means that the church and the spiritual practices affirmed by it (prayer, worship, Bible reading) are painted as the only sources from which we can receive spiritual input. Far too often, our experiences of God outside of this are discounted. However, many of my most treasured and powerful times of spiritual learning have not been in these spaces. They have taken place largely outside the walls of the church, through music, through the stars, through listening to what the world is saying, through conversations with other bearers of the image of God. When such contributions – these formative daily life experiences and interactions – are excluded from church gatherings, we rob and disempower ourselves.

All these things make the Sunday gathering space feel separate from the rest of life, meaning that the pieces of life that would ask questions of what happens within that space (questions which would likely demand change) are simply excluded from it.

Conclusion

All of these practices (in addition to others that have not been mentioned here) create an almost impenetrable resilience in the institutional church, rendering it near-impervious to change. Yet following Jesus is a path almost characterized by constant change. We are saved, but we are also walking the journey of salvation each day. We are meant to be always abiding, but also constantly growing and moving forward, and being challenged in our thinking and practice to be more like the One we follow. Institutions in general are not easy things to change. However, we are not called to be an institution but living stones that can mould and adapt to whatever the kingdom requires at different times. I believe that as the church we need to loosen our iron-fisted grip on traditions, practices, and theology, and instead hold these things collectively with open hands. That way, if God wants to do something different, whatever is no longer necessary can easily be removed, and, conversely, whatever is required for the new season can easily be placed in our hands. And we do not have to be afraid of someone letting go of something in error or taking hold of something that should be left alone, for we are, together, each connected to the Holy Spirit, in concert discerning where we are to go.

It is time to shake off all chains that keep us in stagnation. We were not made for control but for liberation, and if God's dream is for our collective, unbridled freedom, then we need to learn to embrace it too.

5

Poorology

Getting the Seminary into the Slum[1]

Viv Grigg

Resilient Learning Networks
Theology Is Our Response to the Horror of Urban Discontinuities

Some of us in the Micah networks have shared a camaraderie in the struggle over forty years to see the church established in the slums. And then some! Like transforming a slum! We have seen exploding urban poor church movements develop. These often appear very spiritual, but they have little comprehension of the holism of the kingdom of God and its implications in transformative action – thus little wisdom, which is not very spiritual! By the way, there are 1.4 billion slum dwellers living in horrific pain, with the Picasso-like contorted faces of the emotionally damaged, and bodies emaciated through hunger pains – though not every day and not at the level of malnourishment, for there is work, but not enough.

It was my privilege to live in Manila's slums, preaching, and forming a church. I was back there just before writing this. The children have grown, hundreds have been uplifted, and there is a school for eight hundred. But my family, those who adopted me, remain trapped in generational poverty. The people transformed the slum – they gained water and electricity and land rights through struggle and deaths. We rebuilt the houses. But now, like that

---

1. This chapter is derived from V. Grigg, *Slum Dwellers' Theology: Pedagogy in the Slums*, Slum Dwellers' Pedagogy 1 (Auckland: Urban Leadership Foundation, 2018). Used with permission.

poem "The Old Woman Who Lived in a Shoe," out of every window there are children hanging. The husbands and wives work at the same menial jobs as their parents and grandparents; so what have we really accomplished?

From out of our more than thirty years of solidarity with such pain, a cluster of activist-professors have multiplied grassroots training in Slum Leaders' Learning Networks. We have also developed training for slum movement leaders in five continents through the MA in Transformational Urban Leadership. In the process, we have created the domain of urban poor missiology. This involves:

- *Competency-based education*: processes common in vocational education and training (VET);
- *Disruptive innovation*: a new academic domain of urban poor missiology and new patterns of storytelling theology;
- A *new question*: How do we scale up to the millions of new slum leaders?

Credibility and Call

It was Ateneo Park in Manila in 1976. I was twenty-five. My first church planting team were spending the day together. As I looked up at the only cloud in the sky, I heard what was like a voice saying, "Unless you create a master's degree for slum leaders where they have space to think, they will not survive." That was it. Nothing fancy. No design. No structure. Just a command! I saw, in that flash of time, that transformative movements among the poor would not survive without the training of movement leaders at a master's degree level.

It would take us thirty years to work out how to do it. First, we had to live it: to pay the same price that workers in the slums pay; to struggle with all the issues, such as how to enter, how to preach, how to form churches, how to engage with the oppression, and how to fight for land rights.

Resilience is persistence in a long journey over time.

Developing leadership was an even bigger challenge, and so was how to engage in the complexity of social, economic, and political issues. We then spent years recruiting workers, relocating them, and training them, as we formed global and indigenous missions.

All this time we were thinking, writing, and studying. It wasn't until thirty years later that the Encarnação Training Commission launched the MA in Transformational Urban Leadership. There was a shared sense of unity around this vision of master's-level training. Our beards grew and our hair turned grey – except for the Filipinos, who are eternally young!

Structuring the Domain of Urban Poor Missiology

What is the content of the "Seminary in the Slums"? I led Slum Workers' Storytelling Consultations in twenty-two cities in the 1990s. They identified 433 outcomes for effective apostles, prophets, pastor-teachers, evangelists, and deacons.

Within these, I identified twenty-three fields. In developing the MA in Transformational Urban Leadership (MATUL), a group of professors who live or work with the poor reduced these to sixteen courses.[2] These get reduced further in each school to make space for traditional theologians to add in courses on (contextual European systematic) theology and (modernist) exegesis. For harmony's sake these need to be accommodated, and also for the sake of engaging with the classical idea people have of theology.

The grassroots training is similar but simpler, as shown in figure 5.1.

Figure 5.1: Grassroots certificates for oral learner leaders in the slums

---

2. Go to "Master of Arts in Transformational Urban Leadership," http://www.matul.org, for an overview of the course development; to "MA Transformational Urban Leadership," http://www.urbanleaders.org/ma, for the content of the commission gatherings; and to "Establishing a Global Cadre of Educational Practitioner-Scholars: The MATUL Commission," http://www.urbanleaders.org/Portfolio/PortfolioMATUL.html, for further analysis of processes.

Jesus's Seminary in the Slums: Theological Derivation of a Degree Structure

For movement leaders among the poor, the critical space is a thinktank with other leaders. This is the nature of a master's degree.

In 2006, I was in Manila at the launch of the MATUL at Asian Theological Seminary. I contrasted Jesus's style of education and the education of the academy. For Jesus was an educator – a brilliant mind. An executive! A philosopher! An educator who made the people marvel, "Where did he get this learning?" He recruited learners around him. He graduated them with a commissioning service to go and educate the world.

Here is an outline of our Jesus-style education in the slums.

Following Jesus in the twenty-first-century context, this MA in Transformational Urban Leadership is an action-reflection degree built around a process I call "transformational conversations." This involves discerning truth through holistic storytelling. Some academics think this is not kosher. They believe that truth can be found only through Platonic logic. Jesus was smarter. So was Paulo Freire. And Jane Vella. And Drs Corrie de Boer and Chona – who have started a thousand preschools, starting in our slum.

But Jesus was far, far deeper than the educational philosopher Freire. He touched not just *conscientização*, that social awareness of structural evil which burdens the soul of the urban poor person, but also the inner spirit. His syllabus began with forty days of prayer and fasting, so we begin the same way with "Urban Spirituality." This is logical from the wisdom of Israel: "The fear of the LORD is the beginning of wisdom" (Prov 9:10). This puts the MATUL outside and far beyond the usual academy, and at far greater levels of learning than in humanistic academia. We encounter the Holy Spirit in the cross as part of the process of spiritual formation. Learners experience that Spirit in their liberation from sin, from trauma, and from bondage to human philosophies (and false doctrines and traditions that Paul and Jesus so opposed). They are also liberated from oppressive, abusive leaders (often religious). They begin to enter into the liberty of his work, ministering to others.

Then, in the power of the Spirit, Jesus began to preach, build a team, and disciple (all elements of our course in "Urban Poor Church Planting"). What Jesus preached was the kingdom of God; so next is an overview of the Scriptures, "A Biblical Theology of Urban Mission." This particularly references the kingdom of God as it engages with poverty, oppression, societal structures, and other issues for slum dwellers.

Of course, Jesus's declared focus was the poor. In fact, the next course is on "Standing with the Marginalized" – prostitutes, street children, drug addicts, and those HIV emaciated who hide in their quiet, dark rooms. This is serving among people like my sister who could not see, sitting in squalor with little food as her family forgot to feed her, mourning the loss of her husband who had left because of her blindness . . . (Each course has character training objectives; in this case, one expects expansion of gifts of mercy and administration, which are the essential qualities of a deacon/ess.)

Jesus understood the issues of the day. What do you think a rebel leader like Simon the Zealot and a tax collector named Matthew discussed over supper along with John, the son of one of the leading families?

"Why should we pay taxes to Rome?"

"It was your family that agreed with Herod on this!"

"We should do away with them all – though not you, Matthew, you repented!"

Jesus discussed ways of understanding the signs of the times, so our course on "Urban Realities and Theology" helps students understand the social, economic, and political contexts of the city. It helps them understand poverty through the lenses of various urban sociology, urban anthropology, urban economic, and urban geography theories. Wisdom is known by her children! This is always the most requested topic when working with slum pastors: "Why are the slums, slums?"

Now here is a beautiful thing: Jesus expected his disciples to bear much fruit! And you too! "Movement Leadership" grapples with the multiplication of interconnected cells in revival movements and social movements.

Jesus was also very engaged with the rich – because he cared for the poor. In fact, Nicodemus came to him because he was caring for the poor – issues of "Advocacy and Justice," connecting rich and poor, were important to him. And he was involved in healing and caring for the sick and those with leprosy; thus, a course on "Primary Health Care."

A quarter of his teaching was on economics, so "Community Economics" (or "Economic Discipleship") is, of course, foundational to any theological degree (it was in your degree, right?).[3] We also have a course on "Entrepreneurial Leadership," along with developing "Slum Education" initiatives, so that every pastor can train people in small business and each church can become a viable economic unit. This lays the educational foundations for the next generation; and it also solves the property barrier, that cost of church buildings, through shared facilities used by associated schools.

---

3. Urban Leadership Foundation, "Economic Discipleship," 2018, accessed 30 August 2019, http://www.economicdisciple.org.

Jesus mentored. Thus, all these courses are taught by supervised action-reflection methods, with a balance of extensive practicum, classroom reflection, and guided readings. Since in the twenty-first century we do have to interface with the academe (descendant of Plato), the reflections are refined in a final "Integration Project or Thesis."

Sample program: Each school has variations			
YEAR 1			
Semester 1		Semester 2	
TUL 500	Biblical Theology of Urban Mission	TUL 540	Urban Reality and Theology
TUL 505	Language and Culture Acquisition	TUL 550	Service to the Marginalized
TUL 520	Urban Spirituality	TUL 555	Educational Centre Development
TUL 530	Building Faith Communities (Church planting)	TUL 560	Theology & Practice of Community Economics
YEAR 2			
Semester 1		Semester 2	
TUL 620	Leadership in Urban Movements	TUL 640	Entrepreneurial & Organizational Leadership
TUL 630	Community Transformation	TUL 655	Advocacy and the Urban Environment
TUL 650	Commuity Health Care	TUL 670 & 675	Research Project or Thesis

Figure 5.2: A sample programme of courses in the MATUL

This is our humble attempt to follow Jesus-style education in the slums, to get the seminary into the slums!

Global Collaboration

This is a degree that has grown from among the poor. Then we exported it back to the West. Following storytelling consultations of urban poor leaders in twenty-two cities including Mumbai (1993) and Hong Kong (1996), the Encarnação Alliance Consultation of urban poor mission leaders in São Paulo in 2002 concluded that collectively we should develop our own training processes for urban poor workers. At the Encarnação Alliance Consultation in Bangkok in July 2004, we sensed that the Lord was in process of mobilizing fifty thousand people to the slums of Asia, Africa, and South America – indigenous and cross-cultural new workers to meet the needs of deepening poverty, growing migrant populations from rural contexts, and the responsiveness of the urban poor.

In 2002, after twenty years of failed discussions with seminaries, we determined that this idea should be called a "leadership programme" by definition, as against a theological programme (which immediately invokes the addition of seven to nine "core" courses). This defused opposition from the traditional theological faculty, and minimized friction as the new style of contextual, storytelling, oral theologizing took root. I had developed the "transformational conversations" model of doing theology with urban students and in city-wide consultations for a number of years.

In Nairobi, Colin Smith had developed similar ideas in moving a training school based at Carlile College into the slum of Kibera and launching a BA degree. At three other institutions there was an immediate sense of compatibility, and the MA programme was launched at Asian Theological Seminary in Manila (July 2007), Hindustan Bible Institute in Chennai (July 2007), and Azusa Pacific University in Los Angeles (Jan. 2010). Rich Slimbach of Azusa Pacific University brilliantly took the initial programme design and simplified it down into a programme proposal which we used as a basis for consensus between the schools.

Programme directors from these schools were invited into the Encarnação Alliance Commission which met in Chennai in November 2006, and they, plus selected faculty, then met in Bangkok in February 2007 to work on course design processes.

Los Angeles launched in 2010. Dr Colin Smith moved the MATUL at Carlile College into partnership with St Paul's University in 2011, though it has not been sustained. Mission India Theological School launched that year also under Dr Hruda Lahora, the dean. Uganda Christian University launched in 2017. And it grows, though not without turmoil.

Creative Expansion

Schools have creatively diversified the initial design. Hindustan Bible Institute are now looking at an undergraduate version that feeds into an urban master's; Mission India Theological School developed a non-formal delivery of the same programme and integrated other courses into the MDiv; Asian Theological Seminary developed the CTUL and created a pathway from the MATUL to MDiv; Rev Michael Mata at Azusa Pacific University developed a United States domestic version of the programme.

Sustainable Infrastructure

Each school functions within its own operational and financial system (there are no dependencies) and under the accreditation system of its own country.

Differentiating the Domain

A domain of knowledge is usually fed from parallel domains but requires some degree of differentiation to survive.

This domain of "urban poor missiology" is significantly fed by movement leadership studies, but business leadership studies or church growth leadership studies do not define the urban poor movement leadership dynamics. It is a programme in social entrepreneurship, with two courses on economics and entrepreneurship, five internships, and a thesis, that trains students in entrepreneurial skills and organizational analysis. But that also does not make it an MBA.

Differentiating the MATUL Learning Domain
It is/is not a Community Development or Social Work or Transformational Leadership degree. It is a Missions Leadership Degree fed by Community Development, Social Entrepreneurship, Business, Economics, Anthropology.

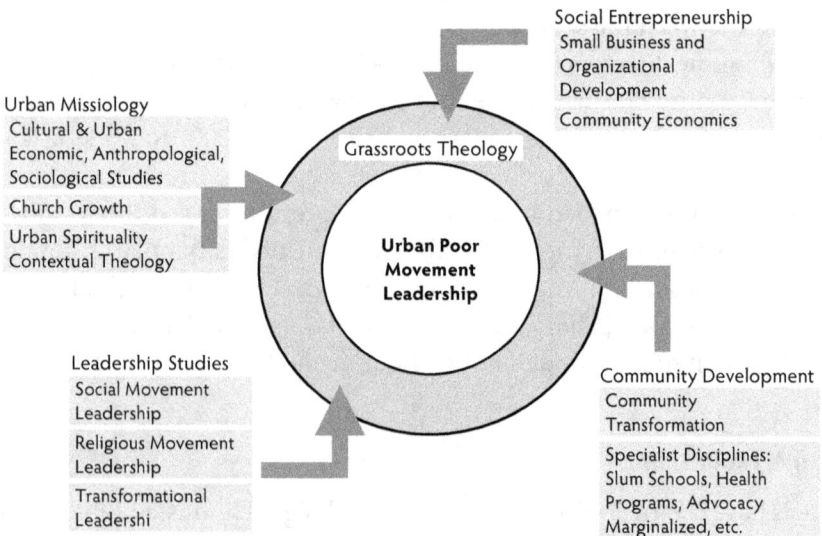

Figure 5.3: Five contributing domains to the domain of "urban poor movement leadership"

Similarly, when community development industry employees see the degree, they presume it is a degree in community development – to train people in how to deliver wealth from West to East. There are five development internships. However, (1) the underlying concept of kingdom growth is from the Scriptures not from the industry standards of the Sustainable Development Goals; (2) it is not based on "round development" or "shalom," where evangelism is identified as a sector, but on the directional holism of Jesus – a holism based on the centrality of proclamation, church growth, and diaconal development as the means of engaging local community needs; and (3) the church planters live by faith and prayer, not fundraising. They live according to the significant biblical principle of manna. This is unintelligible in the development community! There are many other differentiations.

It is a theology degree, with most courses being one-third theology, one-third social analysis, and one-third praxis. The theology is comprehensive, but it is not derived from Augustinian logic. It is derived from contextual engagement and in the midst of it. This theology explores the classic content of ecclesiology, pneumatology, justification, sanctification, and spirituality . . . but it also focuses on the other central biblical themes of poverty, oppression, nation-building, and urbanization. Systematic theologies are sacrosanct to traditional theologians. So is church history and Old and New Testament exegesis. So, in the minds of many theologians, all of these courses must be added to urban theology until there is nothing left for the grassroots pastors to develop their own theologies. The rhetoric of "theology from the margins" means nothing when it comes to the practice of the centre – that centre inherited from the Catholic Church and Protestantism.

The more difficult differentiation is within urban missiology. Is urban poor missiology a separate domain? Or is it just a subset of urban missiology? I choose the first but am ambivalent. Our people, those leaders of slum ministries, won't read this chapter or attend a Micah Network or International Society on Urban Mission conference. These things belong in the upper circuit economy where development workers and theologians hang out. But when we meet together in the lower circuit economy, there is a hum and a buzz in the room. We meet and tell stories. From these stories we integrate theology, and it all makes sense. There is not too much on paper because paper is used by governments to bring legal cases against us, but not much else. We do our business books in our head. We are happy to cross over to the formal upper circuit economy, but we operate within the lower circuit economy.

So community development organizations will buy our people, and so will American urban ministry conference people, and include them to make up their numbers and hear their voices – but we don't belong. We are happy to contribute. But this is *our field of knowledge*.

You are welcome to contribute, if you come as a learner and are willing to live in the slums – otherwise leave us to develop it. The fact that we are graduating with a master's is to learn the formal economy lingo – to learn from it, but not to leave our people.

Conclusions: A Domain Formulated, Multiplying . . .

Urban poor missiology and practice is a domain formulated and multiplying, but fragile . . . as all things among the urban poor are! Expansion is dependent on the communal web of relationships and leadership to sustain them. While we have leadership networking, no leader with access to resources, incarnational experience, and academic credibility has risen up to take over the global catalytic role, despite the mentoring of several. Several have faced unusual catastrophic situations. To scale to a fully-orbed urban poor missiology domain needs a significant increase of structural support.

Breadth of Dissemination

In 2015, the directors of the MATUL programmes, meeting in the yearly MATUL Commission, determined to concentrate their graduates on grassroots development. This means that we are currently in a second phase of exploring how to expand and disseminate the master's level content out to five thousand people in the slums, at a grassroots level of delivery. Each school already had experiments in this direction.

Expanding Grassroots Learning Networks

Since I began living in the slums in the 1970s, there have arisen many hundreds of church multiplication movements within the slums. With the aid of technology, it is possible to reach these pastors and leaders all around the globe. Our desire as a network is to multiply training (networking with existing training models or creating new ones) for these slum leaders through grassroots learning networks in a manner where content is easily disseminated and replicated around the world.

By building personnel and technologically relevant means of transferral, training of these leaders can occur in blocks of six-week courses (the maximum for commitment) on key paradigms. The central dynamic is facilitators on the ground leading face-to-face discussions regarding these paradigms in the local context. From there, leaders are taught how to teach the material themselves, and they go out to teach others in their communities, who also are taught to teach others.

Take one course as an example. During twenty years of setting up storytelling training for semi-literate grassroots slum movement leaders in scores of cities, ten principles of a "Theology and Practice of Cooperative Economics" have been crystallized into economic transformation for slum churches – radically shifting their economic conditions.

In Uganda, Professor J. B. Lukwago has, over ten years, taught these concepts to leaders of 168 churches, resulting in many attempts at economic development and transformation of the role of pastor and flock, as the pastors seek to serve their flocks by helping them become self-sufficient financially.

Strategy for Scaling to Fifty Thousand
Certification Development of an Industry Standards Model

Our mandate from the Bangkok Encarnação Alliance gathering of 2004 has been to train fifty thousand leaders in holistic church-based missional work in the slums. This requires sustainable infrastructure support. Beyond the experiments and theoretical frameworks documented in this study, our desired future is vertically integrated educational infrastructures of urban poor leadership, training from certificates to PhDs, delivered in context at cost-effective levels. Using an industry standards model from vocational education and training (VET), educational systems will do this.

Contrasting Master's/Doctorate and Certificate Level Models

Andrew Sears talks of the contrast between the "Best in the World" model and the "Long Tail" model for maximum volume distribution.[4] At a master's level, we have worked to design a "Best in the World" model. But at the certificate and diploma level, the objective is massification, at minimal cost to recipients, and using platforms accessible by cell phone and Internet cafe.

Outcomes-Based Content

Defined outcomes determine content and delivery style for training. Each partnering organization needs to define its outcomes, and these can be

---

4. "Disruptive Innovation in Higher Education," City Vision University, 2018, accessed 30 August 2019, https://www.udemy.com/course/disruptive-innovation-in-higher-education/.

linked to outcomes for the infrastructure. This is different from classical education, where Aristotelian logic determines the content of courses within defined disciplines.

The content and outcomes for a master's degree have been refined over these fifteen years and have been listed. Much feedback on the outcomes for certificate and diploma training have been collated from multiple sources. It is expected that multiple models will develop, and cross-fertilization between these models is a desired process.

Global Validation

In the vocational training field, training is validated by the employers' confederations. They are the ones who define the skills needed. And they are integrally involved in the design of delivery.

The recommendations here are to utilize the concept of the New Zealand Qualifications Authority framework (there are similar frameworks in vocational training in the UK and Australia). This consists of nine levels of education, where modules between institutions can be validated on their system as at an equivalent level and quality. There are progressions in this model from certificate to diploma to bachelor's to master's to doctorate level education. Ways of defining outcomes at each level are clearly differentiated. We utilize definitions derived from discussions on Bloom's taxonomy.

Lean Start-ups and Unbundling Accreditation

Each country has its own accreditation system, so it has been essential for partners to modify the core concepts of our master's degree to fit with their own context. In Nairobi, the Commission on Higher Education decreed it was a "Transformational Leadership" degree in the field of business. In Manila, additional courses expanded a forty-five-unit degree to fifty-four units. In Brazil, it is designed as a simpler master's, called a *Lato Senso*.

Commitment to evaluation is an essential concept for quality education. The concept of outside evaluation consumes enormous resources and is more expensive than most programmes can sustain. The alternative is involvement of the participants in the programme and course design itself. They can best evaluate much of it. This is part of what is known as "lean start-up design."[5]

---

5. E. Ries, *The Lean Startup: How Today's Entrepreneurs Use Continuous Innovation to Create Radically Successful Businesses*, 1st ed. (New York: Crown Business, 2011).

The accreditation comes from the recipients and from the industry leadership network itself. The concept of a lean start-up is to garner feedback at each step of the development phase. In contrast, traditional education defines the outcomes and course content usually based on past history of what has been taught. In the field of "Transformational Urban Leadership," we are creating a good number of the fields of knowledge as we go. The students themselves have proactively been involved in the programme design. They own it. The MATUL itself is a lean start-up.

However, this has limitations as governments seek control of churches. Often, accredited degrees are needed, so each certificate and diploma given by our partners should be able to be located in a gradated system that confirms competencies from level 3 to level 9.

Technical Requirements: The Knack of Non-complex Delivery

We are focused on creating material from the slums that can be easily disseminated to other slum leaders via mobile phones and tablets. Every pastor and business in the slums owns one. However, our attempts to use cell-phone delivery have not proven effective – at this time. Smart phones are required, and they are expensive, and the cost of downloading is expensive. Nevertheless, we should develop everything in responsive modes.

Computer Cafe Learning Centres

I received the following note from one of our learning network leaders: "My last query is about studying online. Many pastors I have approached about this programme say they would like to join the programme if allowed, but they lack gadgets for assessing the teachings. Some suggested it is possible to have a learning centre, facilitated with computers or screens and Internet. Is it possible for them to schedule time for lessons? How would you advise me on this?" John Edmiston has identified the requirements for setting these up.[6]

An Association of Industry Providers

The key to all of this is for the MATUL Training Commission to become a Commission of Industry Providers that defines outcomes and credits providers. We must expand our network to include leadership and institutions.

---

6. Contact John Edmiston at AIBI Resources, http://www.aibi.org.

Massification of Vocational Training

At the certificate and diploma level we integrate delivery from multiple sources that meet our criteria for effective slum leader education. Thus, we give credibility to certificates from multiple sources internationally, and diplomas where national accreditation processes allow. Four certificates become a diploma recognized by the commission or another body. This follows vocational education and training models.

And Beyond: From Slum Leaders to Institutes for City Transformation

All of these logically fit into urban institutes that need to be developed city by city. Let us press on to see the urban poor reached and the slums transformed across the face of the earth, preparing for Jesus's coming and reigning over the cities.

6

How Do Missionaries Become Resilient?

Preliminary Findings from the Resilient Missionary Study

Geoff Whiteman, Emily Edwards, Anna Savelle, and Kristina Whiteman

The life I live is not easy. There have been seasons that were so hard it was difficult to breathe, but I wouldn't trade this life for anything in the world. In times of great trial is when we can be broken and feel defeated or broken and grab hold of the Father. What I have shared with other new missionaries is to stay very close to him. Breathe God. Talk to him about everything all the time. He will stay close and bring you through the hard times. (Sam, missionary in southern Europe for sixteen years)

In less than a generation, globalization has dramatically changed the world in which missionaries live and minister. At the same time, the world of missions has experienced an equally dramatic metamorphosis. For example, the country that receives the most missionaries is also the country that sends the most missionaries (the United States). These global shifts are also marked by identity shifts whereby more and more missionaries identify with the causes they fight for rather than the denominations and agencies they belong to.

These and many more factors have led to a rise in missionary attrition and a corresponding increase in efforts to intentionally understand and care for missionaries. The largest study of missionary attrition (ReMap II) found the average annual retention rate for agencies was 94 percent. That means every decade the average agency lost one out of two missionaries, and half were for potentially preventable reasons.[1] This is clearly an issue that must be addressed, in efforts informed by both the Christian faith and solid research.

However, reducing attrition is not the same as increasing longevity and well-being – not having cancer doesn't mean you are healthy. Therefore, a mission paradigm focused on retention rather than attrition – on thriving rather than surviving – is essential. The rise in interest in missionary resiliency in recent years reflects the growing need for this paradigm.

Kelly O'Donnell notes:

> Member care, I have learned over and over again, is not about creating a comfortable lifestyle. Nor is it about trusting people instead of trusting God. Rather, it is about further developing the resiliency to do our work well which includes our character, competencies, and social support. It is also about developing relational resiliency, which includes working through the inevitable differences and impasses with international and local fellow-workers. Member care helps to balance the realistic demands of suffering and sacrifice with the realistic needs for support and nurture in our lives.[2]

The aim of this research is to build upon what has been learned through earlier research into missionary attrition and to contribute to the growing body of research into missionary resiliency by exploring this question: How do missionaries become resilient? This chapter reports the preliminary findings from the first phase of combined quantitative and qualitative research.

Methods
Participants

This study consisted of a questionnaire distributed to missionaries (n = 1,044) by snowball method starting in September 2017 and ending in February 2018. The requirements to participate were fluency in English and not being a member of a protected class as defined by the Code of Federal Regulations (45 CFR

---

[1]. R. Hay, *Worth Keeping: Global Perspectives on Best Practice in Missionary Retention* (Pasadena, CA: William Carey Library, 2007); WEA Missions Commission, *Remap II: Worldwide Missionary Retention Study and Best Practices* (Deerfield, IL: World Evangelical Alliance, 2010).

[2]. K. O'Donnell, *Global Member Care*, vol. 1, *The Pearls and Perils of Good Practice* (Pasadena, CA: William Carey Library, 2011), 7.

46 – a minor, incarcerated, or pregnant). After multiple attempts, incomplete answers, and ineligible participants were removed, the final sample size was reduced to a total of 892 participants. *Given the estimated global population of missionaries at 400,000, this sample size has a 99 percent confidence level with a +/- 4.31 percent margin of error.*[3]

Passport and Serving UN Region: The participants in the final sample (n = 892) represent 41 passport nationalities in 17 UN Regions (the unrepresented UN Regions account for 0.8 percent of all sent missionaries). The most prominent regions, accounting for 90.6 percent, are North America (72.6%), Australia–New Zealand (10.0%), and Northern Europe (8.0%). Participants ministered in 148 countries in 21 UN Regions (the unrepresented UN Regions account for 0.8 % of all received missionaries). The most prominent receiving regions, accounting for 68.6 percent, are Eastern Africa (16.4%), South East Asia (11.0%), South America (9.2%), Central America (8.0%), East Asia (7.3%), South Asia (5.5%), West Africa (5.5%), and Western Europe (4.3%). (See table A for details.)

Length of Missionary Service: Ranged from 1 to 58 years (mean = 13.7). 18.5 percent of participants reported serving less than 4 years (n = 165); 24.4 percent reported serving 5–9 years (n = 218); 27.4 percent reported serving 10–19 years (n = 245); and 25.5 percent reported serving 20+ years (n = 228).

Age: Ranged from 21 to 91 (mean = 47.1). 26.8 percent of participants (n = 239) were born after 1981 and belong to the millennial generation; 40.8 percent (n = 364) were born between 1965 and 1980 and belong to Generation X; 30.5 percent (n = 272) were born between 1946 and 1964 and belong to the Boomer Generation; 1.7 percent (n = 15) were born before 1945 and belong to the Silent Generation.

Gender and Relationship Status: 69.7 percent were female (n = 622); 29.4 percent were male (n = 262). While in the field, 60.7 percent were married (n = 540); 27.2 percent were single (n = 242); 7.4 percent got married (n = 66); 2.7 percent got divorced or separated (n = 24); and 1.5 percent were widowed (n = 13).

Church Affiliation: Participants were affiliated with every major branch of Christianity, identifying themselves in the following percentages: 30.8 percent Non-denominational (n = 275); 14.9 percent Baptist (n = 133); 10.0 percent

---

3. Center for the Study of Global Christianity, *Christianity in Its Global Context, 1970–2020: Society, Religion, and Mission* (South Hamilton, MA: Center for the Study of Global Christianity, 2013), https://archive.gordonconwell.edu/ockenga/research/documents/ChristianityinitsGlobalContext.pdf.

Methodist (n = 89); 6.4 percent Non-denominational Evangelical (n = 57); 6.4 percent Pentecostal or Charismatic (n = 57); 5.6 percent Anglican (n = 50); 5.2 percent Reformed (n = 46); 3.9 percent Lutheran (n = 35); 3.7 percent Anabaptist or Brethren (n = 33); 2 percent Restoration Movement (n = 18); 1.7 percent Catholic (n = 15); 1.7 percent Orthodox (Eastern or Oriental) (n = 15); 1.1 percent African Independent Church (n = 10); <1.0 percent Ecumenical or Interdenominational (n = 6); <1.0 percent Seventh-Day Adventist (n = 3); and <1.0 percent Chinese Independent Church (n = 1).

Agency Affiliation: Size of agency with which missionaries were affiliated varied: 7.3 percent worked independently (n = 65); 19.8 percent worked in micro-agencies with fewer than 24 missionaries (n = 177); 17.5 percent worked in small agencies with 25–99 missionaries (n = 156); 27.9 percent worked in mid-size agencies with 100–499 missionaries (n = 249); 7.1 percent worked in large agencies with 500–999 missionaries (n = 63); and 19.1 percent worked in mega-agencies with over 1,000 missionaries (n = 170).

Ministry Function: Participants reported holding a variety of ministry roles, with 75.3 percent reporting multiple ministry functions. The following were the most common: Training or Education (55.5%, n = 495); Social or Community Work (49.3%, n = 440); Support of Existing Local/National Churches (36.0%, n = 321); Support of Mission (administration, support staff, etc.) (33.5%, n = 299); Evangelism among Unreached Peoples (28.9%, n = 258); and Church Planting (28%, n = 250).

Over one in four participants (27.2%, n = 243) chose to write "Other" under ministry functions. The ten most common codes included: Health Care/Medical (18.5%, n = 45); Bible Translation/Literacy (14.0%, n = 34); Leadership (9.5% n = 23); Youth and University Ministry (9.1%, n = 22); Missionary Care and Training (7.0%, n = 17); Orphan Care (6.6%, n = 16); Business As Mission (6.2%, n = 15); Media (4.9%, n = 12); Discipleship (3.7% n = 9); and Worship/Prayer/Creative Arts (3.3%, n = 8).

Procedures

The initial phase of research employed the snowball method and was launched on 19 September 2017 at ResilientMissionary.org/research using an online questionnaire (Resilient Missionary Survey) administered though Survey Monkey.[4] Participant responses were received for five months for the purpose

---

4. An alternative questionnaire was created for cross-cultural workers in creative-access countries with appropriate language for their protected participation. The link for this survey was not published but was included in the automated thank-you email. This survey received

of this project, though the survey remains active so additional participants will be included in future longitudinal studies. The primary means of distribution were social media (Facebook, a blog post) and personal and organizational referrals.[5]

The questionnaire collected basic information about demographics, mission work, sources of stress and support; administered the CD-RISC (Connor-Davidson Resilience Scale)[6] (Cronbach's a = .87); and included a neutral open-ended question: "What else about yourself or your experience as a missionary would you like to share?"

After response collection and anonymization, the quantitative data was analysed using SPSS analytics, and the qualitative data was analysed using ATLAS.ti software. Analysis was done collaboratively by the primary researcher and three research assistants.

Results
Quantitative Analysis

The CD-RISC scores were converted to z-scores and categorized by how many standard deviations each score fell from the mean, resulting in five categories: Lowest CD-RISC (-2), Low CD-RISC (-1), Average CD-RISC (0), High CD-RISC (+1), and Highest CD-RISC (+2). The sample distributed in an even bell curve across these categories: Lowest CD-RISC (3.5%, n = 31); Low CD-RISC (10.5%, n = 94); Average CD-RISC (70.6%, n = 630); High CD-RISC (13.1%, n = 117); Highest CD-RISC (2.2%, n = 20).

CD-RISC Categories: There was little variability based on gender, relationship status, home country, church affiliation, start age, and the number of years on the field. Two patterns found in the demographic data were that (1) increase in age and (2) earlier start year in the field were both associated with increasing CD-RISC scores. For example, Lower CD-RISC had an average age of 44.5 (s = 10.1) and an average year started of 2002.1 (s = 10.5). Higher CD-RISC had an average age of 50.9 (s = 12.8) and started working in the

---

fifty-three complete entries which were included in final counts.

5. An automated referral mechanism was built into the survey to allow participants to nominate those they believed were resilient missionaries. These nominees received an automated email invitation describing the purpose of the study and a link to the questionnaire.

6. The CD-RISC was selected because of its extensive use in previous research (see "Bibliography," at Connor-Davidson Resilience Scale (CD-RISC), http://www.connordavidson-resiliencescale.com/bibliography.php) and the possibility of future research with non-English speakers through the sixty-plus approved translations (see "Translations of the CD-RISC," http://www.connordavidson-resiliencescale.com/translations.php).

average year of 1995.5 (s = 11.5) (See table B for details.) Further analysis on these two patterns is given below.

The two below-average CD-RISC categories reported working primarily in the UN Region of South East Asia, whereas the three categories with average and higher-than-average CD-RISC scores reported working primarily in the UN Region of East Africa.

It is significant to the research team that the Highest CD-RISC category was the only group in which Evangelism among Unreached Peoples as a role was most commonly listed (45%).

Sources of Support: Included among the three most common supports in all groups were Wife/Husband/Child(ren) and Friendship with Co-workers. However, the Lowest CD-RISC was the only group to list Books/Blogs/Podcast as the most common source of support (35.5%).

It is significant to the research team that Friendship with Nationals was a commonly listed source of support in every category except Lowest CD-RISC, and percentages increased from 34% to 55% as CD-RISC scores increased (see table B for details).

Sources of Stress: The three most common sources of stress for the Lower CD-RISC category were Feeling Inadequate (16.8%), Financial Pressures (10.9%); and Unrealized Goals (10.9%). For the Low, Average, and High CD-RISC categories, Conflict with Co-workers was most common. For the Low CD-RISC category, Feeling Inadequate (12.2%) and Cultural Stress (12.2%) were the next most common sources of stress. For the Average CD-RISC category, Over-Worked (13.1%) and Cultural Stress (11.2%) were the next most common. For the High CD-RISC category, Over-Worked (12.9%) and Financial Pressures (10.9%) were next. For the Highest CD-RISC Category, Financial Pressures, Language Barriers, and Unrealized Goals were tied as the most common sources of stress (11.5%). (See table B for details.)

Age and Start Year: Pearson's correlation analysis revealed a statistically significant positive relationship between CD-RISC scores and age: $r(888) = .122$, $p = .000$, $R2 = .015$. (Higher CD-RISC scores were related to older ages.) The correlational analysis also revealed a statistically significant negative relationship between CD-RISC scores and the year individuals began working on the field: $r(889) = -.122$, $p = .000$, $R2 = .015$. This means that higher CD-RISC scores were related to earlier start dates in the field, though not necessarily beginning their work at younger ages: $r(875) = .017$, $p = .615$, $R2 = .0003$.

Multiple Roles: The missionaries in this sample held many different ministry roles on the field, and 75.3 percent of participants held more than one role in their ministry. Use of Pearson's correlation found that higher CD-RISC scores were significantly related to a higher number of roles held in ministry: $r\,(885) = .069$, $p = .04$, $R2 = .005$.

UN Regional Groups: There were no statistically significant differences between participants' home/passport UN Sub-Region on CD-RISC scores: $F\,(5, 883) = 1.07$, $p = .375$, eta squared $= .006$. However, an analysis of variance (ANOVA) examination demonstrated a statistically significant difference in CD-RISC scores between UN Regional Groups worked in. Individuals who worked in the Americas were more likely than those who worked in Africa to have higher CD-RISC scores: $F\,(4, 884) = .261$, $p = .046$, eta squared $= .011$.[7]

Stressors and Supports: An analysis was done of overall reported sources of stress and sources of support (see table B for details). The top three reported sources of support were relational: Co-workers (60.7%), Wife/Husband/Child(ren) (58.1%), and Nationals (47.9%). The top three reported sources of stress were Conflict with Co-workers (41.9%), Over-Worked (37.6%), and Financial Pressures (31.6%).

It is significant to the research team that relationships with co-workers are mentioned as prominent sources of both stress and support.

Qualitative Analysis

After the demographic information and stress/support, this survey contained a neutral, open-ended question: "What else about yourself or your experience as a missionary would you like to share?" Of the participants, 52% (n = 465) chose to answer this question. The wide-ranging answers were coded and analysed according to the five CD-RISC categories; co-occurrence of Positive/Negative perspective; and other code groups.

Low CD-RISC: This group (8.9%, n = 41) was most frequently associated with codes including Specific Stresses (51.22%), Stress due to Ministry/Role (24.39%), and Unmet Expectations (21.95%). Interestingly, this category also had the highest incidence of reporting Specific Supports (21.95%), coming in at twice the average for respondents overall (10.11%).

Average CD-RISC: This group (71.1%, n = 327) was most frequently associated with codes including Specific Stresses (31.10%), Negative Perspective (20.73%), Positive Perspective (17.99%), and Trust in God as Key (17.38%).

High CD-RISC: This group (14.6%, n = 67) was most frequently associated with codes including Specific Stresses (33.82%), Negative Perspective (25%),

---

7. The United Nations divides the world into five Regional Groups and twenty-two Sub-Regions.

Organization (25%), Stress due to Ministry/Role (20.59%), Trust in God/Relationship with God as Key (19.12%), and Positive Perspective (19.12%). Only the mentions of their sending organization were significantly higher than the average.

Highest CD-RISC: This group (2.0%, n = 9) was most frequently associated with codes including Trust in God/Relationship with God as Key (50%), Positive Perspective (41.67%), Importance of Calling (33.33%), and the practice of Prayer or other Spiritual Disciplines (33.33%).

It is significant to the research team that every single response (100%) mentioned spiritual supports in this open-ended question. They were most likely of all groups to mention helpful personal traits such as flexibility, interpersonal skills, boundaries, etc. (41.67%).

Positive or Negative Perspective: The open-ended question was designed to be neutral, yet some responses had ether a Negative Perspective (20.6%) or a Positive Perspective (18.7%). Out of the five most frequent co-occurrences with Negative Perspective, three relate back to stress, with over 50 percent listing a specific type of stress and one-third listing stress in their role or ministry. Additionally, Negative Perspective frequently co-occurred with comments about Unmet Expectations (27%), Conflict (24%), and Overall Stress (24%).

The most predominant co-occurrences with the Positive Perspective, on the other hand, had to do with Specific Support Systems (25% of answers) and two types of Spiritual Support (over 50%), Gratitude (23%), and "Living in Tension" (23%).

It is significant to the research team that those in the Highest CD-RISC category reported over twice the rate of Positive Perspective reported in other categories, and none of the Highest category reported a Negative Perspective. Those in the Lowest CD-RISC category reported a Negative Perspective at over twice the rate of the group overall.

Supports and Stressors: Over 40 percent of answers related either to expressions of Specific Stress in missionaries' lives (32.69%), to Overall Stress (13.12%), or to both. Conflict, a common source of stress, was mentioned by 10.11 percent of respondents. Over 50 percent mentioned Spiritual Supports that had been helpful to them, with high incidences of mentions of how important their Relationship with God and/or Trusting in God has been (17.42%) and of God's work within their frailties or weaknesses (13.98%). Many mentioned Specific Support Systems (13.76%).

It is significant to the research team that those in the Lowest and Low categories were more likely than other categories to mention Specific Stresses (such as Stress about Family, Safety, or Ministry/Role), while no participants in the Highest group mentioned either Specific Stresses or their Overall Stress level.

Living in Tension: Of great interest to the research team was the frequent expression (9.68%) of statements coded as "Living in Tension." These answers expressed both positive and negative – both challenge and hope – held at the same time. For example: "We may face lots of difficulties and challenges, but if we remain faithful to our task God will bring marvellous things out of it."

Discussion

First, the research team is grateful to the missionaries who participated in this study. What they have shared with us is more than data in a spreadsheet – they have shared their stories, the joys and heartbreaks that have accompanied their missionary experience. We are honoured by this precious gift and desire to steward this data in ways that will better serve the global missionary community.

The initial findings from this phase of research suggest that it is important to discover how missionaries become resilient. This robust set of data will require further analysis in future publications. For the sake of length, this report will focus on only one of several significant findings.

There are multiple ways to interpret the statistically significant correlation between CD-RISC category and age (.001 level). One interpretation is that for missionaries, resiliency functions more like a skill or virtue than an inherent trait. That is to say, missionaries may be able to develop their capacity for resiliency. If that's the case, then each adversity becomes an opportunity to engage in resiliency-promoting habits and attitudes that allow missionaries, one day at a time, to persevere with joy.

In order to discover what these habits and attitudes might be, we need to understand how missionaries are transformed by the tribulations they endure. We need to understand the role of relationships – who are the people that come alongside, and how are they supportive? We need to understand the specific ways missionaries personally respond to adversity in ways that build their resiliency. Ultimately, as Christians, we believe that Jesus Christ, through his death and resurrection, is the Resilient One. So how are missionaries abiding in him, participating in his mission, and appropriating his resiliency?[8]

---

8. Of the 892 missionaries who participated in the initial questionnaire, 244 also participated in a written interview that addressed these very questions. The analysis of the written interview was expected to be completed in 2018/2019.

Table A: Missionaries sent and received, by UN region[9]

UN Group	UN Region	Sample Sent	%	All Sent	%	Diff.	Sample Rec'd	%	All Received	%	Diff.
Africa	Eastern Africa	6	0.7%	4,428	1.1%	-0.4%	148	16.4%	33,185	8.3%	8.06%
Africa	Middle Africa	0	0.0%	2,360	0.6%	-0.6%	7	0.8%	24,520	6.1%	-5.36%
Africa	Northern Africa	0	0.0%	432	0.1%	-0.1%	18	2.0%	3,730	0.9%	1.06%
Africa	Southern Africa	11	1.2%	8,330	2.1%	-0.8%	36	4.0%	15,460	3.9%	0.11%
Africa	Western Africa	6	0.7%	5,156	1.3%	-0.6%	48	5.3%	16,690	4.2%	1.13%
Americas	Caribbean	2	0.2%	1,783	0.4%	-0.2%	31	3.4%	10,545	2.6%	0.79%
Americas	Central America	3	0.3%	8,170	2.0%	-1.7%	72	8.0%	20,030	5.0%	2.95%
Americas	Northern America	640	72.4%	135,166	33.8%	38.6%	25	2.8%	40,180	10.0%	-7.28%
Americas	South America	9	1.0%	48,399	12.1%	-11.1%	83	9.2%	71,410	17.9%	-8.68%
Asia	Central Asia	0	0.0%	72	0.0%	-0.0%	26	2.9%	600	0.2%	2.72%
Asia	Eastern Asia	5	0.6%	26,937	6.7%	-6.2%	66	7.3%	19,460	4.9%	2.43%
Asia	South Asia	7	0.8%	10,452	2.6%	-1.8%	50	5.5%	13,550	3.4%	2.14%
Asia	South-East Asia	7	0.8%	8,567	2.1%	-1.3%	100	11.0%	20,280	5.1%	5.98%
Asia	Western Asia	2	0.2%	1,045	0.3%	-0.0%	30	3.3%	5,360	1.3%	1.97%
Europe	Eastern Europe	2	0.2%	5,540	1.4%	-1.2%	38	4.2%	32,120	8.0%	-3.83%
Europe	Northern Europe	72	8.1%	29,345	7.3%	0.8%	20	2.2%	14,859	3.7%	-1.50%
Europe	Southern Europe	2	0.2%	47,155	11.8%	-11.6%	36	4.0%	17,150	4.3%	-0.31%
Europe	Western Europe	19	2.1%	50,685	12.7%	-10.5%	39	4.3%	25,930	6.5%	-2.17%
Oceania	Australia and New Zealand	89	10.1%	5,000	1.3%	8.8%	12	1.3%	6,019	1.5%	-0.18%
Oceania	Melanesia	0	0.0%	335	0.1%	-0.1%	19	2.1%	5,560	1.4%	0.71%
Oceania	Micronesia	0	0.0%	123	0.0%	-0.0%	1	0.1%	1,380	0.3%	-0.23%
Oceania	Polynesia	2	0.2%	520	0.1%	0.1%	0	0.0%	1,982	0.5%	-0.50%
	Total	884		400,000	100%		905		400,000		

---

9. Working in multiple regions accounts for the discrepancy in the Sample Received column. Dual Citizens (n = 5) are removed from the Sample Sent column.

How Do Missionaries Become Resilient? 75

Table B: Key demographic and psychographic characteristics of resilience groups (calculated by standard deviation)

	LOWER CD-RISC	%	LOW CD-RISC	%	AVERAGE CD-RISC	%	HIGH CD-RISC	%	HIGHER CD-RISC	%
Mean Age	44.5		44.8		47		49.6		50.9	
Start Year	2002.1		2002.9		2001.3		1998.4		1995.5	
Ministry Type	Social / Community	26%	Training / Education	22%	Training / Education	21%	Training / Education	22%	Training / Education	21%
	Training / Education	23%	Social / Community	18%	Social / Community	19%	Social / Community	19%	Social / Community	20%
	Support Existing Churches	17%	Support of Mission	16%	Support Existing Churches	14%	Support of Mission	13%	Evangelism	16%
	Church Planting	9%	Support Existing Churches	14%	Support of Mission	13%	Support Existing Churches	14%	Church Planting	13%
	Evangelism	7%	Evangelism	12%	Church Planting	11%	Church Planting	12%	Support Existing Churches	11%
	Support of Mission	9%	Church Planting	7%	Evangelism	11%	Evangelism	10%	Support of Mission	7%
SUPPORTS	Family	19%	Coworkers	20%	Family	20%	Coworkers	18%	Local friendships	17%
	Coworkers	16%	Family	17%	Coworkers	18%	Family	17%	Coworkers	17%
	Books, blogs, podcast	11%	Local friendships	10%	Local friendships	12%	Local friendships	14%	Family	15%
	Support from home	10%	Retreats or Vacations	9%	Support from home	9%	Spiritual disciplines	11%	Spiritual disciplines	9%
	Local friendships	9%	Spiritual disciplines	8%	Spiritual disciplines	8%	Support from home	9%	Support from home	8%
	Spiritual disciplines	7%	Support from home	7%	Retreats or Vacations	7%	Visits from Friends/Family	4%	Books, blogs, podcast	6%
	Personal Studies	6%	Books, blogs, podcast	6%	Books, blogs, podcast	6%	Retreats or Vacations	4%	Personal Studies	6%
	Exercise	5%	Caring Leader	5%	Personal Studies	5%	Books, blogs, podcast	5%	Visits from Friends/Family	6%
	Caring Leader	3%	Visits from Friends/Family	4%	Caring Leader	3%	Personal Studies	3%	Retreats or Vacations	5%
	Visits from Friends/Family	3%	Personal Studies	3%	Visits from Friends/Family	3%	Excercise	4%	Corporate Worship	5%
STRESSORS	Feeling Inadequate	17%	Conflict w/ Coworkers	13%	Conflict w/ Coworkers	13%	Conflict w/ Coworkers	14%	Financial Pressures	12%
	Financial Pressures	11%	Feeling Inadequate	12%	Overworked	13%	Overworked	13%	Language Barriers	12%
	Unrealized Goals	11%	Cultural Stress	11%	Cultural Stress	11%	Financial Pressures	11%	Cultural Stress	12%
	Overworked	10%	Overworked	10%	Financial Pressures	9%	Cultural Stress	10%	Unrealized Goals	10%
	Cultural Stress	9%	Language Barriers	9%	Feeling Inadequate	9%	Feeling Inadequate	8%	Conflict w/ Coworkers	12%
	Conflict w/ Coworkers	8%	Unrealized Goals	7%	Language Barriers	9%	Language Barriers	8%	Overworked	8%
	Needs of Children	6%	Financial Pressures	7%	Needs of Children	7%	Needs of Children	6%	Mental/Emotional Health	8%
	Maintaining Spiritual dis.	6%	Needs of Children	6%	Mental/Emotional Health	6%	Mental/Emotional Health	6%	Maintaining Spiritual dis.	6%
	Language Barriers	3%	Mental/Emotional Health	5%	Maintaining Spiritual dis.	5%	Maintaining Spiritual dis.	4%	Feeling Inadequate	4%
	Mental/Emotional Health	4%	Maintaining Spiritual dis.	4%	Unrealized Goals	4%	Unrealized Goals	3%	Needs of Children	2%

7

The Gospel and the Future of Cities

A Call to Action

Participants of the Gospel and Future of Cities Summit

Now the LORD God had planted a garden in the east, in Eden; and there he put the man he had formed. (Gen 2:8)

Your people will rebuild the ancient ruins, and will raise up the age-old foundations; you will be called Repairer of Broken Walls, Restorer of Streets with Dwellings. (Isa 58:12)

Also, seek the peace and prosperity of the city to which I have carried you into exile. Pray to the LORD for it, because if it prospers, you too will prosper. (Jer 29:7)

And I heard a loud voice from the throne saying, "Look! God's dwelling-place is now among the people, and he will dwell with them. They will be his people, and God himself will be with them and be their God"... No longer will there be any curse. The throne of God and of the Lamb will be in the city, and his servants will serve him. (Rev 21:3; 22:3)

History and Intent of the Call to Action

There are times in history when it is imperative that God's people come together to pray, seek discernment, and act. Such a time was the gathering of evangelical Christians convened by the World Evangelical Alliance (WEA) and Micah

Global for the Gospel and the Future of Cities Summit, 15–16 October 2016 in Quito, Ecuador.[1]

The gathering was crucial for several reasons. First was the need to build on two seminal evangelical declarations – the Lausanne Movement's 2010 "Cape Town Commitment,"[2] and the 2012 Lausanne/WEA Creation Care Network's "Creation Care and the Gospel: Call to Action."[3] We reaffirm the "Cape Town Commitment" statement on cities that "We must love our cities as God does, with holy discernment and Christ-like compassion, and obey his command to 'seek the welfare of the city,' wherever that may be."[4] The Gospel and the Future of Cities Summit especially wanted to take seriously the concomitant charge that "Church and mission leaders worldwide [should give] urgent strategic attention to urban mission."

We also reaffirm the "Creation Care and the Gospel: Call to Action" statement pertaining to cities, recognizing that "rural and urban design and living" has a significant practical bearing on how to care for creation. We especially wanted to take up the statement's bold challenge to undertake more detailed work to provide in-depth guidance for Christians in this area.

Inspired by these earlier statements; as witnesses to the enormous spiritual, social, economic, and environmental challenges posed by today's rapidly urbanizing world; and in response to the prompting of the Holy Spirit, this call to action seeks to motivate and activate the whole church to more deeply understand, love, and care for cities and their inhabitants from God's perspective, and to become better equipped and effective for urban presence, ministry, work, and witness. The broader world is also challenged by the future of cities in these times. It was this urgency that provided the second reason for convening the Gospel and the Future of Cities Summit in Quito. Immediately following the summit was Habitat III – a global conference on urbanism organized every twenty years by the United Nations that in this instance drew together over forty-five thousand global leaders.[5] The document that was produced through the Habitat III process and signed by all the member

---

1. Formally the Urban Shalom Project.

2. To review the "Cape Town Commitment," go to https://www.lausanne.org/content/ctc/ctcommitment.

3. To review the "Creation Care and the Gospel: Call to Action" statement go to https://www.lausanne.org/content/statement/creation-care-call-to-action.

4. "Cape Town Commitment" II.D.4.

5. The objectives of Habitat III were to "secure renewed political commitment for sustainable urban development, assess accomplishments to date, address poverty, and identify and address new and emerging challenges," and to produce a "concise, focused, forward-looking, and action-oriented outcome document."

governments of the United Nations is entitled "The New Urban Agenda." Its call for more sustainable, resilient, safe, equitable, healthy, and inclusive cities was a historic moment worthy of the church's attention and encouragement.

Indeed, Habitat III galvanized the global evangelical community to join the world and come together to pray for the world's cities, and to discuss and reflect on biblical truths as they apply to cities, integral urban mission, and care of creation in today's historical context. The outcomes of the Gospel and the Future of Cities Summit provided a platform for evangelical delegates attending Habitat III to engage in global dialogue about urbanism from an evangelical perspective undergirded by the consensus generated at the summit. Because the gospel applies to all aspects of life and creation, including the well-being individuals and communities can derive from living in cities; and because evangelical Christians faithfully following the gospel have a historic and abiding concern for cities and their inhabitants, and thus the world's urban future, Habitat III was not an event for Christians to miss.

Our summit drew together theologians, scholars, pastors, Christian leaders, architects, urban planners, community organizers, and creation care practitioners from around the world under the auspices of the World Evangelical Alliance (WEA), the Lausanne/WEA Creation Care Network, Micah Global, and the Urban Shalom Society.

This is a call to action for Christians to engage with urban challenges and opportunities, including UN-Habitat's New Urban Agenda.

Our Convictions

Our discussion, study, and prayer together led us to the following two convictions:

1. Concern for All Forms of Human Urbanism – Be They Large Aggregates Such As Cities or Smaller Aggregates Such As Towns, Villages, or Neighbourhoods – Truly Is a Gospel Issue within the Lordship of Christ[6]

We reaffirmed this primary biblical truth concerning cities articulated in the "Cape Town Commitment," but also sought to explore and expand biblical understandings of urbanism with the following reflections.

---

6. For convenience' sake, we will refer to the range of human settlements – cities, towns, villages, etc. – simply as "the city." For example, when we affirm that "God loves the city," what we really mean is that God loves not just cities, but all varieties of places – cities, towns, villages, etc., that people design and build for human settlement.

God Is a Place-Maker

In the book of Genesis, we learn God created the earth as a good place, and thus a good home for all God's creatures. Creation, then, is a loving gift from the hand of God, and human beings – who are a special and unique part of creation, being made in God's image – are given the inimitable responsibility to be good and faithful stewards of God's gift of creation.

In Genesis chapter 2 we also learn God intentionally "planted a garden in the east, in Eden" for Adam to dwell in. That is, God purposely made a place in creation for Adam and his descendants to inhabit and where they could flourish. Some essential truths we learn from the book of Genesis include that God created people to have a relationship with him, to live in community and right relationship with others, and to live in-placed lives.[7] In other words, people and places go together!

This theme is reflected throughout Scripture and was particularly important for the Israelite people as they entered the promised land. Later, even when they were in exile, God's command to his people was to settle in the land where they had been led, and to work for its prospering (Jer 29).

The incarnation is also an example of God's place-making desire as he seeks to make a home physically with his people. Finally, in Revelation 22 we see heaven coming to earth, in the form of a garden city. This realization points to both the importance God places on the physical environment in which we live and his desire to place-make with us.

God Loves People, Places, and Cities

Because God created and loves in-placed people, God is concerned about the places where people live their lives – which today are modern forms of farms, villages, towns, and cities situated within, and dependent upon, the larger gift of creation.

The character and quality of these places – which people are responsible for designing and building – have a direct impact on the well-being of human families, individuals, and communities. Furthermore, the design of human settlements also affects the integrity and health of the earth's ecosystems, which humans and all other creatures are dependent on for life.

Christians need to be concerned about the design of cities, towns, and villages. Indeed, it is a legitimate, abiding, and imperative concern for Christians because in God's created order people and places are inextricably

---

7. To learn more, see C. G. Bartholomew, *Where Mortals Dwell: A Christian View of Place for Today* (Grand Rapids, MI: Baker Academic, 2011), ch. 1, "A Theology of Place in Genesis 1–3."

tied together. Furthermore, because God is concerned that people dwell in places that are fit for human flourishing, so too should Christians be concerned with the suitability of cities for human flourishing and care of creation.

2. The World Is Facing a Period of Rapid Urbanization Which Is Exacerbating Serious Social, Economic, Cultural, Ecological, and Spiritual Challenges That Must Be Addressed through Integral Urban Mission in Our Generation

This conviction led to these additional reflections.

The Future of Cities

God's relationship with humanity starts by dwelling together in the garden of Eden. Following the fall and restoration of all creation by means of God's love and grace through the death and resurrection of Jesus Christ, biblical history will culminate when God and humanity once again dwell together in righteousness in a perfect place. That perfect place described in the book of Revelation is a garden city on a redeemed and renewed earth.

Cities are complex. Their designs and inner workings can produce many positive things and bless people's lives. At the same time, city realities can grind people up and cause pain and despair. Cities can also cause excessive pollution and transgress the ecological integrity of creation, or they can function within the limits of healthy ecosystems.

Cities will never be perfect places until Christ returns, but in the meantime Christians can pray for, and work towards, designing and making cities that are just, equitable, productive, safe, diverse, healthy, ecologically sustainable, beautiful, enjoyable – in short, places that are commensurate with God's love and goodness. In such places, families, communities, and individuals can flourish.

We also recognize that while 50 percent of the world's population currently lives in cities, with rapid urbanization 70–75 percent of the world's population will live in urban areas within twenty to thirty years. This rapid rate of urban growth creates a fresh, insistent reality that unequivocally calls for an extraordinary response of Christian love and integral mission that is ample and sophisticated enough to respond to the challenges of rapid urbanization and the complexity of the city.

We affirm the great work of many evangelical churches all over the world as they engage with their neighbourhoods, villages, towns, and cities through being sources of light, life, and hope. We recognize, however, that to fully participate in God's reign on earth, and the flourishing of individuals and communities in our generation, we need to go deeper into embracing, understanding, and influencing the physical, social, spiritual, and other inner workings of the city.

A Call to Action: Urban Shalom

Based on these two convictions we call the whole church, in dependence on the Holy Spirit, to respond radically and faithfully to love and care for places – cities, towns, villages, and neighbourhoods worldwide – as participants in, and agents of, God's shalom though the transforming love and power of Christ. We especially call on evangelical leaders, national evangelical organizations, and all local churches to urgently understand, learn, and act at personal, community, national, and international levels to "seek the peace and prosperity of the city," or what we term "urban shalom."

Specifically, we call for:

- Digging deeper into Scripture to learn more truths related to cities from God's perspective and to implement what we learn.
- Applying principles of biblical shalom to develop a vision and practice for urban shalom in integral urban mission. We articulate some principles of urban shalom below.
- Coming closer to God through prayer and other spiritual disciplines so that along with the empowerment of the Holy Spirit we acquire Christian virtues and other spiritual resources to uphold us in our integral urban mission work.
- Supporting, encouraging, and collaborating with our Christian colleagues who are also engaged in integral urban mission work.
- The creation of the common good through seeking to work with our non-Christian colleagues, incorporating the best thinking and practices for city-building from them and other organizations devoted to improving cities. This includes but is not limited to the work of the United Nations Human Settlements Programme, otherwise known as UN-Habitat, and the principles of urban design outlined in the "Charter of the New Urbanism."

Urban Shalom: Some Principles and Practices
Urban Shalom Is a Vision for the City

We recognize God has a picture of the way life should be, and this picture includes cities. Shalom – which is the picture of the way life should be – best equates with flourishing and is concerned with the well-being of the individual in the context of his or her community. Flourishing includes our basic needs being met; a sense of belonging to the land and to each other; the ability to contribute to the common good; living a life full of meaning; the chance to celebrate; and a growing relationship with God.

Passages such as Isaiah 58:6–12; 65:17–25; Jeremiah 29:7; Luke 4:16–20; and Revelation 22:1–5 put this concept into the context of cities, showing that they can be places where the young and old are valued, needs are met, and each is engaged in meaningful work. These passages also point to the role and responsibility people of faith have in developing cities of shalom.

We affirm that the concept of shalom not only guides our involvement in integral urban mission, but also compels us to dialogue and work with non-Christians who are working for the common good in cities.

Urban Shalom Invites a Fresh Call to Discipleship

This vision of shalom cannot simply be another ideology to hold other leaders, governments, and people to. As Christians, we ourselves must become people of shalom, more closely following, joining, and participating with the Prince of Shalom. As Christians, we recognize that we have fallen short of what God requires of us in seeking cities of shalom. We have not given our whole hearts and lives to seeing all relationships flourish. We have not spent enough time sacrificially praying and standing in front of the Lord on our cities' behalf. We recognize that activities that undermine God's shalom – excessive consumerism, greed, and competitiveness, to name a few examples – are deeply ingrained in our lives and can only be transformed through Jesus Christ in the power of the Holy Spirit. We ask for God's forgiveness and seek repentance. We ask God that the church today might become a "sign, instrument and foretaste" of God's coming shalom in the places where we are responsible and have influence.[8]

Given the times in which we live, the call to encounter, follow, and join the Risen Jesus afresh as Prince of Shalom in his mission in the world could not be more urgent and important.

---

8. Lesslie Newbigin, *The Open Secret: An Introduction to the Theology of Mission* (Grand Rapids, MI: Eerdmans, 1995), 233.

Urban Shalom Embraces Economic Equity and Security

God's shalom is absent wherever people are not flourishing with God, other people, and the earth. We recognize that this time in history is one in which cities are seeing a growing and scandalous gap between rich and poor. Condominiums with helicopter pads and swimming pools can sit right next to overcrowded slums with open sewers. Disparity destabilizes urban relationships and our life together, dehumanizing people and destroying creation. Jesus came to "bring life and all its fullness," which is a promise for every urban resident, not just the wealthy ones. Where there are powers and evil forces at work perpetuating disparity and economic injustice we call for prayer and active opposition while working for economic equity and security for all people. This includes overcoming disparity in the spheres of business, education, media, government, art and entertainment, families, and religion. Each sphere has unique challenges and opportunities to seek the shalom of the city.

Given the growing inequalities between rich and poor, and the suffering and instability this is causing the planet, the need to confront the powers that cause economic disparity while working for economic justice, equity, and security for all people is vital and urgent.

Urban Shalom Embraces Diversity

Cities are by their very nature diverse places. Indeed, a city could not function if every person had exactly the same talent or was the same age and gender. We, therefore, welcome diversity in all its complexities, recognizing that Christians can be people of welcome and hospitality, helping neighbours belong together despite differences. We recognize that no individual church or Christian group will be able to respond to all the diverse challenges and opportunities of their city. Strategic alliances, therefore, need to be developed that can share people, resources, and expertise; identify emerging trends and find responses in proactive ways; and help to advocate for specialist, yet connected responses.

Given the expanding cultural and religious diversity of our cities, and the need for human dignity and respect for diversity, the role of shalom-makers and community builders is vital and urgent.

Urban Shalom Cares for Creation

Creation is a gift from God that has an ecological integrity which supports life. God calls us to be good stewards and caretakers of his creation, thereby enabling us to enjoy the fruits of creation to meet our needs, but without overstepping the ecological limits of creation and destroying creation's fruitfulness.[9]

The everyday intersection of most people's lives and God's creation is not a pristine forest, a wild river, a tropical reef, or some other unspoiled part of creation, but their homes and the cities or towns those homes are a part of. Thus, how cities and towns are designed and built; how they function internally (e.g. their transportation systems; their drinking water, waste water, and storm water systems; their energy systems; their solid waste systems; etc.); how they relate to their neighbouring rural/agricultural communities; and how they relate to wild places – land, rivers, lakes, oceans, and so on – has a big impact on the health and integrity of creation. For this reason, urban shalom requires that urban development use models and practices of urban land use, city planning, architecture and design, and building that accord with preserving the ecological integrity of God's creation.[10]

Urban Shalom Involves Urban Design

One of the defining characteristics of the urban context is high densities of people sharing a common place. How this sharing of place is negotiated is a crucial challenge for faith and mission. Given the speed of urbanization the burgeoning of quickly established slums and informal settlements, suburban sprawl, and tower block sprawl are understandable, but can undermine human flourishing. The role of imagination and of designing, planning, and building places amenable to humans living together in harmony with God and place is therefore a critical one. The Judeo-Christian tradition recognizes that seeing urban shalom happen in cities requires deep prayer, imagination, will, and political engagement coupled with commensurate urban design and development.

Given the growing density of populations and the various types of stresses this is causing, the need to design, develop, and, where necessary, retrofit places so they accord with shalom so that communities can flourish is vital and urgent.[11]

---

9. For more in-depth information about the principles of creation care that this call to action upholds and supports, go to https://www.lausanne.org/networks/issues/creation-care.

10. The "Charter of the New Urbanism" and accompanying "Canons of Sustainable Architecture and Urbanism" articulate principles and practices that can be used to design and build places that care for creation. To read these documents go to Congress for the New Urbanism, https://www.cnu.org/who-we-are/charter-new-urbanism.

11. The critical relationship between urban shalom and urban design applies not only to care of creation, but to many other aspects of shalom in the city. Thus, the "Charter of the New Urbanism" and accompanying "Canons of Sustainable Architecture and Urbanism"

Urban Shalom Engages with the Public Square

Christians are explicitly called to be "salt and light" in the world; thus we have a responsibility to contribute to the common good of the city, which requires proactively and constructively engaging in the public square.

We lament that as evangelicals our engagement in the public square has not always come from a place of love and has not always borne witness to God's kingdom or his shalom. It is with regret that we acknowledge the times we have stood in the way of God's purposes in the world, through ignorance, institutional self-interest, individual divergent priorities, or other motivations.

Because of this recognition, we seek to enter the conversation around the future and development of cities with a humility and an openness to truly hear the perspectives and needs of others living in, and served by, the city, and where possible to partner in initiatives. We recognize that we do not have to control initiatives but simply to serve, bringing what we have to offer to the table.

We also acknowledge that many people of faith are already in positions of influence within cities, and as leaders we pledge to encourage and strengthen those leaders to be bearers and influencers towards shalom.

Urban Shalom Develops Relationships and Collaborations for the Common Good

Jesus encourages us to seek out people of peace and to work with them for the benefit of the kingdom. In a rapidly changing world, we acknowledge the need to do this as never before. We seek to develop relationships and collaborations with others who may not share the faith but who are open to its values and the possibility of working together towards the common good. This will allow us to connect with their expertise currently beyond our reach and influence its use towards shalom.

We also recognize the value of organizational partnership and will seek to build connections between churches and local authorities, educational institutions, international organizations, and so forth, for the positive development of the city. This includes but is not limited to the work of UN-Habitat, and the principles of urbanism outlined in the "Charter of the New

---

apply practically to this point too. To read these documents go to Congress for the New Urbanism, https://www.cnu.org/who-we-are/charter-new-urbanism.

Urbanism" and accompanying "Canons of Sustainable Architecture and Urbanism."[12]

Associations for the Common Good of People, Places, and Cities

As people of faith we are not starting from scratch in this endeavour. We have a long history of relevant cultural engagement that reflects gospel and kingdom priorities in cities, from starting hospitals to running schools, to service agencies and NGOs that work all over the world loving, strengthening, and building up the resilience of marginalized people living in cities. We also recognize that people of faith are not the only ones concerned about cities and the experience of people living in them. In October 2016, fifty thousand people gathered in Quito, Ecuador, for UN-Habitat III. They were city planners, architects, leaders of NGOs, politicians, support agencies, academics, activists, advocates, UN officials, engineers, and climate specialists, all with the aim of creating sustainable and liveable cities.

Drawing on the biblical narrative, including the concept of shalom, as well as our own history and learning, we believe there are three important extra-biblical international documents that Christians should be aware of and analyse for the data and information they contain, the practical tools and insights they offer, and the strategic goals they describe regarding cities and their development over the next twenty to thirty years.

"The City We Need 2.0: Towards a New Urban Paradigm" was put together through a civil society consultation process involving twenty-six Urban Thinkers Campuses held in various places around the world.[13] These conferences and other meetings identified ten key principles for city development.

Cities need to:

- Be socially inclusive and engaging;
- Be affordable, accessible, and equitable;
- Be economically vibrant and inclusive;
- Be collectively managed and democratically governed;
- Foster cohesive territorial development;

---

12. To read "The Charter of the New Urbanism" and the accompanying "Canons of Sustainable Architecture and Urbanism" go to Congress for the New Urbanism, https://www.cnu.org/who-we-are/charter-new-urbanism.

13. To review "The City We Need 2.0" go to World Urban Campaign, https://www.worldurbancampaign.org/sites/default/files/Annex%20I_The%20City%20We%20Need%20TCWN%202.0_1.pdf.

- Be regenerative and resilient;
- Have shared identities and sense of place;
- Be well planned, walkable, and transit-friendly;
- Be safe, healthy, and promote well-being;
- Be places of learning and innovation.

The second document is Habitat III's "New Urban Agenda."[14] This document was unanimously ratified in Quito by all member states of the United Nations at the culmination of the conference. It drew heavily on the recommendations of "The City We Need" as well as on expertise from other key stakeholders. We affirm its core vision:

> We share a vision of cities for all, referring to the equal use and enjoyment of cities and human settlements, seeking to promote inclusivity and ensure that all inhabitants, of present and future generations, without discrimination of any kind, are able to inhabit and produce just, safe, healthy, accessible, affordable, resilient and sustainable cities and human settlements to foster prosperity and quality of life for all. We note the efforts of some national and local governments to enshrine this vision, referred to as "right to the city," in their legislation, political declarations and charters.

The third, and very practical, document is the Congress for the New Urbanism's "Charter of the New Urbanism" that opens with the following statements that then lead into specific urban design principles. We affirm the Charter's core understanding of cities and principles for urban design.[15]

> The Congress for the New Urbanism views disinvestment in central cities, the spread of placeless sprawl, increasing separation by race and income, environmental deterioration, loss of agricultural lands and wilderness, and the erosion of society's built heritage as one interrelated community-building challenge.
>
> *We stand* for the restoration of existing urban centers and towns within coherent metropolitan regions, the reconfiguration of

---

14. To review the "New Urban Agenda" go to http://habitat3.org/wp-content/uploads/NUA-English.pdf.

15. To read "The Charter of the New Urbanism" and the accompanying "Canons of Sustainable Architecture and Urbanism" go to Congress for the New Urbanism, https://www.cnu.org/who-we-are/charter-new-urbanism.

sprawling suburbs into communities of real neighborhoods and diverse districts, the conservation of natural environments, and the preservation of our built legacy.

We advocate the restructuring of public policy and development practices to support the following principles: neighborhoods should be diverse in use and population; communities should be designed for the pedestrian and transit as well as the car; cities and towns should be shaped by physically defined and universally accessible public spaces and community institutions; urban places should be framed by architecture and landscape design that celebrate local history, climate, ecology, and building practice.

We recognize that physical solutions by themselves will not solve social and economic problems, but neither can economic vitality, community stability, and environmental health be sustained without a coherent and supportive physical framework.

We represent a broad-based citizenry, composed of public and private sector leaders, community activists, and multidisciplinary professionals. We are committed to reestablishing the relationship between the art of building and the making of community, through citizen-based participatory planning and design.

We dedicate ourselves to reclaiming our homes, blocks, streets, parks, neighborhoods, districts, towns, cities, regions, and environment.

While these documents are holistic in nature, as people of faith we must ask the question: *Do they go far enough towards manifesting a kingdom of God (shalom) agenda in the world?* We proffer this question not out of contentiousness, but sincerely from our commitment to Christian faith as we engage with these globally influential events and documents related to the world's urban future. Where compatibility and common good can be found, we will undertake supportive actions implementing the "New Urban Agenda." And where from a Christian perspective we see deficits in the "New Urban Agenda," we are willing to take divergent actions that we believe are in line with advancing God's vision for urban shalom. We apply the same to the "Charter of the New Urbanism" and to the Congress for the New Urbanism that works to advance the design principles of the Charter.

A Call to Action Is a Call to Prayer

A call to action requires more than words and activities. There is a spiritual struggle over the future of the city that we must not shy away from. We especially encourage prayers for the following:

Engaging Reality: Lord, open our eyes, ears, and other senses to perceive what is happening in our cities, towns, and villages. Help us to find ways to appropriately respond to the realities we perceive and understand.

Lamenting Grief: Lord, help us feel deeply what you feel about the happenings in our cities, towns, and villages. We especially pray for forgiveness where we have been responsible for, or benefited from, holding others back from flourishing in our cities, towns, and villages.

Finding Hope: Lord, our hope is in you and the redemption of all things in Christ (Col 1:15–19). Help us to be your agents of shalom in cities, and for cities. May we be fully empowered for this work by your Holy Spirit, the truth of your Word, the vision of your kingdom on earth, and the assurance of Jesus's return that will consummate the reconciliation and redemption of all creation, including cities, that was initiated with Jesus's resurrection victory over sin and death.

Celebrating Victories: Lord, help us to rejoice over and celebrate the breakthroughs and victories, big and small, that will be won along the way as we take up this call to action for urban shalom.

Agreed together by the participants of the Gospel and Future of Cities Summit, Quito, Ecuador, 16 October 2016.

Part 2

Resilience, Peace, and Justice

8

Biblical Teachings on Social Justice

Manavala Reuben

Justice is at the very heart of the Christian faith, even though this fact is yet to be understood by many Christians. As light and salt to the world, Christians have a role in bringing the needed transformation in social justice.

In order to understand what the Bible teaches about justice, it is necessary to set the term in the context of relationships.[1] Social justice concerns relations between individuals, communities, nations, and the poor. The problem of social justice today is that some people are radically dependent on and controlled by others; as a result, they are not free and do not have the right to self-determination. Some people are denied the right to participate fully in public life; they do not have the opportunity to fight for their rights, and many live in poverty. While the rich have more than enough to satisfy their wants, the poor do not have sufficient to satisfy their basic needs.[2] This chapter examines what social justice is and how it is dealt with from a biblical perspective.

Vocabulary

The phrase "righteousness [sĕd-āqâ] and justice [miš-pāt]" (Ps 33:5) brings together two of the biggest words in the Old Testament. The nearest English expression to the double-word phrase would be "social justice."[3] Justice is taken

---

1. J. Putti, *The Fair Deal* (Bangalore: Kristu Jyoti College, 1993), 434.
2. Putti, *Fair Deal*, 7–9.
3. C. J. H. Wright, *Old Testament Ethics for the People of God* (Downers Grove, IL: InterVarsity Press, 2004), 255.

in the individualistic sense of giving people what they earn or deserve. The adjective "social" is then a reminder that justice is about community; we are not just individuals engaged in a constant competition for power, wealth, and prestige, but we belong to one another because we first belong to God.[4]

Specifically, social justice deals with economic (society's rules and procedures for maintaining efficient and fair commercial markets), remedial (just and fair rules and procedures pertaining to civil and legal matters), and distributive (focusing on assuring a fair distribution of burdens and benefits among the citizens) areas of social concern.[5]

The Theological Basis for Social Justice

Social justice problems are often viewed as law and order problems. Aristotle famously spoke of justice as "rendering to each person their due" – but this simple phrase doesn't tell us what is due to each person.[6]

Retributive theories of justice provide the simplest answers: people should get what they deserve. The Old Testament conception of "eye for eye" and "tooth for tooth" (Exod 21:23–24) conveys the idea. If you destroy somebody else's eye, you deserve to lose the sight of your own eye; and similarly with a tooth, or, in the case of murder, with a life. We can understand that theory of justice perfectly well.[7]

Views of Social Justice

The God of the Bible is the God who delights in and demands justice. From Old Testament days until now, God has commanded his people to exercise justice in their dealings with others.[8]

---

4. P. C. Kemeny, ed., *Church, State and Public Justice* (Andhra Pradesh: Authentic, 2007), 221.

5. The original source for this idea was http://thechristianworldview.com/tcwblog/archives/741. No longer available online.

6. Kemeny, *Church, State and Public Justice*, 218.

7. Kemeny, 218–219.

8. "Our Daily Bread," *RBC Ministries Indonesia*, 16 January 2006.

1. Justice in the Priestly Tradition

Justice in the Noahic Covenant

In the Old Testament, election and covenant are based on the love of God. Human beings are the agents of God's will, being creatures made in the image of God (Gen 1:27). The image of God includes the dignity and dominion of humanity. Humankind's dignity is seen in the fact that they were made for fellowship with God. Humankind's dominion is seen in the fact that human beings share in the sovereignty of God over the earth (Ps 8:4–6).

Humanity's pride and disobedience resulted in the fall. Though the image of God in humanity was not lost at the fall (Gen 5:1–3; 9:5–6), it left people with corrupt and wicked hearts (Gen 8:21).[9] God established the Noahic covenant to show that life is sacred and to guarantee that he would never again destroy life with a flood; human government was brought in to assure order in the world (Gen 8:20 – 9:29).[10]

Justice in the Abrahamic Covenant

The Abrahamic covenant is seen in God's commitment to give Abraham a land as an everlasting possession (Gen 17:7–8) and in the universal promise that "all peoples on earth will be blessed through you" (Gen 12:3).[11]

God does justice and wants justice done. He elected Abraham for being righteous and just. The purpose of the divine election of Abraham (Gen 18:18–19) seems to have been God's planned judgment upon Sodom and Gomorrah.[12] Justice and righteousness are not merely demands but means of bringing God's promised blessing to the nations through Abraham (Gen 18:19–20).[13] The two cities became powerful symbols of human wickedness and divine retribution.[14] God had seen and heard the suffering of the oppressed. He planned to take action on behalf of the wronged and to put things right. Abraham feared for the safety of any righteous people living there and appealed to God, "Will you sweep away the righteous with the wicked?" Abraham was appealing to God on the assumption that God must and would act justly. When God later

---

9. H. H. Barnette, *Introduction to Christian Ethics* (Nashville: Broadman, 1961), 14–16.
10. R. Griffith, *Old Testament Survey*, vol. 1 (Singapore: Singapore Bible College, 2006), 65.
11. Griffith, *Old Testament Survey*, 59.
12. Wright, *Old Testament Ethics*, 259.
13. Wright, 36.
14. B. M. Metzger and M. D. Coogan, *The Oxford Companion to the Bible* (New York: Oxford University Press, 1993), 707.

destroyed those wicked cities, righteous Lot and his two daughters escaped with angelic help (2 Pet 2:7–9). God acted according to his own character.[15]

2. Justice in the Mosaic Covenant (Deuteronomistic)

The Mosaic covenant stressed that Israel bound itself voluntarily to Yahweh, in response to his beneficent deeds.[16] The origin of social justice goes back to the fact that every human being is created in God's image. The Israelites had to learn that each individual is equally important, and for that reason no person was to be oppressed by his or her neighbour.[17] Concern for justice for the oppressed is evident throughout the Scriptures (Deut 15:1–18; 24:14–15). It was especially clear when God established the rules for his covenant people after they were released from Egyptian bondage (Deut 24:18–22). Moses emphasized concern for the underprivileged (Exod 22:22–27; 23:6–9; Lev 19:9–10). Repeatedly, the Israelites were reminded that they were to love those who were foreigners because God loved them, and because they themselves had been foreigners in Egypt (Exod 23:9; Lev 19:34; Deut 10:17–19). Standing for justice means fighting against injustice.[18]

The laws of the Decalogue have universal values indispensable for the fulfilment of the individual and society. Humanity's duty to God is summed up in the first four laws; the remaining six apply to people's duties to others and themselves. The longest of the Ten Commandments is the fourth commandment: "Remember the Sabbath day by keeping it holy" (Exod 20:8–11).[19] The word Sabbath means "to rest." God created all things in six days and rested on the seventh, blessing and sanctifying it.[20] The rest day ordained by God is a special day for us to recall God's amazing creative power and rejoice in his grace in giving us a day free from labour. Just as God loves us and cares for our spiritual, physical, and mental well-being, Christians should not forget that God loves all people.[21]

---

15. Wright, *Old Testament Ethics*, 259.
16. B. W. Anderson, *Contours of Old Testament Theology* (Minneapolis, MN: Fortress, 2011), 206.
17. B. Thorogood, *A Guide to the Book of Amos* (London: Hollen Street, 1977), 47.
18. "Our Daily Bread," *RBC Ministries Indonesia*, 20 February 2009.
19. Andrew Goh, "Impact," *Impact Christian Communications Singapore*, July 2012, 32.
20. Barnette, *Christian Ethics*, 20–22.
21. Andrew Goh, "Impact," *Impact Christian Communications Singapore*, July 2012, 32–33.

3. Justice in the Davidic Covenant (Zion)

The Davidic covenant finds its source in the Abrahamic covenant and is a further expansion of the original promise of offspring to Abraham. God's promise to Abraham of offspring (Gen 12:1–3) from his own body (Gen 15:1–9) which would become a great nation is further explained in his promise to David (2 Sam 7:10–16).[22] The Davidic covenant stresses that Yahweh, by a solemn oath, is bound to David and to his dynasty unconditionally and for ever. In the ancient Near East, the king was fundamentally responsible for securing justice and righteousness. This was accomplished by the administration of the law and the use of royal edicts to release people from social burdens. In difficult cases, the king was the highest court of appeal (Ps 72). However, the king was not the source of the law, but was subject to the revealed Torah (Deut 17:14–20). In Israel, political power was to be exercised under the judgment of God (2 Sam 12:1–14). If a king committed an offence in office, he was subject to punishment, as in the case of David's sin with Bathsheba (2 Sam 11).[23]

4. Justice in the Historical Books

In the book of Esther, we learn that Haman (the highest noble under King Xerxes) expected every royal official to kneel down and honour him. But Mordecai refused to bow to anyone but God. This outraged Haman, who planned to destroy not only Mordecai but every Jew in the whole Persian Empire. Haman convinced Xerxes to sign a decree authorizing the destruction of all Jews and started building a gallows for the execution of Mordecai. Esther confronted this injustice towards the Jews (Esth 3:1–11; 7:1–10).[24]

From the book of Nehemiah (Neh 8:1–8), we learn that Ezra read the books of the law (Pentateuch) aloud to the people. This led the people to commit themselves again to God's law, confess their sins (Neh 9:1–3), and renew the covenant with their redeemer God. In the book of Ezra, we see his distress at the intermarriages of Jewish men with non-Jewish women. He led these men to repent of their sin and to divorce their pagan wives (Ezra 10:17–44). The concern here seems to have been to keep the marriage relationship inviolate.[25]

---

22. Griffith, *Old Testament Survey*, 61.
23. Anderson, *Contours*, 206–207.
24. "Our Daily Bread," *RBC Ministries Indonesia*, 25 October 2011.
25. H. Lockyer, *Nelson's Illustrated Bible Dictionary: An Authoritative One-Volume Reference Work on the Bible, with Full-Colour Illustrations* (Nashville: T. Nelson, 1986), 372.

5. Justice in the Wisdom Literature (Poetical Books)

The requirement for social justice on the part of Israel's kings is expressed in Proverbs (Prov 29:4, 14). King Lemuel's mother warns him against women and wine. She acknowledges the positive value of wine in bringing temporary relief to those in anguish (Prov 31:3–7). However, the responsibility of the king is to fight problems, not to forget them in the temporary pleasures of women or wine. He must look to restore people's rights and to reward those who have been oppressed (31:5). He should campaign for the rights of all who are poor and destitute (31:8). He should ensure a system of justice so that the poor are not deprived of their rights (31:9), whether through ignorance of what they can receive or through inability to engage expensive lawyers to help them. The phrase "speak up for those" implies that the king should speak up for the rights of all, and especially for the poor whose voices are often neglected in society.

This is a call to every citizen of the country to, like Lemuel's mother, pray for the rulers (presidents, prime ministers, politicians, government officials, etc.) of the nation to provide care and be concerned for the poor.[26] The book of Ecclesiastes speaks about the selfish and materialistic age,[27] and also about the lack of compassion, generosity, and justice (Eccl 4:1), and the impoverishing effect of bureaucracy (Eccl 5:8–9).[28] In the Song of Songs, we see King Solomon's relationship with a Shulamite girl (Song 3:6–11), and the justice is that those with abundance must help the needy generously.[29] Job showed concern for the poor during the period in which he was materially blessed. He rescued the poor, fatherless, widowed, blind, lame, needy, and strangers, and opposed the wicked (Job 29:12–17).[30]

6. Justice in the Prophetical Books

The Old Testament prophets' primary message was to the community, calling the nation back to God. Social justice is boldly outlined.[31] The Old Testament prophets raised their voices against oppression, injustice, dishonesty, and corruption, and against the rulers of the ancient world. Ethically, the prophets emphasized the principles of justice, righteousness, mercy, and love. Central to

---

26. "Methodist Message," *The Methodist Message Church in Singapore*, August 2009, 1, 20.
27. Lockyer, *Bible Dictionary*, 318.
28. Wright, *Old Testament Ethics*, 178.
29. C. L. Blomberg, *Neither Poverty Nor Riches* (Grand Rapids, MI: Eerdmans, 1999), 60.
30. Blomberg, *Neither Poverty Nor Riches*, 58.
31. L. O. Richards, *The Believer's Guidebook* (Grand Rapids, MI: Zondervan, 1983), 338.

Amos is the demand for justice; in Isaiah it is holiness. Jeremiah and Ezekiel speak of the responsibility of the individual before God. Hosea stresses love (Hos 10:12). Loving God and loving our neighbour is the heart of the matter. This is also the prophetic word given in the book of Micah. The heart of the matter is the matter of the heart. Micah summarizes the essence of religion in ethical terms: "He has shown you, O mortal, what is good. And what does the Lord require of you? To act justly and to love mercy and to walk humbly with your God" (Mic 6:8).[32]

The book of Amos speaks about oppression of the poor. The rich used their influence to oppress the poor and to extract greater luxuries for themselves (Amos 2:6–7). Poverty is so often linked with injustice, and Amos graphically describes God's anger towards those who oppress the poor (Amos 4:1–2; 5:11–12, 24; 8:4). Corruption was rife, with the use of false measures and tampered scales to cheat customers (Amos 8:5–6).[33] In the modern context we can see how foreign workers are oppressed.

Jeremiah denounced King Jehoiakim for his unjust exploitation of unpaid labour, and described him as a man whose eyes and heart were set only on dishonest gain, and on oppression and extortion (Jer 22:13–17).[34]

Isaiah condemned the authorities in Jerusalem, likening them to the rulers of Sodom (Isa 1:10). The reason, it seems, is that Jerusalem had become, like Sodom, a place of suffering, oppression, robbery, corruption, and violence, instead of showing the justice and righteousness that used to be present there (Isa 1:21–23).[35]

Ezekiel attacked the "shepherds" or rulers, of Israel for their greed and lack of care for the needs of the people (Ezek 34:1–8).[36]

Justice in the New Testament

Matthew has a fondness for comparing Christ with Moses. The old righteousness of the law (Moses) is contrasted with the new law of love (Christ). The new righteousness demands more truthfulness (Matt 5:33–37). The old law says, "Do not swear falsely" (Lev 19:12); Jesus says, do not swear at all. The new

---

32. Barnette, *Christian Ethics*, 29.
33. D. Burnett, *The Healing of the Nations: The Biblical Basis of the Mission of God* (Carlisle: Paternoster, 1996), 84–87.
34. Wright, *Old Testament Ethics*, 274.
35. Blomberg, *Neither Poverty Nor Riches*, 274.
36. E. Käsemann, *Primitive Christian Apocalyptic* (London: SCM, 1969), 274.

ethic of Christ demands non-retaliation (Matt 5:38–42). The old law says, "An eye for an eye" (Exod 21:23–25; Deut 19:16–21); Jesus says, no retaliation at all. The new righteousness-ethic revealed by Christ demands more love (Matt 5:43–48). The old law says, "Love your neighbour" (Lev 19:16–18); Jesus says, "Love your enemies."[37]

The epistle of James is largely an ethical tract. The royal law of love involves sharing of possessions with those in need (Jas 2:8, 14–16). James goes on to denounce the social injustices of the rich who gain their goods through oppression (5:1). He speaks specifically of those who keep back, by fraud, the just and lawful wages of workers. Turning from the oppressors to the oppressed, James urges the reclamation of sinners "until the coming of the Lord."[38]

Conclusion

Justice is not a programme or project; it is the characteristic of God. Justice specifies what is right, not only as measured by a code of law, but also by what makes for right relationships as well as harmony and peace. The Bible speaks of doing justice (Ps 82:3; Prov 21:3), whereas we speak of getting justice. To do justice is to maintain what is right or to set things right.[39]

In a world filled with injustice, we can take the wrongs done to us, submit them to the Judge of the earth, and trust him for ultimate justice. Everyone desires justice, but we must recognize that our human frailty makes it challenging to find true justice.[40] As followers of Christ, the question for us to think about is, what do others see in us? How do we treat each other? How do we relate to each other? Exploitation of the poor, human rights abuses, how our nations deal with foreigners, and how our nations treat so-called enemies – these are all behaviours of injustice. We as Christians need to raise our voices. Standing publicly for what is right is required of us as well. Christians should not repay evil with evil but bless and pray for our enemies.[41] Social justice is thus a critical aspect of a Christian's life. God is interested in people. Christians need to play a lead role in this vital area of social justice. God as the sovereign ruler has absolute authority over justice.

---

37. Barnette, *Christian Ethics*, 58.
38. Barnette, 82.
39. Lockyer, *Bible Dictionary*, 609.
40. "Our Daily Bread," *RBC Ministries Indonesia*, 7 January 2009.
41. "Our Daily Bread," *RBC Ministries Indonesia*, 16 January 2006.

9

Addressing Gender and Leadership Gaps in Development-Oriented Organizations

Amy Reynolds and Nikki Toyama-Szeto

In their pursuit of integral mission, many Christian organizations have made gender justice a priority. Such commitments may translate into actions like having more women and girls in a programme, investing in girls' education, or working with anti-violence efforts. These are all extremely important, given the ways in which women and girls are marginalized around the world. However, gender justice also includes attention to gendered dynamics within one's own organization.

We start by acknowledging that many strong resources exist for Christian organizations wanting to pursue gender justice, even as they are underutilized. We have listed some of these at the end of this chapter ("Resources for Increasing Gender Engagement in Programmes"), but they are not the focus of our chapter. Fewer resources exist for those wanting to create organizations where women and men serve and lead together. While there are some resources that exist for large NGOs (such as work on gender mainstreaming), more work is needed in thinking about the how and why of empowering women to lead in Christian missions and development, at both local and/or global levels.

Why Gender Justice Matters
The Example of Early Christian Community

It began with a seemingly simple problem. The early church in Acts had committed to taking care of the vulnerable in their midst. This often meant those who did not have a male family figure to provide for them – the widows and the orphans. Through the collection of resources (Acts 2), the early church shared what it had and provided for these women. However, as the church grew, the Greek widows were overlooked. Perhaps it was an issue of language or of visibility. But Acts 6 clarifies that it was only the Greek widows, not the Hebraic ones, who were being overlooked.

What is notable here is the response of the Jewish disciples. Many will simply increase the representation of the wronged party as a solution. They did not set up and create an advisory council of Hellenistic Jews to advise – and retain the power themselves. Rather, there was a giving over of power to rectify the situation. A new group of Hellenistic disciples was given leadership over the distribution of the resources to all, including all decision-making. This included handing over the distribution of food to the Hebraic and the Greek widows. It was an extraordinary divestment of power, which was largely concentrated in Jewish hands, to those who would be able to best see those who had been invisible.

This specific example in Acts presents a guide for a leadership response to an issue. In other examples, it is notable to see the ways in which Paul in his writings affirms the power of a diverse body of Christ working in unity (1 Cor 12:12–31; Eph 4:1–16). These exhortations affirm the unique contributions of many, adding to the fulfilment of the purposes of the whole.

The example of the distribution of food to the Greek widows highlights the increased effectiveness that comes when there are leaders from the community that is being served – increased programmatic effectivity.

Accomplishing Mission

As organizations committed to bringing shalom, it is important to recognize that gender equity in leadership is also connected with missional effectiveness and stewarding our resources faithfully. As detailed more in *Missional Effectiveness*,[1] Christian non-profits that have diversified their leadership acknowledge that they have become more productive, engaged broader perspectives, and

---

1. J. Curry and A. Reynolds, *Missional Effectiveness: Achieving Institutional Goals and Mission* (Wrentham, MA: Gordon College, 2016).

witnessed greater professionalism among men and women. That is, groups note the positive ways increased gender equality in leadership allows them to (1) steward and use the gifts that women bring and (2) change dynamics in positive ways among all leaders. In a recent issue of *Transformation*, Julie Ma writes "Women in the Global South are called to make serious contributions to Christian mission. Their potential is often buried in culturally hostile environments. Therefore, men and women need to be keenly aware of God-given gifts and opportunities."[2]

In the United States, research has found that women often practise more collaborative leadership than men; teams with women have a less top-down approach. One of the positive effects of this is that more people are included in the decision-making, resulting in more robust decisions. In many ways, women's leadership characteristics may be particularly advantageous.[3]

Theological Foundations Undergirding Gender Diversity Convictions

The Christian community has often not done a good job of valuing the gifts of women, and women's leadership still meets resistance around the world. It will be difficult and a challenge to both promote and support women in leadership. New and uncomfortable questions or discoveries may arise. A strong theological foundation provides helpful navigation through these challenges. These same capacity-building skills also often extend to helping organizations benefit from a more diverse set of leadership styles across cultures, nationalities, and ethnicities.

To better understand helpful theological frameworks for organizations advancing the leadership of women within their organizations, Reynolds and Curry interviewed some large Christian non-profits, mostly focused in the United States, but often serving around the world. We suggest several key core theological values that prompt attention and action around gender justice.[4]

---

2. J. C. Ma, "The Role of Christian Women in the Global South," *Transformation: An International Journal of Holistic Mission Studies* 31, no. 3 (2014): 203.

3. B. M. Bass and B. J. Avolio, "Shatter the Glass Ceiling: Women May Make Better Managers," *Human Resource Management* 33, no. 4 (Winter 1994): 549–560.

4. A. Reynolds and J. Curry, "Best Practices for Attracting, Promoting, and Retaining Female Leadership in Christian Organizations" (Gordon College, Wrentham, MA, January 2017), https://gordonedu.sharepoint.com/WebLinks/Shared%20Documents/Provost/WILNS_PhaseIII Final_Jan2017.pdf?&originalPath=aHR0cHM6Ly9nb3Jkb25lZHUuc2hhcmVwb2ludC5jb20 vOmI6L2cvV2ViTGlua3Muа3MvRWNCYTNhTVd3ODFHaGRRKSEI4UHNMck1CenVSZGsxengyb 0JtaXItZTE1Qkg5Zz9ydGltZT1wYUQ2VjQzcjEwZw. All quotations from the following interviews come from this report.

The first is an emphasis on community, and the belief that real community engages everyone. Do we believe that we need all voices in our organizations? Groups that pursued a Christian sense of gender justice did so based on a belief that everyone's voice was really needed, as individual differences helped to bring communities closer to Christ. The commitment was based on the idea that Christianity is really a corporate call, and that we do that with one another. Leaders in these organizations recognized that Christianity is a corporate rather than individualistic faith. There was a deeply held belief that we understand God's work better when we hear different people's perspectives. People pursued inclusion of men and women in leadership (within the organization, but also within communities they worked within) because they believed it provided a fuller picture of God and God's kingdom and that they needed the experiences, perspectives, skill sets, and approaches to leadership that women brought to the table.

Second is a desire to model the kingdom of God in the most authentic way possible. Our communities should reflect a vision of God's people in our pursuit of mission and witness. The reality is that, to date, men's voices have guided many of the trajectories of our organizations and churches. The groups pursuing gender justice did so in part to provide a corrective. One mission leader noted that "If we're made in the image of God, male and female and all ethnicities and tribes . . . I am actually not doing you a service . . . by giving you this really narrow space." Through modelling better inclusion of women and men leading in our organizations, we provide better examples for others of a more gender equal world where women's voices matter.

Justice is a value that is not just pursued on behalf of others, it brings those others into the conversation to pursue something together. The Micah Network focuses on groups that serve under-resourced or marginalized populations; this often centres around girls and women. We know that the systems and structures we work within are deeply flawed, and many Micah actors are committed to reforming those structures to better reflect God's design for right relationships. How we run our organizations matters. As one male development leader noted, having only men at the table means that "you are perpetuating a systemic imbalance of power that organizations will have to correct in a very intentional way in order for there to be any progress towards something like equality."

Communities focused on making sure women and men are able to follow God and the call of the Holy Spirit in their lives are often more likely to seek gender reconciliation and challenge gender norms. Leaders of such organizations often note a desire to not limit the work of God in the lives of women, and a belief that God calls women to the same leadership and pursuit of shalom as men. Empowering women means giving women the freedom to follow God in all the ways that God calls them. Evelyn Miranda-Feliciano noted in her reflection on Deborah's reign (as described in the book of Judges) that there is "no effort to take special significance from the fact that the judge and the prophet was a woman . . . This seems to say that God, the Lord of history, takes it for granted that at some point in a people's life, women may rule and exercise power."[5] We restrict the use of God's gifts when women aren't empowered and encouraged to use the leadership gifting they have. However, groups that want to be faithful stewards need to recognize the leadership gifts of women that have often been ignored and underdeveloped.

We found that organizations that are able to pursue gender justice have a theological statement that makes clear their commitment to gender justice and the reasons why they value men and women leading together. This will be different for different organizations, but we would encourage all organizations to clearly name this. A widespread understanding of this statement, by both members of the organization and external partners, is key.

Cultural and National Contexts

At the same time, the empowerment of women can be confined by theological convictions. And so it is possible to pay attention to the elevation of women's leadership in ways that affirm the community's convictions. In thinking about just and God-honouring relationships, the reality is that each of us faces different realities, obstacles, and opportunities in our culture and context.

Different cultures have different gender expectations. The gospel is unique in its ability to both affirm culture (that aligns with God's kingdom) and to be prophetic with regard to the cultural norms that compete with God's kingdom orientation.[6] Understanding and applying some of these, within the theological convictions and the cultural norms of a country, are key. It does not do any good to promote a universal solution, when gender is very culturally specific. Here, we list a number of different cultural challenges faced in specific contexts, drawing in part on articles from *Transformation: An International Journal of*

---

5. E. Miranda-Feliciano, "Women in Revolution: The Philippine Version," *Transformation: An International Journal of Holistic Mission Studies* 6, no. 2 (1989): 10.

6. N. Toyama-Szeto, The Daniel Project Directors Report, 2011.

Holistic Mission Studies (published on behalf of the Oxford Centre for Mission Studies) written by women in Africa, Asia, and Latin America.[7]

Various Challenges

The history of colonialism has changed gender dynamics across cultures. In most places, this has often meant increased gender inequality. For example, in the Philippines, evangelical leader Evelyn Miranda-Feliciano notes that before Spain occupied the country, women would inherit property, engage in commerce/business, have agency in decisions about family and children, and serve as priestesses. However, "three centuries of Spanish rule crushed that freedom and egalitarianism."[8] Moving continents, Nigerian scholar Pamela Olubunmi-Smith notes that "Throughout Africa, women have played significant roles in virtually every sphere of life, but neo-colonial structures and social attitudes have threatened to render their contributions to African societies inconsequential."[9] The church has unfortunately also been part of this process in many cases. Hannah Kinoti, a religious studies scholar in Kenya, notes that "one of the features of the initial missionary education to girls in Africa was to prepare them to be good Christian wives and mothers . . . the tendency to ingrain the message that 'a woman's place is in the home' through special 'homecraft' subjects tended to inhibit Evangelical women from wider horizons."[10]

One of the ways we often see gender inequality manifested is in the idea that women should play a private role, and not be involved in leading in the political sector or in other spheres of society. Kinoti notes that evangelicalism has often prioritized a more private than public role, much to its shame, for both men and women; however, women are even more impacted by this. Olubunmi-Smith argues, "while the Church has advanced the cause of women by acknowledging and reinforcing the community of women within the church through evangelization, it needs to be more proactive in championing the cause

---

7. It should be noted that women's voices – especially from Asia, Africa, and Latin America – are not well represented in this journal. Since its inception, only about 12 percent of articles in the journal have been authored by women, and they disproportionately are on issues dealing specifically with family and gender.

8. Miranda-Feliciano, "Women in Revolution," 81.

9. P. Olubunmi-Smith, "Feminism in Cross-Cultural Perspective: Women in Africa," *Transformation: An International Journal of Holistic Mission Studies* 6, no. 2 (1989): 11.

10. H. Kinoti, "Evangelical Women and Politics in Africa," *Transformation: An International Journal of Holistic Mission Studies* 11, no. 4 (1994): 7.

of women outside the church."[11] While groups like the Micah Network aim to remedy this public–private split with engagement with integral mission, the evangelical church still suffers from some of these ideas, with women often not receiving the support and encouragement to engage in politics and social affairs more broadly. However, this looks different in different settings. In research comparing gender norms among evangelicals in Brazil and the United States, for example, Brazilian evangelicals were more likely to support women in politics, although US evangelicals were more likely to accept women's shared leadership in the home.[12]

As a consequence of history, women often struggle across contexts to imagine themselves as leaders. Sometimes women deal with imposter syndrome, and even those who hold leadership roles are hesitant to exercise leadership. Although it is manifested in different ways in different cultures, often women are taught or encouraged to be humble, to be silent, to be less than men.[13] Julie Ma, who spent a decade at the Pacific Theological Seminary in the Philippines, notes that "the foremost challenge for women is found in the establishment of their identity in a given social setting. Cultural practices are hard to die, and how women are viewed and treated in many parts of Asia, Africa, and Latin America still remains a formidable challenge."[14] We would add North America and Europe as well, even if the challenges are different. For example, Ma also notes, "Another practice shaped by the teachings of Confucianism in Asia is that men are described as the 'sky' while women are the 'earth.' This is not just a yin-yang relationship, with its complementarity in roles, but a matter of injustice and discrimination. For example, even today, in some homes, mothers and children do not eat at the same table when there is a guest of the father."[15]

Moving Forward

However, in spite of those challenges, we also want to highlight two different types of resources in specific cultural contexts to help us think about leadership differently. The first is the numerous examples we have across culture of women

---

11. Olubunmi-Smith, "Feminism," 16.
12. A. Reynolds, "Evangelical Feminism in Brazil and the USA," in *Brazilian Evangelicalism in the Twenty-First Century: An Inside and Outside Look*, ed. E. Miller and R. J. Morgan (Cham: Palgrave Macmillan, 2019), 177–199.
13. N. Toyama-Szeto and T. Gee, *More Than Serving Tea* (Westmont, IL: IVP, 2007).
14. Ma, "Role of Christian Women," 196.
15. Ma, 196.

leading even when denied power. One provocative example that changes the way we think about leadership (and the top-down perspective) comes from Lisa Espineli Chinn and Miriam Adeney.[16] They describe the Filipina domestic. In cities around the world, but notably in Asia and the Middle East, Sunday is when the Filipina domestics have the day off. They can be seen in the parks, meeting with friends, sometimes having church. While various Christian organizations have faced obstacles engaging with the women in traditional Muslim households, these Filipina domestics are gossiping the gospel in the kitchen. They say that the future of Singapore is in the hands of the Filipina, because she is the one caring for the next generation, praying over the children in her care. While this example isn't an example of leadership per se (though some might say that it is), the example stirs the imagination with regard to the ways in which women can be playing highly strategic roles when our lenses of what is "strategic" are decolonized from the trappings of wealth, privilege, and power.

A second example, also from the contexts of the Philippines, comes from the history of political engagement by women. Similar (but different) examples can be found in most histories of justice. Miranda-Feliciano, an evangelical leader from Silang, Cavite, notes the strong example from the Philippines of women being active in the revolution. She writes, "Women made a distinctive contribution towards bringing that [peace and unity among differences]. From the baby girl sucking her mother's breast, to the midwife, to the high-society grandmother, to a girl peanut vendor, to the nun facing the tanks, to the resplendent icons of Mary, to the brave women of media and election computers, and to Corazon Aquino herself."[17]

Many women have been active in movements to bring about not just women's equality and rights, but greater justice. In Brazil and other parts of Latin America, for example, women's movements were often key in dismantling dictatorships or pushing for democratic political change. Olubunmi-Smith notes the importance of different women's associations in uprising through Africa in the twentieth century, highlighting the commitments of feminist movements to human rights for all.

---

16. Lisa Espineli Chinn, conversation with Nikki Toyama-Szeto, Madison, WI, 2009.
17. Miranda-Feliciano, "Women in Revolution," 11.

Strategies for Encouraging Women to Lead and Seek Gender Justice

As Christians committed to God's kingdom, we need the voices of women in leading our organizations. At the same time, we recognize that what this looks like culturally (and the obstacles) may vary. In this third section, we want to highlight strategies that organizations, small and large, might consider. We recognize this task is culturally specific. We have seen well-meaning teams rush to appoint women leaders to positions of influence, but fail to fully support and appreciate the ministry contexts (and therefore challenges) for those leaders. Paying attention to the gaps between external culture, organizational culture, and personal leadership culture will strengthen the effectiveness of women in their organizations.

Policies or Protocol

For different organizations, there will be different pathways towards encouraging and supporting women in leadership within our organizations. However, among a diversity of organizations (mostly based in the USA) that work throughout the world, we found a few practices that helped them in their quest to have women and men leading together. As previously mentioned, one of the central things organizations can do is create and share a theological statement about the value of women and men serving together; this statement needs to be both clear and widely distributed/known. Most Christian organizations lack this. Many people do not know their organization's commitment or approach to gender, and given the variance among Christian communities, boldly supporting women's leadership and gifts is necessary.

Another is to enforce harassment and discrimination policies. It can often be hard or off-putting to hold people accountable for abuse. We worry about what might happen to the organization itself if a male leader is known for his abuse or harassment of women. However, clearly setting expectations and regulations that harassment and abuse will not be tolerated is necessary; and to be willing to expose leaders and others who violate these protocols is vital.

We also need to invest resources in leadership development for women. Admittedly, among organizations working in under-resourced areas, the idea of investing more resources in the development of staff can seem unrealistic. This may simply look like making sure the resources you do invest in staff development have a gender lens. It may mean that programmes you develop in communities to help provide theological training target both men and women. Simply making sure women are central in your leadership and community development programmes can make a difference. Sometimes, this involves non-monetary practices, such as making sure that female staff are mentored. Granting time and permission to invest in their personal development might be sufficient.

Encouraging women leaders to connect with other women leaders (outside the organization or within) can have multiplicative benefits – the personal development or encouragement of the leader, the expansion of the network of the organization, and the volunteer wisdom that comes from peers advising leaders. Have senior staff commit a proportion of their time to the development, mentoring, and training of women in the organization, and formally state such to avoid accidental bias or disproportionately mentoring men. In larger organizations, formal mentoring structures tend to help, since informal mentoring structures usually lead to the concentration of resources into male leaders.

When it comes to funding, men and women face different constraints and opportunities. Many models were created by men, in a masculine style. We found that organizations may need to direct a significant amount of financial resources to buffer some female leaders (especially if they lack the same resources). This is true for organizations where leaders raise their own funding, as well as for those with paid positions.

Organizations should be flexible and agile in incorporating women. Women are often dealing with challenges that come from leadership (and navigating leadership models that are gender based) and balancing other demands (family, expectations). Women may also deal with many more demands and expectations outside the organizational setting. Perhaps it is the roles they play in their families, communities, and churches. For some, this is seen as a liability. However, a flexible organization recognizes the tremendous asset it is to have a leader who has multiple touchpoints, and adjusts what her role might look like. These demands may make someone a stronger leader for a greater diversity of constituents, furthering the mission of the organization. Integration of the leadership task with all areas of life is key to the sustaining of women in leadership. An excellent resource for women to have an integrated leadership approach is the McKinsey Women in Leadership Project.[18]

---

18. McKinsey Leadership Project, available at https://www.wgea.gov.au/data/wgea-research/women-in-leadership-lessons-from-australian-companies-leading-the-way.

Organizational Culture

Rethink what it means to be a leader. What are the characteristics of leadership that your organization intentionally, or unintentionally, holds up? And are any of those characteristics gender bound? For one parachurch organization, it was surprising to discover that the very traits that the ethnic minority women in their organization brought to leadership matched some of the best leadership theory of the time. Jim Collins talks about the level 5 leader who blends a fierce personal will with a personal humility,[19] and these characteristics often described the ethnic minority women in their organizational pipeline. However, because these women didn't match the culture's "leadership narrative" of loud, charismatic, preaching leaders, they were overlooked until the organization began to apply the findings from leadership research. In our research and experience with US mission-oriented non-profits, we heard multiple female leaders express these concerns.

Regardless of size or location, we found that having senior leaders – especially men – model healthy relationships and speak out vocally in their support of women as leaders is key. We had a number of female staff and leaders talk about the importance of having male leaders speak about the need for women and men to serve together and the importance of having women leading. Women also mentioned the importance of having men put them in public positions and support their voice in public ways.

Women often lack the type of networks men have in the workplace. The leaders we spoke with reported a lot of respect and appreciation for men who showed they valued professional interactions with strong women, and who were not afraid to mentor or engage with women in significant and God-honouring ways.

As an organization, think about your history. What are the images and examples (the heroes or heroines) of your organization? As you tell the stories of the early days, or of the work, or of the types of ways in which God has worked in and through your organization, who are the protagonists of those stories? Sometimes it can be powerful for organizations that are trying to grow the capacity of their women in leadership to find stories of the women and make them a part of the retelling. We noted earlier the way self-doubt can hinder female leaders. By finding ways in which women have contributed or participated (or led, in various and creative ways), it creates the space for women leaders to step with freedom into a story that God has been writing.

---

19. J. Collins, *Good to Great: Why Some Companies Make the Leap . . . And Others Don't* (New York: HarperCollins, 2011).

Accountability

Try to regularly collect data on your organization. A number of leaders and organizations often think they are doing a better job of having women lead than they actually are; others are unaware of gender dynamics in their organizations. Note the number of field staff or community leaders who are men and women when you evaluate a programme. Look at the gender distribution of men and women serving on your boards and leadership teams. Annually look at the data as an organization and evaluate if your numbers represent your values. Some organizations noted that once they had reached the levels they wanted, they were less diligent in keeping themselves accountable, and they lost the gains they had made.

People need to be able to discuss the gendered experiences they have in their organizations, even if it is uncomfortable. It is especially important to recognize that women have different experiences based on race/ethnicity and other status markers (which may vary in our different contexts). Often, people do not talk about sensitive issues because they are uncomfortable. Ask women in your organization (and if you are a woman, ask other women) about their experiences. Provide a forum for people to discuss what is difficult about leading or serving in your organization, as well as some of the opportunities that might exist. We found groups that would sometimes read books together about gendered issues, and then discuss challenges or structural realities in their organizations. As Christians, we often need anti-bias work to see our own prejudices and false assumptions. We would note that conversations between past leaders and current leaders could be helpful. It is essential that these conversations are carefully formed to foster honest feedback.

Conclusion

Organizations will benefit from the increased participation of women at all levels of leadership that align with the organization's culture and theological beliefs. The research has shown that perspectives from a variety of social locations result in more robust decisions. While some organizations desire to increase the participation of women in leadership from a strategic viewpoint, it is important that Christian organizations have clarity on their theological foundations (and limits) for doing so. Inviting women to lead in authentic ways (if we believe that women bring something to the table that men do not, we would want to preserve that authenticity) will cause the fruitful dissonance that marks healthy organizations. And a strong theological foundation will help anchor the organization through the growing pains that may precede mutual partnership.

Challenges for increasing the sphere of influence for women in leadership within organizations are found in the external environment and culture, theological framing, organizational dynamics, relational/familial expectations of women, and one's own internal obstacles. Paying attention to the context – the gender expectations and norms, and the community's values – is key to creating situations to help set up organizations and leaders for flourishing. Many organizations are committed to the expansion of women's leadership in their organizations, but competing priorities or organization urgencies push it further down the list.

This process may start by your organization asking several questions and thinking about your theological and missional commitments. What does your organization believe God says about men and women? What does the larger culture (in which your organization operates) say about men and women? Where are the places where these views (God's views and culture's view) align, and where are the gaps?

The reflection on one's own context that relies on data and the inclusion of many voices is important. What are the obstacles to women succeeding in leadership in your organization? What does the data suggest, and what do women themselves say? Which strategies mentioned here might be worth pursuing?

We invite and welcome further dialogue and research about how organizations seeking to do integral mission can use models of shared leadership to help their organizations accomplish mission, and how to encourage women in these leadership roles.

Resources for Increasing Gender Engagement in Programmes

Development Associates International (DAI) Institute. 2018 (current version). Women and Men Serving Together. Video Course. https://institute.daintl.org/courses/women-and-men-serving-together/.

Lutheran World Relief. "Learning for Gender Integration Initiative (LGI)." 2016. https://jliflc.com/resources/learning-gender-integration-initiative-lgi/.

Tearfund. "Transforming Masculinities: A Training Manual for Gender Champions." 2017. https://learn.tearfund.org/en/themes/sexual_and_gender-based_violence/resources_and_publications/transforming_masculinities/.

World Vision Solomon Islands. "Channels of Hope Gender: Community Vision for Change Project Evaluation." 2015. https://www.wvi.org/church-and-interfaith-engagement/publication/channels-hope-gender-community-vision-change-project.

Zengele, Patricia Bongi. "Hand in Hand: Bible Studies to Transform Our Response to Sexual Violence." Tearfund 2015. https://learn.tearfund.org/en/themes/sexual_and_gender-based_violence/resources_and_publications/transforming_masculinities/.

10

Deeper Understanding for More Resilience in the Work for Peace and Justice

Vilma "Nina" Balmaceda

How does the blessing of shalom/*eirene* incorporate justice, and how does the pursuit of justice build the sort of godly relationships that are present in a healthy community? The eternal call to do justice is inherently intertwined with Jesus's call. In this chapter, I hope to contribute to a deeper understanding of the biblical teachings on peace and justice, with the desire to encourage resilience among Christians working with the most vulnerable communities. I hope these reflections will contribute to mobilizing faith communities to support justice and peace initiatives in their respective contexts.[1]

Why Should Christians Be Resilient in the Pursuit of Justice and Peace?

Being resilient can be understood as being "capable of withstanding shock without permanent deformation or rupture."[2] Just a few days before writing this, I had the privilege of visiting a number of Christians working in some of the most dangerous neighbourhoods of Central America. Between smiles

---

1. I would like to acknowledge my good friend Chip Zimmer with whom I published "Our Calling to Pursue Peace and Justice" earlier last year. Several sections of this chapter are based on our collaboration for that article. See V. Balmaceda and C. Zimmer, "Our Calling to Pursue Peace and Justice," *Journal of Latin American Theology* 12, no. 1 (2017): 101–116.

2. See "resilient," *Merriam-Webster Online Dictionary*, accessed 19 September 2019, https://www.merriam-webster.com/dictionary/resilient.

and tears, joy, and, yes, I must admit, fear for my own safety, I walked with them through streets filled with children, teens, and women trying to survive one more day. The impact of injustice is obvious in the lives of people who work hard and yet live in infrahuman conditions. Many of those teens will join a *mara* or gang; others will be caught by organized crime; a number of them will die before they turn twenty-five. Christians working among people in miserable material conditions tend to understand well the call to build a better world, often at a high price: the pain for the suffering of their fellow humans – especially children, teens, and mothers – and the frustration they feel with what they perceive to be the indifference of many other Christians.

On the other hand, some well-intentioned Christians tend to assume that, since perfect justice will only be achieved when the Lord returns, opportunities to build more just and peaceful societies in this broken world are limited to a few hot-button issues. Confronting widespread violence, corruption, and other forms of abuse is not a priority in their agenda.

And yet, several of the prophets of the Old Testament as well as Jesus and his disciples in the New Testament bravely confronted the authorities and the people with messages from God that required them to seriously reconsider their attitudes and behaviour regarding all spheres of life in light of the demands of God's justice.

At a time when our world is hit hard by the effects of great social and economic injustice and by the increasing rise of nationalist and authoritarian tendencies that feed hate and discrimination against those who are different and more vulnerable, the challenge to build more just and peaceful communities remains difficult and demands great resilience from those who dare to take God's kingdom and his justice seriously. Like Jesus himself – in the context of a very broken reality, living under an abusive and violent empire – we are called to pray, "your kingdom come, your will be done, on earth as it is in heaven."[3] This means that, even when we know that we will not be able to see a perfect society in our time, God cares about the conditions in which people live, and there is much that God can do through his people to confront the prevailing expressions of deception, coercion, violence, greed, corruption, and abuse of power in today's societies.

Building up resilient Christian workers requires several important factors. In this chapter, I will address only one of them. In my inquiries with brave Christians working for justice throughout Latin America, it has become very clear that a deep understanding of the principles of shalom and justice in the

---

3. Matt 6:10.

Bible constitutes one of those relevant factors that enable them to be resilient in the face of adversity. Not only that, such deeper understanding demands a rereading and a reinterpretation of biblical teaching, which will probably confront some commonly held assumptions about God's will that tend to obscure the otherwise very clear call to pursue justice. God himself calls us to care about justice because justice is one of his character traits and, as creatures made in his image, we are to reflect his character.

With the hope of contributing to such understanding, I will try to dig deeper into the relationship between justice and peace and God's will for human society. I start by considering the meaning and collective implications of the biblical concept of "shalom" (Old Testament) / *eirene* (New Testament) and how it cannot be separated from justice. A discussion on the qualities of biblical justice follows, inviting us all to reflect on its implications for our daily lives as Christian members of diverse societies.

The Blessing of Shalom/*Eirene*

Some may be more familiar than others with the beautiful Hebrew blessing "shalom." *Eirene* is its equivalent in the New Testament. As a word derived from the Greek term *eiro* ("to join"), it has the emphasis of joining together what has been severed or disturbed. *Eirene* is a powerful biblical term that emphasizes the restoration of relationships previously broken. Like shalom, *eirene* and its implications for our daily lives tends to be reduced if not ignored altogether.

A first common misconception about shalom/*eirene* is that these terms mean peace, understood merely as the absence of conflict. For many evangelical believers, it is peace in very individual terms, in the context of a vertical relationship between God and the believer that excludes the community. But examining these terms provides an opportunity to discover a richness and breadth that will help us understand why justice is so important in God's eyes. Some may think – and this may even be a cultural challenge – that avoiding talking about difficult issues in order to "preserve the peace" is a good thing. This, however, may actually prevent the possibility of resolving an issue, by not being willing to have an honest discussion about it. How much more serious this issue can become when the situation is actually a great injustice.

"Shalom" in the Old Testament is interpreted not only as "peace," but also as "completeness," "soundness," and "well-being." While these terms may sound familiar to those coming from individualistic cultures, Christians must be careful not to miss the collective implications. Shalom is used in the Bible "to describe the ideal state in which the community should function."[4] Depending on the context, shalom can also be understood as "restitution," "reparation," and even "fulfilling a contract." It is always about relationship, caring for it and restoring it when something has gone wrong. In addition, it is often used in the Bible when praying for the welfare of another person, as well as when praying for the good of a city or country. In addition to harmony and concord, *eirene* equally refers to a state of national tranquillity.[5]

Shalom has strong associations with truth, justice, and righteousness. This suggests that the biblical conception of peace is much more than just a passive state of mind, or escape from the real world. Rather, the blessing of shalom/*eirene* is receiving from God an active and dynamic attitude towards life that cannot remain silent in the face of cruelty and abuse. The fruit of such an attitude and effort is the result of God's blessing acting through his human instruments. Shalom/*eirene* is a state in which all relationships are as God designed them to be. In consequence, the blessing of shalom/*eirene* does not refer only to our inner peace with God – which, of course, is important as the foundation of who we are and what we want to do – but is a notion that can only be fully understood in community, as a blessing meant to be enjoyed collectively.

Understanding that God's will is that his people pursue shalom/*eirene* on earth has important implications for how we should care for and bless one another and the world around us, particularly those who are victims of injustice. Since in this fallen world we will never attain complete shalom/*eirene*, we need to be resilient, so that we can join in efforts towards restoring God's original intent in our community and the wider society.

In contrast to Lerner, who insists that humans need to believe that the world is inherently a safe and just place, biblical teaching does not assume shalom/*eirene* as the premise that all human beings are essentially good and that everything will be fine as long as we remain optimistic.[6] To the contrary, recognizing that too much hurt and injustice exist in the world, and that violence, corruption, abuse, and greed steal people's very lives, God's will is that his people become active in confronting undue suffering and work to sow the seeds of justice and peace.

---

4. D. Van Ness and K. Heetderks Strong, *Restoring Justice* (London: Routledge, 2015), 6.

5. See *The NAS New Testament Greek Lexicon*, Bible Study Tools, accessed 19 September 2019, https://www.biblestudytools.com/lexicons/greek/nas/eirene.html.

6. M. Lerner, *The Belief in a Just World: A Fundamental Delusion* (New York: Plenum, 1980), 11–15.

The Life and Death of Jesus of Nazareth Invites Us to Be Resilient in Our Pursuit of Justice

Throughout his life, Jesus of Nazareth exemplified a serious concern for doing justice and showing compassion, particularly in the lives of those suffering the most. His sacrifice on the cross was offered on our behalf to honour all the demands of God's eternal justice. Only because of that sacrifice can humans have shalom/*eirene* with God.[7]

This peace with God provides the context for us to have peace with others[8] and empowers us to be resilient as we pursue a ministry of justice,[9] peacemaking,[10] and reconciliation.[11] Jesus promises to give us his peace, a peace that passes human understanding.[12] I recently had the opportunity of seeing this with my own eyes, observing how Christian men and women cultivate shalom/*eirene* beyond all human understanding, by teaching children in the garbage dumps of *La Terminal* (where the poorest of the poor separate garbage for recycling purposes) and in *La Limonada*, one of the most dangerous neighbourhoods in Guatemala City, in the hope that by helping them read, write, and do maths, and learn about the love of Jesus of Nazareth, those children and teens will not end in a *mara*, in prison, or killed. I have also seen it in the lives of Christians who work tirelessly with children who have been victims of sexual violence and other forms of cruelty in the Andean countries, sharing with them – in the midst of humanly hopeless situations of material deprivation and emotional neglect – that God wants to renew their lives, filling them with dignity, empowerment, and the blessing of shalom/*eirene*. But the toll in the lives of those Christian workers is immense and they need to be resilient, and it is important that local communities of faith understand their needs and contribute to caring for them.

The sacrifice of Jesus of Nazareth also enables us to seek shalom/*eirene* in relation to our planet. We are accountable to God for stewarding this beautiful planet that he has given us.[13]

Pursuing shalom/*eirene* is only possible because of the sacrifice of Jesus of Nazareth, but it is also a responsibility of God's people. Therefore, a full

---

7. Rom 5:1–2; 2 Cor 5:18–19; Col 1:19–20; 1 Tim 2:5–6.
8. 1 Pet 3:10–12; Rom 12:17–21.
9. Jer 22:16; Mic 6:8.
10. Matt 5:9.
11. 2 Cor 5:18–20.
12. John 14:27; Phil 4:7.
13. Gen 1–2; Rom 8:18–21; Col 1:15–20.

understanding of biblical peace speaks of the need to build relationships in which God's will and purposes are made apparent. When we cultivate shalom/*eirene* in our interpersonal relationships, we become capable of confronting issues of injustice openly and dealing with disagreement in an honest way, rejecting corruption, violence, and unethical coercion but not running away from real conflict to right a wrong. While the specific ways in which Christians will fulfil this responsibility will look different in different contexts, an honest concern for justice and shalom/*eirene* needs to become part of Christian identity in contextually appropriate forms. But pursuing peacemaking and doing justice are tough work and can be very dangerous in most parts of the world. Pursuing them may not, in the end, make us "happy," at least in the sense that happiness is popularly understood. But seeking God's kingdom and his justice does bring the blessing of shalom/*eirene* to our communities.[14]

What Happens When We Pursue Justice?

The idea of justice encompasses four elements: distribution, power, equity, and rights.[15] This is especially relevant when we think of human rights. When we pursue justice, we focus on ensuring that people receive fair shares of that to which they are entitled because of their dignity as human beings, because every person has been created in the image of God. This means working towards ensuring that power is legitimately acquired and used; that courts and other fora in which disputes are resolved be impartial; and that adequate protections be given to those who are most vulnerable. As Marshall has concluded, "[J]ustice entails the exercise of legitimate power to ensure that benefits and penalties are distributed fairly and equitably in society, thus meeting the rights and enforcing the obligations of all parties."[16]

Biblical justice includes these elements with the purpose of restoring relationships. Again, on the cross, Jesus of Nazareth fulfilled all the demands of God's justice to redeem us. God did not discard the demands of justice. We must not assume that justice is not important in the delicate labour of helping people restore their communion with each other, and helping people be restored in their relationships with their families, their communities, and the wider society. While going back to the way things were before the harm

---

14. Matt 6:33.

15. C. D. Marshall, *The Little Book of Biblical Justice: A Fresh Approach to the Bible's Teachings on Justice* (Intercourse, PA: Good Books, 1989), 6–7.

16. Marshall, *Little Book*, 7.

was inflicted is often not humanly possible, we need to look for ways to repair the harm done to all parties as much as possible.

Mishpat is one of several Hebrew terms for "justice." This term is particularly important because it confronts another common misconception. Contrary to what many Christians think, justice in the Bible is not an abstract concept. *Mishpat* involves two very relevant concerns: primary justice and rectifying justice. Primary justice is the presence of relationships that reflect and uphold the inherent rights of human beings due to their equal dignity as bearers of God's image. Rectifying justice is the system that corrects and restores those inherent rights when they have not been adequately upheld. This is a clear reference to God's concern for human responsibility regarding the administration of justice and justice through other public institutions (e.g. just laws fairly applied, judicial procedures without bias, appropriate police function); the need for a corrective component (e.g. sentences and fines for transgressors that do not destroy human dignity but uphold the rights of the victims and those of the offenders); and a restorative component (e.g. victims and offenders coming together to resolve the damage caused by the offenders' actions). God sent courageous prophets to confront Israel's leaders both for failing to implement primary justice and for impeding the work of rectifying justice through bribery and favouritism.[17] These ancient Hebrew concerns carry over into the New Testament. Jesus of Nazareth pronounced striking condemnations of Israel and its leaders for attending to the details of the law while neglecting the most important matters of God's law, which are "justice, mercy and faithfulness."[18]

Another relevant term is *tsedaqah*, which has been commonly translated in modern languages as "righteousness." As with "shalom," there are various other renderings, depending on context. *Tsedaqah* can also be translated as justice, fairness, doing the right thing, equity, and integrity. The term connotes human well-being, as well as right behaviour. One of God's names, attributed to the Messiah by the prophet Jeremiah, is *Yahweh Tsidkenu*, which means "the Lord is our Justice."[19] And the beautiful tradition in the Hebrew culture of helping the poor as a responsibility before God is also known as *tsedaqah*.[20] Another

---

17. Deut 27:19; Mic 7:3; Isa 58:6.
18. Matt 23:23.
19. Jer 23:6.
20. See Jer 22:16 and the powerful connection between pursuing justice for the poor and the vulnerable and knowing God. It is worth noting that the highest level of *tsedaqah* implies walking alongside those in need until they are able to stand on their own feet.

common misconception in this regard is to think that God wants us to give charity to the poor, while what he demands is that we do justice by enabling them to find opportunities to stand on their own feet.

Nicholas Wolterstorff has argued that "justice . . . prevails in human relationships insofar as persons render to each other what they have a right to."[21] In other words, justice is present when people are treated with the respect their worth requires. For Christians, this brief sentence can serve as a summary of what all of Scripture has to say about "justice," whether at the interpersonal level or at the collective level. For Scripture describes all human beings as made in God's image and commands us to love others as we love ourselves. Viewed from this perspective, the Ten Commandments are a summary of what it means to treat God and others "justly," rendering to others, including God himself, "what they have a right to." If shalom/*eirene* includes the "steady state" of primary justice that exists when the peace of God is present, rectifying justice amounts to the equilibrium-restoring actions that, when fully and rightly pursued, move God's people towards shalom/*eirene*.

Justice is corrective; it imposes consequences to our wrong behaviour to help us discern right from wrong. It therefore has a punitive dimension, as expressed in Romans 12:19 and Exodus 34:6–7. But God's justice also has a very clear redemptive purpose in the lives of human beings. After committing terrible crimes, David cried to God, "Deliver me from bloodguilt . . . and my tongue will sing of your *tsedaqah*."[22] Following this same principle, John the Apostle encouraged believers to repent and be resilient with the promise that "If we confess our sins, he is faithful and just and will forgive us our sins and purify us from all unrighteousness."[23]

Conclusion: True Justice Is Never Separated from Compassion

The pursuit of biblical justice means, first of all, that individuals and communities accept their responsibility, that they are able to admit wrongdoing and confess and seek forgiveness and reparation, not denying their responsibility for the presence of injustice in their land.

Second, pursuing biblical justice means recognizing that justice exists in close relationship with compassion, so much so that the two concepts are

---

21. N. Wolterstorff, *Justice in Love* (Grand Rapids, MI: Eerdmans, 2011), 89–90. See also N. Wolterstorff, *Justice: Rights and Wrongs* (Princeton: Princeton University Press, 2008).

22. Ps 51:14. Translated by V. Balmaceda and C. Zimmer.

23. 1 John 1:9.

often juxtaposed in the Scriptures. God expects his people to act justly and mercifully.[24] God places them side by side in order that they might influence one another in our daily lives.

Justice has also very relevant implications for our personal walk with God. God's justice demands are to be taken seriously as we come to his presence. He said through Isaiah, "Is not this the kind of fasting I have chosen: to loose the chains of injustice and untie the cords of the yoke, to set the oppressed free . . . ?"[25] God's justice demands make us realize that we need to change our hearts as well as our words and actions; caring for those in our communities who suffer injustice shows that we love our neighbours.

Justice demands that we be impartial, but also partial. This is an interesting paradox. On the one hand, we are clearly commanded, in both Testaments, not to show favouritism.[26] Rectifying justice includes the concern for procedural fairness in the way justice is administered in court and equivalent fora. On the other hand, God also takes the side of widows, orphans, foreigners, and the poor. The reason why God shows such favouritism is precisely because those people are not treated with impartiality. God rectifies justice by singling out the most vulnerable groups in society. This is completely consistent with Jesus's teaching. He said that when the sheep and goats are separated on the day of judgment, how we have responded to the hungry, the thirsty, strangers, the naked, the sick, and prisoners is the criterion for who gets placed in which fold.[27] This does not mean that our acts of justice will save us, but rather that our "works" – as reflected in our treatment of those who suffer injustice in our day – are an indication of who we truly worship, mammon[28] or God.[29] This is the basis for a deeper understanding – and not merely in Platonic terms – of what Jesus affirmed after reading the promise of Isaiah 61 in the synagogue and his announcement that "Today this scripture is fulfilled in your hearing."[30]

If God's justice demands require that we treat people according to their worth and render to them what they are due, it follows that when we work for the rights of the needy we are not merely showing compassion or charity, and neither should we reduce our responsibility to the most vulnerable to

---

24. Mic 6:8; Zech 7:9; see also Matt 23:23.
25. Isa 58:3–10.
26. Lev 19:15; Zech 7:9; Jas 2:1.
27. Matt 25:31–39.
28. Matt 6:24.
29. Jas 2:14–26.
30. Luke 4:16–21.

mere acts of charity. Failing to care for the poor and the vulnerable is not just stinginess; it is unrighteousness. Failing to pursue ways to correct the injustice that steals them of opportunities is also unrighteousness. It is a failure of our obligation to give people what they are due, to treat them with the respect they deserve – the broad definition of justice. Doing justice involves the righting of wrongs (rectifying justice) and the creation of a community of righteous relationships (primary justice).

11

God's Preference for the Poor

The Bible and Social Justice in Ireland

Patrick Mitchel

In Ireland, the word "Bible" has had a tempestuous history.[1] On the one hand, the use of the Bible can lead to generous acts of grace and mercy to those in need; on the other hand, there exists a long history on this island of claiming "biblical" justification for attitudes and actions contributing to bitter sectarian conflict, the misuse of power, and exclusion and demonization of "the Other" where God "is on our side" and not yours.[2]

My interest in this chapter is to analyse and reflect critically on those "threads of grace" – how the Bible inspires and informs acts of generous justice among Christian communities. Particular focus will be on the relationship between the Bible and selected contemporary expressions of Christian social justice in Ireland – here understood as actions motivated by a theological framework that are intended to serve others in need, particularly the alleviation of poverty and suffering by challenging injustice and fostering dignity and self-sufficiency for the powerless.

Before discussion of particular examples of contemporary practice, some historical perspective is necessary. The historical context will take the form of a brief overview of particular "echoes" from the past regarding the Bible and social

---

1. This chapter was first published as P. Mitchel, "God's Preference for the Poor: The Bible and Social Justice in Ireland," in *Ireland and the Reception of the Bible: Social and Cultural Perspectives*, ed. B. A. Anderson and J. F. Kearney (New York: T&T Clark, 2018), 193–210. Reproduced here with permission from Bloomsbury.

2. For some examples of destructive use of the Bible, see P. Mitchel, *Evangelicalism and National Identity in Ulster, 1921–1998* (Oxford: Oxford University Press, 2003).

justice in Irish culture and history that continue to be heard in the present. Of prime significance here are the controversial events of the nineteenth-century Protestant "second Reformation" and Catholic "counter-Reformation" in which the Bible and social action played a pivotal, and highly contentious, part. I will sketch the legacy of this era in terms of changing attitudes to the Bible in Irish culture up to our post-Christendom and postmodern present.[3]

From this historical context, the discussion will focus on two broadly representative contemporary organizations with strong links to distinct Christian traditions. They are Trócaire,[4] the official overseas development agency of the Catholic Church in Ireland; and Tearfund Ireland,[5] a sister organization of Tearfund UK[6] launched in the Republic of Ireland in 2008. Tearfund is well established as a global relief and development agency operating within an evangelical Christian ethos. Obviously, many other organizations could be selected, but comparing and contrasting these two Irish Christian development agencies will provide a useful route into discussion of how the Bible is used within each organization in shaping and informing its vision and praxis of social justice.

Sketching the Bible in Irish Memory and Culture from the Nineteenth Century to the Present

Conflict tends to demand our attention. Certainly the "Bible war" of the 1820s, the development of Protestant missions, and Catholic resistance during the nineteenth century has been well documented.[7] This is for good reason: it was during this period that two polarized and oppositional national identities emerged with religion embedded as the ultimate marker of belonging. Within

---

3. "Irish culture" is a contested term. For our purposes it refers to the Republic of Ireland and does not include Northern Irish culture with its distinct relationship to the Bible.

4. See the official website of Trócaire: http://www.trocaire.org/.

5. See the official website of Tearfund Ireland: http://www.tearfund.ie/. For its statement of faith and vision and values see https://www.tearfund.ie/vision-and-values/.

6. Tearfund UK was formed in 1968 and is now one of the largest non-governmental organizations in the UK.

7. For example, D. Bowen, *Souperism: Myth or Reality? A Study in Souperism* (Dublin: Mercier, 1970); D. Bowen, *The Protestant Crusade in Ireland, 1800–70: A Study of Protestant–Catholic Relations between the Act of Union and Disestablishment* (Dublin: Gill & Macmillan, 1978); I. Whelan, *The Bible War in Ireland: The "Second Reformation" and the Polarization of Protestant–Catholic Relations, 1800–1840* (Madison, WI: University of Wisconsin Press, 2005); M. Moffitt, *Soupers and Jumpers: The Protestant Missions in Connemara, 1848–1937* (Dublin: Nonsuch, 2008); M. Moffitt, *The Society for Irish Church Missions to the Roman Catholics, 1849–1950* (Manchester: Manchester University Press, 2010).

a broader context of moral reform and evangelical advance in Britain and America,[8] Protestants of various hues in Ireland engaged in a remarkable period of urgent missionary and educational activity to bring moral and spiritual reform to the native Catholic population through the work of a range of Protestant societies formed with the intention of rescuing large numbers of Irish Catholics from ignorance and spiritual slavery.[9] To this specifically spiritual factor behind polarization can be added others: the wider context of increasing political threat to Protestant minority rule from Catholic Emancipation; the organizational revitalization of the Catholic Church; violent agrarian reform movements like the Rockite rebellion in West Limerick;[10] the Tithe War of 1831–1838; the rise of formidable leaders of Catholic popular opinion like O'Connell and Bishop James Warren Doyle; Catholic millennialism in the form of Pastorini's prophecies of the downfall of Irish Protestantism by around 1821–1825;[11] counter-versions of Protestant millennialism;[12] and a deep-seated Protestant belief that unfamiliarity with or opposition to the Word of God was linked to political rebelliousness.[13] All of these acted to catalyse an astonishing range of evangelical Protestant missionary activity during the nineteenth century.

Our particular interest is in the contested association of the Bible with social justice within that story. The methodology of Protestant evangelism revolved around the central place of Bible reading and the Bible in popular education. This was based on a confidence that the Scriptures alone would speak powerfully to Irish Catholics perceived to be deliberately kept in ignorance of the liberating power of the gospel by their Church. The promotion of the Bible "without note or comment" was not perceived as a "neutral" educational

---

8. J. Wolffe, *The Expansion of Evangelicalism: The Age of Wilberforce, More, Chalmers and Finney* (Nottingham: Inter-Varsity Press, 2006).

9. Whelan traces their origins and development in chapter 2 of Whelan, *Bible War*, 53–85.

10. G. Curtin, "Religion and Social Conflict during the Protestant Crusade in West Limerick 1822-49," *The Old Limerick Journal* (Winter 2003): 43–54.

11. J. S. Donnelly, *Captain Rock: The Irish Agrarian Rebellion of 1821–1824* (Cork: Collins, 2009).

12. See Kelley for discussion of how Nangle's famous Achill Mission was, in part, motivated by his millennial thought. T. J. Kelley, "'Come Lord Jesus, Quickly Come!': The Writing and Thought of Edward Nangle, 1828–1862," in *Protestant Millennialism, Evangelicalism and Irish Society, 1790–2005*, ed. C. Gribben and A. Holmes (Basingstoke: Palgrave Macmillan, 2006), 99–118.

13. J. Liechty and C. Clegg, *Moving beyond Sectarianism: Religion, Conflict, and Reconciliation in Northern Ireland* (Dublin: Columba, 2001), 88.

methodology by Catholic leaders.¹⁴ Within an increasingly sectarian conflict, the Bible came to be viewed, in Catholic eyes, as a foreign and Protestant book, a tool of political and religious oppression. As one Catholic pamphlet writer put it, "The Bible, without note of comment, is not less a means of Protestant dominion than the Orange Yeoman's military array – Bibles as mere sheets resolve themselves into a question of power and triumph, religion and truth as altogether extrinsic."¹⁵

Neither (to put it mildly) was later Protestant alleviation of suffering during the Famine seen in disinterested terms, being inextricably linked to the charge of "souperism."¹⁶ For example, Moffitt, in her detailed research on the work of the Society for Irish Church Missions to the Roman Catholics (ICM) during the Famine, describes an era of sectarian bitterness, court cases, public condemnations, riots, exaggerated claims of missionary success on one side against apocalyptic warnings about converting on the other, and social ostracism of converts that occasionally overflowed into violence.¹⁷ This picture of sectarian warfare in the rural west was replicated in the Dublin slums.¹⁸ Moffitt argues that while the ICM's work in feeding thousands of starving people who would have otherwise perished during the Famine should be acknowledged, this good work has been completely lost in public memory because the ICM did link alleviation of suffering with the wider goal of eradicating Catholicism, and converts did benefit in terms of relief, employment, housing, education, and knowledge of the Scriptures.

Moffitt's findings are consistent with how Protestant mission and the "Protestant Bible" continued to be strongly resisted by Catholics, particularly in rural communities, into the late twentieth century. Examples include itinerant preachers distributing Scriptures being run out of towns, and new converts within the modest growth of evangelicalism in the Republic since the late

---

14. Whelan, *Bible War*, 269.

15. G. Ensor, *Letters Showing the Inutility, and Exhibiting the Absurdity, of What Is Rather Fantastically Termed "the New Reformation"* (Dublin: R. Coyne, 1828), 41.

16. The accusation of "Souperism" can be defined as Protestant mission to Catholics exploiting a context of desperate poverty in order to gain converts through the provision of material aid.

17. Moffitt, *The Society*, 266–284.

18. J. Prunty, "Battle Plans and Battlegrounds: Protestant Mission Activity in the Dublin Slums, 1840s–1880s," in *Protestant Millennialism, Evangelicalism, and Irish Society, 1790–2005*, ed. C. Gribben and A. R. Holmes (Basingstoke: Palgrave Macmillan, 2006), 119–143.

1970s sometimes being denounced from pulpits at Mass or perceived as joining some sort of cult.[19]

Finally, it is worth "fast-forwarding" to contemporary attitudes to the Bible and Christianity within a post-Christendom Ireland where the plausibility and credibility of Christianity has been profoundly undermined.[20] Elsewhere I have written that, in dramatic contrast to the past, "Many people in modern Ireland are convinced that 'religion is bad for you' and are determined to construct a society free from its negative influence. This impulse strongly resonates with . . . John Rawls who argued that the public square should form an 'overlapping consensus' consisting only of 'reasonable' points of view (rather than 'comprehensive doctrines' such as religious beliefs) that could be accepted as such by all participating groups."[21] In other words, there is now, for many, a pervasive "hermeneutic of suspicion" regarding "comprehensive doctrines" such as the belief that the Bible represents divine revelation. In such a context, churches (and their Bibles) are now increasingly viewed by many as an irrelevant if not malign influence on public life. Rather than the Scriptures dealing in public truth, they are taken to represent the personal views and prejudices of an increasingly marginal proportion of the population. All this is to say that in Irish history the Bible is not a neutral book and there exist significant barriers to its reception in contemporary culture. Ireland is not unique in this regard within post-Christendom Europe, but it does have a particular and complex relationship to the Bible.

With that relationship in mind, it is time to press ahead into description, comparison, and contrast between two current expressions of social justice in Ireland based on their self-understanding, with theological and practical comments developing retrospectively out of that comparison.[22] The focus of discussion will be not so much the details of what is done by the organizations but how the Bible and theology inform praxis.

---

19. On these issues, see P. Mitchel, "Evangelicals and Irish Identity in Independent Ireland: A Case Study," in *Irish Protestant Identities*, ed. M. A. Busteed, F. Neal, and J. Tonge (Manchester: Manchester University Press, 2012), 155–170; see also 162–163.

20. For further discussion see S. Murray, "Post-Christendom, Post-Constantinian, Post-Christian . . . Does the Label Matter?," accessed 19 September 2019, https://amnetwork.uk/wp-content/uploads/2019/07/After-Christendom-Does-the-label-matter.pdf.

21. P. Mitchel, "Sex, Truth and Tolerance: Some Theological Reflections on the Irish Civil Partnership Bill 2010 and Challenges Facing Christians in a Post-Christendom Culture," *Evangelical Quarterly* 84, no. 2 (2012): 155–173.

22. Analysis is based on extensive published documents on both organizations' websites.

Two Contemporary Expressions of the Bible and Social Justice in Ireland

1. Trócaire and Catholic Social Teaching

Trócaire was established in 1973 by the bishops of Ireland who simultaneously issued a pastoral letter on development. In it they describe utterly inadequate aid and trade relationships between the rich West and poor countries in the Majority World, and follow this with a brief account of why Christians should be engaged in addressing such wrongs. This appeal has two foundations. One is a call for Christian personal discipleship of obedience to Jesus and love of others in need.[23] The other is a call for fairness that puts an obligation on governments of rich nations to act for global justice, since "The earth and its good things belong to all the people of the earth and no nation has the right to build its own prosperity upon the misery of others."[24] While not developed, there is a strong implicit critique of unrestrained capitalism here. Wealth is not to be viewed as a private resource to be protected and selfishly accumulated, but as a gift of God to be shared.

This original Pastoral Letter is best set in the double context of the decline of the Catholic Church as a mass provider of social services in Ireland and simultaneously dramatic developments in Catholic social thought globally: Vatican II; the conference of Latin American bishops in Medellín in 1968; the rise of liberation theology; the development of the concept of solidarity with the poor; and a willingness to confront and challenge unjust secular authority in the cause of social justice all lie in the background. These developments led to a tension, visible in Trócaire's work today, I believe, between an emphasis on Catholic Social Teaching (CST) as a body of universal principles and an increased awareness of and emphasis on social justice being informed and shaped by local contexts and other strands of thought – for example, as we shall see, human rights legislation. Fahey argues that "The very notion of Catholic social thought as a unitary, general and universally valid set of principles, laid out in Rome and handed down to the faithful everywhere, was implicitly abandoned and replaced by a more fragmentary, variable and democratically sensitive approach."[25]

---

23. Based on two texts: Matt 25:40 and 1 John 3:17–18.

24. "Pastoral Letter of the Bishops of Ireland Establishing Trócaire," 1973, accessed 19 September 2019, http://www.trocaire.org/whatwedo/pastoral-letter-bishops-ireland-establishing-trocaire.

25. T. Fahey, "The Catholic Church and Social Policy," in *Values, Catholic Social Thought and Public Policy*, ed. B. Reynolds and S. Healy (Dublin: Conference of Religious of Ireland, 2007), 155–156.

Consequently, on the one hand, Trócaire is one of Ireland's largest non-governmental organizations and has an explicit Catholic basis and structure. It is an episcopal trust, under the overall direction of the bishops and with strong local connections to individual parishes where it is seen as an important global witness to the gospel.[26] On its website, the strongest links to an overtly Christian and biblical basis for its mission can be found in links to (very impressive and highly professional) local parish resources.[27] In some of these resources core principles of CST are highlighted.[28] In 2014, Executive Director Éamonn Meehan argued how CST, and development of CST by Pope Francis, informs the work of Trócaire globally. He stated: "I believe that in the work we do, we are the minds, the hearts, the arms, the legs of the Irish Church in transmitting this love and compassion [of God] to the furthest corners of the world."[29] It is therefore evident that Trócaire is self-consciously inspired by Christian values and the social teaching of the Catholic Church in its overall mission.

Yet, on the other hand, the organization's overriding focus is rights-based development within a firmly "this-world" horizon. Fahey argues that Trócaire's "work in the field is drained of any overt Catholic message and its inspiration in Catholic thinking is held firmly in the background."[30] The organization's six core themes (sustainable livelihoods; human rights; gender equality; HIV; climate change; emergency relief) are framed within a general theme of justice rather than being developed around specific biblical themes. For example,

---

26. Trócaire receives around €30 million each year from the Irish public, mainly through its annual Lenten campaign. É. Meehan, "Faith in Action: Trócaire and the Future of the Church in Ireland," iCatholic Player, 5 October 2014, accessed 19 September 2019, http://www.icatholic.ie/irish-catholic-eamonn-meehan/.

27. Resources which develop theological application from core biblical material include the "Just Faith" programme developed by Trócaire with the Offices of Evangelisation and Ecumenism in the Archdiocese of Dublin, various Lenten materials, and "The Cry of the Earth: A Call to Action for Climate Justice; A Pastoral Reflection on Climate Change from the Irish Catholic Bishops' Conference," 2014.

28. A three-minute video was used by Executive Director Éamonn Meehan to launch his talk at the "Pope Francis and the Future of the Church in Ireland" conference hosted by the *Irish Catholic* on 4 October 2014 (Meehan, "Faith in Action"). Eight principles of CST listed in the video are human dignity; solidarity; the common good; subsidiarity; rights and responsibilities; option for the poor; stewardship; and participation. For resources on Catholic Social Teaching see the online list of papal, conciliar, and other official documents at "Major Documents," Catholic Charities of St. Paul and Minneapolis, accessed 19 September 2019, http://www.cctwincities.org/page.aspx?pid=441, and https://www.cctwincities.org/wp-content/uploads/2015/12/Key-10-Principles-of-CST_1-pager.pdf. CST is summarized in a compendium of the Social Doctrine of the Church by the Pontifical Council for Justice and Peace on the same web page.

29. Meehan, "Faith in Action."

30. Fahey, "Catholic Church," 157.

there is little talk in Trócaire's many publications, as far as I have been able to find, of themes such as the kingdom of God; future hope; the New Testament's eschatological structure for Christian ethics; sin; forgiveness; the uniqueness of Christ; new life in the Spirit; the church as the people of God; and so on. The three elements of CST that Trócaire highlights are dignity (all people are created in God's image and are therefore due respect); option for the poor (putting the poor and vulnerable first); and the common good (everyone is included with a right and responsibility to promote the community's good and to benefit from it). These are applied in ways to support (good and valuable) development objectives of helping practically those in need. The same can be said in general for how the Bible is used in a presentation on CST.[31] Verses used include classic "justice" texts such as Isaiah 58:6, 10 (fasting as loosing the bonds of injustice); Micah 6:8 (do justice, love mercy, walk humbly with your God); Proverbs 31:8–9 (speak out for those who cannot); Luke 4:18–19 (good news to the poor); and Luke 10:25–37 (parable of the Good Samaritan). These texts are applied within a broad *creational* framework to support general rights-based teaching on the value of all human life which compels those with resources to help those without. In similar vein, Trócaire's "Vision and Mandate" envisages "a just and peaceful world" where people's dignity is ensured and rights are respected. Such a world will exist when "basic needs are met, and resources are shared equitably; people have control over their own lives; and those in power act for the common good."

My point is not to make any comment on the merit of rights-based development, nor on the undoubted professionalism and quality of Trócaire's work. It is simply to say that it is primarily political and legal, is semi-detached from CST, fits relatively comfortably within the values and narratives of secular aid agencies, and "backgrounds" explicit biblical and theological themes. This approach means that "on the ground" Trócaire is a non-missionary organization. Fahey argues that the "secular nature" of its mission is reflected in its staff, hired primarily for their expertise in development, resulting in the fact that "the organisation's worth lies in its technical competence and commitment, not in its denominational colour."[32] Fahey's point carries weight when one examines Trócaire's numerous excellent advocacy publications (many of them submissions at governmental and EU level) as opposed to its Parish Resources.

---

31. "An Introduction to Trócaire and to Catholic Social Teaching," accessed 19 September 2019, https://www.trocaire.org/sites/default/files/images/anintroductiontotrocaireandtocatholicsocialteachingpower.pdf.

32. Fahey, "Catholic Church," 157.

Reference to CST, use of the Bible, and even discussion of Catholic teaching on sexual ethics in its work on HIV/AIDS is virtually absent. In general, the organization adopts a consistent and strong rights-based approach to global development. One example is the organization's analysis of the Millennium Development Goals (MDG). Trócaire criticizes the "failure to embed the MDGs within existing human rights commitments, standards and principles . . . the MDGs miss the point that every woman, man and child on the planet . . . is inherently endowed with moral entitlements to a dignified life . . . *These moral entitlements are enshrined in international human rights law*."[33]

If there is a "duality" to Trócaire's identity and praxis – that it is explicitly informed by broad Christian values and CST and yet these strands lie implicitly well in the background of the organization's work – why this is so is a larger question on which I can only speculate here.[34] Possibly, given the legacy of Irish history discussed earlier, there is a deep-seated reservation in Irish culture about explicitly connecting social justice with any form of Christian mission that could be perceived as an overseas version of "souperism." Perhaps another relates to the negative perceptions of the Bible (and Christianity) discussed above within a post-Christendom liberal secular democracy. Also, in the important work of global development, it may be pragmatically much easier to make progress in helping others if "religion" (and particularly the Bible) is kept firmly in the background.

2. Tearfund and Integral Mission

While considerably smaller, Tearfund Ireland (hereafter simply Tearfund) shares many similarities with Trócaire. Tearfund is also a professional and experienced faith-based development organization which depends to a significant degree on support from local churches across Ireland, and is a member of Dóchas, the umbrella body of Irish development agencies. It also prioritizes aid to the poorest and most vulnerable people in the world through focus on four areas (some of which overlap with Trócaire): emergency relief; forgotten children; vulnerable women; and HIV. Like Trócaire, Tearfund offers resources and training for churches in Ireland to engage with issues of social

---

33. Justin Kilcullen, "Foreword," in Trócaire, *My Rights Beyond 2015: Making the Post-2015 Framework Accountable to the World's Poor* (Dublin: Dublin City Resource Centre, 2013), 4, emphasis mine; accessed 19 September 2019, https://www.trocaire.org/sites/default/files/resources/policy/trocaire-my-rights-beyond-2015.pdf.

34. I did contact Trócaire to discuss these themes, but it was not possible to arrange a meeting.

justice.³⁵ As with Trócaire, Tearfund recognizes that the causes of poverty are complex and that bringing justice involves both aid to relieve suffering and action to address the root causes of injustice. Likewise, Tearfund places significant emphasis on sustainability and empowerment at a local level. Finally, like Trócaire, Tearfund roots its call to action in the belief that "all people should be treated justly and equitably. We are committed to seeking the restoration of relationships that are unjust and inequitable, and seek to ensure the dignity and flourishing of every human being and society as a whole."³⁶

At this point, it is clear that the two organizations share significant points in common. However, on closer examination noticeable differences begin to appear, both in the praxis of overseas development and especially in how the Bible shapes and informs that praxis. At the heart of these differences lies Tearfund's understanding of "integral mission." Numerous resources on integral mission exist in Tearfund's own publications and partner organizations; I will simply offer a brief synopsis here.

First, some very brief context. For decades the precise relationship between evangelism and social responsibility has been a major topic of discussion and debate within the global evangelical world of which Tearfund is a part – with a continual tension between those who want to protect the primacy of individual faith, repentance, and forgiveness of sin through the atoning work of Christ, and those who want to widen what they see as an overly "narrow" understanding of the gospel to include God's redemptive work to redeem creation, establish his kingdom rule, and rescue people from injustice in the "here and now."³⁷ The history of that debate is not our concern here, save to say that the key issue is whether "social action" is an integral component of the gospel or a secondary (and therefore distinct) implication of that gospel. This is no academic debate. On the one hand, behind conservative concerns lies the ghost of Rauschenbusch³⁸ and fears of "downgrading" Christian mission so that

---

35. "In Ireland," accessed 19 September 2019, https://www.tearfund.ie/in-ireland/.

36. "Justice," under "Our Values," accessed 5 June 2020, https://www.tearfund.ie/vision-and-values/.

37. Some resources on this discussion are T. Chester, *Good News to the Poor: Social Involvement and the Gospel* (Leicester: Inter-Varsity Press, 2004); D. Hughes and M. Bennett, *God of the Poor: A Biblical Vision of God's Present Rule* (Carlisle: Authentic, 2007); J. A. Grant and D. A. Hughes, eds., *Transforming the World? The Gospel and Social Responsibility* (Nottingham: Inter-Varsity Press, 2009); M. Hoek and J. Thacker, eds., *Micah's Challenge: The Church's Responsibility to the Global Poor* (Milton Keynes: Paternoster, 2008).

38. Walter Rauschenbusch (1861–1916), author of *Christianity and Social Crisis* (1907); *A Theology for Social Gospel* (1917); and *The Social Principles of Jesus* (1918). Debate continues as to whether he has been unfairly caricatured, but for many evangelicals his name is intrinsically

social action takes centre stage over and above proclamation of the gospel of Jesus Christ. On the other hand are concerns of socially engaged evangelicals, particularly beyond the West,[39] who are passionately convinced that the gospel is not dualistic, dividing the spiritual from the physical.

Tearfund belongs in the latter category and defines integral mission as "the work of the church in contributing to the positive physical, spiritual, economic, psychological and social transformation of people," with particular focus on the poor.[40] Dewi Hughes,[41] in discussing Tearfund's statement of faith[42] (which is adopted by Tearfund Ireland), outlined a theological rationale for integral mission. Mission must be understood within the biblical narrative of creation, fall, redemption, and consummation, with the church "in the time between the arrival of the Holy Spirit's new redemptive power on earth following Christ's resurrection and the consummation of all things when Christ returns."[43] This means that the call of the church is to declare Jesus as the one "who forgives the sins of those who believe in him," but *also* that "this initial experience of Jesus [is] a door into a growing understanding of his lordship" in the power of the Spirit for *all* aspects of life. Further, this puts the church as a "caring, inclusive and distinctive community of reconciliation reaching out in love to the world" at the *centre* of Christian mission. Hughes argues that "the church is not the means by which Tearfund can deliver 'development' to the poor but the most convincing evidence that we now have of the outworking of God's purpose to redeem his creation." While churches are frequently broken and imperfect, it is Tearfund's "privilege to be continually looking for such churches within the worldwide Evangelical community that we may encourage them in their integral mission," since "showing mercy and acting on behalf of the

---

associated with the "social gospel" that is perceived to turn the good news of the kingdom of God into merely a societal reform movement.

39. It is significant that some of the earliest advocates of holistic mission among evangelicals in the latter half of the twentieth century included people like C. René Padilla from Argentina. Padilla is a key figure in both Tearfund and the Micah Network's "Declaration on Integral Mission" (2000). For his views see C. R. Padilla, "What Is Integral Mission?," 1–5, accessed 19 September 2019, http://www.dmr.org/images/pdf%20dokumenter/C._Ren%C3%A9_Padilla_-_What_is_integral_mission.pdf.

40. Jason Fileta, ed., *Live Justly: Global Edition* (Portland, OR: Micah Challenge / Tearfund, 2017), 6.

41. Dewi Hughes was, until recently, Tearfund UK's theological adviser for nearly twenty years.

42. "Statement of Faith," accessed 5 June 2020, https://www.tearfund.org/about_you/jobs/tearfund_statement_of_faith/.

43. Hughes, "Theology of Integral Mission," accessed 5 June 2020, https://arkaidawareness.weebly.com/the-social-gospel.html.

poor belongs to the essence of the church . . . a church that does not care for its poor is not a true church."⁴⁴

In terms of development, Tearfund's praxis is also drawn explicitly from the Scriptures. Hughes contends,

> We accept as consistent with the Bible the development community's analysis of poverty as a lack of empowerment, opportunity and security and emphasise that the poor are denied power, opportunity and security by the rich and powerful . . . Showing mercy to the poor, therefore, often requires a lot more than a handout although in an emergency a handout/alms may be required. To show mercy requires a whole range of different actions and gifts needed to reduce the vulnerability of the poor. These actions and gifts also cost money.⁴⁵

It is evident that the objective of a theology of integral mission is to knit together Christian mission, development, and the local church into a coherent rationale for praxis. Tearfund Ireland's values reflect these priorities, self-confessedly driven by the "belief that God through His word, character and the person of Jesus Christ calls the church and Christians to active involvement in ending poverty and seeking justice for people who are marginalised and vulnerable."⁴⁶ Hoped-for outcomes include practical needs being met, increasing participation and empowerment of the poor, advocacy to challenge structural injustice, personal understanding of individuals as made in the image of God, local church engagement in service to the poor alongside worship and witness – all inspired by Christ's example: "His word steers us and His presence steadies us."⁴⁷

Tearfund's vision for integral mission locates the organization within a wider network of evangelical organizations and theologians sharing similar commitments. In true evangelical fashion, biblical scholar Chris Wright is emphatic that holistic mission must be cross-shaped in that it is only in the cross that guilt, sin, the powers of evil, victory over death, alienation between human beings, and the reconciliation of all of creation are achieved. This is

---

44. Hughes, "Theology of Integral Mission."

45. Hughes.

46. "Our Values," under introductory paragraph, accessed 5 June 2020, https://www.tearfund.ie/vision-and-values/.

47. "Our Values," under "Christ-Centred," accessed 5 June 2020, https://www.tearfund.ie/vision-and-values/.

the "mission of God."⁴⁸ "It is a mistake, in my view, to think that, while our evangelism must be centred on the cross (as of course it has to be), our social engagement has some other theological foundation or justification . . . So it is my passionate conviction that holistic mission must have a holistic theology of the cross. That includes the conviction that the cross must be as central to our social engagement as it is to our evangelism."⁴⁹

Wright's comments are strongly aligned with the ethos of the Micah Network which was developed by an international group of Christian organizations to campaign for delivery of the MDGs. Its "Declaration on Integral Mission" states, "If we ignore the world we betray the word of God which sends us out to serve the world. If we ignore the word of God we have nothing to bring to the world. Justice and justification by faith, worship and political action, the spiritual and the material, personal change and structural change belong together. As in the life of Jesus, being, doing and saying are at the heart of our integral task."⁵⁰

It is worth noting here that, in regard to the MDGs, Tearfund's policy response lacks mention of a political rights-based approach to development. The organization affirms the value and importance of rights, but says that "Christian organisations need to be fully aware of human rights, but with a distinctly Christian perspective. Christians and the church may be called to accept injustice and violation of rights against themselves but at the same time to be committed to actively seeking justice and upholding other people's rights. It is a motivation of love rather than law."⁵¹

So, while Tearfund and Trócaire share many similarities as Christian, faith-based organizations which affirm the truth and authority of the Bible, it is clear that on closer inspection significant differences exist in both theology and praxis. Most, if not all, of these differences lie in the organizations'

---

48. For further discussion see C. J. H. Wright, *The Mission of God: Unlocking the Bible's Grand Narrative* (Downers Grove, IL: IVP Academic, 2006), http://www.loc.gov/catdir/toc/ecip0616/2006020882.html. Wright is a key figure in global evangelicalism and played a central role in drafting Tearfund's statement of faith as well as the "Cape Town Commitment" agreed at the Third Lausanne Congress on World Evangelization 2010.

49. Wright, "Reaffirming Holistic Mission: A Cross Centered Approach in All Areas of Life," accessed 5 June 2020, http://www.lausanneworldpulse.com/themedarticles-php/61/10-2005.

50. From the "Micah Network Declaration on Integral Mission," accessed 19 September 2019, http://www.micahnetwork.org/sites/default/files/doc/page/mn_integral_mission_declaration_en.pdf.

51. P. Stephenson, "From Needs-Based to Rights-Based Approaches," Tearfund Learn, accessed 19 September 2019, http://tilz.tearfund.org/en/resources/publications/footsteps/footsteps_61-70/footsteps_66/from_needsbased_to_rightsbased_approaches/.

distinct Catholic and evangelical identities. Rather than Catholicism's dual source of revelation, evangelicals hold to the Reformation's notion of *sola scriptura* whereby the Bible is "supremely and uniquely authoritative for our belief and behaviour."[52] This means that, for Tearfund, the Bible is explicitly at the forefront of its mission and vision of how development is to happen in practice. Close attention is paid to the content of the biblical narrative and the new covenant role of the church as a subversive community of God's people embodying kingdom life in the Spirit within a sinful and unjust world.[53] Themes of personal conversion, the cross, and activism (working on behalf of the poor) are all evident in Tearfund's vision and mission. While professional advocacy to powerholders is an important part of the organization's work, there appears to be less emphasis on a "top-down" rights-based approach to development but more a "bottom-up" emphasis of change at the local level. This reflects an evangelical ecclesiology of the church as a "gathering community" of believers who have committed their lives to the risen Lord; what Hughes calls "an ordered society under the government of Jesus."[54]

Concluding Reflections

It is time to offer some concluding reflections on the Bible and Irish culture in light of our overall discussion.

First, given a widespread (and often justifiable) contemporary negative reaction against Ireland's damaging experience of nineteenth-century religious conflict and subsequent experience of all-pervasive forms of Christendom,[55] it is important that "threads of grace" not be cut out of the overall picture. Those threads include people from many church groupings being inspired to confront injustice and work for fairness in Ireland and overseas by voices in the Bible which demonstrate a radical commitment to the poor and marginalized. Just two organizations have been focused on here, but thousands of others could be listed, across all sorts of charities, religious congregations, local churches, and parachurch organizations, not to mention innumerable acts of

---

52. "Statement of Faith," accessed 5 June 2020, https://www.tearfund.org/about_you/jobs/tearfund_statement_of_faith/.

53. See D. A. Hughes, *Power and Poverty: Divine and Human Rule in a World of Need* (Downers Grove, IL: IVP Academic, 2008).

54. Hughes, *Power and Poverty*, 200.

55. By this I refer to both Catholic and Protestant forms of Christendom within the island of Ireland.

individual self-giving and compassion by individuals.[56] They reflect a deep-seated characteristic of Christianity to serve those in need that, I suggest, has had a profound global impact and continues to influence and shape Irish culture. Increasingly the important contribution of faith-based organizations (FBO) to global development and to social provision "at home" is being recognized by policymakers acutely aware of the limitations of government social provision.[57] It would be a fascinating area for further research to attempt to quantify the contribution of FBOs to the common good in Ireland.[58] From personal experience of church life in Ireland, my sense is that the level of engagement in social action is pervasive but patchy and often not thought through theologically.[59] It would seem that there is room here for organizations like Trócaire and Tearfund increasingly to use their expertise in developing social justice partnerships overseas in local contexts here in Ireland.

Second, picking up on Moffitt's point about mission being done primarily for the needs of Protestants rather than the poor, *motives* for engaging in social justice are of paramount importance. The astonishing organizational efforts of many nineteenth-century Protestants in feeding the poor were fatally tainted by their connection with aggressive evangelism.[60] Similarly, Fahey is persuasive in arguing that even though the Catholic Church's contribution to social action in Ireland has been enormous (particularly in education and hospitals), it tended to be pragmatic, as a means to an end (the dissemination and safeguarding of faith), rather than to combat social inequality or to reform society. This meant that it tended to reinforce social divisions rather than challenge them and it

---

56. One local church I know of did an "audit" of its members' involvement in areas of social concern. The results were an astonishing list of activity across youth, children, community development, counselling, care for the elderly, overseas development, human rights, religious freedom, and so on, for a relatively modest-sized group. Such findings could be multiplied many times over via churches and Christian organizations nationally.

57. For an overseas example (Nigeria) see O. O. Olarinmoye, "Faith-Based Organizations and Development: Prospects and Constraints," *Transformation: An International Journal of Holistic Mission Studies* 29, no. 1 (Jan. 2012): 1–14. For discussion of this trend in the UK see S. Furness and P. Gilligan, "Faith-Based Organisations and UK Welfare Services: Exploring Some Ongoing Dilemmas," *Social Policy and Society* 11, no. 4 (Oct. 2012): 601–612.

58. The work of St Vincent de Paul Society would be a significant example in this regard.

59. Reid also makes this point: J. Reid, *Faith Expressing Itself through Love: An Applied Theology of Evangelical Social Action for Today's Ireland* (Saarbrücken: Lap Lambert Academic, 2012), 87.

60. This is in contrast to the positive Famine legacy of the Society of Friends/Quakers who provided a remarkable level of aid to the starving "without strings attached." Their generosity probably lay behind their inclusion as one of the named denominations in the 1937 Constitution. See Reid, *Faith Expressing*, 73.

was the Church that tended to resist social change rather than initiate it.⁶¹ The "dark side" of this level of control was abuse and marginalization of the most vulnerable in society who did not fit into the "imagined community" of Irish Catholic identity. It is significant how transparent both Trócaire and Tearfund are in aid being given impartially on the basis of need alone.⁶² This sort of vision is vital for any Christian organization attempting to engage in social justice in Ireland today. It would be all too easy to see "care for the poor" become a means to an end – perhaps attracting funding or the growth or reputation of the organization, for example. The Bible itself is a powerful resource here regarding the central place of love as a basis for all of Christian life.

Third, while (many) Catholics may approach issues of social justice through the lens of CST and the Magisterium of the Church, and (many) evangelical Protestants come to the issues via a theology of integral mission, both traditions agree that God is a God of the poor and that they are therefore called to God's mission of justice and love in a broken world, both overseas and at home. Unrestrained capitalism has wreaked havoc on the Irish economy⁶³ and contemporary Ireland is now one of the most unequal societies among OECD member states.⁶⁴ In this context, all those who claim to follow the resurrected Jesus as Lord are called to challenge all forms of oppression and to help relieve human suffering in all its diabolical manifestations. God is not indifferent to the plight of the poor, the hungry, the illiterate, the victims of war and prejudice, and those oppressed by military, political, and economic

---

61. Fahey, "Catholic Church," 146–150. For example, Fahey notes that schools and religious congregations themselves reflected status distinctions in their structures.

62. On impartiality Tearfund states that their "own Christian affiliations do not affect the provision of needs-based assistance but rather affirm a calling to respond based on need alone (Matthew 25:31–46)," "Tearfund Quality Standards for Emergency Response," accessed 19 September 2019, http://www.tearfund.org/~/media/files/tilz/topics/dmt/field_guides/tf_quality_standards_field_guide_-_second_edition_-_july_2015_final.pdf?la=en. Similarly, for Trócaire, see Niamh O'Byrne, "Strengthening Humanitarian Principles," Trócaire, 16 July 2012, accessed 19 September 2019, http://www.trocaire.org/opinion/strengthening-humanitarian-principles. Both organizations are committed to international codes on impartiality and good governance in development.

63. Irish national debt is, at the time of writing, over €200 billion (up about €160 billion since 2006). It costs over €8 billion to service this debt annually. Over €60 billion was paid into insolvent banks. See A. Beesley, "National Debt and Its Servicing Still Weigh Heavily on State," *The Irish Times*, 16 October 2014, accessed 19 September 2019, http://www.irishtimes.com/news/politics/national-debt-and-its-servicing-still-weigh-heavily-on-state-1.1965128.

64. Ireland performs poorly across five categories of poverty, education, labour market inclusion, social cohesion and equality, and generational equality. See "Ireland Has One of the Worst Levels of Social Justice among OECD Member States," Social Justice Ireland, 11 January 2011, accessed 19 September 2019, http://www.socialjustice.ie/content/policy-issues/ireland-has-one-worst-levels-social-justice-among-oecd-member-states.

tyranny. The church has no choice but to dive in and help those whose worldly address lies within one of the many suburbs of hell. It has no choice but to accept the partnership with God in the creation of a better world.[65]

---

65. D. S. Ferguson, *Biblical Hermeneutics: An Introduction* (Atlanta: John Knox, 1986), 194.

12

Worship and Justice

Spirituality that Embodies and Mobilizes for Justice[1]

Sandra Maria Van Opstal

Christian worship is the communal gathering of God's people in which we glorify God for his person and actions. This encounter with God includes gathering together, encountering the triune God in the Word and sacrament, and sending the community out into the world as agents of his love and justice. This chapter highlights the importance of worship in forming people who walk humbly with God and love mercy and do justice. Worship is formative, so we must ask, what are we forming? What we include in or exclude from our worship practices in preaching, prayer, music, and arts informs our theology and our embodied faith. In this chapter, I examine the importance of spirituality that embodies and mobilizes for justice, the challenges in breaking people free from idolatry in worship, and the implications for the church and its role in the world. I rely on case studies from local congregations, denominations, and organizations both for illustration and to help suggest some best practices for those seeking to build bridges at the intersection of worship and justice.

There are churches that make worship a priority and yet the worship doesn't result in transformed disciples with increased compassion and love

---

[1]. Sections from this chapter were first published in (or have been adapted from) my two books S. Van Opstal, *The Mission of Worship* (Downers Grove, IL: InterVarsity Press, 2012); S. Van Opstal, *The Next Worship: Glorifying God in a Diverse World* (Downers Grove, IL: InterVarsity Press, 2016). Reproduced here with permission from InterVarsity Press, www.ivpress.com.

for neighbour. What does it look like for us to develop practices of worship that mobilize our communities towards justice and to model just practices in our worship? While there are some dialogues on contextualized worship and/or multicultural worship, they often employ approaches that model little more than tokenism and appropriation. I start by exploring the theological intersection of worship and justice and then move to worship and formation. The strategies I propose are rooted in worship that embodies hospitality, solidarity, and mutuality. I conclude by reimagining worship that does more than entertain us.

Theology at the Intersection of Worship and Justice
The Law
The law was given to God's people so that they might live lives that embodied his character and the way of his kingdom. When the Lord gave his law to the people, its very foundation was the intersection of worship and justice. The description in Deuteronomy of God being for the systemically marginalized, sandwiched between the commands to love God and to love the most vulnerable, makes it clear that loving others is at the core of knowing and loving God:

> And now, Israel, what does the LORD your God require of you, but to fear the LORD your God, to walk in all his ways, to love him, to serve the LORD your God with all your heart and with all your soul, and to keep the commandments and statutes of the LORD . . . He executes justice for the fatherless and the widow, and loves the sojourner, giving him food and clothing. Love the sojourner, therefore, for you were sojourners in the land of Egypt. You shall fear the LORD your God. (Deut 10:12–20 ESV)

The Prophets
The words of the prophets, such as Micah, Isaiah, and Amos, reoriented God's people to the reality that social righteousness is central to a life that is pleasing to God. Through their words they attacked the abuse of power and condemned Israel's worship. We hear their strong words about worship without justice:

> I hate, I despise your religious festivals;
> your assemblies are a stench to me.
> Even though you bring me burnt offerings and grain offerings,

> I will not accept them.
> Though you bring choice fellowship offerings,
> I will have no regard for them.
> Away with the noise of your songs!
> I will not listen to the music of your harps.
> But let justice roll on like a river,
> righteousness like a never-failing stream! (Amos 5:21–24)

Like a prosecuting attorney, Amos was charging the people with their failure to live lives of true worship. While Amos was clearly addressing their idolatry, which is mentioned two times, he highlighted their injustice and abuse of the poor by mentioning it five times. He charges them with the following five things: (1) being self-important; (2) using wealth as a means of indulging in luxury; (3) neglecting the poor; (4) treating people like commodities; (5) perverting justice in the courts which ultimately led to idolatry. Like other prophets, such as Isaiah and Micah, after describing the abuse and evil of society he appeals to God's people to repent of these sins. He doesn't give them a way out either, making it clear that indirect oppression is no more acceptable than direct oppression; it is still sin against God himself. Continuing to worship through rituals when not living justly only adds to their transgression. Amos 5 clearly argues that true worship cannot exist without justice.

The sharp language used in this passage conveys the revulsion of God. The Lord is saying to these "worshipers," "I can't stand your worship, I can't stomach the stench." The Israelites were sitting in their own filth and probably had no idea how bad they smelled. It was like being on a road trip for more than twelve hours and getting used to your odour. You do not realize how bad you smell! The Lord goes on to say through Amos, "I will not look at you." Their worship had become a mechanical means of appeasing their God. They had pretty buildings, pretty objects, pretty songs, but they were not beautiful to the Lord because they lacked justice. There is a clear movement in the text that encompasses all the senses: from smelling to seeing to hearing. At this point the Lord just says, "Shut it! Away with your singing." Their soulless worship was a burden to the Lord, and he was totally disgusted. How might the Lord experience our worship today?

We gather in pretty buildings with pretty music and neglect the vulnerable people we drive or walk past on our way there. We produce "Christian" products without ever asking about the work conditions of those who manufactured them. True worship is not about style or form. True worship has little to do with music, offerings, or services – it is about seeking God and living in response.

We need to be cautious and hear this clear warning from Amos. The ethics of a worshipper matter; our lives must overflow with righteousness and justice. Our religious lives are busy – and we can think we're doing well because of all our activities; but true worship requires mercy and justice towards others and obedience to God's commands. Mark Labberton writes that "human beings are created to reflect God's glory by embodying God's character in lives that seek righteousness and do justice. Worship turns out to be the dangerous act of waking up to God in the world, and then living lives that actually show it . . . True worship includes the glory and honor due to God – Father, Son and Spirit. It also includes the enactment of God's love and justice, mercy and kindness in this world."[2]

When was the last time you heard a sermon on Amos or any other prophet as a part of the "worship" discussion at church? How might the Lord experience us today if he smelled, saw, and heard our "worship"? We may need to repent that our focus has been on the style of worship rather than on the content of our worship, which includes God's teaching about justice. Compare how much time and money we have spent consuming "Christian" worship with the attention we have given to caring for the needs of the poor. He might say to us, "Shut up!"

The Great Commandment

Living a life committed to justice for all people makes sense to those who grow up with or among displaced, silenced, or systemically oppressed communities. Growing up with family in both Argentina and Colombia, I developed an awareness of the poverty and injustice in the world. As we were Catholics, social action was taught as a key worship activity of my Christian upbringing. We learned that our love and worship, anchored in Matthew 22:37–40, was intertwined with a call to love our neighbour: "'Love the Lord your God with all your heart and with all your soul and with all your mind.' This is the first and greatest commandment. And the second is like it: 'Love your neighbour as yourself.' All the Law and the Prophets hang on these two commandments." Along with the greatest command from the lips of Jesus, my Catholic foundations highlighted the Sermon on the Mount as a lens for worship. The life and words of Jesus painted a compelling picture.

---

2. Mark Labberton, quoted in B. D. Jones, *Dwell: Life with God for the World* (Downers Grove, IL: InterVarsity Press, 2014), 136.

The apostles continue to give testimony to the centrality of the great commandment by questioning a love for God that does not include and intersect with love for our brothers and sisters. The themes in Acts, James, as well as 1 John continue to draw us into reorientation and repentance. The following calls from 1 John are piercing:

> By this we know love, that he laid down his life for us, and we ought to lay down our lives for the brothers. But if anyone has the world's goods and sees his brother in need, yet closes his heart against him, how does God's love abide in him? Little children, let us not love in word or talk but in deed and in truth. (1 John 3:16–18 ESV)

> Beloved, let us love one another, for love is from God, and whoever loves has been born of God and knows God. Anyone who does not love does not know God, because God is love. (1 John 4:7–8 ESV)

> If anyone says, "I love God," and hates his brother, he is a liar; for he who does not love his brother whom he has seen cannot love God whom he has not seen. And this commandment we have from him: whoever loves God must also love his brother. (1 John 4:20–21 ESV)

Love for God encompasses love for the fatherless, the hurting, your brothers and sisters, your neighbours. Loving them requires seeing, naming, and standing in their pain, as well as tangibly responding to the things that affect under-resourced or marginalized populations.

My prayer is that we will cultivate worship with our time by serving the marginalized; that we will cultivate worship through our finances by giving to ministries that will advance the mission of God; that we will cultivate worship with our influence as global citizens in advocating about issues such as education, sex trafficking, and immigration. In order to cultivate a passion in our communities and to mobilize for justice we must ask ourselves what we are doing to intentionally form that theological understanding in them.

Worship Is Formative
Influence of Worship

People often visit me in Chicago. When I prepare for them, I ask them what they enjoy doing. I want to know if they are fans of sports, museums, shopping, or entertainment. Knowing what they want allows me to craft tours that will fit their desires. I love taking people to places they want to go. As a Chicago native,

I also know that there are places where they need to go. There are foods they must eat and sights they must see to fully experience our great city! There is a restaurant in my neighbourhood that invented a plantain and steak sandwich called a Jibarito. Whenever friends come back to visit, they beg me to take them there again. While they wanted the deep-dish pizza, they needed the Jibarito. A good guide takes you to places where you want to go, but a great guide takes you to places where you need to go.

Worship leaders take people where they want to go. We help them enter into God's presence and encounter God in ways that are familiar and comforting. In addition, we take them to places where they need to go to understand God more deeply. We guide them into a fuller experience of God's character, which is a difficult task that takes both theological and experiential wisdom. When worship practices miss this second step, it forms disciples who are self-centred.

Challenges to Change

In *The Mission of Worship*, I wrote: "Worship often begins by taking people where they want to go. We all want to experience God in ways that are familiar. Our way of relating, whether to God or people, develops naturally out of our personalities, experiences and preferences. This preferred way of relating with God affects how we approach congregational worship."[3] It is important for our felt needs to be met in worship so that we can "connect" with God in ways that are relevant to us as individuals. This allows us to have an authentic experience with God – sincere, genuine.

> A few years ago I introduced a Kenyan worship song for a missions Sunday at my church. Although the congregation seemed to enjoy the new form of worship, I could see them nervously smiling as they danced. After a few minutes in Kiswahili, I transitioned into a song with which they were more familiar. With eyes closed, feet planted, and hands lifted high, the congregation came alive at a new level. I knew I had them when their arms hit the sky! . . . While it is natural to desire an experience of God that "fits" us, we can sometimes be egocentric or community-centric instead of God-centric.[4]

---

3. Van Opstal, *Mission of Worship*, 9. Copyright © 2012 by Sandra Maria Van Opstal. Used by permission of InterVarsity Press, www.ivpress.com.

4. Van Opstal, *Mission of Worship*, 10. Copyright © 2012 by Sandra Maria Van Opstal. Used by permission of InterVarsity Press, www.ivpress.com.

When it comes to the modern consumer of worship, comfort is king! In *The Mission of Worship*, I said,

> I am sure we can all recall conversations when we have either heard or said, "I was not feeling worship at that church." About this consumer approach to worship Pam Howell . . . writes:
>
> "Can you imagine the Israelites, freshly delivered from slavery, before a mountain that trembles violently with the presence of God (Exod. 19), muttering: 'We're leaving because we're not singing the songs we like. Like that tambourine song, how come they don't do that tambourine song anymore?'
>
> "'I don't like it when Moses leads worship; Aaron's better.'
>
> "'This is too formal – all that smoke and mystery. I like casual worship.'
>
> "'It was okay, except for Miriam's dance – too wild, not enough reverence. And I don't like the tambourine.'"
>
> This scene seems absurd, given that these ex-slaves had been liberated by God himself. God's people were not evaluating worship; instead they were filled with awe, fear and hope. However, many today come with a list of preferences and a self-centred attitude toward worship.[5]

As created beings, we want to meet God in real ways, to experience repentance, healing, freedom, restoration, and joy. Each of us comes with our own issues from the week and we need to come just as we are. This type of space in worship is needed; but if our worship is just about staying in our familiar, comfortable experiences, we will get stuck. If we truly hope to go deeper in our worship with God, we may need to exchange where we *want to go* for where we *need to go*. Worship is not about entertaining ourselves, it is the communal gathering of God's people in which we glorify God for his person and actions. The repetition of prayers, the rehearsing of songs, and the challenge of the Word form theological emphases from which we live.

Strategies for Change

As Christian leaders we are therefore presented with the challenge to confront the idolatry of preference in our communities and develop practices that lead

---

5. Van Opstal, *Mission of Worship*, 10–11. Copyright © 2012 by Sandra Maria Van Opstal. Used by permission of InterVarsity Press, www.ivpress.com.

God's people to embrace the fullness of Christian worship as displayed in the Psalms and modelled in the Scriptures. We lead in the reality of a consumer-driven approach to local congregations and its impact on the decisions we make as to how much we can stretch our people. If changes in a local congregation require a significant degree of intentionality, organizational changes require even more effort and at many levels. We need to identify the stakeholders and the existing structures that are ripe for change.

Over the past decade, as I have consulted with churches, universities, and institutions, I have heard some common reasons why people do not want to implement change. After many hours of conversation on change management, I am left with a few learning points. First, interpret! Leaders serve as interpreters of an experience for their communities. Changing culture requires us to explain the changes along the way, otherwise our silence leaves space for the wrong interpretation. Even if people don't like what we are doing, they will know what we are doing and why.

Second, get feedback along the way. This is not something that can be done on our own; it needs the involvement of the whole community. Leaders must pay attention to the dynamics of the congregation. We must also make sure we are listening to a variety of voices, and if we are intentionally trying to help the community lean into the work of compassion and justice, we must pay special attention to those who are often marginalized and most impacted by the injustices and ask if our approach is honouring their community's story.

Third, we must be intentional about what we are creating. Each worshipping community must pursue a specific approach that makes sense for its context.

Lastly, when introducing change, it's important to acknowledge those who've gone before us. The last thing we want to communicate to our communities is that what they have done does not have any worth.

Leading worship that mobilizes for justice requires leadership that is willing to take calculated risks. The leaders need to be willing to do the following: connect change to the mission or big picture; gather a group of stakeholders affected by the change; have them work together; get the buy-in of the top tier of leadership; develop a vision of what things will look like in five years, and then communicate, communicate, communicate; and empower and help people to find their place and contribution.[6]

---

6. Steps based on Dr Kotter's "8-Step Process for Leading Change," Kotter Inc., accessed 19 September 2019, http://www.kotterinternational.com/the-8-step-process-for-leading-change/.

Worship that Embodies and Mobilizes for Justice
Solidarity in Worship Mobilizes for Justice

In *The Next Worship*, I tell the story of Quest Church:

> Quest Church of Seattle is a multi-ethnic church of nine hundred primarily composed of Asian American and white congregants. They are committed to community, reconciliation, compassion, justice and a global presence. While their church is only about 15 percent Latino and African American, they are committed to walking in solidarity with one another. They have an annual "faith and race" class and interweave the issues of the world into their worship experiences. Quest regularly incorporates global lament during the pastoral prayer portion of worship. They spend time naming the global realities and standing with the communities in prayer. One Sunday evening they hosted a special event focusing on the 270 Nigerian schoolgirls kidnapped by Boko Haram terrorists on April 14, 2014. Quest leaders invited people to a prayer space with prompts toward lament and protection.[7]

I go on to say,

> Solidarity means we identify with one another in the practices of lament and joy; we join in empathetic grieving and rejoicing. This is not a new practice or idea; the Scriptures clearly call us to solidarity. Reflect on the following passages and imagine congregational worship that lives into this reality of solidarity . . . We stand with one another in lament that leads to hope. We rejoice with one another when we see glimpses of the power of the gospel transforming situations. In solidarity we hope for this coming reality:
>
>> "Then I saw 'a new heaven and a new earth,' for the first heaven and the first earth had passed away, and there was no longer any sea. I saw the Holy City, the new Jerusalem, coming down out of heaven from God, prepared as a bride beautifully dressed for her husband. And I heard a loud voice from the throne saying, 'Look! God's dwelling place is now among the people, and he will dwell with them. They will be his people, and God himself will be

---

7. Van Opstal, *Next Worship*, 65-66. Copyright © 2016 by Sandra Maria Van Opstal. Used by permission of InterVarsity Press, www.ivpress.com.

> with them and be their God. He will wipe every tear from their eyes. There will be no more death or mourning or crying or pain, for the old order of things has passed away.' He who was seated on the throne said, 'I am making everything new!'" (Revelation 21:1–5)
>
> This type of solidarity in worship transports us from the reality of the not yet. It reminds us of the kingdom to come. We can envision a place where we all as one body draw in closer to the glory of our God.[8]

We also learn to stand with one another in the pain and depth of the now. Solidarity is not just a feeling; it can and should be practised through word and deed. It should be practised as we stand with one another in protest against injustice. It should be practised through repentance and forgiveness. Worship can and should be a catalyst. These catalytic events can often be painful but powerful.

When Christians respond publicly to current events, it is evident that we have strikingly different perspectives based on our cultural and social location. Our reactions reveal how polarizing our viewpoints can be. We stand not with one another but on opposite sides. It's fantastically horrible to see how Christians treat one another across those differences. Ideally the experience of being in a diverse community with one another would create a space of reconciliation and solidarity in which empathy and understanding could be developed, particularly for those who are most deeply impacted by systemic injustice. However, even in homogeneous communities, we want to imagine what worship that embodies justice in standing in solidarity could look like.

Worship practices that help us stand in solidarity bring us beyond what we do and what we experience to the effects of injustice on others. The decentring of our space for the centring of those who have been systemically marginalized is in itself a practice of justice. We can do this singing and praying for people with our words and songs. We can also do this by singing and praying with people as we utilize the songs they share with us. I must caution that taking songs from people without the relationship and long-term commitment to stand in solidarity with them can be experienced as tokenism and appropriation. Many of the multicultural models of worship for diverse churches in North America, as well as for "global conferences" that are primarily led by Western-influenced

---

8. Van Opstal, *Next Worship*, 65–66. Copyright © 2016 by Sandra Maria Van Opstal. Used by permission of InterVarsity Press, www.ivpress.com.

leaders, employ an approach to inclusive worship that is disembodied. Songs and prayers are selected from song books at random, or because of accessibility, but they are not connected to the narrative nor in dialogue with the people. Embodied solidarity requires us to stand with them (proximity), not merely stand for them.

Mutuality in Worship Embodies Justice

Mutuality moves beyond standing with people and takes us to learning from one another. Mutuality acknowledges that there are not students and teachers, but co-learners. Reciprocity honours the reality that the entire body is necessary, and all play a meaningful role in the community. The differences we bring in gender, culture, social location, abilities, and age should be acknowledged, honoured, and embodied, or represented somewhere in our worship. This act of mutuality in designing worship practices embodies justice and forms disciples who understand what Martin Luther King, Jr said about justice and mutuality:

> We must all learn to live together as brothers [and sisters] or we will all perish together as fools. We are tied together in the single garment of destiny, caught in an inescapable network of mutuality. And whatever affects one directly affects all indirectly. For some strange reason, I can never be what I ought to be until you are what you ought to be. This is the way God's universe is made; this is the way it is structured.[9]

As worship leaders we can help people experience this reality in worship. In *The Next Worship*, I tell the following story:

> At a worship gathering of global leaders we worshiped to a song called "Magdan Lik," which was given to us by some of my friends at St. Samaans Church, also known as the Cave Church in the Mokattam (Garbage City), just outside Cairo, Egypt. This community undergoes tremendous persecution as a religiously and socioeconomically marginalized community. The faith I saw them exhibit under systemic oppression was grounded in their legacy story of Simon the Tanner, who literally moved Mokattam

---

9. Martin Luther King, Jr., "Remaining Awake through a Great Revolution," The Martin Luther King, Jr. Research and Education Institute, Stanford University, accessed 19 September 2019, https://kinginstitute.stanford.edu/king-papers/publications/knock-midnight-inspiration-great-sermons-reverend-martin-luther-king-jr-10.

mountain in prayer (prophet of Baal style) . . . Choosing that song was significant to me for a couple of reasons. First, I had been profoundly changed by my partnership with Egyptian Coptic Christians, and I wanted to expose American Christians to their depth of faith and compassion. Second, I wanted the participants to hear the Arabic language being used to worship Jesus. Too often we associate certain sounds, rhythms and images as being un-Christian, when they are merely un-Western. Hearing the language and rhythms, and seeing the Arabic characters on the screen, was a teaching moment for many attendees and a healing moment for many Arabic speakers who felt alienated by the American church.[10]

Worship is a way of connecting our lives with the lives of Christians in a completely different context in order to learn what it might be like to tell God "All my life is yours" in the midst of persecution and poverty.

Embodied Justice/Decolonization of Worship

Mutuality goes even deeper than inclusivity and appreciation: these relationships of reciprocity facilitate the decolonization of worship. Liturgical structures and practices that embody justice intentionally seek to decentre communities that have historically been in power by naming the practices and theology they imposed on indigenous communities. This is especially true for nations that were "Christianized" by European missionaries or later "evangelized" by American missionaries. The effects of political colonization on continents like Africa, Latin America, and Asia were also seen in their theological colonization and have been documented at length. Worship was colonized. As faith was brought to the nations, so were dress codes, hymnals, and "proper" liturgical practices coming from Lutheran, Anglican, Dutch reformed, and other European traditions. The folk music, instruments, stories, and narratives of the people were stripped away and seen as less reflective of the Bible. It was godlier to use an organ than drums, so missionaries and schools actually shipped organs and pianos to ensure that "correct" forms of worship were being practised. Global worship practices are currently shaped by a small group of worship movements on three Western continents (North America,

---

10. Van Opstal, *Next Worship*, 67–68. Copyright © 2016 by Sandra Maria Van Opstal. Used by permission of InterVarsity Press, www.ivpress.com.

Europe, and Australia), continuing the pattern of theological colonization that impacts the health of the entire church.

Decolonizing worship is the work of asking why Christian practices from the Majority World mirror both Western liturgical forms and modern contemporary Christian expressions, and of acknowledging the impact of that reality on the whole church. Reflection, acknowledgment, and repentance of the oppressive ways in which worship has been imposed on Christians around the world historically will ultimately also result in our liberation. We will be able to see what we have missed and are missing.

Like O-negative blood types, the universal theological donors are Western evangelicals. This universal donor is always translating books into other languages, planting churches in other countries, setting up seminaries on other continents, or gathering "global assemblies" with planning teams that have been highly influenced by the West. We never seem to have the same intentionality to receive from our global friends. Today more than ever the North American church is in need of a remedy to the blind spots in our theology that are shaped by our practices and ultimately impact our formation as Christ followers. We need to be formed by the liturgical practices of the global church, but first we must find churches that have not simply adopted North American forms. We must ask why there are so many churches around the world that just want to mimic the famous worship bands from the United States or Australia.

The American evangelical church witnesses the growth of the church in Latin America, Africa, and Asia as it hopes for a vibrant revival in its own churches. Churches of colour in urban settings as well as immigrant churches also show huge promise to be the future of the church in America. Worship has been at the root of the growth in the non-Western, non-white settings. Pentecostal prayer forms and new songs telling the stories of communities' encounters with God are springing up; revival and reclaiming of indigenous instruments and dancing are finding their way to our ears. The de-Westernization and breaking free of the shackles of forms of worship that were used as means of colonization and oppression is in full force. We in the West should not be scared but blessed. We are in need of the spiritual practices of our southern brothers and sisters.

We must ask ourselves, what theological truths does post-colonial worship liberated from the power of Western colonizers contribute? What can contextualized practices in worship look like in a post-colonial church? What harm do we inflict on the majority church located in the Majority World if we continue to export a practice of worship that is theologically and socially located in the West? What is the loss to Western Christianity if we don't listen to the voices of the global church in worship and formation?

Conclusion

How can we say we love God? How can we offer to him songs and words, how can we have a multi-billion-dollar worship industry, and yet be so detached from the issues of injustice that are rampant in our countries and in our world? We can do this because we have practised a spirituality that does not embody or mobilize for justice. We have worship concerts, worship schools, programmes in church music, that have no integration of worship as formation. We see worship leaders as musicians and not as pastors, prophets, or guides who lead people where they need to go instead of where they want to go. We've made worship about us. For some this may mean holding on to traditions for safety and comfort; others seek new forms of worship for entertainment and free expression. The Scriptures call us to a worship that results in justice. To be a follower of Christ is to have a spirituality that embodies and mobilizes for justice.

13

Proclamation and Demonstration

CB Samuel

I always say that I belong to the old school, which means I prefer the microphone when it's fixed to a stand and not to me. And I prefer to open the Word of God. So, if you are uncomfortable with that style, let me tell you that too is the old style and it will remain. And for many, proclamation too is old school! This tension between the end of the era of proclamation and its continued usefulness is increasing. In this age of major communication leaps through advanced technological achievements and alternative methods of teaching, I still believe that proclamation has a significant and strategic place in Christian mission. Our bad experiences of proclamation or preaching are no reason to throw away the "baby with the bath water."

When I was invited to speak here the subject was "resilience." And I hope we can consider stories of communities in resilience. In our telephone conversation, I expressed to Sheryl my apprehension that many institutional experiences of resilience are of *individual resilience*, which we are good at. However, what we intend to hear are the cases where whole communities stand for a cause. This is the desperate need in many of our nations around the world. We need to revisit the significant evangelical traditions and models of community resilience, such as William Wilberforce, John Wesley, and others who shaped powerful movements for change. The biggest hindrance to promoting resilience has been the reduction of all Christian engagement in society to institutional engagement. Most of our people, however, are not in institutions, they are in society. And we need to reinvent ourselves if we are talking about resilience because institution-spurred resilience is not the only resilience. There is a lot of resilience happening in my country by people who are not in political parties, who are not in institutions, but purely because they belong to the people who are being victimized and marginalized. Unfortunately, what has happened over the years is that every good intention to be usefully engaged is channelled into "forming an organization" or "joining an institution." That's the death of the good intention. We end up spending most of our time managing the organization itself, rather than the vision which spurred us to start. It's very important for us, therefore, to always ask the question, "What goal are we trying to reach?"

My brief here is to consider the subject of proclamation and demonstration. Biblical images of proclamation are intentional actions to call for resilience. This is clearly portrayed by the prophetic traditions, including Jesus himself. We should never shy away from an opportunity to proclaim if we stand in the prophetic tradition. When we proclaim, we are actually prompting, instigating, or spurring resilience.

Proclamation Is Not a One-Event Activity

Contrary to popular opinion, Jesus's way of proclamation is not a one-event activity. Recently my daughter gifted me with a new phone. Her reason for getting me a bigger and smarter phone was, she said, "You do a lot of work on your phone, more than on your computer; so it would be good for you to have a slightly bigger phone." In this way she sold the idea of a good phone to me. What she was doing here was what I think we mean when we talk of "proclamation": we tell others and ourselves about the benefit of something. However, when I got the phone, the first thing I did was to look for the manual on how to operate it. And that was a part of that proclamation, of that selling, because if I took the phone based on what was told to me, I would never understand the benefits of it until I read the manual. It said, first, "Don't use the phone before charging it for so many hours"; then it said, "You can do this, do that." And it was then that I entered a new world of so many things that the phone could do.

Proclamation, to begin with, was basically the advertisement part. If I carried the phone with me, you might look at it and say, "Wow, CB, you've got a very good phone," and I might say, "Yeah, it's a good phone."

"And what do you use it for?"

If I replied, "Nothing, I just carry it with me," soon you would begin to laugh at me and say, "CB is the one who carries a very good phone and doesn't know how to use it!"

That is why the world is laughing at Christians. They look at us proclaiming something of Jesus of Nazareth, but they don't see anything of him in us. And that is a real problem of proclamation. We have stopped by thinking that proclamation is just advertisement. Announcement is the first step in proclamation – but proclamation is much more than that.

Last week I was privileged to visit some of the staff of EFICOR (an Indian evangelical civil society organization) working in a small village in a western state of India. During a brief interaction with the local villagers (a marginalized, poor community) I asked them: "What is your dream? Thirty years from now, where do you want to be?" They looked confused and blank. I have seen a similar response many times among poor communities. They say, "We have no dream at all; we are just here in the present." Interestingly, all that they hope for is "we just want our children to live."

"What is Christian engagement," I asked myself, "if it doesn't enable people to dream again?" In today's world, there are quite a few people whose main job is to destroy people's capacity to dream. Proclamation allows us to enter into such situations and initiate a conversation that ignites the ability to dream. And that is precisely what Jesus did.

Resilience is understood to have five stages. The first is creating awareness: of people becoming aware of their condition. You can't create resilience unless people are aware of their condition and realize they are in a place which has to be changed. Perhaps they have seen others change. The second stage of resilience is when they make a commitment to get out of that situation. Then they learn about things, they meet people, and they negotiate with others for change.

The third stage is when they take action to change. Any move that starts with awareness and commitment and doesn't move to action actually could be resistance to resilience. Action is when one converts one's desire into reality. I think that one of the dangers in religion in general is that we misunderstand resilience as survival. No wonder Karl Marx wrote, "Religion is the opium of the people." Religion – and Christianity is no exception – ends up teaching people to smile rather than get out of the situation. We engage with communities with the attitude "The world won't change, it's a bad place, so you should just smile." That is not the same as resilience. *Christian faith is not about survival. Resilience is about creating not the capacity to smile, but the desire to get out of that situation.*

Once people choose to act, the next stage of resilience is that they begin to acclimatize themselves to the new changes. The New Testament captures this stage with words such as "put off" and "put on." And then, in the fifth stage of resilience, they come to realize that this is the new normal. This is how they will be the people of the kingdom of God.

I think it's very important to notice that in the Gospels, this is the model of Jesus. He comes into a situation, *takes a group of people, and works with them until they become the salt and light of the earth. They become the change-agents. Though today we have forgotten this important aspect of Jesus's way, it is still the methodology of God to bring resilience.*

The Process of Resilience: A Case Study from Jesus

Let us look at the process which Jesus used with his followers.

First, Jesus started his work of creating a community of resilient people among those John the Baptist had invested in. *John created an environment of resilience.* John came from the same place as Jesus – Nazareth in Galilee – which had a bad reputation: nothing good came out of that place. This wasn't because nothing good did actually come out of it, but because the good that came out of it was not acceptable to certain people from Jerusalem. Nazareth was the place of revolutions; many people had already come from Nazareth claiming to be the Messiah. So everybody thought of Nazareth as a troubled area. There are places like that in every country – hotbeds of hope. Nazareth was not like the places we usually belong to – the Jerusalems, the centres of religion, where religious life is what we do. In Nazareth people were waiting for the Messiah; they were pregnant with hope, but also wanting to do something.

John, like Jesus, started off saying, "Repent, for the kingdom of God is at hand." And I believe that biblical proclamation starts with a call to repent. In the last ten years I have not heard this word "repent" in the church I go to. We don't like to use it. Yet the Bible is clear that there is no question of proclamation without calling people to repentance. You are part of a system you need to get out of if you want to change. Resilience happens when we begin by saying, "I hate the system that I am part of." Unfortunately, today we are comfortable where we are. So John called the people who came to him to repent in specific areas. John was not the best person to be a pastor of your church. He said to those who came to be baptized, "You brood of vipers, who warned you? Why are you coming for baptism? Set your life right!" This is such a contrast to what happens today, where there is competition to outdo each other in reporting the number of baptisms each year! Today we want to attract people, so we dilute the demands of obedience.

I love the fact that we have so many young people under thirty years of age at this Micah Global gathering. Usually we don't actually respect our young people, because we think that they don't think. Instead we believe that our role as a church is to babysit them, to keep them busy with entertainment. So when we say, "This is a youth-friendly church," what we mean is that our entertainment level has gone up. We are scared to challenge our young people to give themselves to the stipulations of obedience that proclamation requires for experiencing resilience. But we have got our young people wrong.

I work with three different Christian groups of young people: church youth fellowships (senior high and undergraduate youth), young adults (working young people), and students of a vibrant university (outside the purview of the church). I believe our concentration on church youth is lopsided. There are many who don't come to our churches who are very interested in engagement and are keen on sacrificing self-interest to achieve the common good. Such young people don't want to be entertained but engaged. This morning, a friend of mine sent me two pictures of protests largely led by young people. They are the ones who are on the streets. They have learned to get beaten, and they are learning to stand and even go to prison if required. Their expectation of the church is that it should be a place where we are in touch with reality and are broken about the things that people are broken about.

John (and Jesus) was leading such a movement when he went on telling people, "Repent! Get your act together!" It's very important for us to understand that all proclamation begins with this call to repent. The cultures we belong to, the institutions we are a part of, the churches we belong to, are very often anti-kingdom of God. And note that John was located in the wilderness – and that people went all the way there into the wilderness to see him. They were not going for a conference; they went to meet a person called John. John prepared the way; Jesus met him there. And most of Jesus's first disciples were John's disciples. John had already prepared the way for Jesus by creating a community that was aware and ready for resilience.

I think *the church should relocate to where there have been preparations for resilience.* We simply go out to places, but I don't think that is what Jesus had in mind. He said, "And when you go to a place, if they accept you, stay there. If they don't, keep moving." I think there is a very important principle to identify here: find locations of resilience. Find where preparation is going on.

While the proclamation begins with a call to repent, it is followed by the announcement "The kingdom of God is here." What a lovely phrase! Yet it is totally misunderstood and misused by most people today. We have different versions of the kingdom of God that are far removed from Jesus's understanding of it. Jesus was not introducing a new phrase; he connected to the hope of the people. Thus resilience begins when we connect to the hope of the people and understand what they are looking forward to. The "kingdom of God" was a common term which Jesus used to proclaim his mission. *Proclamation is hard work. It means using the language of the people, their aspirations, and their hopes to communicate the purpose of God. It requires us to unlearn much of what we learned in our seminary education. Resilience is created by communicating hope to people.* That's what Jesus did when he talked about the kingdom of God. I think it is good for us to revisit our cities, to walk in their streets, and to learn the language of the people again. Much of our vocabulary is far removed.

We are totally out of touch with the questions people are seeking answers to. Often we are in our workplaces, immobile and irrelevant. I used to say to my colleagues in the Christian organization I worked in that the worst invention in the world is the chair. Once you come to the office you think that you are stuck to your chair. It is time for us to take out the chairs from our offices. We need to be outside! Then we will meet people, and we will talk with them.

If we are going to be people who build resilience through our proclamation, it is very important that we be connected to the language and lives of others. It is very important to know their dreams and aspirations. And we must try to enable them.

Jesus then calls people to follow him, and proclamation includes this call to discipleship. Let us look at Luke 5 to see one great example of the process of discipling in the life of Peter.

When I came to Christ many years ago – in 1971 – I asked my friend through whom I came to know Christ, "OK, so what do I do next?" He was confused – he didn't know the answer. Eventually he said, "Come to church on Sundays." Then he added, "Read the Bible every day, and pray every day. Be in fellowship with others. And you should share your faith with others." I said, "Is that all? That looks very easy!" But I thought to myself, "It must have been very different when people followed Jesus." So I started reading the Scriptures to find out what people did when they followed Jesus. That opened my eyes as to why our movement of proclamation is flawed and doesn't transform society.

In Luke 5 following Jesus begins with a call: "Come, follow me, and I will make you fishers of men." In other words, I will use you as an instrument (perhaps to cause resilience in society).

Peter followed him. Use your imagination as you read the verses that follow which introduce us to a series of events in Peter's life. You can't read the Scriptures without imagination.

Peter went home that day bringing with him a big catch of fish.

Peter's wife and mother-in-law would have looked at him and said, "You got a big catch today; was it good?"

Peter said, "It was bad, actually. But then, you remember the rabbi we talked to, the one we met in Jordan? He came there."

"What did he do? Does he know how to fish?"

"I don't know if he knows how to fish. But he told us to throw out the net, and we caught this huge number of fish!"

"So tomorrow, are we going to have more fish?"

"No, tomorrow there'll be no more fish; it's over. Today is the last day of fishing. He told us to follow him, so I've left the nets behind."

"What are you going to do now?"

"I don't know. We're going to follow the rabbi; you know some of us are following him."

"Where are you going to meet? Will it have a whiteboard with a marker? Will there be PowerPoint presentations?"

"We don't know how it's going to be, but perhaps after two weeks we'll come back and tell you what it means to follow this rabbi."

And so perhaps he came back after two weeks. Luke tells of many incidents that followed. Picture Peter reporting the first lessons of discipleship to his family members. Peter's mother-in-law and wife would have been excited and asked him, "Peter, what happened? How was it with the rabbi? Where did you meet? Which room did you take?"

"There was no room."

"What do you mean, no room?"

"He's not like John or the Pharisees. This rabbi is different. We walked on the road."

Athol Gill, the Australian missiologist, titled his book on the messianic lifestyle *Life on the Road*. If we are to be instruments of resilience, our visibility as followers of Jesus must increase. For Peter it must have been, "Monday to Saturday we were walking on the road." It was a busy two to three weeks of learning on the road.

The discussion could have gone like this. Peter might have begun his narration of what happened by saying, "The first day when I left here we went out and saw a man with leprosy on the street."

"What did the rabbi do?"

"He touched him!"

There would have been silence in the house. Then they would have said, "Did you touch him? Because you know that, as a Jew, you're not supposed to touch certain people."

"Yeah, I know that, but then who tells Jesus?" Peter replied.

"Did you touch him?"

"Well no, not this time. But I think I will have to touch them soon."

What was Jesus doing? Following Jesus is about transforming our minds. Most Christians in my country have not been transformed. Christian faith, for many, is like the icing on the cake. It has not changed us in the inside. But change is what happened when Jesus proclaimed. He took his followers into situations which challenged them. I'm afraid that most of us can talk about a lot of the issues faced by the marginalized but, if not for our institution, have never actually been located among them. And that's why I have often noticed that many people who retire from Christian development agencies have nothing to do with the poor afterwards.

The next lesson for Peter was in a home where Jesus healed a paralyzed man. Peter might have said something like, "We went to a home and were sitting there, when suddenly mud started falling on our heads! We looked up and saw these men sending down another man with a rope from the roof! They were sending him to Jesus for healing."

Peter's wife asked, "Did Jesus heal him?"

"He did, but before that he said, 'Son, your sins are forgiven.'"

This was not the done thing. Peter's mother-in-law would have looked at Peter and said, "Oh! You're not supposed to forgive. Who can forgive? Only God can forgive."

"That's what the Pharisees said," replied Peter. "But Jesus said that this was done so that you will know that the Son of Man has the right to heal."

Jesus was reinterpreting God for Peter. But Peter had to learn that when you walk with Jesus, your understanding of God begins to change. Jesus defined God differently: he touches the wrong people; he is sitting in the wrong places.

Our understanding of God has still not changed in many parts of the world today. But change is what happens when you follow Jesus. That's what resilience does: it begins to change the way we think.

Then they said to Peter, "What else did you do?"

"I'll tell you tomorrow morning," replied Peter.

"No, we want to know now!"

"Well, the next thing that happened was that we were walking along the street and saw Matthew the tax collector."

"Did you tell Jesus about the tax collector? Did Jesus look at the tax collector and say, 'Woe unto you tax collectors, for fire will come!'"

"No," said Peter, "I had no chance to tell him anything. Jesus told Matthew, 'Follow me.'"

"What do you mean, 'Follow me'? Didn't you tell him we don't accept certain people?"

This is very important for us! We have categories of people we shun – the oppressed, the oppressor, even the upper caste, and so on – but Jesus does something totally different. He breaks our ways of including people in the community of God. Later, we notice how God worked when he moved to bring Saul, the persecutor, to himself. God does it differently; this is a new community of God. I think our language sometimes betrays our hatred of people, but that is not the way of the kingdom of God.

I could go on. This is what proclamation meant for Jesus. As Peter heard Jesus proclaiming the good news of the kingdom of God, he began to see that proclamation is revealed in demonstration. Any proclamation that does not have demonstration is no proclamation at all. And any demonstration that does not have an interpretation of the demonstration is no demonstration at all. We do both hand in hand; and that is what we call "integral mission."

To close, one of the biggest casualties of integral mission is that the gospel itself is no longer seen as integral in character. This is very important for us: *the gospel is integral in character.* You can't present a spiritual gospel and separate all the actions out as something else. The proclaimed gospel is integral in character. And the more integral our gospel is, the more integral our mission will be. May God help us to be such a community in our proclamation and demonstration.

14

What Is Required?

Florence Muindi

I found no better definition of integral mission than the mission of Jesus as stated in Isaiah 61. It comes out in three main points: preaching the good news to the poor; facilitating their restoration by giving them their dignity (and for me it is a sustained dignity, as they participate and own their own development); and empowering them to become the righteousness of God. It is clear God has been at work, and the mission of Jesus has been ongoing through his disciples and through the people who have been discipled thereafter until this day, even to our current generation.

Every September we hold a holistic-centred conference in Nairobi and the Global Missions Health Conference of Africa. It happened just last week, and we had people from twenty-five nations in attendance. Various ministries from different countries in Africa were represented and shared their experiences, with more than four hundred people attending. It was very refreshing for me to see the Majority World leading and initiating ministries in areas that are having an impact in line with the mission of Jesus. They are multiplying, they are expanding, and they are taking responsibility for raising global holistic ministries. And I stand to testify to a holistic awakening, that God himself is stirring and making disciples of all nations – especially in the nations where poverty is prevalent. Christians are baptizing people in the name of the Father and of the Son and of the Holy Spirit and teaching people all that the Bible teaches us. This is a participation in the manifestation of Isaiah 61, with an authority that is bringing about transformation in the areas that can be witnessed. I think there is no greater joy for all of us than to find fulfilment in being part of what God is doing and together joining that. Unfortunately, not everyone can be part of this. Unfortunately, not everyone can come alongside and experience what God is doing and be part of the manifestation of Isaiah 61, and it is in these countries that God is inviting us to be part of that manifestation.

God invites us to a process of integral mission. So we ask, "What does it take?" What does it take for us to join God and actually become a part of what he is doing in the nations today? What does it take for our organizations to strategically align themselves with what God is doing so that we can be a part of that manifestation?

Here I will respond to those questions. I will share my story. I will share in a very vulnerable way five things God has taught me – the essentials for taking part in what God is doing and becoming a part of the transformation process.

Father, I pray that, as we engage with what you are inviting us to, you will cause it to settle in our spirits and you will invite us into that process; and that together, Lord, we can be counted worthy to take our place and see transformation happen in the nations. In Jesus's name. Amen.

The First Is *Salvation*

This is the first essential and vital step that we have to take. I recall the time I invited Christ as Lord and Saviour into my life. I remember I was forgiven, and I felt that forgiveness. I was only a young child – I was eleven years old. But I remember I became a part of the redeemed. I remember I could feel the difference – the before and the after. I could not experience this and keep it to myself because it moved me to want to tell others of what had happened to me. I knew the old Florence in me had passed away and the new had come. The change began to manifest itself in me. I began to find it very difficult to go to bed thinking about a neighbour who was alone. She was an elderly widow and I thought, "She is alone in her house across the valley with nothing to eat." I found it very difficult to see our neighbours' clothes hanging nearby, as they were tattered and torn, and they would dry them at night in order to reuse them without even water to clean them in. I began to know the compassion of Christ being expressed through me for the people around me who were hurting.

Sharing the gospel by word and deed became my passion. The two go together. How can they not go together? Wherever he went, Jesus did good, and Jesus in us will do good. That is the vital step that we have to take. I know this is familiar to most of you, but I know it also must be familiar as it is sad if we are seeking integral mission based on human love, human ambition, or other things that quickly fade away and cannot be sustained. The Spirit of Christ in me compels me to love the lost and to love my brothers and sisters as I love myself, because Christ in us is the testimony of sin forgiven – of the free gift of eternal life in the heart of missions and continually being manifested in word and deed. We cannot transform unless we are transformed. We cannot participate in what God is doing unless we know Christ and are walking with him.

The Second Is *Surrender*

I realize there is a difference when we refer to Christ as Saviour and when we refer to him as Lord and Master of our lives. It was not until I was about to graduate from high school that I realized it actually takes surrender. My father recently died in a tragic traffic accident and in my time of grief and mourning – the loss of someone who was my hero, my provider – I began to battle with questions of purpose. What is my reason for existence? Why do I live? Why am I here today? What does it mean that I no longer live but Christ?

Jeremiah 29 tells me God has a plan for me: a plan to give me a future and a hope. And Romans tells me that plan is pleasing and perfect. But how do I get on board? I was struggling to know what God had called me to do. How could I identify with Jesus and sign in for that? I remember long days of reflection and seeking God and the Word and asking God again and again, "What is my purpose?" One night at 2 a.m. I got on my knees sobbing and told the Lord, "I've seen it. I get it." And I enlisted for that. From that time onwards I fully surrendered. I began to call him my Lord and my Master. It was no longer my story, my rights, my dreams, but God's dreams. I signed into them. Use me wherever, however, for your glory.

That decision dethroned me and enthroned Christ. I remember writing it down and entering into a covenant with him. And I asked my Lord to guide me; that if I began to move away from that perfect will, that he would correct me. If my covenant was broken, I would rather be with Jesus in glory than be in this world to serve myself or another. That night I fully surrendered. It was no longer about my projects, my moves, myself, but about him and him alone.

This was thirty-seven years ago: thirty-seven years of living a surrendered life. It wasn't until I came to that place of full surrender that I began to hear the voice of God. I began to understand who he is. The Spirit of God was released in me so I can move as he moves and be where he wants me to be, doing what he wants me to do.

Soon after that I got to know clearly that God was calling me to cross-cultural mission. It was time for me to be equipped and trained in a process that would lead me to be effective in mission. So I went to medical school and then public health school and later I took a position in cross-cultural missions, to be able to serve the poor and the vulnerable in ways that preach the good news to them. I wanted to serve in ways that would give them life, and life in abundance. That became my focus. When my husband proposed to me, that purpose was discussed. God had called me to serve the poor and the vulnerable. How could we do this together, because that was my covenant and my commitment? When I was exploring post-graduate studies, or having children, or making any investment, that was the guiding factor. It was a non-negotiable focus. My Lord has called me, and my Master is expecting me to be on the front lines serving the poor and the vulnerable, that they may have life.

This is about total surrender to an eternal mission – for a purpose. We choose to be where he wants us to be. We choose to be fully surrendered in obedience. We choose for him to use us without us getting in the way. We allow the Spirit of God to manifest himself in the places where he has positioned us. We desire his glory, that we may bear much fruit. We surrender, so that we may be able to be unified with Christ and unified with one another. We are unified in his kingdom purpose. We choose his way, that we may have impact.

The Third Is *Seeking Prayer*

Do you know we journey to where he leads us? It is his vineyard. We take our position in the place where the harvest is ready because he is the Lord of the harvest.

I serve in a ministry known as Life in Abundance International. Every Monday, we take time to fast and pray; to seek God together; to hear him in what he is leading us to do in that week and over the coming days. I could tell you story upon story of how on a Monday morning God has revealed what we should do and, in a corporate way, led us to specific communities. He has led us into places we never imagined we would go – even closed countries, giving us specific details.

I am so thankful for my grandmother, because she modelled prayer for me. I pray that we too might be people who model prayer to those we lead, those who look up to us, because prayer is key. I recall inviting my grandmother to come and live with us for a time because I was in clinical practice and doing my residency. I had had our first baby and I wanted her to help take care of the baby. I would go into her room in the middle of the night to nurse the baby and would find her on her knees praying audibly so that I could listen and participate. She would pray for the sick and those suffering from disasters. She would pray for things that would happen later that week that would be put out in the news. She would connect with God and intercede for things even before they happened. She would sometimes begin to pray for a patient with leukaemia I was looking after without her even knowing that I was taking care of the patient. She would pray for healing, and I would then see that patient walk out of hospital in answer to a prayer that I had heard a week before. This was all because of a grandmother who was led by the Spirit. She waited on God and invited herself to take that place for intercession so that, with spiritual discernment and authority, she could speak into things that hinder the kingdom of God. She would pray that the kingdom of God would come. She prayed for me for the first twenty years when I was in cross-cultural missions. She would call me and rebuke me. She would inform me of things that were yet to come as we pursued God in the ministry and in the life in abundance.

My grandmother died four years ago at the age of 104, and she was still a woman given to prayer. She would still be on her knees every day, interceding that the kingdom of God would come in places that are so dark.

I believe God invites us to that lifestyle of prayer. I believe he wants to reveal so much more to us than we can take on by knowledge, discussions, and consultations. There is so much more that he wants to reveal to us. He wants to lead us to specific places. He wants to order our days, and he wants to open and close countries. He wants to give us the hearts of men and women, if only we would locate ourselves in that sacred place. It is possible to know his will. It is possible to continually hear his voice. It is possible to journey step by step in his will, if we would. Because he wants to lead. He wants to continually reveal himself to us at that personal level because he is a loving Father. He is the one who has invited us, and he wants to be Lord of the harvest.

The Fourth Is *Sacrifice*

Here I mean a life of sacrifice. It costs. Jesus turned to the crowd and said, "If anyone comes to me and does not hate his own father and mother and wife and children and brothers and sisters, yes, and even his own life, he cannot be my disciple. Whoever does not bear his own cross and come after me cannot be my disciple" (Luke 14:26–27 ESV).

I had no idea God would call me to leave my country, Kenya. I had seen Western missionaries leaving home. But I am African. I thought, "It is pastors and evangelists who go and plant churches, but I am a medical doctor." I thought, "It is men who go, but I am a woman, and I am married, and I have a six-month-old baby who is asthmatic. How can you be calling me to go on cross-cultural mission, to Ethiopia, and to serve at a leprosy-affected community?" And the Lord said, "Go, I am sending you to your Samaria. Yes, go and make disciples."

I began to resist. I began to say, "My mother is a widow. There are ten of us in our family. We are in need. I need to work and support my family." But the Lord would say to me, "Surely I say to you, unless a kernel of wheat falls to the ground and dies, it remains only as a single seed. But if it dies, it produces much seed, much fruit."

One of the rights I found it very difficult to release was the right to own a home. When we went to the mission field it weighed on me continually – that I did not have a kitchen or a place where I could fix a meal for my children or my husband. And, specifically, I just wished we could stay in one place. I remember going to a retreat and taking a piece of paper and writing, "Today I want to die to the right of owning a home." I tied it to the end of a helium balloon and watched it rise as I released that right. If we die to our rights and move on we realize that more rights come to claim us and we have to die again. It really is a lifestyle of continually dying to our rights and continually, daily, counting the cost. And we count the cost and we count it again.

I remember one time sitting in an airport in Khartoum in Sudan where we were doing some work in the Darfur area. I had been held captive for three days in the Darfur area, and at that particular time I was feeling shamed, emotionally. I was feeling broken inside and wondering, "How will I ever put myself back together?"

It costs. When you think it has cost much, it has yet to cost more. The finish line is ahead. Do not begin to sit in one place; we have to keep moving. This is loving him more than life. It is counting the cost and staying on the wave of the movement of God wherever he leads, without compromise.

If you are feeling there is no cost in following him, it may just be time to check again. Maybe you have been skirting around and compromising the purpose of God. Maybe you have been making your own way, so you do not come into contact with that cost. Because the kingdom of God is taken by violence, and we have to seek it by addressing that warfare. That will mark our paths.

I am reminded of Jim Elliot who said, "He is no fool who gives what he cannot keep to gain what he cannot lose." He was one of a team of men who travelled to Ecuador in 1956 to introduce peoples to Christian faith. All five men were killed by the indigenous people shortly after they landed. That initial contact cost them their lives. Jim died at the age of twenty-nine, and his widow Elisabeth Elliot published several books that included letters and journals. Jim had written those words long before he had gone to the field. Indeed we are no fools, even if we give our lives spiritually long before we give them physically, that there may be eternal purpose.

The Fifth Is *Strategy*

For many of us, this is where we want to focus. What is the method? What is the implementation plan? What does the project look like? So we begin there before we even realize it begins with us. We focus on the how, the when, and the where. But God first wants to complete his obedience in us.

I confess I made mistakes myself. I started out working hard in ministry in that slum community among those with leprosy. I grew the Bible studies, so that I had three Bible studies running every Saturday morning. And within a week I was serving that community, dressing their wounds, doing home visits, encouraging them in different ways, and getting involved in development work. Then I would have Bible students come to our home regularly with their children. I was totally immersed, and within the first five years my family and I began to be known and respected, sought after in this needy community of about five thousand people.

And then the Lord brought me to my knees and showed me there is a better way. It was not going to be me taking charge to provide medical care and even physical and spiritual care, and to manage all those relationships. Instead of me being a hero, it was going to be a response that would make his Bride, the local grassroots church, the hero.

My strategy changed from that time on. We are involved in a strategy that lifts up the local church to become relevant, and decreases my role, so that Christ may increase. It helps the vulnerable to become empowered in their own development. It bestows dignity on the least of these whom Jesus speaks of as brothers and sisters, and it keeps their focus on the local church. It deals with root causes and provides lasting solutions for the affected, removing me from doing things for them, to them, or even on them. It prevents others from falling into the same difficulties, as it institutes preventive measures in these communities so that they can be restored and transformed, and sustained in their transformation.

I know it is not as simple as giving for the day. I know it is not as simple as taking charge, as it involves equipping, training, mobilizing, and trusting people. But there is no other way we are going to have sustained impact that establishes the kingdom of God in communities unless we step out of the way and enthrone Christ in the communities where he has invited us.

This commitment has given us a three-year partnership with the communities to which we go, with the clear intention to exit from the beginning. We continually push them to take on the responsibility, so we train them in the things that we have come to do, and we choose to step back. We can make sure the local church is the one that becomes famous, the one that becomes sought after, because that is where the solution is. This is basically given to us in Isaiah 61. It is God blessing us and asking us to align ourselves with his Word.

Over the last twenty years I have watched God grow that work from the initial family-based work in the first community to us now having a hundred staff members in twelve countries in Africa and two countries in the Caribbean, and offices in the United States and Europe. These serve about 92,000 people from the different communities, and we have partnerships with more than 270 local churches, and also groups of local churches in the countries where God has placed us. We seek to empower others and partner with local churches; and within three years we step back and allow them to be discipled by the local church. It is entrusting nationals with the responsibility. It is having Ethiopians for Ethiopia, people from Sudan for their work in Sudan, Egyptians for Egypt. It is allowing them to take their position with authority so that Christ may be known. We simply come alongside as facilitators and enablers to invest in them so that they can be obedient to what God has called them to be.

God invites us to practise the mission of Jesus, and his yoke is easy and his burden light. He invites us to preach the good news to the least of these, to address their shame and their oppression. The end result is righteousness rising in the places where he has sent us. And when we put the church at the centre we see God at work, bringing his glory to the nations. We seek to empower the poor and the vulnerable to become the righteousness of God.

I've offered just one example. I would encourage you to take the time to look again, to revisit and review your strategy. Who is it glorifying? Who is it enthroning? Who is receiving the glory, and what is the impact of this?

These five commitments – salvation, surrender, seeking a life of prayer, sacrifice, and strategy – are the essentials for taking part in what God is doing and becoming a part of the transformation process.

15

Beyond Compassion to Solidarity

Peter McVerry

I'd like to share my story with you. I've been working with homeless people in Dublin, the capital of Ireland, for the last forty-odd years. I'd like to share how I started and how it has developed. But above all, I'd like to share with you how working with homeless people has changed me – because they have totally and radically changed me: they have turned me inside out and upside down; they have challenged my values, at least some of my prejudices, and the way I see Ireland and the world. They have challenged my understanding of God, they have changed my relationship with God: they have done everything for me.

So, to begin at the beginning, I went to live and work in the inner city of Dublin in 1974. The inner city of Dublin at that time was by far the most deprived area in the whole of Ireland: the housing was terrible, the education was very poor, kids were growing up with no prospect of employment. It was a situation of great despair and much hopelessness, so three of us moved in to see if we could make a difference. But homelessness itself wasn't the issue. Very quickly we realized that the real issue was that young people were leaving school, at the very latest by the age of twelve, and were hanging around the streets all day long. Their parents were unemployed and couldn't give them any money. So what were these kids doing? They were doing a little bit of robbing, and by the time they got to sixteen and seventeen, they were doing a lot of robbing, and they were going to jail. So we opened a youth club for all the kids in the area. We opened a crafts centre where they could learn various crafts. They were able to sell what they made and make a bit of money, and we were able to employ a few of the kids making the crafts.

Then I came across a nine-year-old sleeping on the streets. We realized we needed to do something for this kid. So we opened a small hostel for six boys up to the age of sixteen – it was all boys then; there were no girls on the streets in those days. I thought no more of it. This wasn't the beginning of a lifetime working with homelessness, this was just one more project for the kids of the area. I ran that hostel for a couple of years, but the kids were leaving at sixteen and were then going back onto the streets because there was nothing else for them. So then we had to open a hostel for the over sixteens. Then we had to open a second hostel. Then we had to open a hostel for the over eighteens. Then the drug problem hit Dublin and we had to open for fourteen- and fifteen-year-olds. Some fourteen- and fifteen-year-olds were coming to us on heroin, so we had to open a drug detox centre – and then the problem: where did the kids go when they detoxed? Did they go back onto the streets? If so, they'd wasted their time detoxing. So we had to open a drug-free after-care house where they could live for six months in supported, supervised accommodation; but where did they go after the six months? We had to get some apartments together where they could live independently for twelve months with support from our staff.

So one thing just led to another; I never planned anything in my life, I just went from one year to the next. There is a need; you try to meet that need; and when you meet that need, new needs emerge, and you try to meet those needs.

So, from that nine-year-old kid sleeping on the street, we now have about twenty hostels in Ireland for about a thousand homeless people. We have three hundred apartments so we can give a homeless person the key to a door and say, "This is yours for the rest of your life – you never ever need to become homeless again." We have two drug treatment centres, we have a drop-in centre, we have a youth cafe. If forty years ago I had seen how this was going to develop, I'd have run the other way! But luckily all I saw was one year at a time, and we went from that.

Who are these homeless young people?

I'd say that most of the homeless people today are simply unable to afford their own accommodation. The cost of accommodation in Ireland has risen and risen, to a point where many people can no longer afford it. However, some homeless people have a serious drug and alcohol problem, and it is those homeless people with a drug problem who have changed me.

Many of them have had horrific childhoods. Let me tell you a few stories (though some stories are much worse).

A young man lived with his mother and sister. He and his sister were very close to each other. His mother was an alcoholic, and also a mental health patient. When he was twelve years of age his mother stabbed his sister to death in front of him. So he left home. We don't know where he was for five years – he was sleeping on the streets of Dublin. He turned up at our door when he was seventeen. He has lived with us since because he now has serious mental health problems.

Another young fellow was fourteen years old, but every time he went home his mother slammed the door in his face and said: "Go away – you're not wanted here." How do you cope with that at fourteen years of age?

Another young man was twelve years of age. His mother was a drug user, and every morning before he went to school he had to go into town and buy the heroin his mother needed for the day, and then he had to come back and help her to inject it because she couldn't get the needle into her vein – if you've been injecting for a long time it becomes hard to find the vein. So, not surprisingly, by the age of fifteen he himself was injecting heroin and he was homeless.

Finally, a young man knocked on my door late at night. He was eleven years of age, stoned, and said: "Can I stay?"

I said: "No, you can't stay – you're only eleven. And anyway," I added, "you have a home to go to."

"Can't go home," he said.

"Why can't you go home?" I asked him.

"Just can't go home."

I talked to him for a bit, persuaded him to go home, put him into my car, drove him up to his house, and said: "There you are – in you go."

"Can't go in," he said.

"Why can't you go in?" I asked him.

"Just can't go in."

I talked to him a bit more and discovered his alcoholic parents were sending him out every night into prostitution, and he had to come back with a certain amount of money, otherwise he'd get a beating. He had no money that night, so he was going to get a beating.

These young people have had horrific childhoods. Some of them take drugs.

Why do they take drugs? These young people take drugs for different reasons from other young people, who might do so out of curiosity, to see what they are like, or under peer pressure. These young people take drugs to forget. To forget their childhood memories, to suppress the feelings that are associated with those memories. And drugs work. Best thing ever, if you don't want to remember painful memories.

One young girl said it very poetically shortly before she died of a drugs overdose: "Wouldn't it be wonderful if you could run so fast that your memories couldn't catch up?"

They're using drugs to run away from their memories. So what happens when they come off drugs? When they come off drugs, all those memories, and the feelings associated with them, all come flooding back to the surface – with a vengeance.

One young man who came down to our detox centre came off drugs, went back to Dublin, and was doing very well – until his granny died. When he went to her funeral he found himself sitting in the front row of the mourners – beside the uncle who had abused him as a child. All the memories and feelings came flooding back in the middle of that funeral service. I was there, up at the altar, and I saw him get up off the bench and literally run down the centre aisle of the church and out the front door. The next day he killed himself.

For them, coming off drugs is hugely traumatic. People look at them in the city centre in Dublin and say, "Why don't they stop taking drugs?" It's really not as simple as that. They need all the counselling, all the therapy, and all the support we can give them if they are to come off drugs.

So, what have they done for me? I'll mention just a couple of things. The first thing is that they have taught me never to judge anybody. We can never judge anybody because we don't know what's going on in anybody's life or anybody's childhood.

One guy who lived with us was seventeen and a big fellow, and every time the staff asked him to do something he'd throw a punch at them. The staff came to me and said: "Get rid of this fellow; he's mad, we can't work with this; someone's going to get hurt, so throw him out." But before I got around to throwing him out, I was talking to him on his own and he broke down in tears. He said: "You know, in my home when I was growing up it was 'Do this, do that' or thump, thump, thump, you got punched around the house as if you were a punching bag." As soon as he said that, everything fell into place.

When the staff asked him to do something, what did he see? He saw his own father in front of him, and he reacted the only way he knew how to react to his father: he threw the first punch before his father could get a punch in. Once we understood that, we were able to work with him; we didn't throw him out, and he lived with us for three or four years before moving on to his own accommodation. Here was someone we could have written off. We could have said: "Impossible to do anything with him" because we did not understand where he was coming from.

There's a little phrase in the Gospel: "Do not judge, and you will not be judged." Growing up, I always thought it meant that if you go through life not judging people, then, when you die and go before God, God won't judge you. But I don't think that's what it means any more. What am I doing if I judge one of these young people? If I say: "There's a little scumbag," or "There's a little junkie robber," what am I doing? I'm actually judging myself, because I know that if I had been born into their circumstances, I would be exactly the same. And if they had been born into my circumstances, they would be the priest coming up to visit me in prison. I didn't choose the family I was born into; they didn't choose the families they were born into – it could so easily have been the other way around. So, when I look at them – maybe sitting in a corner stoned out of their faces, maybe out robbing to feed their drug habit – I see part of myself in them, because "there but for the grace of God go I."

They have taught me never to judge anybody, and I had grown up believing God was a judge. It was the image of God that I was given. God was a judge, and your relationship with God depended on how you kept the laws, rules, and regulations that God had laid down and which were interpreted by the church.

But then a young homeless fellow said to me once: "The very thought that there might be a God depresses me." As I tried to figure out what he meant, I came to realize that he was believing in a God who was a judge – and this young homeless fellow had broken every commandment in the book, and a few more that hadn't been invented yet! And so he felt that God was up there looking down on him and saying: "There is someone I couldn't love, someone I have no time for, because he's a bad person." He believed that if he died and went before God, God would say: "Go away from me, you bad person."

I knew that kid very well; he had grown up in a horrific home where he experienced a lot of violence and abuse. So I was saying to myself: "If there is a God, this young person must have a special place in God's heart because of what he has suffered as a child. And if he ever died and went before God, God would have a big, warm welcome for him because of what he has suffered. And yet he is telling me, 'The very thought there might be a God depresses me.'"

So the God I came to believe in was no longer the judging God. God does not judge us – God forgives us again and again and again. And so, for me, God became the God who cares, the God of compassion.

As I look at my own life, I see that I have been given so much by God. I have been given good family, good education, good opportunities in life; but there are so many people who have not had those opportunities or gifts. And so now, for me, God is the giver of the gifts, not a judge. The very many gifts God has blessed me with have made me very grateful to God – grateful for the place God has given me in this world. My relationship with God totally changed – from being one of worrying whether I was on God's side or not, to simply praying: "Thanks for all I have received." There is nothing else to say to God except "Thanks."

Another thing they've done for me is to make me angry, and I'm glad to be angry – I always say that when I lose my anger I'll be no use to homeless people. They have made me angry because we as a society have failed them. Ireland is the fifth wealthiest country in the world, it has the fastest-growing economy in the European Union, and fifty thousand millionaires live there. And yet we have a growing number of homeless people. There is something radically wrong. We Christians are supposed to be angry at things like this. We are supposed to be angry because this world is not the way God wants it to be, and we should be angry enough to want to change it. A large part of my work is therefore lobbying governments, trying to raise awareness among people about the injustice of homelessness in a country like Ireland.

I sometimes think we can't understand the Gospels unless we are angry. Jesus was angry – when he threw the buyers and sellers out of the temple; when the Pharisees would not allow him to heal someone on the Sabbath because it was breaking the law; when he called the Pharisees "You hypocrites!" Jesus was angry, and we should be angry too – angry enough to want to change things. For me, anger and love go together. You cannot love somebody who is suffering unnecessarily without being angry at what is causing the pain.

Of course, anger can explode destructively. But anger can also be used very effectively and constructively.

Another thing they've taught me is what the hardest part of being homeless is. I always thought the hardest part of being homeless was not having a bed for the night, having to find a doorway or something to sleep in; but it's not. You can get used to that. What's the hardest part of being homeless? We had a guy live with us for a few years. When he was eighteen he left us and went to live with his girlfriend. After about a year they split up and he went onto the streets of Dublin because he had nowhere else to go. After a couple of months on the streets he threw himself into the river. To his dismay, he was rescued and brought into hospital, where I went to see him. He said to me: "I can't go on living like this." I asked: "What do you mean?" He said: "I can't go on living, knowing that nobody cares." That's the hardest part of being homeless: to know that if you disappeared off the streets, no one would even notice you were gone. Your life has no meaning, it has no value to anybody else – you have totally lost your self-esteem, your dignity.

People say to me, "What do you do for homeless people?" I say: "We can give some of them accommodation, we can give some of them drug treatment, and we can give some of them counselling. But what we are really trying to do is give them the message that they are just as important and just as valuable as anybody else. If we are not giving them that message, we may as well pack up and go home because the rest isn't worth it."

How do we give them that message? Well, most of our services for homeless people are very nice services. The accommodation is very good; it's got bright, painted pictures on the walls. In most of our hostels every homeless person has his or her own room, and in some of our hostels every room has an en suite. We say that this is deliberate because the service you offer homeless people sends a message to them: this is how we value you; this is what we think you are worth. So, if you pack homeless people into a run-down building where the paint is peeling off the walls and you pile them in, as many as you can get in a room, you might be giving them a bed for the night, but you're destroying their dignity. They'd be better off sleeping on the streets.

Sometimes people in Ireland ask me: "Should you give money to people begging?" I say: "I don't know." Sometimes I think you should, sometimes you shouldn't. But there's something you can do that's more important than giving money: when you pass by, say "Hello." What does that do?

Imagine sitting on the street begging, with thousands of people passing you by. Where are they all looking? They are all looking anywhere except at you. They're looking down at their feet and straight ahead; they are looking the other way. You are sitting there, and thousands of people are passing you by as if you were invisible.

How does that make you feel? It makes you feel like a non-person. So if somebody just comes up to you and says: "Hello, how are you? What's your name? What are you doing?," that person is treating you as a person.

I said this to a group of women once, and sometime later a woman came up to me in the street and said: "I was at that talk you gave and I heard what you said, so I decided to try it." She was walking along one day, and her two-year-old saw a guy begging. So she gave her son €2 and told him, "I want you to go and put that in the cup in front of that man sitting down there." She went up to the man and said: "Hello there, how are you? It's freezing cold. What's your name, and how's business?" She made a little bit of small talk and then she said: "Look, my son has something he wants to give you." And the boy went up and put the €2 in the cup, whereupon the homeless man put his hand in his pocket, took out a chocolate bar, and said: "And I have something to give your son." What was the homeless man responding to? It was the fact that he was treated as a human being. That's what our work is about.

But why Ireland? Ireland is a very compassionate country with very compassionate people; if there is a tsunami or an earthquake our aid contribution per head of population is one of the highest in the world. Why is it that in a country where people are so compassionate the numbers of homeless people continue to grow?

I think the issue is that we need to move from compassion to solidarity. There are two differences between compassion and solidarity. In *compassion*, I decide who I will be compassionate towards – maybe a homeless person I see passing on the street, maybe those suffering from a disaster I see on television. I get to decide that this person, or this cause, deserves my contribution. And usually the person or the organization I give to, that I am compassionate towards, is one where I feel the recipients are deserving.

But in *solidarity* I do not decide who I will be compassionate towards. It is the pain of others that causes me to be compassionate. I don't decide that this person is deserving and that person not deserving – it is their pain that causes me to reach out to them. And so they are the ones who tell me who to be compassionate towards.

The other thing about compassion is that I decide how I will be compassionate – maybe I will give a donation to a homeless charity at Christmas, or some of my time to working as a volunteer. I decide how I am going to be compassionate. But in solidarity it is the pain of people that tells me what to do. And so people might give big cheques to a homeless charity at Christmas, but if there is any attempt to open a shelter for homeless people in their neighbourhood, they could be the first out picketing to prevent it.

No – we do whatever is necessary to alleviate the suffering of others. We take their suffering on our shoulders, and therefore do everything we can to lift their suffering off their shoulders as if it was on our shoulders. And that costs, and it challenges; and so in Ireland, and in other parts of the world, we have to move from compassion to solidarity with those who are in pain. And the gospel message is a movement from compassion to solidarity.

When I say I believe in God it means nothing, absolutely nothing, until I describe the sort of God I believe in. Islamic State fighters believe in their god – so passionately that they are prepared to become suicide bombers in obedience to him. But the god they believe in is a god who wants to destroy and kill. The God we believe in is the God revealed by Jesus – a God who cares, a God of compassion. Every human being is a child of God, and therefore God's family is the whole human race.

Jesus had a dream. Jesus dreamt that there would be no one in this world who was hungry and was not given food, no one who was thirsty and not given drink, no one who was naked and not given clothes, and no one who was in prison and not visited. Jesus had a dream that we, the human race, could live together as the family of God. In a family of four children, the parents don't give three of their children a nice big steak for their dinner and give the fourth child bread and jam. No, whatever food is available is shared by everybody.

And yet, in the family of God, one billion people go to bed hungry every night. Every one of those one billion people is God's beloved child. No parent wants to see his or her child go to bed hungry every night. And God does not want to see his children going to bed hungry every night. And in a family of four children, the parents don't give three of them a nice warm bed for the night, and tell the fourth child to sleep outside in the back garden. No, whatever rooms are available are shared by everybody. And yet in almost every city in the family of God there are people living on the streets. Every one of those people living on the streets is God's beloved child. No parent wants to see his or her child living on the streets, and God does not want to see his children living on the streets.

What makes us Christians? What is our identity as Christians? What makes us Christians is not that we obey certain laws that are different from those of other religions. What makes us Christians is that we share Jesus's dream – a dream of building a world in which every child of God can live a happy and fulfilling life, which is what every parent wants for his or her child. We dream of that world – a world of justice and peace. And just as Jesus was crucified, we too will be crucified by those who do not want to share their wealth. Again, the claim has been made at this Micah Global conference which we are attending that eight people in this world own as much wealth as the poorest half of the world's population; in 2016 it was sixty-four people, and in 2012 it was 360 people.[1] More and more of the wealth that is being created is rising to the top. It is estimated that by 2040 one person in this world will own 1 trillion US dollars. Do you know how long it would take to spend 1 trillion US dollars? You would have to spend 1 million dollars every day for three thousand years.

So there are those in our world who do not want to share their wealth with those who are in need, and they will persecute us just as they persecuted Jesus. There are those in power who want to use that power for their own self-interests and not for the common good, and they will persecute us. If we seek to build a just world, we will be persecuted; we will be crucified.

Finally, young people sometimes say to me: "How do you know there's a God?" This is what I say to them: imagine somebody sitting at a riverside on a lovely sunny day enjoying the peace and quiet out in the sun. And there's a little child playing on the riverside beside that person. All of a sudden, the child falls into the river, but the person jumps in, pulls the child out, and saves the child's life.

---

1. See the Oxfam International report, "An Economy for the 99%," accessed 25 May 2020, https://www.oxfam.org/en/press-releases/just-8-men-own-same-wealth-half-world.

What will the parents of that child do? The first thing, of course, is go to the hospital or wherever the child is and reassure themselves that their child is all right. And what's the next thing they will do? It is to find that person and thank him or her for saving their child.

I say to young people: if you want to know if there's a God, there's no point looking up into the sky; instead, look around you, at the pain, the suffering, and the distress of so many people. Reach out and try to take some of that pain, suffering, and distress off their shoulders. And what will God do? God will want to find you, he will want to thank you for what you've done for his children. So I tell young people: you will not find God in your churches, and you will not encounter God in your prayers and your hymns, unless you first find God and encounter him in the suffering, pain, and distress of those around you.

Question Time

Question addressed to Peter McVerry: You can see why I invited Father Peter to come and join us. You talked about anger. Peter, how does that now translate for you? You've been working with the poor and the homeless, but now this work could be like pouring water into a bucket with a hole. How do you actually change the injustice in the system?

I think there are only two ways to change a system. Either you have a revolution – and I'm not advocating that in Ireland just yet – or you work through the normal democratic process. You get people to make different decisions. So a lot of my time is spent lobbying and advocating on behalf of the homeless. The government in Ireland can't stand me; I'm a pain in their neck!

And the way to change policymakers must come from the grassroots. It's through giving those ordinary people information and knowledge about homelessness and pointing out the injustice so that they then will put pressure on the government, in order to make the changes that are necessary. So I don't think that I can just work in a silo, running services for homeless people, without trying to create a bigger change. My purpose in life is to become redundant – I will have succeeded when I can go and play golf every day because there will be no more homeless people in Ireland. That is my purpose, my aim, my objective: to change our society so there will be no more homelessness.

Question addressed to Peter McVerry: So this transition from caring for the poor is not a transition because you don't stop caring. What made you decide you had to be more vocal? What was the driving factor that drove you to that vocal point of engaging?

It was the experience of homeless people. We had young homeless people who had maybe broken a window and got arrested, and they were taken down to the police station and got beaten up by the police. I would say to myself: two crimes have been committed – one of criminal damage and one of assault. The person who committed the assault, the police officer, is a respected member of society and will probably be promoted. The person who committed the criminal damage is probably going to be arrested, prosecuted, and maybe go to jail. There is something very wrong here. Again, say there is a young lad who runs and his trainers get torn; he has no way of replacing them, so he goes down to a big store and robs a pair of trainers. People say, "That's wrong." But I would say, "If that's wrong, it is even more wrong to put that young person into a situation where he has no choice but to go down to the store and rob for the trainers."

So my experience of homeless people gave me that sense of the injustice that was being experienced by homeless people, and I wanted to change that. And to change that I had to challenge the police, I had to challenge government, and I had to challenge many of the people who are respected in our society. When you have become accustomed to privilege, equality feels like oppression. So many people in our society live very comfortable lives. And to try to challenge them that there is something radically wrong with the society they are living in and that has been so good to them, economically and socially, is to challenge them to look at themselves and their society – this is going to make you very unpopular.

Question addressed to Peter McVerry: And what about your church in this whole journey? Do they think you are a bit of an outsider, or have they embraced your radical lifestyle and also your outspoken character?

I've been very supported by my Catholic church, particularly since Pope Francis came in, because he's on the same wavelength as I am. I think for a long time the church's attitude to me was, "We're delighted you're doing it, and we're glad it's not us!" So I think they were supportive in that sense – they weren't criticizing me, but it was very much an outlying ministry within the church. It was something that was peripheral to the church's main job of preaching, getting people into churches, performing the sacraments, and so on.

Now, with Pope Francis, I think the church is coming round to seeing it as at the heart of the church's ministry, at the heart of the church. Young people today in Ireland are moving away from the church just as they are in most of the global north. This baffles me. Thousands of people spent the whole day listening to Jesus. They forgot they were hungry – clearly what

Jesus was saying was not irrelevant to the people he was talking to. And the church's message is supposed to be the continuation of the message of Jesus. But instead of thousands of people coming to the church to hear what it has to say, they're all walking away. What has gone wrong? I think they are walking away because they do not experience the church as caring and compassionate. Young people today experience the church in Ireland as something that's cold, distant, legalistic, judgmental, and condemning. That's the way they see the church, and they don't want anything to do with it – and they're right not to want anything to do with it.

How do you preach or proclaim a God of compassion? You can't proclaim a God of compassion from the pulpit. You can only proclaim a God of compassion by being the compassion of God. So, if we want to bring that God of compassion to the world, we have to be the compassion of God to the world. And young people particularly, when they look at our church, they don't see that. They don't see the compassion of God. They see judgment and condemnation, and so they walk away. It's time to recover and show the solidarity and compassion of Jesus.

Part 3

Resilience, Spirituality, and Compassion

16

"My God, My God, Why Have You Forsaken Me?"

The Necessity of Lament for Spiritual Resilience in Contexts of Poverty and Injustice

Clinton Bergsma

Our faith maintains that Yahweh is loving, all-powerful, and concerned about the marginalized. However, these claims are inevitably questioned when we encounter poverty and injustice. Communities that have an integrated spirituality, and the Christians serving them, often face the risk of losing their faith when disaster strikes or poverty persists and passionate prayers go unanswered. This chapter argues that the biblical process of lament is a proven way of holding on to faith when it seems as if God has disappeared from the scene or has not acted along the lines of his promises and character. Lament allows us to throw our accusations and questions at God while simultaneously drawing us closer to him and the people we are trying to serve. It is thus a necessary tool for building spiritual resilience in the often theodicean contexts of poverty and suffering.

The spiritual practice of lament has largely been overlooked in modern times. While there is increasing interest among Christian psychologists regarding the use of lament as a process of dealing with grief and trauma, as yet there appears to have been little exploration of lament's potential contribution to situations of poverty and injustice. Poverty naturally raises questions of theodicy, and lament offers itself as a powerful and appropriate process for maintaining spiritual resilience in situations of injustice and poverty.

Lament and the Historical People of God
Lament in the Biblical Narrative

The practice of lament is integral to the experience of God's people throughout the biblical narrative.[1] The Scriptures never attempt to hide the awkward things that suffering and confused people said about God to God.[2] The exodus event, so prominent in the Hebrew mind, began with a cry of lament,[3] and the pinnacle event in the story of salvation hears Jesus cry out with a confused and pained voice: "My God, my God, why have you forsaken me?"

Though redemption always begins with a lament in the biblical narrative,[4] those historical cries of the people of God often remain unjoined by twenty-first-century Christians seeking the redemption of the world.[5] Surely lament has something to teach us about how the divine–human relationship is to be worked out in the tensioned here-but-not-yet. Lament is not a footnote in the narrative of God's restorative work; it is an indispensable thread in the story of Yahweh and his people.

Yahweh and Lament
Against God to God

Perhaps one of the most striking features of lament is that it is a complaint to Yahweh about Yahweh – it paradoxically "clings to God against God."[6] Lament believes that God has not acted as he should have, but it cannot see any place to bring that complaint to other than Yahweh himself, and as such is a movement towards God.[7] Lament maintains God as lover while also questioning whether this is how lovers truly act.[8] It looks at what is happening in light of the promises

---

1. C. Westermann, *Praise and Lament in the Psalms* (Atlanta: J. Knox, 1981), 263.

2. C. C. Broyles, "Psalms of Lament," in *Dictionary of the Old Testament: Wisdom, Poetry and Writings*, ed. Tremper Longman III and Peter Enns (Nottingham: Inter-Varsity Press, 2008), 395; Westermann, *Praise and Lament*, 264.

3. W. Brueggemann, *The Psalms and the Life of Faith* (Minneapolis, MN: Fortress, 1995), 106.

4. Brueggemann, *The Psalms*, 99.

5. Westermann, *Praise and Lament*, 264–265.

6. Westermann, 273.

7. Westermann, 273.

8. D. J. Cohen, *Why O Lord?* (Milton Keynes: Paternoster, 2013), 52.

and abilities of God and declares that, frankly, Yahweh cannot wash his hands of the matter.[9]

Prayers of invocation, then, assume that God is interested and intimately involved (somehow!) in the drama. Lament is an inevitable outcome for people who experience the brokenness of life in the company of a Friend and Father who claims to be able to intervene and has promised to restore everything. To avoid lament is either to live in denial of the injustice that exists[10] or to attempt some illusion of honest relationship with God.

A God Who Is Willing to Listen

"There is no god like Yahweh" was the catch-cry of ancient Israel, but there is also no one who listens like Yahweh.[11] When we lament, "we seek an audience with the most-high God," and he willingly condescends – even if our complaint is irrational or tarnished with hypocrisy.[12]

It is significant that the editors of the Scriptures never sought to sanitize or censor the material they presided over. Rather, the inclusion of lament throughout the biblical canon is indicative of a God who hears his people hope that "the infants of my enemies would be smashed upon the rocks" and permits rather than discourages such language even though he desires otherwise.[13] Yahweh is not only big enough to restore all things, he is big enough to hear all things. He listens to the complaints of his bride and gives her room to scream her unfair tirades at him, for he is not indifferent to her suffering. Indeed, Yahweh has had his share of grief.

A God Acquainted with Sorrow

Yahweh is "a God acquainted with grief and sorrow."[14] He has not stood immune to the suffering of his beloved creation. The impact of the fall touched God himself. Perhaps for the first time in all eternity, the heart of God was pierced

---

9. Broyles, "Psalms of Lament," 395. See also W. Brueggemann, "The Costly Loss of Lament," in Brueggemann, *The Psalms*, 101.

10. Brueggemann, *The Psalms*, 102; Broyles, "Psalms of Lament," 394.

11. C. R. DeGroat, "The New Exodus: A Narrative Paradigm for Understanding Soul Care," *Journal of Psychology and Theology* 37, no. 3 (2009): 187.

12. Broyles, "Psalms of Lament," 394.

13. Cohen, *Why O Lord?*, 79; cf. Matt 5:43–48.

14. W. Brueggemann, *The Message of the Psalms: A Theological Commentary* (Minneapolis, MN: Augsburg, 1984), 52.

with pain and regret,[15] and the suffering continued outside the garden of Eden. The pursuit of his beloved into a world of darkness saw Yahweh imploring his people time and time again through the prophets to return to his loving embrace.[16]

While the Psalms describe humanity's cries to a patient, listening God, the prophets detail Yahweh's pleas with an impassionate, uninterested, and fickle humanity. It's no wonder, then, that lament ultimately draws us closer to Yahweh. Yahweh not only permits and listens to our complaints – he understands and identifies with the very grieving of our hearts.

A Time to Lament

While some scholars have attempted to place the individual psalms of lament in their correct historical context, the task has proved elusive and tenuous.[17] A unique benefit of this is that the psalms take on an abiding quality as their expressions of the ups and downs of the divine–human relationship aren't tied to any one place or situation.[18] While there is a particular linguistic and cultural flavour to them – which importantly grounds them in the history of humanity and prevents them from becoming abstract ideology – the questions and sentiments they posit are timeless.[19] These songs of distress provide words for those whose hearts have been too numbed by pain to speak, their voices hoarse from crying.

Laments also express a wide range of sentiments and situations in the divine–human relationship: anger, despair, questioning, confusion. Some are individual, some are corporate.[20] Still others are set in the context of daily life and natural disasters.[21] When all of the biblical laments are placed together, the impression is that there are no issues or distressing situations outside the boundaries of lament.[22] When God's promises appear impotent in light of the

---

15. Gen 6:6.

16. E.g. Hos 2.

17. W. S. La Sor et al., *Old Testament Survey: The Message, Form, and Background of the Old Testament*, 2nd ed. (Grand Rapids, MI: Eerdmans, 1996), 431–432.

18. Cohen, *Why O Lord?*, 11.

19. D. D. Hankle, "The Therapeutic Implications of the Imprecatory Psalms in the Christian Counselling Setting," *Journal of Psychology and Theology* 38, no. 4 (2010): 276.

20. Broyles, "Psalms of Lament," 385.

21. Brueggemann, *The Psalms*, 76.

22. Brueggemann, *Message of the Psalms*, 52. See also Cohen, *Why O Lord?*, 6.

world we live in – whatever the context may be – lament is an appropriate process of addressing the predicament.

The Enabling Gift of Lament
Healing through Screaming

Lament's first enabling gift is the granting of a necessary permission to "scream."[23] It is well accepted by psychological experts that disclosing emotional trauma directly improves mental and physical health.[24] Contrastingly, suppressing the emotional outworkings of our distress has a negative impact on mental and physical health.[25] As a PTSD sufferer who witnessed horrific things as a soldier in East Timor explained, "you're paying for it [emotionally] at the time, it's just on credit. Once you're out of the situation and you let the façade down, it's payday."[26] Interestingly, a recent study has suggested that the health benefits of emotional disclosure can be enhanced when people are provided with "response training" or a structured process through which to deal with their distress.[27]

Lament permits the initial and at times repeated "scream" that is fundamental to healing from situations of distress, while also providing a framework and a process through which the healing can occur.

As a Movement

While despair, trauma, suffering, and theological conundrums often cause us to freeze, circle, or wander aimlessly, lament is a process that allows us to

---

23. R. Hicks, *Failure to Scream* (Nashville: Thomas Nelson, 1993), 134.

24. J. W. Pennebaker and S. K. Beall, "Confronting a Traumatic Event: Toward an Understanding of Inhibition and Disease," *Journal of Abnormal Psychology* 95, no. 3 (Aug. 1986): 274; D. Westen, L. Burton, and R. M. Kowalski, *Psychology*, 4th ed. (Milton, Queensland: John Wiley, 2006), 588; S. J. Lepore et al., "It's Not That Bad: Social Challenges to Emotional Disclosure Enhance Adjustment to Stress," *Anxiety, Stress and Coping* 17, no. 4 (2004): 341.

25. Hicks, *Failure to Scream*, 34–35; K. N. Snow et al., "Resolving Anger toward God: Lament as an Avenue toward Attachment," *Journal of Psychology and Theology* 39, no. 2 (2011): 131; D. G. Benner, *Healing Emotional Wounds* (Grand Rapids, MI: Baker, 1990), 68; C. Ringma, *The Seeking Heart: A Journey with Henri Nouwen* (Brewster, MA: Paraclete, 2006), 104.

26. "Australian Army PTSD Doco: Casualties of War, Part 3," YouTube, 27 July 2008, accessed 2 October 2019, https://www.youtube.com/watch?v=CZ505b1x2As; see also Hicks, *Failure to Scream*, 8.

27. A. Konig, A. Eonta, and S. R. Dyal, "Enhancing the Benefits of Written Emotional Disclosure through Response Training," *Behavior Therapy* 45, no. 3 (2014): 344–357.

move forward without abandoning those feelings or the chaos that ensues.[28] There is a wonderful paradox here, as David Cohen aptly describes: "The shape, or structure, of psalms of distress can be viewed as juxtaposed to the lack of structure, or containment, often resulting from personal distress. In this way these psalms offer an engagement which paradoxically invites the distressed person to embrace the chaos caused by distress through a structure."[29]

Grieving is never a straightforward process,[30] and while there are loosely recognized "stages" of grief, most people do not move through them in a sequential, orderly fashion.[31] While there is a "sense that mourning can be finished . . . there is also a sense in which mourning is never finished."[32] Lament provides a framework through which emotional and spiritual trauma can be expressed, while also moving the participant, even with tidal emotions, towards a place of resolution.[33]

Lament allows the necessary emotional disclosure while providing a process through which healing can take place, for to stagnate at the scream is harmful – and not just for the larynx. There must be movement (even if it ebbs and flows) towards healing, but the healing process must not be rushed.[34] The regular use of lament provides a gentle but guiding framework that healing from distressing situations requires.

Holding Truths in Tension

Lament doesn't always result in resolution, and at times resolution is only partial. However, lament enables the distressed person to "hold" the suffering. David Cohen undertook a small study using lament as the process through which unresolved grief was expressed. While none of the participants felt complete resolution, they all experienced a decrease in distress. Cohen suggests that this "underlines the significance of lament as a process for holding distress rather than necessarily resolving it."[35]

---

28. Brueggemann, *Message of the Psalms*, 54.
29. Cohen, *Why O Lord?*, 35.
30. Benner, *Healing Emotional Wounds*, 72.
31. J. W. Worden, *Grief Counselling and Grief Therapy* (Hove: Brunner-Routledge, 2001), 25.
32. Worden, *Grief Counselling*, 47.
33. Hankle, "Therapeutic Implications," 276.
34. Benner, *Healing Emotional Wounds*, 73.
35. Cohen, *Why O Lord?*, 145; see also 80.

The holding of distress rather than its removal is a consistent conclusion to the laments in the biblical account. Job never received clear answers to his questions, and no doubt the memories of his dead children and that fateful day remained long after the conclusion of the narrative. Yet Job 42:3 finds Job describing a peace and a deeper understanding of God and his own self. This is prior to the positive concluding section where Job receives riches and children again.[36] His words weren't fatalistic so much as a strangely joyful acceptance that there was something "too wonderful for me" going on.[37]

Some may argue this is a type of "meaning making" or "suspended growth."[38] I suggest that there is a delicate difference. Meaning has not been made: "I still don't understand why God let this happen," yet growth has somehow continued: "I feel less distress." The difference is subtle, yet important. "Holding distress" allows the lamenter to preserve a number of truths in tension while also assisting the imprecator to have hope and move forward in life. This is an important aspect of lament for situations of repeated or unresolved distress.

Lament and the Majority World
The Broader Impacts of Poverty

It is universally accepted that poverty has an adverse effect on human flourishing. Northern aid and development organizations typically separate the physical and spiritual realms and implement interventions that focus entirely on physical deficiencies,[39] and Christian development organizations are not immune from this unfortunate dichotomy.[40] However, almost all indigenous cultures and peoples of the Majority World see life as completely interconnected.[41] When disaster strikes or generational poverty persists in this context, it is highly likely that significant spiritual questions will arise.[42]

---

36. Job 42:10–17.

37. Job 42:3; see also Pss 10; 22; 55.

38. Bowlby in Worden, *Grief Counselling*, 35.

39. B. L. Myers, *Walking with the Poor: Principles and Practices of Transformational Development* (Maryknoll, NY: Orbis, 1999), 4–5.

40. Myers, *Walking with the Poor*, 7.

41. J. Ife, *Community Development in an Uncertain World: Vision, Analysis, and Practice* (Cambridge: Cambridge University Press, 2013), 97–98.

42. Myers, *Walking with the Poor*, 87; J. D. Aten, "Disaster Spiritual and Emotional Care in Professional Psychology: A Christian Integrative Approach," *Journal of Psychology and Theology* 40, no. 2 (2012): 132–133; Ife, *Community Development*, 237.

Further, the impact of poverty extends beyond the tangible needs of the poor and affects mental health.[43] I have met people in rural Indonesia who have buried two, sometimes three, children from preventable diseases. It is not possible to remain unaffected by these types of repeated trauma, and it is not unusual to see coping behaviours such as addiction and violence follow.[44]

While it is often harmful to attempt programmes that ignore local spirituality, passing over the spiritual questions of communities can be especially counterproductive – particularly for communities where spirituality is fundamental to life.[45] Programmes built on such a foundation will be woefully inadequate, and so space must be created for theodicean questions when engaging with communities that acknowledge spirituality and are experiencing the trauma of poverty or disaster. Lament is well placed to contribute significantly to contexts such as these.

The Potential Contribution of Lament

Spiritual and emotional care in development and disaster relief must be suitable to the particular spiritual worldview of the affected community – it cannot be "parachuted in" from the global north context.[46] However, this does not imply that principles cannot be taken from a process such as lament and appropriately contextualized. Indeed, the use of lament in the global north demonstrates its adaptability across cultures, for its origins lie in the Middle East. Lament is unique in that it is a process that has significant parallels with modern approaches to grief and trauma counselling, yet has a uniquely spiritual emphasis so important in the Majority World.[47]

Lament enables the imprecator to move to a place of peace even when the situation at hand has not yet resolved – a regular phenomenon in situations of poverty. While a particular community's access to water might improve

---

43. M. Funk et al., *Mental Health and Development: Targeting People with Mental Health Conditions as a Vulnerable Group* (Geneva: World Health Organization, 2010), 28ff., accessed 2 October 2019, https://www.who.int/mental_health/policy/mhtargeting/en/.

44. V. Murali and F. Oyebode, "Poverty, Social Inequality and Mental Health," *Advances in Psychiatric Treatment* 10, no. 3 (2004): 216–217. See also R. Trudgen, *Why Warriors Lie Down and Die: Towards an Understanding of Why the Aboriginal People of Arnhem Land Face the Greatest Crisis in Health and Education since European Contact* (Darwin: Aboriginal Resource and Development Services, 2000), 59, 172–173.

45. J. Ife and F. Tesoriero, *Community Development: Community-Based Alternatives in an Age of Globalisation* (Frenchs Forest: Pearson, 2006), 247. See also Aten, "Disaster Spiritual," 132.

46. Aten, "Disaster Spiritual," 132–133.

47. Cohen, *Why O Lord?*, 65. See also Snow et al., "Resolving Anger," 133.

with the assistance of a development organization, issues such as conflict may remain relatively unaltered. Life has improved, but it may well still be incredibly difficult, and so an element of distress continues. However, regular lament has the potential to enable people in poverty to hold that continuing distress without their spiritually shaped worldview crumbling. This is crucial for communities of faith, without which hope may be lost and coping behaviours like addiction and violence develop. Lament has the potential to contribute significantly to a community's empowerment, healing, and holding of distress.

Lament and the Christian Global North
The Disconnect

While the inclusion of a section exploring lament and the Christian global north in the context of community development may appear out of place, the theme is worthy of exploration. While most Northern Christians make the odd donation to their favourite aid organization, there is little difference in overall posture towards the poor between those who describe themselves as "deeply religious" and those who would call themselves "non-religious."[48] We've somehow managed to have a "pious spirit" while ignoring the "real world."[49] Walter Brueggemann links this to a lack of lament:

> It is a curious fact that the church has, by and large, continued to sing songs of orientation in a world increasingly experienced as disoriented. That may be laudatory. It could be that such relentlessness is an act of bold defiance . . . a great Evangelical "nevertheless" . . . but . . . it is my judgement that this action of the church is less an Evangelical defiance guided by faith, and much more a frightened, numb denial and deception that does not want to acknowledge or experience the disorientation of life. The reason for such relentless affirmation of orientation seems to come, not from faith, but from the wishful optimism of our culture.[50]

The world is a "frightening and disorienting" place for many people – particularly for the poor and vulnerable. But the Northern Christian is currently permitted to dance to only one band – Enlightenment optimism

---

48. R. J. Sider, *Rich Christians in an Age of Hunger: Moving from Affluence to Generosity*, 20th anniversary revision ed. (Dallas: Word, 1997), 40.

49. G. H. Stassen and D. P. Gushee, *Kingdom Ethics: Following Jesus in Contemporary Context* (Downers Grove, IL: InterVarsity Press, 2003), 449.

50. Brueggemann, *Message of the Psalms*, 51.

and its lead vocalist (the marketing jingle) – while the dissenting body of theodicy lies bound and gagged behind an overworked smoke machine. Northern Christians may not ask theodicean questions or show doubt as it may be indicative of an impermissible crack in the proverbial amour of God.[51] In a recent American study, 52 percent of people who disclosed their anger towards God to a friend said that the response they received was that "it is wrong to have negative feelings towards God."[52] There currently appears to be little room in the Northern Christian mind for confusion, doubt, or anger towards God.

Failure to Lament

This failure to lament has a direct impact on our posture towards the poor, for they become a physical theodicy that is best left out of sight in darkened alleyways and overseas slums. Sider seems to suggest that the failure of the Christian global north to be deeply troubled by social justice is an issue of biblical education: "Most wealthy Christians have failed to seek God's perspective on the plight of our billion hungry neighbours . . . There are millions of Christians who will take any risk, make any sacrifice, forsake any treasure, if they clearly see that God's word demands it."[53]

While I agree with Sider that a corrected understanding of Scripture would increase the average evangelical heart for the poor, I would argue it runs deeper than that. I would suggest that the global north perhaps needs to combine biblical lessons with learning how to shake a fist at Yahweh. Again, Brueggemann: "A community of faith that negates lament soon concludes that the hard issues of justice are improper questions to pose at the throne [of God], because the throne seems to be only a place of praise . . . [and they] are left with only grim obedience and eventually despair. The point of access for serious change has been forfeited when the propriety of this speech form is denied."[54]

Permitting only positive words in the context of relationship with Yahweh results in and relies on an illusion that there is no injustice, no poverty, no suffering – or worse, that Yahweh has nothing to say or do about these issues. In

---

51. Brueggemann, 52.

52. J. J. Exline and J. B. Grubbs, "'If I Tell Others about My Anger toward God, How Will They Respond?' Predictors, Associated Behaviours, and Outcomes in an Adult Sample," *Journal of Psychology and Theology* 39, no. 4 (2011): 310.

53. Sider, *Rich Christians*, 40.

54. Brueggemann, *The Psalms*, 107.

this setting, one must ignore not just the injustice, but the one who is enduring the injustice. It allows us to hear of terrible disasters and suffering without feeling much empathy, and allows us to pray about injustice to a supposedly all-powerful and all-loving God without any complaint in our hearts.

I clearly remember a time when I believed that the poor somehow didn't feel the pain of suffering as deeply as I did – until I began meeting people like the village leader in rural Indonesia who had lost his wife and three children to cholera; until I sat with a leper colony and heard them express a quiet but deep pain at being isolated by their community. These situations (among many others) forced a choice upon me: give up on the notion that the poor don't feel pain, or give up on Yahweh who seemingly stands by while they suffer. Lament has helped me to hold this tension while I attempt to sit with the poor in the presence of God. Failing to lament fosters a terrible disconnect between the Christian global north and our suffering family in the Majority World.

Reconnecting through Lament

Learning to lament, and using lament as a regular, spiritually formative practice, will help integrate issues of social justice, both local and international, into the global north agenda.[55] Songs of lament strip away the false filters we build for ourselves, and "dangerously" help us to see the world as it really is.[56] As we open ourselves up entirely before God, with rational thoughts and irrational thoughts, with words of praise and lament, we become "liberated" towards God and our neighbour.[57] Lament forces us to measure up our story against others, opening our eyes to our shared humanity.[58] It enables us to advocate for those who are suffering to the One who promised he would remove all suffering,[59] while also throwing the same challenging questions at ourselves: how have I contributed to the suffering? Why do I "stand far off"?

Lament builds solidarity between the global north and our suffering family in the Majority World – but it also builds solidarity with Yahweh in declaring that the world is not as it should be. It allows us to be immanent

---

55. Brueggemann, 106.
56. Brueggemann, *Message of the Psalms*, 53.
57. A. Gill, *Life on the Road: The Gospel Basis for a Messianic Lifestyle* (Scottdale, PA: Herald, 1992), 119.
58. Broyles, "Psalms of Lament," 386.
59. Westermann, *Praise and Lament*, 276.

and understanding of suffering as Yahweh is.[60] The regular use of lament can prepare the global north for times of disaster and news of disaster, as the process becomes embedded in our way of engaging with a broken and suffering world.[61] It is perhaps the antidote that donor fatigue requires, for it reminds us that the redemption of the world remains incomplete, and fosters an expectation that it is the task of Yahweh (and, in turn, his people) to address the brokenness. Lament has the ability to help us to break down the false assumption that we know what God is doing in the world, forcibly reshaping our response to questions of theodicy. Perhaps one day a posture of embrace with silent tears of solidarity will replace the theologically correct propositional statements and calls to repentance that Christians (myself included) have trotted out in times of suffering.

Lament and the Practitioner
The Impact of Working with the Poor

We turn now to consider lament and the community development practitioner, for to be at the front end of poverty alleviation inevitably fosters questions of theodicy and issues of mental health. The very nature of development work is emotionally taxing, and many feel isolated and relatively unsupported. It is a common sentiment among community development practitioners that "there is nowhere to take the . . . [mess and problems], but home."[62] It is a complex task involving the balancing of the many varied views of stakeholders, the impossibility of helping everyone, and the evil of having to choose who will be assisted and who will be passed by. There is a constant dilemma of one's own wages and expenses coming out of project budgets meant to help the poor. It is no wonder that there are high rates of staff turnover in our sector.[63]

Failure to Lament

The consequences of failing to deal with the distress and theological dilemmas associated with engaging with poverty first-hand are the same as for ignoring anguish and theodicy elsewhere: practitioners can become "easily blindsided

---

60. Hicks, *Failure to Scream*, 170.
61. Brueggemann, *Message of the Psalms*, 67; Cohen, *Why O Lord?*, 75.
62. P. Hoggett, M. Mayo, and C. Miller, *The Dilemmas of Development Work: Ethical Challenges in Regeneration* (Portland, OR: Policy, 2009), 60.
63. Hoggett, Mayo, and Miller, *Dilemmas*, 62.

in particular situations and . . . involved in strange compensatory behaviours."[64] Practitioners can become outcome-oriented and rush or impose projects in hopes of allaying a fear of not making a difference.

This dilemma is particularly sharp for Christian practitioners raised in the environment of the Christian global north outlined above, practitioners who have had it drummed into them that Christ has triumphed over sin and that "there really are no other crises to be had."[65] It is understandable then that, as Melba Padilla Maggay writes, "There is something about the daily exposure to poverty and other ills of society which tends to tear away faith and make agents of change some of the most cynical people around."[66]

Unresolved distress from helping the poor significantly increases the risk of coping mechanisms such as violence, control, addiction, and emotional withdrawal beginning to take over as the formative characteristics of the practitioner. Being indefinitely angry at God has been demonstrated to result in mental and physical deterioration,[67] which is unacceptable for people who are attempting long-term work in contexts that are ripe with theodicy.

The Potential Contribution of Lament

In dealing with the difficult task practitioners face, Robert Chambers recommends taking time to reflect on others who have done great things,[68] Jim Ife proposes reflective journaling,[69] and Bryant Myers suggests a mix of theological reflection, moderated expectation, and detachment, among other things.[70] Myers's proposal that comes closest to the process of lament – counselling and psychological help – is a final option reserved for "critical incidents."[71] While I greatly respect these authors and appreciate that Myers highlights spirituality as important to the practitioner, I believe their suggestions fall short of practitioner needs.

Lament offers Christian practitioners a way to be truly incarnational in approach while holding the distress and bringing the mess and pain to the

---

64. Ringma, *Seeking Heart*, 104.
65. Ringma, 108.
66. Myers, *Walking with the Poor*, 163.
67. Snow et al., "Resolving Anger," 130.
68. R. Chambers, *Rural Development: Putting the Last First* (Harlow: Longman, 1983), 216.
69. Ife, *Community Development*, 305.
70. Myers, *Walking with the Poor*, 162–163.
71. Myers, 166.

One who sees the things they see and travels with them on the road, who will hear their hardest criticisms, weep with them, think no less of them for their despair, and gently remind them – when they're ready – that it *is* his problem to sort this mess out.

Then, and *only* then, am I ready to hear an inspirational story, recite a popular fatalistic poem ("Lord, grant me the serenity . . ."), and head back into the fray with a reckless and abandoned love. It's shaking my fists at a loving Yahweh that allows me to slowly open my hands to embrace the disfigured and downtrodden. It's his listening to my despair that enables me to sit with the despairing without abandoning my faith.

Perhaps that's too self-reflective, too much "I." But in the absence of research and qualitative studies in the area of lament for community development, I put myself forward as an example of a practitioner who finds lament to be a most helpful and sustaining tool.

Conclusion

Lament has been, for the most part, a tool left on the shelf of Christian antiquity. I have argued that we need to dust it off and get comfortable with using it if we hope to maintain spiritual resilience in the face of the theodicies that contexts of poverty create. Avoiding lament will ultimately require us to abandon either our faith or our empathetic relationships with the marginalized. The task before us requires the regular practice of lament throughout our organizations and the people they touch.

Thankfully there is a wonderfully obsolescent nature to lament as it drives us closer to the day when "crying will be [needed] no more." I long for the day when lament will rightfully be a dust-gathering relic. Until then, however, I hope you will join your voice to mine as I continue to cry out to Yahweh, with the poor and – I hope – increasingly the global north: "How long, O Lord?"

17

Building Resilient Communities

The Importance of Integrating Mental Health and Well-Being in Effective Development Thinking and Practice

Becca Allchin, Stephanie Cantrill, and Helen Fernandes

Mental health is central to building resilient communities and realizing progress towards the Sustainable Development Goals. Effective promotion of mental health and well-being globally strengthens progress in sustainability, equality, and resilience. As well as this, the exclusion experienced by people as a result of psychosocial disability makes them a vulnerable population. Mental health is intersectional as it is both affected by and compounds other social determinants of health and well-being. Mental illness is a cause and a consequence of poverty. Transformational development's focus on holistic restoration promotes the mental health of individuals, families, and communities, and upholds the identity of those affected by mental ill health as made in the image of God. Mental health promotion and inclusive development are important justice responses in the restoration of God's kingdom.

This chapter reflects on TEAR Australia's learning through research and explores the place of mental health in strengthening community resilience and development.

Introduction

Mental health, once largely an invisible issue in international development, is now being framed as "one of the most pressing development issues of our time."[1] It has been gaining recognition as crucial to realizing the Sustainable Development Goals (SDGs).[2] Such a focus across the SDGs recognizes the importance of mental health and well-being to strengthen progress in sustainability, equality, inclusion, and resilience.[3] The World Health Organization (WHO) advocates for a justice approach to addressing mental health that promotes both holistic support for people with mental illness and wider community mental health support.[4] Mental health promotion activities, such as building social cohesion, enabling social and economic well-being, and individual and family coping mechanisms, build community resilience. While community resilience is increasingly prominent within community development research, mental health is an emerging focus in community development.[5]

Mental health is foundational for both community functioning and individual well-being.[6] Rather than the absence of illness, mental health is understood in the broader context of social determinants of health and is seen in an individual's, family's, community's, or nation's positive sense of well-being, connectedness to others, and ability to have agency and experience meaning. Good mental health is understood through a cultural lens and shaped by worldview, spirituality, inequities, and infrastructure.[7] As a result, mental health and well-being promoting strategies are found outside specific

---

1. FundaMentalSDG, "UN Development Agenda 2030: Call to Action for Mental Health Indicators," Public Statement, accessed 27 September 2019, www.fundamentalsdg.org/uploads/3/8/5/0/38504573/brief_mental_health_in_un_agenda2030.pdf.

2. N. Votruba et al., "The Importance of Global Mental Health for the Sustainable Development Goals," *Journal of Mental Health* 23, no. 6 (Dec. 2014): 283–286.

3. T. Izutsu et al., "Mental Health and Wellbeing in the Sustainable Development Goals," *Lancet Psychiatry* 2, no. 12 (Dec. 2015): 1052–1054.

4. World Health Organization, "Comprehensive Mental Health Action Plan 2013–2020," accessed 27 September 2019, http://www.who.int/mental_health/action_plan_2013/en/.

5. F. Berkes and H. Ross, "Community Resilience: Toward an Integrated Approach," *Society and Natural Resources* 26, no. 1 (2013): 5–20.

6. H. Herrman et al., "Introduction: Promoting Mental Health as a Public Health Priority," in *Promoting Mental Health: Concepts, Emerging Evidence, Practice: A Report of the World Health Organization*, ed. H. Herrman, S. Saxena, and R. Moodie (Melbourne: Department of Mental Health and Substance Abuse; The Victorian Health Promotion Foundation; The University of Melbourne, 2005), 2.

7. S. Sturgeon and J. Orley, "Concepts of Mental Health across the World," in *Promoting Mental Health: Concepts, Emerging Evidence, Practice: A Report of the World Health Organization*, ed. H. Herrman, S. Saxena, and R. Moodie (Melbourne: Department of Mental Health and

mental health goals and seen in many community development and resilience-building activities. This view of supporting individuals, communities, and nations to live to their potential is captured in Myers's understanding of transformational development which seeks positive change in the whole of human life: materially, socially, psychologically, and spiritually.[8] Development such as this seeks to enable all to recover their true identity as made in the image of God with intrinsic value, charged with the tasks of caring for the world and enabling the people that depend on it to flourish.[9] This work helps to address the search for meaning, identity, and worth, foundational for good mental health and well-being.

Attention to mental health in community resilience work is vital as the absence of good mental health leads to vulnerability to mental health conditions, and to communities being less cohesive and adaptive, and more vulnerable to shocks and disruption.[10] Exclusion is also often experienced by people as a result of mental illness and such exclusion can lead to poor outcomes in other areas of health, economics, and social cohesion.[11] This negative cycle results in communities with greater inequity, instability, and disadvantage experiencing higher rates of mental illness.

Community resilience has been defined as the existence, development, and engagement of community resources by community members in order to thrive in an environment characterized by change, uncertainty, and unpredictability.[12] This community-level capacity to bounce back in the face of adversity requires social and family cohesion, adaptability, and support infrastructures. Building community resilience is considered crucial in enhancing community development outcomes. Imperiale and Vanclay suggest that effective development programmes understand and seek to strengthen the resilient social processes communities put into action to address the negative

---

Substance Abuse; The Victorian Health Promotion Foundation; The University of Melbourne, 2005), 59.

8. B. L. Myers, *Walking with the Poor: Principles and Practices of Transformational Development* (Maryknoll, NY: Orbis, 1999).

9. Myers, *Walking with the Poor*.

10. V. Lehtinen et al., "The Intrinsic Value of Mental Health," in *Promoting Mental Health: Concepts, Emerging Evidence, Practice: A Report of the World Health Organization*, ed. H. Herrman, S. Saxena, and R. Moodie (Melbourne: Department of Mental Health and Substance Abuse; The Victorian Health Promotion Foundation; The University of Melbourne, 2005), 46.

11. Izutsu et al., "Mental Health," 1052–1054.

12. Berkes and Ross, "Community Resilience," 401–416.

social and economic impacts they experience.[13] In addition, mental health frameworks and mental health promotion strengthen a deeper understanding of the factors which contribute to building these social processes and thus community resilience.[14] The growing body of evidence for effective actions people and communities can take to promote mental health and well-being[15] aligns with the desired outcomes of community development highlighting the value in cross-sector learning.[16]

TEAR Australia recently brought together a research project which explored the place of mental health in community development, reflected upon current approaches and challenges, and created a platform for the lived experience of mental illness to be heard. The research is the collective efforts, experience, and knowledge of a range of stakeholders, including three TEAR partners who are implementing community-based mental health programmes; communities of practice within Australia and globally; and communities, families, and people with lived experience of mental illness in Afghanistan, India, and Nepal. The research findings have challenged and expanded TEAR's understanding of the place of mental health in community development and its centrality in building community resilience.

This chapter seeks to reflect on TEAR's learning, and further explore the place of mental health in strengthening community resilience and development.

The Intersectionality of Mental Health

Mental health cannot be separated from health, since "there is no health without mental health."[17] Having mental ill health increases an individual's risk of poor physical health, early death, and injury, while, in reverse, mental ill health is

---

13. A. J. Imperiale and F. Vanclay, "Experiencing Local Community Resilience in Action: Learning from Post-Disaster Communities," *Journal of Rural Studies* 47 (2016): 204–219.

14. L. Oades, *Building Community Resilience and Wellbeing Report* (Wollongong: Mental Health Commission of NSW, 2014).

15. R. Kobau et al., "Mental Health Promotion in Public Health: Perspectives and Strategies from Positive Psychology," *American Journal of Public Health* 101, no. 8 (Aug. 2011): e1–9; Herrman et al., "Introduction"; S. Mnookin, *Out of the Shadows: Making Mental Health a Global Development Priority* (Washington, DC: World Bank Group and World Health Organization, 2016), accessed 27 September 2019, http://documents.worldbank.org/curated/en/270131468187759113/Out-of-the-shadows-making-mental-health-a-global-development-priority; R. Burgess and K. Mathias, "Community Mental Health Competencies: A New Vision for Global Mental Health," in *The Palgrave Handbook of Sociocultural Perspectives on Global Mental Health*, ed. R. G. White, S. Jain, D. Orr, U. Read, 2nd ed. (London: Palgrave Macmillan, 2017), 211–235.

16. Oades, *Building Community Resilience*.

17. M. Prince et al., "No Health without Mental Health," *The Lancet* 370 (2007): 859–877.

precipitated or prolonged by health conditions.[18] Like health more broadly, mental health is intersectional.[19] Social determinants within any context, such as gender, low education, social status, caste, poverty, conflict, and disaster, and other compounding reasons for exclusion, affect mental health outcomes on an individual, household, and community level.[20] As a result, mental health is an important cross-cutting focus for development.[21]

Gender

Gender disadvantage is an example of this as more women are affected by mental ill health, such as depression, than men. While a significant proportion of women in low- and middle-income countries (LMICs) experience perinatal mental ill health,[22] mental health is often a neglected component of maternal health care.[23] Recent evidence has also shown that there are strong links between antenatal depression and increased likelihood of preterm birth and low birth weight.[24] Investments in integrating mental health in perinatal interventions have been shown to be effective in reducing depressive symptoms and improving infant outcomes.[25]

Gender-based violence and its mental health consequences affect more women in LMICs than men.[26] The resulting psychosocial disability and

---

18. Votruba et al., "Importance," 283–286; Prince et al., "No Health," 859–877; J. Eaton et al., "There Is No Wealth without Mental Health," *The Lancet Psychiatry* 1, no. 4 (2014): 252–253.

19. J. S. Seng et al., "Marginalized Identities, Discrimination Burden, and Mental Health: Empirical Exploration of an Interpersonal-Level Approach to Modeling Intersectionality," *Social Science and Medicine* 75, no. 12 (Dec. 2012): 2437–2445.

20. V. Patel, "Mental Health in Low- and Middle-Income Countries," *British Medical Bulletin* 81 (2007): 81–96.

21. Votruba et al., "Importance," 283–286; G. Thornicroft and V. Patel, "Including Mental Health among the New Sustainable Development Goals," *British Medical Journal* (20 Aug. 2014): 349.

22. J. Fisher et al., "Prevalence and Determinants of Common Perinatal Mental Disorders in Women in Low- and Lower-Middle-Income Countries: A Systematic Review," *Bulletin of the World Health Organization* 90, no. 2 (1 Feb. 2012): 139–149.

23. S. Mnookin, *Out of the Shadows: Making Mental Health a Global Development Priority* (Washington, DC: World Bank Group and World Health Organization, 2016), accessed 27 September 2019, http://documents.worldbank.org/curated/en/270131468187759113/Out-of-the-shadows-making-mental-health-a-global-development-priority; P. J. Surkan et al., "Maternal Depression and Early Childhood Growth in Developing Countries: Systematic Review and Meta-Analysis," *Bulletin of the World Health Organization* 89, no. 8 (1 Aug. 2011): 607–615; A. Rahman et al., "Grand Challenges: Integrating Maternal Mental Health into Maternal and Child Health Programmes," *PLOS Medicine* 10, no. 5 (2013): e1001442.

24. Surkan et al., "Maternal Depression," 607–615.

25. Rahman et al., "Grand Challenges," e1001442.

26. Patel, "Mental Health," 81–96.

poor development outcomes for women and their children furthers gender inequity.[27] Development programmes that focus on women's empowerment, leadership, skill building, or health – including reproductive health – will be strengthened by the integration of mental health across all programmes.

Poverty

Growing evidence shows that mental ill health and poverty interact in a negative cycle especially in LMICs.[28] Poverty is both a cause and a consequence of poor mental health.[29] People living in poverty are at increased risk of mental illness due to the stress of living in conditions of deprivation; increased risk of trauma; increased obstetric risks; social exclusion; and lack of food security. Having a mental illness has been linked with increased health spending, loss of income and employment, stigma, and exacerbation of poverty and vulnerability.[30]

The systemic root causes of poverty and inequality are the strongest contributing factors to developing mental illness and undermining self-determination and community cohesion.[31] As a result, social inequality and multidimensional poverty must be addressed as part of a community development approach, both to contribute to prevention of mental illness and to strengthen recovery and inclusion of people with psychosocial disability.[32]

In order to strengthen recovery and development outcomes for people with mental illness, community development approaches that build stronger economic security – such as savings and livelihood opportunities – need to be

---

27. World Health Organization, "Gender Disparities in Mental Health: WHO Fact Sheet," accessed 27 September 2019, http://www.who.int/mental_health/prevention/genderwomen/en/.

28. C. Lund et al., "Poverty and Common Mental Disorders in Low and Middle Income Countries: A Systematic Review," *Social Science and Medicine* 71, no. 3 (Aug. 2010): 517–528; C. Mills, "The Psychiatrisation of Poverty: Rethinking the Mental Health–Poverty Nexus," *Social and Personality Psychology Compass* 9, no. 5 (2015): 213–222; V. Patel and C. Lund, "Mental Disorders: Equity and Social Determinants," in *Equity, Social Determinants and Public Health Programmes*, ed. E. Blas and K. A. Sivasankara (Geneva: WHO, 2010): 115–134.

29. Eaton et al., "There Is No Wealth," 252–253; C. Lund et al., "Outcomes of the Mental Health and Development Model in Rural Kenya: A 2-Year Prospective Cohort Intervention Study," *International Health* 5, no. 1 (Mar. 2013): 43–50.

30. Lund et al., "Outcomes," 43–50.

31. Patel and Lund, "Mental Disorders," 115–134.

32. Lund et al., "Poverty," 517–528; S. Rosenfield, "Triple Jeopardy? Mental Health at the Intersection of Gender, Race, and Class," *Social Science and Medicine* 74, no. 11 (Jun. 2012): 1791–1801; J. F. Trani et al., "Mental Illness, Poverty and Stigma in India: A Case-Control Study," *BMJ Open* 5, no. 2 (23 Feb. 2015): e006355.

inclusive of people with mental illness and their families.[33] Poverty-reduction initiatives, including cash transfers, can achieve better mental health outcomes and improve the social determinants that inhibit inclusion.[34]

In order to contribute to resilient individuals, households, and communities, development programmes need to seek to understand the intersectionalities that predispose people to developing mental illness, and impact upon people's lived experience of mental illness.[35]

Mental Health, Relationships, and Households

A further area of learning for TEAR has been regarding mental health and relationships.

The research highlighted participation in family and community life for people with psychosocial disability as central for self-esteem, sense of accomplishment, and increasing self-worth. Through being given opportunities to contribute to meaningful household and community activities, people spoke of rediscovering their valued roles, responsibilities, sense of identity, and potential. People with mental illness often experience deep stigma which severely limits their engagement with community and undermines their identity, sense of self-worth, and ability to contribute.[36] Social isolation is also a risk for deteriorating mental health and suicide.[37]

---

33. A. Carroll et al., "Promoting the Rights of People with Psychosocial Disability in Development Research and Programming," *Development Bulletin* 77 (2016): 25–30.

34. V. De Menil and A. Glassman, *Making Room for Mental Health: Recommendations for Improving Mental Health Care in Low- and Middle-Income Countries* (Washington, DC: Center for Global Development, 2016), accessed 27 September 2019, https://www.cgdev.org/publication/ft/making-room-mental-health-recommendations-improving-mental-health-care-low-and-middle.

35. De Menil and Glassman, *Making Room*.

36. M. Koschorke et al., "Experiences of Stigma and Discrimination of People with Schizophrenia in India," *Social Science and Medicine* 123 (Dec. 2014): 149–159; F. Mascayano, J. E. Armijo, and L. H. Yang, "Addressing Stigma Relating to Mental Illness in Low- and Middle-Income Countries," *Front Psychiatry* 6 (2015): 38; G. D. Sayed, *Mental Health in Afghanistan: Burden, Challenges and the Way Forward; Health, Nutrition and Population (HNP) Discussion Paper* (Washington, DC: World Bank, 2011), accessed 27 September 2019, http://documents.worldbank.org/curated/en/692201467992810759/Mental-health-in-Afghanistan-burden-challenges-and-the-way-forward; S. Amresh et al., "Impact and Origin of Stigma and Discrimination in Schizophrenia: Patient Perceptions," *Research and Action* 1, no. 1 (2011): 67–72; A. C. Sweetland et al., "Closing the Mental Health Gap in Low-Income Settings by Building Research Capacity: Perspectives from Mozambique," *Annals of Global Health* 80, no. 2 (Mar.–Apr. 2014): 126–133.

37. D. Pevalin and D. Rose, Institute for Economic and Social Research, University of Essex, *Social Capital for Health* (NHS Health Development Agency, 2003), accessed 27 September 2019, http://repository.essex.ac.uk/9143/1/socialcapital_BHP_survey.pdf; Office of the Deputy Prime

While negative community attitudes fuel stigma and discrimination, stigma is also often internalized. The result of such "self-stigma" is shame and humiliation which decreases the likelihood people will seek opportunities for participation.[38] A key process in transformational development is seeking to enable all people to recover their true identity as made in the image of God with intrinsic value. McNair[39] advocates that in keeping with 1 Corinthians 12:22–26 people with disabilities are seen as (1) created in the image of God; (2) created with a purpose; (3) indispensable, even if they seem weaker; (4) worthy of special honour, although they are thought to be less honourable. Creating platforms for people with psychosocial disabilities to be seen as image-bearers of God and key contributors in their communities enables development programmes to reflect these values and to shape the work to be transformative on an individual, household, and community level. In programmes this could inform inclusion approaches in creating opportunities for people with psychosocial disabilities to join and participate in collective community activities.

The research illustrated how mental ill health interrupts relationships and everyday life, creating strain and disharmony, and creating a state of vulnerability for the household. The symptoms of the illness, the search for and effects of treatment, as well as stigma in the community, can all contribute to negative effects on family functioning.[40] Family members can, as a result, experience disconnection, disturbed life patterns and routines, compounded economic stress, and relationship and parenting strain, making them vulnerable

---

Minister, *Mental Health and Social Exclusion: Social Exclusion Unit Report Summary* (London: Office of the Deputy Prime Minister, 2004), accessed 27 September 2019, http://www.nfao.org/Useful_Websites/MH_Social_Exclusion_report_summary.pdf.

38. M. Semrau et al., "Stigma and Discrimination Related to Mental Illness in Low- and Middle-Income Countries," *Epidemiology and Psychiatric Sciences* 24, no. 5 (Oct. 2015): 382–394; G. Thornicroft et al., "Evidence for Effective Interventions to Reduce Mental-Health-Related Stigma and Discrimination," *Lancet* 387, no. 10023 (12 Mar. 2016): 1123–1132.

39. J. McNair, "Disability and Human Supports," *Christian Journal for Global Health* 2, no. 2 (2015): 10–15; J. McNair, "A Christian Model of Disability," *Disabled Christianity*, 20 September 2017, accessed 27 September 2019, http://disabledchristianity.blogspot.com/2017/09/a-christian-model-of-disability.html.

40. E. A. McKay, "Mothers with Mental Illness: An Occupation Interrupted," in *Mothering Occupations: Challenge, Agency, and Participation*, ed. S. A. Esdaile and J. A. Olson (Philadelphia: FA Davis, 2004), 238–258; M. Funk et al., *Mental Health and Development: Targeting People with Mental Health Conditions as a Vulnerable Group* (Geneva: World Health Organization, 2010), accessed 27 September 2019, http://www.who.int/mental_health/policy/mhtargeting/en/.

to mental health changes of their own.[41] As family life is the key place where child development happens, these stressors can particularly affect outcomes for children.[42] Families and households are core elements in building resilient communities. Adopting holistic family approaches that take account of all members can strengthen families affected by mental illness, thus strengthening communities. Such initiatives could include family support groups and inclusion of family members into counselling, self-help, and advocacy groups.

Community relationships are also significantly impacted by mental ill health. Negative local beliefs about mental illness that impact individuals with mental illness and their families also affect the whole community, as they seek healthy and contextual ways to conceptualize and discuss mental illness and mental health and well-being. Often people experiencing mental illness are labelled as socially inadequate and experience stigma and discrimination from the community, resulting in social distancing and a breakdown of community relationships.[43] Our research showed the general lack of awareness of, and the misinformation about, mental illness and mental health that exists in most communities which can lead to poor health outcomes, lack of support, and exclusion. The findings also demonstrated the importance of community awareness and strategies to strengthen communities' mental health literacy.

Previous studies indicate that raising awareness about mental illness within a community context shapes communities' responses to it – directly promoting stigma reduction and strengthening inclusion.[44] Initiatives which utilize locally acceptable words and contextually appropriate concepts build the

---

41. L. Hayes et al., "Quality of Life and Social Isolation among Caregivers of Adults with Schizophrenia: Policy and Outcomes," *Community Mental Health Journal* 51, no. 5 (2015): 591–597; A. Muralidharan et al., "Stigma: A Unique Source of Distress for Family Members of Individuals with Mental Illness," *Journal of Behavioral Health Services and Research* 43, no. 3 (Jul. 2016): 484–493.

42. T. Solantaus, A. Reupert, and D. Maybery, "Working with Parents Who Have a Psychiatric Disorder," in *Parental Psychiatric Disorder: Distressed Parents and Their Families*, ed. A. Reupert et al., 3rd ed. (New York: Cambridge University Press, 2015), 238–247.

43. Koschorke et al., "Experiences of Stigma," 149–159; Semrau et al., "Stigma and Discrimination," 382–394; Thornicroft et al., "Evidence," 1123–1132; C. Lauber and W. Rossler, "Stigma towards People with Mental Illness in Developing Countries in Asia," *International Review of Psychiatry* 19, no. 2 (Apr. 2007): 157–178.

44. V. Pinfold et al., "Active Ingredients in Anti-Stigma Programmes in Mental Health," *International Review of Psychiatry* 17, no. 2 (Apr. 2005): 123–131; N. Mehta et al., "Evidence for Effective Interventions to Reduce Mental Health-Related Stigma and Discrimination in the Medium and Long Term: Systematic Review," *British Journal of Psychiatry* 207, no. 5 (Nov. 2015): 377–384.

mental health literacy capacity of the community.[45] It is critical that awareness-raising includes lived experience voices[46] and is broader than just mental illness signs and symptoms and about where to go for treatment.

Community inclusion involves establishing welcoming communities where each individual's participation is valued for its unique contribution.[47] Promoting good understanding of mental illness, community cohesion, and respectful community relationships assists in strengthening participation and inclusion of people with psychosocial disability. These are central components of building a resilient community.

Mental Health Promotion as a Resilience-Building Tool of Community Development

TEAR's research has also shown that effective community development that promotes holistic well-being can contribute to mentally healthy and resilient communities. Social disintegration of community (characterized by lack of social support, violence, migration, substance abuse, and breakdown of social and family cohesion) is associated with an increased rate of mental illness.[48] Conversely, communities with high levels of cohesion, including trust, reciprocity, and participation, have protective capacities for the mental health or well-being of a community.[49]

Mental health determinants are located in the same social and economic domains that community development programmes are working within. These include access to supportive social networks; stable and supportive family, social, and community environments; access to a variety of activities; having a valued social position; having opportunity for self-determination and control of one's life; and access to meaningful employment, education, income, and

---

45. J. Eaton et al., "A Structured Approach to Integrating Mental Health Services into Primary Care: Development of the Mental Health Scale Up Nigeria Intervention (Mhsun)," *International Journal of Mental Health Systems* 12 (2018): 1–12.

46. K. Mathias et al., "Under the Banyan Tree: Exclusion and Inclusion of People with Mental Disorders in Rural North India," *BMC Public Health* 15 (1 May 2015): 446.

47. M. Salzer and R. Baron, *Well Together: A Blueprint for Community Inclusion; Fundamental Concepts, Theoretical Frameworks and Evidence* (Melbourne: Wellways, 2016).

48. Lehtinen et al., "Intrinsic Value," 46.

49. Lehtinen et al., 46; A. Morgan and C. Swann, eds., *Social Capital for Health: Issues of Definition, Measurement, and Links to Health* (London: Health Development Agency, 2004); K. McKenzie and T. Harpham, *Social Capital and Mental Health* (London: Jessica Kingsley, 2006); A. Cooke et al., *Mental Well-Being Impact Assessment: A Toolkit for Well-Being* (London: National MWIA Collaborative, 2011).

housing.⁵⁰ Hence programmes that address these determinants alongside wider issues of power, inclusion, and social justice are also contributing to mental health promotion and resilience-building.⁵¹

Community development programmes can contribute to stronger and more cohesive societies that work together to solve problems, adapt to common issues, and strengthen peace and well-being. Partnership with churches and local faith institutions, and building strong self-help groups (SHGs), support groups, or other collectives, can create such spaces for building relationships and trust, togetherness, and cooperation, and contribute to well-being.⁵² While SHGs are known for their positive role in community economics, they also play a role in overcoming social isolation and contributing to social, personal, and spiritual development.⁵³ These benefits are important for strengthening a sense of individual and community agency and cohesion which contribute to good mental health and resilience. Collectives form a crucial medium for embedding community resilience, which often emerges in times of crisis and contributes to sustainable development.⁵⁴

Through understanding a mental health promotion framework, development programmes can see how their work contributes to community resilience and well-being. Including measurement of well-being and quality of life can help to reinforce the importance of the activities such as self-help groups and livelihood activities, and strengthen organizations beyond their poverty alleviation outcomes.

Mental Health Treatment Access as an Equity Issue

While there is significant literature about the treatment gap, access issues, and the lack of appropriate medical services,⁵⁵ TEAR's research raised the

---

50. Cooke et al., *Mental Well-Being*; Oades, *Building Community Resilience*.

51. H. Fernandes et al., "Inclusion of People with Psychosocial Disability in Low- and Middle-Income Contexts: A Practice Review," *Christian Journal for Global Health* 4, no. 3 (2017): 72–81.

52. S. Cromie et al., *Psycho-Social Outcomes and Mechanisms of Self-Help Groups in Ethiopia* (Dublin: TEARFund Ireland, 2017).

53. S. Cromie et al., *Psycho-Social Outcomes*.

54. Imperiale and Vanclay, "Experiencing," 204–219.

55. C. Hanlon et al., "Challenges and Opportunities for Implementing Integrated Mental Health Care: A District Level Situation Analysis from Five Low- and Middle-Income Countries," *PLoS One* 9, no. 2 (2014): e88437; N. P. Luitel et al., "Mental Health Care in Nepal: Current Situation and Challenges for Development of a District Mental Health Care Plan," *Conflict and Health* 9 (2015): 3; B. Saraceno et al., "Barriers to Improvement of Mental Health Services in

importance of treatment access as an equity and human rights issue and crucial for recovery. Treatment is valued not as an end in itself, but because it enables people to engage in their meaningful activities and in family and community life. Therefore it is important to consider linking people to medical treatment and services for people with psychosocial disability through the lens of a social and rights-based model of disability.[56]

There has been great achievement by the global mental health movement in raising global awareness of mental illness. The WHO "Mental Health Action Plan 2013–2020" shows international commitment to tackling the burden of mental illness and has helped to drive government action[57] The development sector being named as an actor in the plan highlights its role in working on the social determinants for health, advocacy for the vulnerable and marginalized, and mobilizing civil society. Development programmes can play a crucial role in promoting access to treatment, advocating for services, and raising awareness among communities. Organizations don't need to be specialists or have a lot of technical knowledge about mental illness to see how mental health affects development, or to include people affected by mental illness into programmes.

Integrated Community Approaches to Addressing Mental Health

This journey of learning has led TEAR to conclude that multiple approaches are required in considering mental health as an important and often forgotten part of effective community development in order to maximize the inclusiveness and resilience of communities. There is a need to promote pathways to inclusion and to support people with psychosocial disability and their families as vulnerable people in communities. This includes enabling access and ensuring that all development programmes are inclusive. There is also a need for programmes to consider how they can promote mental health and well-being for whole communities, recognizing that much of the

---

Low-Income and Middle-Income Countries," *Lancet* 370, no. 9593 (29 Sep. 2007): 1164–1174; P. Ventevogel, "Integration of Mental Health into Primary Healthcare in Low-Income Countries: Avoiding Medicalization," *International Review of Psychiatry* 26, no. 6 (2014): 669–679.

56. S. Mattner et al., "Self-Determination: What Do People Who Experience Severe Mental Illness Want from Public Mental Health Services?," *International Journal of Integrated Care* 17, no. 3 (2017): 50; S. Porsdam Mann, V. J. Bradley, and B. J. Sahakian, "Human Rights-Based Approaches to Mental Health: A Review of Programs," *Health and Human Rights* 18, no. 1 (Jun. 2016): 263–276.

57. World Health Organization, "Mental Health Action Plan, 2013–2020," accessed 27 September 2019, http://www.who.int/mental_health/action_plan_2013/en/.

work of community development programmes is already working towards resiliency and community health. These approaches are mutually reinforcing, and integrating both types of approaches can strengthen their effectiveness in building resilient communities.

The practical suggestions included in table 17.1 are implications for community development organizations and programmes. The compilation of these has been a collective piece of work and represents input from organizations working in community mental health programmes in Afghanistan, India, and Nepal; people with lived experience of mental illness in India and Nepal; and some of our insights along the way.

Table 17.1: Implications for Practice: Inclusion and Mental Health Promotion Approaches

Implications for Practice: Inclusion and Mental Health Promotion Approaches	
For Your Organization	
1.	Development projects and activities can have either a positive or a negative effect on core protective factors for community mental well-being: Enhancing protective factors requires it to: • Enhance control • Increase resilience and community assets • Facilitate participation • Promote inclusion
2	Support staff in your organization to develop skills in communication, listening, and providing psychosocial support at a community level.
3.	NGOs could build awareness about mental health into any health training or community health initiatives. This should be done using the language which local communities use to talk about emotions or the signs and symptoms of mental illness.
4.	Development programmes play an important role in promoting access to mental health support and can provide a stronger role in ensuring linkages to existing services or advocating for services. Find local sources of knowledge about mental illness and psychosocial disability in your context: • Government or other services (medical or benefits available) • NGOs with specific programs or Disabled Persons Organizations (DPOs)

Implications for Practice:	
Inclusion and Mental Health Promotion Approaches	
For Your Organization	
5.	Skill building in life skills, mental health promotion, youth resilience, parenting support groups, and other community-based programmes are effective approaches to promoting good mental health and supporting recovery for people experiencing mental illness. Think about ways these could be built into existing or new programmes.
6.	If your organization works with SHGs, think about how to open up spaces for discussions about mental health and well-being within groups: • Conversations about what helps people feel emotionally/mentally well and what things affect that.
7.	Look for ways to include people with lived experience of mental illness as part of your work – as staff, and as project volunteers. Learn from their stories and recognize that they are key sources of knowledge and advocacy within your organization and at the community level.
8.	Mark World Mental Health Day (10 October each year), and give key and simple messages: • There is no shame in mental illness. • Mental illness is treatable. • There are mental health services nearby. • Family can help people with mental illness by listening to and including them. (Raising awareness in a respectful way can help break down stigma.)
9.	Consider the mental health of your organization's staff. Start conversations about mental health in the workplace.
For Your Programmes	
10.	People with mental illness are often hidden – think of ways to include them during baseline surveys and when projects are mapping vulnerable groups in the community. Ask who might help you know where to meet these people. You don't necessarily need to identify individuals but households that are vulnerable.
11.	Think about which groups in your communities are vulnerable – because of physical disability, gender, caste, and socio-economic status – and focus work on those groups. As vulnerable groups are more likely to experience mental illness, working with these groups can help prevent this.

	Implications for Practice:
	Inclusion and Mental Health Promotion Approaches
12.	Explore and utilize innovative ways to create space for hearing the views of those with psychosocial disability throughout community development processes. These voices are needed to shape programmes and effect change.
13.	Utilize key educators and advocates in your programme to understand more about mental health and to incorporate it into their community messages and activities.
14.	Work with religious and community leaders so that leaders feel equipped to support people with mental illness and their families, and so that leaders have the knowledge to respectfully discuss mental illness in the community and create inclusive environments.
15.	Work with existing or develop new lived experience groups, support groups, or Disabled Persons Organizations (DPOs).
16.	Adopt holistic family approaches in programmes that enhance family relationships, such as family support groups, and include family members in counselling, self-help, and advocacy groups.
17.	Think about ways in which people with mental illness (and their family members) could be welcomed into SHGs. Contributing meaningfully to the family and community can prevent people from developing mental illness and can help people with mental illness to recover well. Being a member of an SHG and engaging in livelihood opportunities are effective approaches for supporting recovery and inclusion.
18.	Incorporate information on mental health in women's leadership and empowerment programmes. Women are particularly vulnerable.
19.	Incorporate information about mental health in maternal and child reproductive health programmes. Include health messages about mental health in any family planning or perinatal activities.
20.	Include learning about mental illness and how to discuss emotion in school programmes and curricula. Many good resources are available in multiple languages and could be translated.

Conclusion

This journey of learning for TEAR Australia has expanded our understanding of the place of mental health in community development and its centrality in building community resilience. The intersectionality of mental illness with poverty and gender and its effect on self-worth and relationships make it a crucial cross-cutting issue that should be addressed in transformational development programmes. In addition, mental health awareness and promotion activities contribute to healthy resilient populations. For communities to be truly resilient and to reflect the image of God they need to include people with mental ill health as a vital part of society.

Further Reading and Resources

Mental Health Innovation Network: http://www.mhinnovation.net/
Contact Tearfund Australia: info@tear.org.au

18

Indigenous Voices

The Spiritual Strength of the Peoples of Abya Yala[1]

Jocabed Reina Solano Miselis

In a community in the Gunadule nation, the song of a leader in the congress house is heard:

> The ancestors built their huts; they had good huts, but without order, and without the compact forms of what we have today. Then Ibeorgun taught the elders to build better huts, and to better define all the parts that make up the hut; and to give them each an identity.
>
> The pole that you put in the centre of the hut is called *buwar* – a pole that is solid, straight, hard to rot, and too heavy for one person to lift. *Uusor* is another important pole, and the *nagubir* poles rest on each of its sides. The other poles that permit the central pole to really be the *buwar* are called *baggu* and *nagubir*. These lesser poles hold up and sustain the *buwar*, making the whole hut strong and solid. The strong pole is supported by the smaller and weaker ones, so that the stoutest pole gives strength to the weaker ones, and at the same time it gains its vigour and strength and stature from them.

---

1. This chapter by Jocabed Reina Solano Miselis was first published as chapter 4 of G. J. Hill, *Salt, Light, and a City: Ecclesiology for the Global Missional Community*, vol. 2, Majority World Voices (Eugene, OR: Cascade, 2019). Used with permission.

The poles speak to one another. The strong pole, the powerful *buwar*, says to its pole friends:

> I cannot do this alone. I cannot hold up the weight of the hut alone. I am strong, but you are the ones who give me your resistance and flexibility to hold up the hut, the whole house, so that the wind cannot blow away the hut, and so the earthquake will not smash it. This is why I need you, *dior*, even though you are the smallest. I need *magged* to help me, and my friend *saderbir* must also give me a hand. We all need the support and strength of each other.
>
> Only the union of our strength will make those who sleep beneath us happy. I give my hand to *dior*; it in turn gives a hand to *magged*; *magged* offers its spine to *saderbir*; and in that way we all give each other a hand. We all need *sargi*, the great vine; for the *sargi* will unite us so that we don't each go our own way. We strong poles need the smaller ones.
>
> When we are all united by the *sargi*, the great *bejuco* (a vine), then we feel we are stuck together, and we have the capacity to hold up the weight of the *sosga*, which covers our bones. We cannot allow one to carry all the weight, even if it is the strongest. We all have to bear the weight of everyone. United we must defend ourselves against the aggressive wind and the earthquakes which will shake us. The house belongs to all of us who lend our shoulder to keep it firm.[2]

Beginning with this story, I would like to pose some questions that have important implications for our being and doing church and Christian community. What do indigenous peoples have to offer the church? Are they a "mission field" or are they a place where God is already at work? How should the encounter with indigenous peoples change the way in which we live out our faith?

I also want to offer some brief reflections that have emerged from my walk in community with others, recognizing the diverse face of God with my indigenous sisters and brothers in Abya Yala (the continent of America)[3] who live and resist from our own indigenous spiritualities in a world that wants to impose its hegemony. And we as the church are not exempt from this world.

---

2. Narrative (song) sung in the congress house of the Gunadule nation.

3. Abya Yala is a term adopted by indigenous peoples from around Latin America to refer to the entire American continent. It means "fully ripe land" or "land of life blood."

As my Gunadule people would say, they want to kill the Gunadule spirit. In the words of Boaventura de Sousa Santos, this is epistemicide, that is, the destruction of the knowledge of the nations in the hands of European and North American (displaced Europeans) colonialism and imperialism. This destruction is far from the heart of the gospel, and Jesus strongly denounces it. This is because the gospel that is born from the heart of Jesus brings life, not death; and abundant life at that (John 10:10).

Therefore, to know and value the heart and the symbolic universe of indigenous peoples – where God's presence is overflowing – is to accept the invitation of the gospel to look at the kingdom of God beyond our own theological borders, and to reimagine new ways of being the church. Here is where I believe it is necessary for us to continue deepening our faith and theology, while engaging out of a theology of encounter and mis-encounter.

Meaningful dialogue can emerge from this encounter and this new way of seeing the church, the gospel, and the kingdom. I propose a conversation about our understanding of the church from the plurality of the Christian faith; in other words, exploring and valuing the interculturality of the church and of the ways of being the church.

What are some key features of this emerging intercultural conversation? And what do indigenous spiritualities and faith teach the worldwide church? Here are three key points:

1. Indigenous voices offer an integral (and holistic) vision of community, with respect to its social and cosmic environment. Consider the song of the Gunadule nation with which we began this chapter. All living beings are in interdependent relationships and need each other. The interdependent relationships of all living beings affect our lives positively or negatively. Here the voice of the earth also echoes. We need to learn from this cosmic coexistence.

2. Indigenous voices offer a new way of understanding social relations in contrast to the modern and capitalist ways of life that permeate Christianity today, which are strongly infused with utilitarianism, individualism, consumerism, patriarchy, and a cannibalistic competitiveness.

3. Indigenous voices offer another way of understanding the encounter with different cultures, not from a colonial perspective, but rather from a place of conviviality, coexistence, recognition, and valuing our plurality and diversity – just as the gospel calls us to do. "There is neither Jew nor Gentile, neither slave nor free, nor is there male and female, for you are all one in Christ Jesus" (Gal 3:28).

The issue from the beginning then is that we must realign our life together with the other, and not just with other human beings but with the whole cosmos. Starting with our faith as Christians, this realignment should be a fundamental part of our faith and belief and no longer shaped around a colonizing logic. For many peoples, and in this case especially for indigenous peoples, just hearing the word "mission" has a colonizing logic. But more than that, our lack of recognition of the presence of God among all peoples – and in this case among the indigenous peoples of Abya Yala – impedes our ability to see the face of the Creator through mysterious ways that we do not know.

God was here before Christianity. For this reason, the question is not "What can the church do for indigenous peoples?" but rather "What must the church learn from indigenous peoples?" This question reflects the heart of Jesus Christ.[4]

One day I dreamed that I could dance, celebrating God in profound harmony with the earth. From the wind I heard God's voice, from the fire I could see God's sparkle, from the water I saw myself reflected, from the dust I smelled myself, and when I woke up everything was colourful.

---

4. This presentation was given at the 7th Triennial Micah Global Consultation, 10–14 September 2018, CCT Training Centre, Tagaytay, the Philippines.

19

The Gospel and Resilience in the Pursuit of the Common Good

D. Zac Niringiye

It is a joy and privilege to be part of Micah 2018. I begin with a confession. I am one of those people who over the years, particularly during the years when I served with the International Fellowship of Evangelical Students (IFES) and Church Mission Society, attended many Christian conferences. And then I got very tired of them, especially conferences of evangelicals, and decided to take a break. You might then wonder, "Why this particular one?" I am actually excited about Micah 2018. Micah for me is a movement seeking the renewal of faith; it is a renewal of gospel living – to act justly, love mercy, and walk humbly with God (Mic 6:8). This, for me, is life. This is not just another conference; it is life.

The other thing I really love about Micah is this: we gather here as restless people. We are a people who are discontented with the status quo. However, not only should we be restless; we should also be troubled. I'm going to add to that troubling. I'm going to share my restlessness, and suggest some ways of thinking that may disrupt. I'm going to suggest that we learn a new language, because some of the old language has not worked and is not working. Rather than enable engagement with the challenging call in the gospel, more often than not it has led us astray. Can we find some new ways of speaking – indeed, some fresh ways of telling the story? The question of the common good is one such new language and challenges us to rethink and reimagine the imperative in the gospel for believers in the world.

My own life is testimony to disruption. I was serving as a bishop in the city of Kampala in the Church of Uganda (Anglican tradition) when I came to the conclusion that the immediate cause of social injustices in my country is the fact that the state is being run and ruled by people who steal public resources and abuse power with impunity. In a word: thugs; leaders who steal and kill with impunity. It is a case of thugs in charge of state power. I pondered for a long time what this meant for my life and calling as a bishop in Uganda. I came to the conclusion that I would serve the cause of the gospel and the church by quitting serving the Church of Uganda and the city and country in an ecclesiastical office in order to engage in gospel-grounded advocacy and activism for social justice, which meant entering the fray of politics.

The theme for my talk is "The gospel and resilience in the pursuit of the common good." Over many years, the Sermon on the Mount in the Gospel of Matthew, and very specifically the Beatitudes, has been a great inspiration to me in reflecting on the implications of the gospel for public life:

> Now when Jesus saw the crowds, he went up on a mountainside and sat down. His disciples came to him, and he began to teach them.
>
> He said:
>
> "Blessed are the poor in spirit,
>   for theirs is the kingdom of heaven.
> Blessed are those who mourn,
>   for they will be comforted.
> Blessed are the meek,
>   for they will inherit the earth.
> Blessed are those who hunger and thirst for righteousness,
>   for they will be filled.
> Blessed are the merciful,
>   for they will be shown mercy.
> Blessed are the pure in heart,
>   for they will see God.
> Blessed are the peacemakers,
>   for they will be called children of God.
> Blessed are those who are persecuted because of righteousness,
>   for theirs is the kingdom of heaven.
>
> "Blessed are you when people insult you, persecute you and falsely say all kinds of evil against you because of me. Rejoice and be glad, because great is your reward in heaven, for in the same way they persecuted the prophets who were before you.

"You are the salt of the earth. But if the salt loses its saltiness, how can it be made salty again? It is no longer good for anything, except to be thrown out and trampled underfoot.

"You are the light of the world. A town built on a hill cannot be hidden. Neither do people light a lamp and put it under a bowl. Instead they put it on its stand, and it gives light to everyone in the house. In the same way, let your light shine before others, that they may see your good deeds and glorify your Father in heaven." (Matt 5:1–16)

Questions of the Current Global Social Context

Questions matter. Part of the problem with the evangelical tradition is that we are preoccupied with answers but we don't ask questions. As CB Samuel has said, "Jesus is the answer, but what's the question?" Have you heard this – theologians, are you there? A dear friend once described for me who theologians are: "Men and women who answer questions no one is asking." Lord have mercy! I wish it were not true. But most of our theological centres are preoccupied with questions that no one is asking. The questions we ask matter. I therefore propose four questions that we ought to grapple with, questions that I believe arise from our current global social context.

First, "Why don't we Christians pursue the common good?" Why is it that we do not pursue the well-being of all in our societies and our countries?

Just in case you think that's a fallacy, check your country, especially if it's a country where Christianity is the majority faith. Even for those who come from countries where Christianity is a minority, the common good is hardly a concern. Have you noticed how preoccupied we are with our self-preservation, with our own wealth and well-being, with the mission to convert the world to Christianity? So, when we enter public space, we are contesting for our space, our views, and not the views of the other. Consequently, Christian communities all over the globe are part of the problem of conflict. In Africa we know this. Churches have become killing fields – and not just through genocide in Rwanda in 1994 or Kenya's post-election bloodletting in 2007/8; the story has been replicated in many places in the world. Why don't we Christians pursue the common good?

The second question is, "What is the common good?" It is fair to say that as evangelicals the language of 'the common good' is not part of our vocabulary, possibly because we do not care. It is difficult to find evangelical literature on the common good. When I was at a major evangelical liberal arts college, one of the high-flying colleges in the United States of America, I went to the political science department to engage with the head of the department on the question of the common good as an imperative in the gospel. But he was really surprised that as an evangelical Christian I wanted to discuss the common good. Yet our commitment to the gospel demands that we ask the question: "What is the common good according to the gospel?" The issue here is whether the gospel presents us with a vision of life in the world that ought to be shared by all, irrespective of whether they believe the gospel as a common good; and how that vision is to be pursued and realized in public life. Put simply, what does the gospel story teach us about what we owe one another as members of the same society? Indeed, how does God intend for us to live together as human beings who share the same earth?

The third question, which necessarily follows the second, is this: "Does the gospel compel us as believers to pursue the common good, that is, the well-being of all in the world?" I'm not discussing heaven today – I worry that we evangelicals talk too much about heaven. Lord have mercy! Let's talk about this world, this place where we are – the earth. Does the gospel compel us to pursue the good of all?

The fourth question is, "What does resilience in the pursuit of the common good entail for us as the children of God?"

These are big and significant questions, and I can't hope to answer them thoroughly here. I hope that the least I can do is show how essential they are to our faith and life in the world. I have become persuaded that part of the reason why Christians do not pursue the common good is the story we live by: the version of the gospel story that we believe and proclaim is a distortion of the authentic gospel story. So that's the first thing I want to say: we are grounded in flawed and false versions of the gospel story.

Second, I suggest that when we look at the gospel story there is no doubt that not only is the gospel story the common good, but in the gospel there is the common good. We can boldly enter the public square to commend what the gospel teaches about the common good.

And then, third, I suggest that we can therefore relentlessly pursue this common good, inspired by Jesus, the embodiment of the good news.

The Power of Stories and Narratives

We experience life as story. We all live particular stories – defining narratives. How we live our lives is essentially the performance of narratives. These are the stories we live by; the stories that give structure to our understanding of the world, shaping our vision of life; they are the lens we use for making sense of the past; for living in the present – this moment and this place; and for shaping our vision of the future. Visions and dreams of life are grounded in stories; those visions and dreams (which constitute our imagination) shape our actions and mis-actions. Emmanuel Katongole has made the same point in his book *The Sacrifice of Africa: A Political Theology for Africa*:

> Stories not only shape how we view reality but also how we respond to life and indeed the very sort of persons we become. In other words, we are how we imagine ourselves and how others imagine us ... Who we are, and who we are capable of becoming, depends very much on the stories we tell, the stories we listen to, and the stories we live. Stories not only shape our values, aims, and goals; they define the range of what is desirable and what is possible. Stories, therefore, are not simply fictional narratives meant for our entertainment; stories are part of our social ecology. They are embedded in us and form the very heart of our cultural, economic, religious, and political worlds. This applies not only to individuals, but to institutions and even nations.[1]

Our lives, as individuals, communities, and institutions, are stories. We all live in particular stories.

Africans and others who come from oral traditions possibly appreciate this truth about stories and narratives best! Let's teach North Americans and Europeans – Westerners – how to tell stories and the power of narratives. And I plead with those from the global north who systematize experience and who have taught the rest of us systematic theology: please take a back seat and let us from the Majority World teach you how to read the Bible as story. I recall visiting a big theological school in the US and asking them, "What would happen if you cut out courses on systematic theology?" Of course they didn't like it, especially the professors of systematic theology. But I actually believe that "systematic theology" is one of the problems with our theological colleges. I even dare to say that one of the problems with Western theology is that they read the Bible as a book. And yet we know that the Bible is a library of books. And it's a story, a powerful story, a composite of many stories: God's story; the

---

1. E. Katongole, *The Sacrifice of Africa: A Political Theology for Africa* (Grand Rapids, MI: Eerdmans, 2011), 2.

story of humanity; and the story of the community seeking to live by God's story. It's not a book to read; it's a book that reads us. It is a story to live by.

Consider the songs we sing in our churches and fellowships when we gather. When I enter church services I listen to the songs we sing, which are the stories we tell ourselves and each other. It's tragic. It is "I love you, Lord." We sing songs that are individualistic and focused on "I, me, and you." Why don't we sing, "*We* love you, Lord," and "*We* have seen the Lord"?

Thus we are socialized into this story of individualism. Even when we are together we don't know how to sing together. Gathering for corporate worship is the place for telling stories. The privatized and individualistic gospel story we have received is a tragedy! The way we have told it and received it is a distortion – it has been told as a story of the individual, and as only good for the "spiritual" salvation of all who believe. To put it crassly, it's simply a passport to heaven. This narrative has misled us into ignoring the common good – the good of all, believers and unbelievers.

A Quest for the Authentic Gospel Story

In her presentation at our Micah Global gathering, our dear sister Melba Maggay spoke deeply and wonderfully about how we are formed in life: how our lives are shaped by what she characterized as deep structures. Coming from an oral tradition, I want to think of these simply as narratives, stories. It seems to me that God is inviting us to find different ways of talking about this story, to a quest for an authentic gospel story.

I propose that there is a problem with the deep structures that undergird our faith praxis. I will be bold: we live a distorted version of the gospel story. I therefore suggest that we rethink the gospel story we have received, the story we tell of ourselves, and how it has located us in the world.

We have told ourselves that the primary responsibility the gospel story places upon believers is mission. So we go out into the world as missionaries. We even ascribe missionary character to God. We say that God is in his world as a missionary. Hence, we go to the Gospels and we find the Great Commission: "Therefore go!" But, as scholars have told us, "therefore go" is a mistranslation of that text; it ought to read "as you go." Of course, translations themselves are grounded in stories. Because that translation came as a result of the dominance of Western Christianity in the world, it was read as "therefore go." And so Africans, who have received these translations, have taken this as the gospel truth, and we have crafted our lives and churches around the Great

Commission. But I submit that the missionary paradigm has veiled our eyes to the common good in the gospel.

I suggest that we've got it wrong. The gospel story that we have received and told of ourselves is, I suggest, a truncated version of the real gospel story. It is not the full gospel we are called by Jesus to engage in, and live out in the world, as salt and light. It is not the full gospel declared by Jesus the Nazarene and the apostolic church. Those declared "blessed" in Matthew 5 clearly care about the earth and all who inhabit it. The "Great Commission" is not the primary imperative in the gospel. Rather, the biblical narrative, the gospel story, is an "invitation" into its blessedness. So it should be "the Great Invitation" rather than the "Great Commission."

All people – and I mean all – need to hear it, see it, touch it, and experience it. This is why we are "evangelicals." We are to let the "light shine before others, that they may see your good deeds and glorify your Father in heaven" (Matt 5:16). The gospel of Christ is an invitation to both the believer and the unbeliever to a vision and a way of life in the world that is good for all; it embodies the vision of how God intends us to live together, in our plurality, in the world; it is the story of the good that ought to be common to all. And the gospel story is good not just for all humanity, but for all creation. These theologies of dominion, of stewardship of the earth, have done damage to the earth and the gospel. Why? Because we think we have dominion in the earth. No! Again, this is something we can learn from the aboriginal peoples, First Nations, and indigenous peoples. Indigenous peoples don't think they "own" the land; the land owns us. It's powerful.

The true gospel story – as lived, communicated, and embodied in the person, life, and work of Jesus – is the gospel of the common good. It is good news for all humanity and for the flourishing of all creation. The gospel story teaches us about the One who "causes his sun to rise on the evil and the good, and sends rain on the righteous and the unrighteous" (Matt 5:45). In bearing witness to the gospel of Christ, the believer and the believing community become the visible presence of Christ in the world, because the One who is the light of the world shines through them. Resilience is a call and commitment to faithfulness in and to the gospel, pursuing how God in Christ intends us to live together, and living it out daily, individually, and in our communities, in wider society.

20

Against All Odds – and Ends

Ruth Padilla DeBorst

Buenos días! As usual, and in true Latin American fashion, before diving into our topic I must begin by bringing you greetings. Greetings from your sisters and brothers of Casa Adobe, the intentional Christian community to which my husband, James, and I belong in Costa Rica. In this community, which includes refugee families from El Salvador and Venezuela, a young Nicaraguan searching for a vocation, a Lutheran minister and her teenage son, and a few other people here and there, we are learning what it means to live, day in and day out – from Monday to Sunday, from shared meals to dirty dishes, from music night to community organizing, from composting to bridging cultural differences – as a body of followers of the servant King. I also bring you greetings from CETI, the Community of Interdisciplinary Theological Studies we lead, with staff, faculty, and students from across Latin America and beyond. And from INFEMIT, a global community of theologian practitioners who accompany Micah and seek to nourish the church for Christian witness in all areas of life.

It is unending. The stream of need is incessant, and it seems to be channelled directly towards him. He has healed many; but there are always more people with disabilities, more people with leprosy, more blind people. He has encouraged many; but there are always more excluded women, more discouraged workers, more alienated foreigners. He gives himself away daily, teaching, healing, expelling demons, and restoring broken relationships. He feels pain in compassion for the hurting people who are like sheep without a shepherd, vulnerable to the abuse of immoral religious, civil, and military leaders. Roman taxation has impoverished them to the bone. Roman troops have occupied their land and rendered it fruitless. Temple leaders appear more interested in swollen coffers than in offering comfort to their parishioners. The picture is grim, no matter how much light he sheds on it. Many people follow him; but most do so out of self-interest, and even his most intimate friends do not quite understand what he seeks to accomplish.

Sound familiar? Obviously, none of us is living under the iron first of Rome – although other empires do rule our world today. And few if any of us identify that readily with shepherd and sheep imagery. Yet most, if not all, of us are working for justice, peace, and the well-being of people, seeking to make God's love known and to further God's good purposes. And I dare say many of us – me included – suffer from mild to severe Messiah complexes. We are *so* committed we believe that *we* must remedy all the world's problems! Are we not sometimes – or pretty often – burdened by the sheer intractability of the problems faced by our families, communities, nations, and planet? Are we not sometimes – or pretty often – plagued by discouragement at the enormity of the challenges, at the slow pace of change, at the limited fruit of our labour? Are we not tempted at times to give up out of extreme exhaustion?

I was asked to reflect here on resilience in compassion. We'll take a peek into a moment in Jesus's life to see how he tackled the enormity of the task against all odds and to glean some insights regarding how we can persevere in ministry without burning out in the process. We will be aided in this search by the testimony of Mother Teresa and of Monseñor Romero, twentieth-century followers of Jesus who faced difficult odds but persevered in service till the end.

Down. He is truly down. His beloved cousin, the one who had opened the way for his work in Judea, had been imprisoned for denouncing the immorality and abusive power of the ruler. But he has just received the news: because of the spite of the queen, John has been beheaded! His friend's life has ended abruptly, and Jesus knows he needs time away from the crowds. He needs to withdraw to mourn within his intimate circle, to cry out to his Father: why? Why did he have to die so young? What right did Herod have to end the life of God's prophet so violently and shamefully? Why? He yearns for some silence in order to utter his inarticulate cries and gain some perspective in conversation with his Father.

However, on this occasion, Jesus is not to be granted the grace of space, not even once he has crossed the Sea of Galilee in search of it. Crowds of needy people have followed him. They want more from him. No rest. No respite. (Sigh.) Setting aside his personal condition, Jesus compassionately turns his attention to the needs of others. It is late in the day and people have travelled from far away to join him. So Jesus asks Philip: "Where shall we buy bread for these people to eat?"

"What, feed all these people!" Philip is shocked. "It would take more than half a year's wages to buy enough bread for each one to have a bite! How could you even begin to think of such a thing!"[1]

You surely recognize the story. The story of disciples who see all the logical limitations. Hear, for example, Andrew's realistic assessment: "Here is a boy with five small barley loaves and two small fish, *but how far will they go among so many?*"[2] The story of a boy who opens his little lunch box and offers his modest meal. The story of Jesus, who takes the morsels, gives thanks, and distributes basketful after basketful of bread and fish to thousands of children, women, and men. The story of outrageous overabundance and leftovers. The story of a Teacher-Healer who resists being enthroned and withdraws again to a mountain by himself, now finally able to talk things through in the intimacy of the Community of Love.

Unexpected ends. All sorts of odds. Jesus, the stone- and woodworker from Nazareth, faced it all. He felt pain over the plight of his people. He most likely wondered how his calling as the awaited Messiah, the anointed saviour of Israel, was to truly rescue his people. He cried at the death of his friend Lazarus. He shed tears of compassion over Jerusalem. One can imagine how he must have wrestled with the limitations of his ministry: he could not respond to every need. He could not heal every ailment. No matter how much he persisted, as a passionate and compassionate witness to God's love, he – even he – could not solve all the world's problems through his ministry. And that awareness must have haunted him for as long as he lived. And then, in his darkest hour, as he anticipated the end of his earthly life after a tortuous and extremely humiliating trial and execution, he acknowledged his weakness: he pleaded that the cup of suffering be withdrawn.

Mother Teresa, the Albanian-Indian nun, is known for having founded the Missionaries of Charity, a religious order dedicated to serving the poorest of the poor. Today, this order has over seven hundred missions in 130 countries, and provides soup kitchens, centres for family assistance, orphanages, schools, hospitals, and homes for people with diseases such as leprosy, AIDS, and tuberculosis. We may or may not agree fully with her mode of ministry, yet Mother Teresa has been upheld as a model of selfless and compassionate service to the most vulnerable people. The smile of this tiny, wiry woman is still recognized worldwide over twenty years after her death. Yet these are her words: "The smile is a mask, a cloak that covers everything."

---

1. See John 6:5–7.
2. John 6:9, emphasis added.

What did Mother Teresa find a need to cover? Why did she describe her smile as a mask? Her prayer journal reads:

> So many unanswered questions live within me I am afraid to uncover them – because of the blasphemy. If there be God – please forgive me – when I try to raise my thoughts to Heaven . . . there is such convicting emptiness that those very thoughts return like sharp knives and hurt my very soul . . . I am told God loves me . . . and yet the reality of darkness and coldness and emptiness is so great that nothing touches my soul. Did I make a mistake in surrendering blindly to the Call of the Sacred Heart?[3]

Facing poverty, illness, deprivation, and suffering day in, day out, had taken a toll on her soul. Words like "dryness," "darkness," "loneliness," and "torture" are spread throughout *Come Be My Light*, the book in which Brian Kolodiejchuk compiled much of the correspondence between Mother Teresa and her confessors over a period of sixty-six years. As she took on the pain of others, Mother Teresa was unable to remain the impassive donor or distant benefactor. Her world was not divided into "us" and "them," the "haves" and the "have-nots." In contrast to worldly standards of belonging and value, she recognized a new "us," a people joined in brokenness and need for salvation. In the midst of her "dark night of the soul," she knew she was not some high and lofty minister who knew all the answers or owned all the solutions. She was one of those needy people. And only God could satisfy her thirst. Hence her yearning.

What about us, in this second decade of the twenty-first century, in a planet of rising waters and raging fires, in a world of resurgent nationalisms, blatant racisms, exclusionary ethnocentrisms, in communities racked with conflict and war? How can we combat exhaustion and nourish perseverance? What do we learn from Jesus and Mother Teresa? I suggest we are called to renew primarily three things: our sense of identity, our sense of sight, and our sense of time, all in light of God's identity, God's vision, and God's timing. Nothing more. Nothing less.

---

3. Mother Teresa and B. Kolodiejchuk, *Mother Teresa: Come Be My Light; The Private Writings of the "Saint of Calcutta"* (New York: Doubleday, 2007), 187.

A New Sense of "Us": Renewing Our Limited and Communal Identity in Light of God's Sovereign and Communal Identity

Recognizing God as the only Creator, Sustainer, and Saviour of the world puts us in the right place as human beings. Although we are created in the image of God, we are not the ultimate creators, sustainers, nor saviours of the world. We are created beings, part of the wonderfully rich and diverse creation community, moulded and sustained by the Word and the Spirit of the Community of Love.

As such, first, we are limited. Philip could not feed those thousands of hungry people. Mother Teresa could not assuage the hunger of every last poor person with whom she came into contact. We cannot cover all the bases. Neither are we meant to! The frustratingly good news is that neither you nor I can save the planet from the consequences of humanity's plunder. We cannot solve all the conflicts nor guarantee peace with justice the world round. We cannot usher in God's kingdom, the new heaven and the new earth. We need to renew our understanding of our identity and reconcile with our limitations. Do we want to persevere against all odds and carry through to the end? Then let's respond to Jesus's invitation: "Come to me, all you who are weary and burdened, and I will give you rest . . . For my yoke is easy and my burden is light."[4] When Jesus was burdened by the murder of his cousin by a corrupt government, when he was overwhelmed by the needs of people and overworked in responding to them, he withdrew to pray. We too need to take time out from the whirlwind of activity, projects, and programmes in order to take our questions to God, wrestle with and even complain to our loving Father about all that is wrong in the world, allowing that conversation to help put things in perspective, and wait on the Spirit to grant us rest. Only before God are we able to recognize and be at peace with the reality of our limitations.

Second, God's communal identity marks our identity as members of the creation community. God does not stand alone as a unitary, self-contained being. God is Community: Father, Son, and Holy Spirit. Likewise, all humans are beings-in-community, beautiful and wonderfully made, unworthy of God's love but recipients of it, regardless of the size of their bank account – or lack thereof – the letters before their name, the colour of their skin, or any other such humanly constructed distinguisher. Recognizing this dimension of our identity can rescue us again from an inflated sense of self and the consequent burden for that which is beyond the capacity of any one of us and which can only be tackled jointly, alongside others. Do we want to persevere against all

---

4. Matt 11:28, 30.

odds and carry through to the end? Then let's resist all forces that would set us apart from or above the people we serve. Like our Lord, let's move into the neighbourhood and there nourish a limited number of Spirit-led, lasting, life-transforming relations.

A New Sense of Sight: Revising Our Value System

In a world imprisoned by the illusion that bigger is always better, we need to refresh our vision in order that we might see the infinite value of that which is small, specific, local, personal. It was ludicrous to think that two fish and five chunks of bread could feed thousands. So instead of giving up his food, the logical thing would have been for the boy to hide behind a tree and eat on his own. And Andrew could easily have dismissed the boy's offer as naïvely simplistic. It is ludicrous to even imagine the possibility of abundance when our eyes see only deprivation. It is ludicrous to think that the sovereign God of the universe would choose to work through small, finite, and insignificant people like me and you. Yet God is the God of small things, of seeds planted deep in the ground that sprout in unexpected ways.

We need new eyes. Eyes to see beyond what *is* to what *should be*, what *can be*, what *will be*. Take, for example, the customary way in which we identify ourselves. Look at our name tags: they include our name and a country – the country of our birth or the country in which we currently live. And look at our displays of flags. These colourful pieces of cloth represent the nation states according to which we have become accustomed to classifying the world. Flags capture our imagination and bind us into submission to national and exclusionary constructs. The issue, you see, is that modern countries, with their flags, their borders, their structures, and authorities, are constructed and maintained, all too often, on the blood, sweat, and tears of people. We receive them as natural. That is the way things *are*; and we have a hard time seeing beyond. We need new eyes so we can recognize, as did the psalmist, that the entire earth belongs to God. No land is my land; no land is your land. No land, for that matter, belongs to any particular nation state – these modern constructs which society expects us to defend patriotically at all costs, to the detriment of the lives of their inhabitants and of the very land they claim as sovereign possession. All land belongs to God. And we, as God's children, must proclaim this, in bold word and consistent lifestyle, as eyewitnesses and life-witnesses of God's sovereign and loving rule within which the entire creation is invited to thrive. A new world is possible, not thanks to human savvy or willpower, but thanks to the never-ending love and grace of God, who has not abandoned, and will not abandon, the work of his hands. And one day, every tribe and every people group, women and men from all corners of this beautiful and bleeding planet, will fall to their knees and celebrate the rule of the servant King. We need eyes to see the world today in light of that day.

Meanwhile, while we await that day, we'd do well to heed this advice: "If you can't feed a hundred people, then feed just one. And we ourselves feel that what we are doing is just a drop in the ocean. But the ocean would be less because of that missing drop."[5] Do we want to persevere against all odds and carry through to the end? Then let's be the boy who offered his lunch. Let's see the potential of seeds sown, words of comfort offered, a touch, a listening ear. Let's not cease to do good, even if it does not repair national crises. Let's offer the insignificant, and wait on God's Spirit to do with it as God pleases.

A New Sense of Time: Recognizing into Whose Purposes We are Invited

In a world enamoured with the adrenaline rush of the instant, immediate, ever-present virtual reality, we need to recast our sense of time and recognize that we are invited to be witnesses of an agenda that is not merely ours. The drama of God's good purposes for the world began long before we entered it, and it will continue long after we depart.

Óscar Arnulfo Romero served as archbishop of El Salvador during the escalation of a civil war which was actually a proxy confrontation between the blocs of the global Cold War using Central American soil as their testing ground and Central American people as the cannon fodder on their chessboard. As a pastor to a people torn apart by army and guerrilla recruitment, kidnappings, mass killings, and emigration, Romero counselled the needy, preached the gospel, advocated, and spoke up for justice. Days after demanding that the army cease the violence, while he was administering Communion, he was murdered. He was a witness of God's purposes for God's world and God's people against all odds, in life and in death. You see, in most evangelical circles the concept of "witness" has become watered down to mean "giving verbal explanation of one's beliefs." Yet in biblical terms, "witness" means "martyr," one who puts one's own body on the line to attest to the life-truth on which one is grounded.

---

5. These words are attributed to Mother Teresa, but are "significantly paraphrased versions or personal interpretations of statements Mother Teresa made; they are not her authentic words." See "Quotes Falsely Attributed to Mother Teresa and Significantly Paraphrased Versions or Personal Interpretations of Statements That Are Not Her Authentic Words," Mother Teresa of Calcutta Center, accessed 2 October 2019, https://www.motherteresa.org/08_info/Quotesf.html.

Do we want to persevere against all odds and carry through to the end? Then let's pray that God's Spirit may grant us a new sense of time and help us recognize our small yet valuable place in God's good plans for the world God loves. Let's live as witnesses, prophets of a future that is not our own.

Martin Luther King Jr., another prophetic witness to God's good purposes, once said: "The arc of history is bending toward justice" (paraphrased).[6] God's future is one in which none have too little, and none have too much (and believe it or not, there *is* such a thing as having too much!); a new world in which *having* is not the measure of value, and justice, being in right relations, is of utmost importance; a new world devoid of deprivation and overflowing with abundance and gratitude; a world in which two fish and five loaves feed thousands and no one goes hungry; a world in which God's will is fulfilled.

Truly, our brother and Lord, the Messiah Jesus, did get tired. At times, he felt overwhelmed. He spent time wrestling with God and asked that the cup of suffering be taken from him. Yet he persevered, fulfilling the part of God's mission entrusted to him while he was on the earth. And through his self-giving and his triumph over death, he opened a new chapter in the history of humanity. We live on this side of the empty tomb; and no matter how dark the horizon may look, we can trust that a new day will dawn. Not by our efforts, but by God's overabundant grace. Meanwhile, may God's Spirit continue granting us all renewed identity, new sight, and a new sense of time so that we may stand against all odds and even against all ends in full confidence that there is not death but abundant life at the end of God's story.

---

6. "The arc of the moral universe is long, but it bends toward justice" is Martin Luther King Jr.'s paraphrase of a portion of a sermon delivered in 1853 by the abolitionist minister Theodore Parker.

21

Resilience and Disaster and the Church's Response

Johannes Reimer

Disasters: Where Do They Come From?

Our English word "disaster" comes from the ancient Greek and may be translated as "bad star." The ancient Greeks believed that disasters, both natural and human-made, appeared because of a bad constellation of stars. The astrologically influenced worldview of the Greeks gave the people a sense of divine interference when disasters interrupted their normal lives. We find similar ideas in many other cultures. In Germany we still say "hell is loose" when we face disasters. A disaster is in principle negative, often uncontrollable by humans, a fate beyond human influence.

In today's more sophisticated worldview we know that many of our natural disasters are made by humans. To a great extent, humanity causes nature to react. Think of global warming and the effect this has on our world. We are right, therefore, to discuss the cause of disasters in the world and the role of the church of Christ in preventing them, on the one hand, and creating, if possible, resilient communities around the world, on the other.

Hell Will Not Prevail

Jesus promised Peter that he would build his church and added, "and the gates of Hades will not overcome it." The gate in an ancient city was the place where the kings and judges sat and determined the destiny of their people. To say "I will build my church, and the gates of Hades will not overcome it" means nothing less than that Jesus's church will keep hell out of the world. Does this apply to disasters? If a disaster is a human-made "hell," it does indeed. Hell originally describes a never-ending disaster beyond human control. Jesus's promise is beyond comprehension. What kind of church does he see? How does the church he is building keep hell out of the gate?

Jesus Is Building the *Ecclesia*

The church Jesus promised to build is called *ecclesia*, a term seldom used for a religious gathering in the ancient world. It stands for a community called out of their daily life to accept responsibility for the sociocultural space they live in. In the Greek city-state, the *polis*, *ecclesia* was the local parliament which decided all community-related issues. Calling his church *ecclesia*, Jesus suggests it is a fellowship of people called out of the world to accept responsibility for the world. In Matthew 5:13–15 he calls his followers the salt of the earth and the light of the world. And he sends them to the ends of the world to make all *ethne* his disciples living under his life-giving rule. Jesus sends his disciples as the Father has sent him (John 20:21) to reconcile the world to God (2 Cor 5:18–20).

The church Jesus is building is not of the world, but in the world, responsible for the life of the world in all its dimensions. The disasters of the world are directly related to the church's divine responsibility. The church's mission includes ending all injustice and "hell"-related corruption in whatever form it may appear.

To be honest, the church of today is anything but the *ecclesia* of Jesus. Instead of being responsible for the world, it has widely withdrawn itself from the world. Most of our evangelical churches seem largely preoccupied with their own internal issues. The world is considered a sinful place and church members are advised to leave the world altogether. The aim is to be prepared when Jesus returns and takes us home to heaven. And, of course, the church does not want to see the sinners in the world perish. The mission of the majority of evangelicals is, therefore, evangelism of the individual, saving precious souls, and not so much transformation of the world. Relief, development, and transformation might be diaconal expressions of some church members, but they are not the heart of God's intention. Mission is first evangelism, as the

Lausanne Covenant of 1974 states.¹ Social engagement is viewed as an ethical consequence of evangelism.²

There are, of course, churches that have been actively involved in holistic transformation, but the vast majority of evangelicals have entrusted all social engagement into the hands of individuals starting Christian NGOs and expected them to respond to disasters in social as well as economic arenas. This has become one of the greatest problems, as I see it. Without the church in the community, the gates are wide open to hell, and disasters do not decrease but seem to increase daily. Why? And what is the role of the church in all of this?

The World without a Responsible Church

What happens when the church leaves the public square?

The New Testament calls the church of Christ a royal priesthood (1 Pet 2:9–10). It has a clearly defined threefold political mission: (1) to be a dedicated priest interceding for the world before the throne of God; (2) to be a prophetic voice to the world's powers, calling the world to justice and truth and pointing out corruption; and (3) to be an active royal agent of change engaged in community transformation.³

Whenever the church leaves the world it takes things away with it, including its prayer support, its critical voice, its exposure of the powerful in their wrongdoing, and its role as an active agent transforming local communities into places of the common good in fullness of life under God's divine rule. All these thing go when the church withdraws. The church builds a wall between the world and the powers of hell. Take the church away, and the gates of the world will be taken by hell. Disasters are among the dark consequences.

But does not the church have its hands and feet in Christian NGOs? Christian NGOs are not, in all honesty, in a position to substitute for what God has assigned to the church. God has never advised his people to create NGOs. They are a direct result of a church neglecting its mission. Born in the disobedience of the church to God's calling, NGOs may strive to become the extended arms of *ecclesia*. In reality, however, they exist in the constant danger of leaving the church altogether and becoming social businesses fulfilling the

---

1. See J. R. W. Stott, *The Lausanne Covenant: Complete Text with Study Guide* (Peabody, MA: Hendrickson, 2012), 4.

2. Stott, *Lausanne Covenant*, 5.

3. For more see J. Reimer, *Missio Politica: The Mission of Church and Politics* (Carlisle: Langham, 2017).

will of those who support their enterprise. And being donor-centred they will soon destroy more than they build. Glenn J. Schwartz, in his widely read book on charity, convincingly proves that well-meaning charity destroys dignity and creates dependency.[4] Bringing the church back on the scene as the major agent of God's mission creates a healthy environment not only for the world, but also for all those (Western) NGOs without patterns of a responsible kingdom spirit.

To summarize: without the church, the world turns dark, because the light is gone. The world without a church is less fruitful, because salt is not available, and, as a result, God the Father is not praised (Matt 5:13–16).

How Should the Church Respond to the Disasters in the World?

The church of Christ is confronted by increasing numbers of disasters in the world today. What can and must the church do? How should the church respond? According to Jesus's intention of building his church in the world, it must respond in important ways.

First, the church must return to its Christ-given ecclesial nature. To do so, the church will have to repent of how it relates to the world. We do well to remind the church of what it is and what Jesus intended by creating it.

Second, the church must accept its missional task and accept responsibility for the world. It will critically observe the world around it and become a prophetic voice exposing the powerful of the world in their irresponsible exploitation of our world's natural and social capital for their own profit.

The church will engage in creative and royal community and creation care in the name of God the King, building his kingdom, step by step, in all four corners of the world. It will do so as God's divine royal agent, accompanying critically all those NGOs involved in the very same mission of transformation.

And it will be a great priest, spending intentional time in prayer for the world, expecting God's divine protection and direct involvement in our destiny. The promise of Jesus is unprecedented: the recovery of the church will push hell out of the gates of the world, and communities will become more and more resilient to disasters.

---

4. G. Schwartz, *When Charity Destroys Dignity: Overcoming Unhealthy Dependency in the Christian Movement* (Bloomington, IN: AuthorHouse, 2007).

Part 4

Resilience, Mobilization, and Partnerships

22

Building Resilience with Local Churches and Communities

Jané Mackenzie, Chris McDonald, Stanley Enock, and Mari Williams

> I have learnt that the best way to succeed is to find ways of making the community do the things themselves. Then they will produce the information and strategies themselves. (Community facilitator in Zimbabwe)

Tearfund has been working with poor and vulnerable communities for more than fifty years. Our vision is to see each person living to his or her full potential and able to *cope with shocks or stresses without crisis, and to recover quickly.*

This chapter will unpack some of the learning and reflections gleaned by our staff, peer agencies, partners, and community members about how we can partner with churches and communities to build resilience. This is an evolving process. Our aim in this chapter is to reflect and share where we are at, and to share our learning and plans going forward.

Tearfund believes the local church has a significant role to play in helping communities to build their resilience. This is called church and community transformation (CCT) and is one of our corporate priorities. Within CCT there are many different approaches and processes, all of which have the aim of seeing transformation in communities, recognizing the role the church has to play. This chapter focuses on our CCT resilience approach, which is an approach that can be used alongside, in response to, or after existing CCT approaches. It is helpful where there is a recognized need in the context to engage with disaster preparedness and mitigation. This approach emphasizes the role of the church, participation of the community, analysis of vulnerability, appreciating the potential within the community, and practical application. This is not just about following an approach but also appreciating partnership and valuing networks to encourage learning, best practice, reflection, and sustainability. By putting resilience at the centre of this CCT approach we are really seeking to learn together what resilience means for us as an organization, our partners, and for the local contexts within which we work.

This is not the work of one person or partner but comes out of our partnership with many different organizations, practitioners, and people who exist within churches and communities who are willing to share and learn together.

In this chapter we use the following acronyms and phrases:

- PADR: Participatory Assessment of Disaster Risk
- CCT: church and community transformation
- CCM: church and community mobilization
- CCT resilience approach: the approach which this chapter focuses on
- NGO: non-governmental organization

Learning from Zimbabwe

During the El Niño crisis in Zimbabwe in 2016 we wanted to respond in a way which went beyond just focusing on the hazard, but looked deeper at the drivers of vulnerability and what opportunities might exist within the community to mitigate the impact of El Niño and other risks the community might face. These communities were already involved in a CCT approach called church and community mobilization (CCM). CCM starts with the church so that they can work with the community to identify their dreams, and to recognize and utilize their resources to make these dreams a reality.

We wanted to respond to El Niño in a way that didn't conflict with CCM and create dependency. It was therefore decided that we needed more explicitly to explore risks with CCM by introducing a simplified Participatory Assessment of Disaster Risk (PADR).[1] By adding a simplified version of PADR to CCM it encouraged communities and churches to identify their vulnerabilities with underlying causes and, from this, work together on risk mitigation measures and prepare for and respond to future disasters. The value of this approach was in promoting preparedness by anticipating hazards and making adaptations to

---

1. A community-based process to assess and reduce risk.

reduce their impacts, by creating an environment for partnership, reflection, action, and mutual learning in order to build resilience.

We have called this our CCT resilience approach as it is not as detailed as PADR and has emphasis on the role of the church and facilitation. This was introduced as a pilot project to three communities in Zimbabwe that had already been through CCM through a training workshop. It had a strong emphasis on practical outworking and on critical reflection on facilitation and participation. This was important, because while we want to be facilitative and participatory, this doesn't necessarily mean that we actually are! Therefore we built peer-to-peer feedback on facilitation and participation into the training. What this approach brings to CCM is an emphasis on facilitation, participation, and inclusion as essential, emphasizing that resilience cannot be built unless we intentionally involve those most vulnerable to hazards. And in order to achieve this we must be sensitive to facilitate in a way that considers participation and power. The value of adding this to CCM is that the church and community are already organized and have a recognition of their capacity and of the value of working together. Therefore adding in this additional approach can utilize CCM to also build resilience.

This approach has also been used in Uganda and Haiti, with plans to scale up to other contexts.

Overview of the CCT Resilience Approach

This CCT resilience approach is bringing together our experience of working with churches globally to create a flexible, simple, community-led approach to resilience. Our aim is that churches and communities assess their own risk, vulnerability, and capacity, and identify actions that they can take to reduce that risk, where possible using local skills and knowledge, and where appropriate making use of external support. The aim of this approach is to set in motion a learning culture which facilitates resilient actions and reveals where additional support might be needed.

To do this we have proposed an approach with the steps outlined below, with accompanying games and Bible studies. This is not to be prescriptive, and we encourage facilitators to use other related tools and Bible studies that they feel will work better in their context. Once field-tested and refined, the tools will form part of Tearfund's resource *Reveal: Tools to Support Community Transformation*.

This CCT resilience approach benefits from the existing strengths of our PADR process. Most of our CCT approaches aim to have facilitators from the church and community level, so a simplified version will be more readily adopted and owned at this level. We believe the social capital that exists within churches and communities is significant in building resilience, so this approach recognizes the value of networks for ownership, follow-up, and expertise. This adaptation links Bible studies to each step and focuses not just on carrying out the steps, but also on emphasizing the importance of inclusion and participation. Many of the tools within each step existed already in our publications, but some have been created specifically to encourage church- and community-level engagement.

CCT Resilience Approach

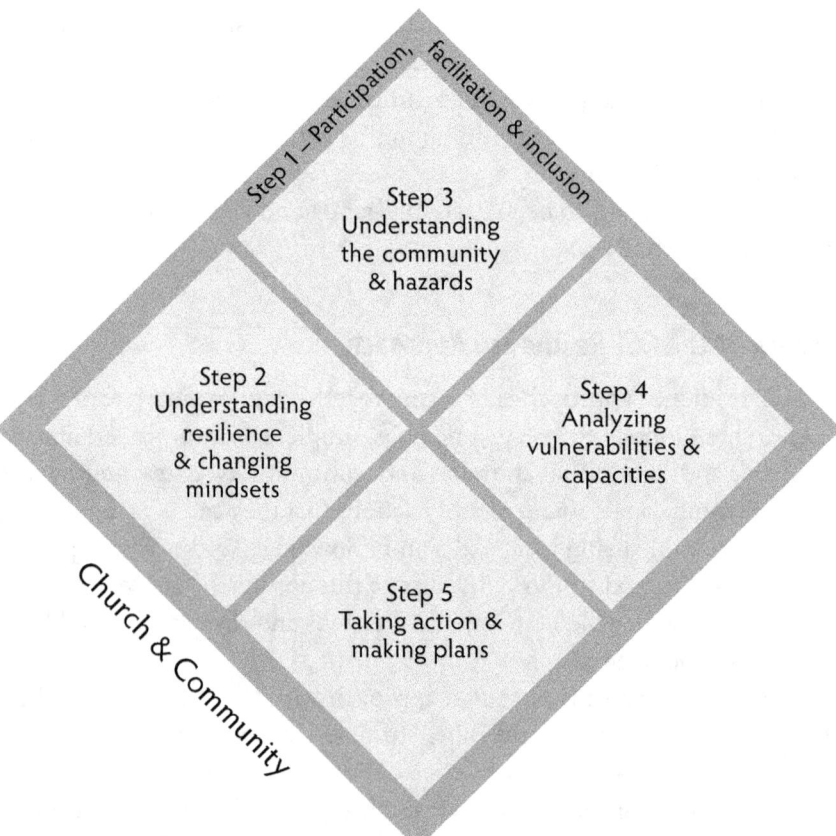

Figure 22.1 CCT Resilience Approach

- *Step 1: Facilitation, inclusion, and participation*
    Facilitation skills and tips
    Activity: Inclusion
    Bible study: God's purpose for humankind
    Activity: Participation/contested chairs
- *Step 2: Resilience and the disaster cycle*
    Bible study: God of justice and mercy
    Activity: What do we mean by resilience?
    Activity: The need to prepare – reducing the effects of disasters
- *Step 3: Getting to know the community and hazards*
    Tool: Getting to know the community
    Tool: Identifying potential hazards
- *Step 4: Vulnerability and capacity assessment*
    Game: Making the longest line
    Bible study: Elisha and the jars
    Tool: Vulnerability and capacity assessment
- *Step 5: Taking action*
    Bible study: Assessing the city
    Tool: Minibus planning exercise

Step 1: Facilitation, Participation, and Inclusion

This emphasis is "Their ideas, not ours. Their change, not yours." We believe that lasting change can be achieved only by making sure we listen to the community and take time to understand the context. Therefore good facilitation is essential and foundational to this process and creates space for people to rethink the problems they face (both now and in the future). This is about more than just a facilitator's skills; it is a fundamental belief that people can solve their own problems given the right support. Our learning globally within CCT and beyond demonstrates that the role of facilitator is crucial in drawing out the wealth of knowledge in the local church and community. There is a clear link between good facilitation and impact.

We must seek to ensure representation from different parts of the community, especially the poorest and those most impacted by disasters, and to guide them through the different steps of the process. Our approach is to empower, not to teach, and to be open to hearing unexpected things. We are willing to focus on any risk that the community wants to discuss, and to not necessarily focus on the most obvious. The workshop doesn't have to be about "disasters" or "climate change"; it could be about local markets or advocacy. This

CCT resilience approach is to create a space to be open to the issues that affect the community the most. This may reveal issues that need additional support and training, such as advocacy or dealing with sensitive or taboo subjects. Support for this may be sought within the partner or other organizations in the area, or from related technical publications such as other tools within Tearfund's resource *Reveal: Tools to Support Community Transformation*.

It is important that we take time to understand the power dynamics within the community and what barriers there might be to all people participating. An important consideration is that we explore how different people and groups are vulnerable to hazards. Not everyone will be affected in the same way, so we must consider who are the most vulnerable.

Step 2: Resilience and the Disaster Cycle

We all come with our own appreciation of resilience. Therefore it's important that we take time to hear and understand how the community understand resilience. We have found that using a collection of images can be a good way to facilitate people to describe their understanding of resilience and encourage them to move beyond outside definitions to their own experience of resilience in their own words. Finding local words for resilience is key and helps to expand our resilience understanding to be more holistic.

Exploring how we might respond to disasters, and using the disaster cycle, encourages us to think beyond response to preparedness, mitigation, and recovery.

Step 3: Getting to Know the Community and Hazards

The purpose of this step is to create space for exploration of the community and reflection on the hazards and disasters they might face. Doing a transect walk and developing a community map gives a good base to uncover hazards in the next step and is a reference point for further discussion.

Following the step above and using a timeline we focus on the hazards that are most likely and most impactful. Analysis is encouraged of the human impact (life and health), the social impact (community structure or education), the constructed impact (buildings and infrastructure), the environmental impact (resources such as water and land), and the economic impact.

Step 4: Vulnerability and Capacity Assessment

Having identified significant hazards, we then consider who is most vulnerable and why. Following this we explore and emphasize that there are capacities within the community, the aim being to reduce the vulnerabilities and strengthen the capacities in order to mitigate the risks associated with the identified hazards and to respond to the possible disasters. This information is used to identify both mitigation and preparedness responses.

Step 5: Taking Action

Having identified responses to hazards the final step is to make realistic and robust plans so that action is owned and taken by the community.

Framework of Resilience

Resilience is wider than disaster risk reduction (DRR). While a significant "disaster" can be a catalyst for churches wanting to engage with communities around preparedness, and often the church and other local actors are the first responders in communities, we need to broaden our approach and practice to be around resilience. DRR is a starting point, but this and other approaches need to engage wider aspects. Through this process which is more open there is scope for actions and hazards to be identified, and from here the partner and community can assess what relevant experience and inputs are needed to take that action. These may exist within the community, or facilitators could draw upon Tearfund's global learning. For example, when this process was carried out in Haiti, it was identified that they needed to engage with the local government. In order to achieve this, they could either engage with others in Haiti who had experience of advocacy, or draw on Tearfund's advocacy guide for churches.

The concept of resilience is universal, but it needs to be contextualized based on various socio-economic and other factors. In Zimbabwe, when leading a reflection on resilience, it became clear that meeting people's livelihood needs was essential in resilience. Achieving resilience without sustainable livelihoods is a big challenge. This aligns with the recent Zimbabwe evaluation that states that unless people's daily needs are met, engagement with this process and CCM will decline. This highlights the reality that we need to look at the underlying factors that help people better cope with shocks and stresses. DRR tends to be hazard-focused (on big known risks like earthquakes, droughts, or floods). Resilience, on the other hand, is people-focused and also helps people deal with increasing uncertainty/variability (e.g. from climate change). Therefore it is important we hold a broader framework of resilience, as explored below.

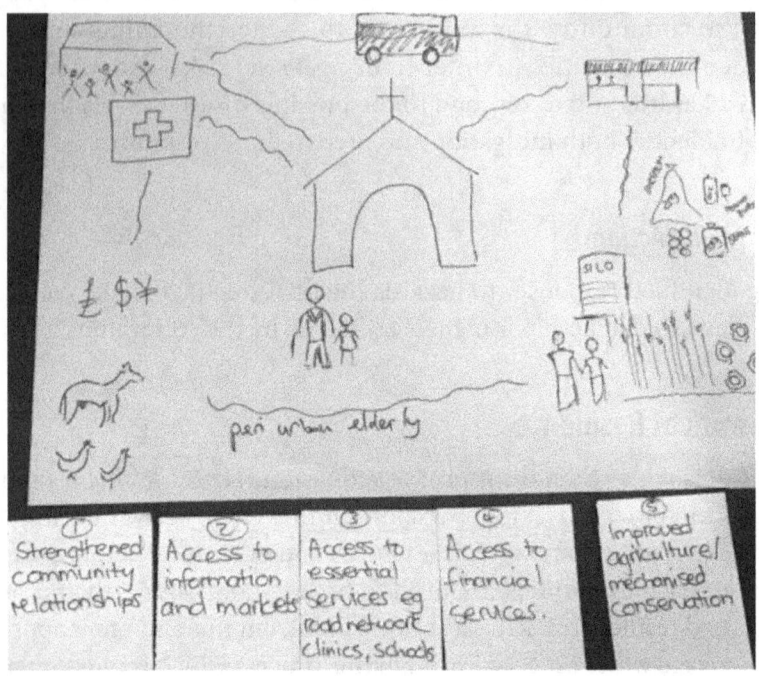

Figure 22.2: Workshop in Zimbabwe on resilience which explored what a resilient community looked like.

Tearfund understands the ability of people and communities to *cope without crisis and recover quickly* as being founded on six pillars, as shown below in figure 22.3:

Disaster risk management includes DRR and disaster preparedness where the emphasis is on reducing and managing *known risks*. It describes efforts by governments, civil society, the private sector, and the wider international community to reduce the impact of shocks and stresses, recognizing that all have a role as part of a system. National governments have primary responsibility to reduce both exposure and vulnerability of their citizens to shocks and stresses – including risk-reducing development policy, early warning, action for anticipated large-scale hazards (such as a storm or drought), disaster response, and recovery. However, Tearfund and our partners can play a part in influencing and assisting governments to help the most vulnerable as well as aiding individuals and communities in identifying, assessing, and managing what they consider to be the most important risks.

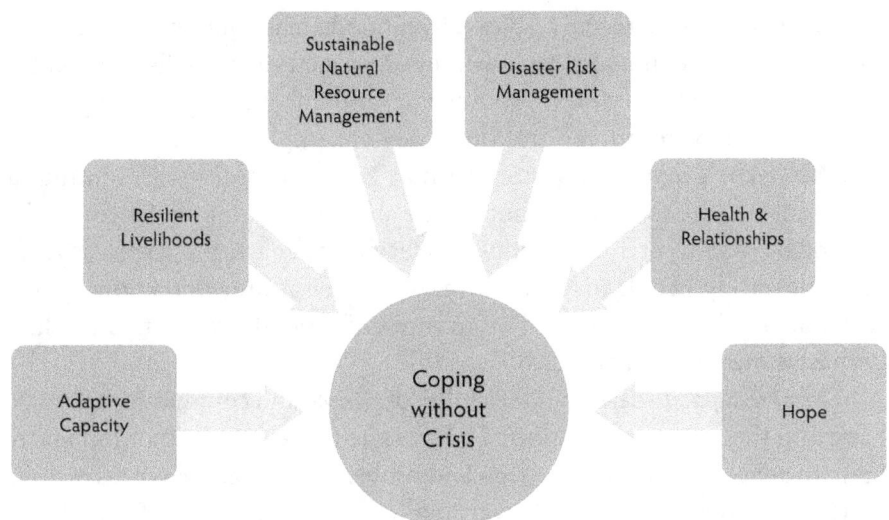

Figure 22.3: Tearfund's resilience framework

Resilient livelihoods describes income and food sources that are secure, risk-diversified, and flexible. "Secure" here describes predictability of return. For example, the return on agricultural livelihoods, beyond weather variability, may be linked to security of land tenure (and dispute resolution), invasive pests and diseases, violent conflict leading to lack of land access, uncertainty in the cost of inputs, and sale price of produce. "Risk-diversified" describes having several different income streams which are not all susceptible to the same known risk. For example, if there is a risk of drought where the primary household livelihood is rain-fed agriculture, having income from another less-drought-affected livelihood, say, repairing bicycles, means that the household does not lose all its income in times of drought. "Flexible" describes being able to choose different livelihood strategies depending on the opportunities available. It is aided by strengthened market access to buy and sell, adding value to products and services, savings to smooth variation in income and expenditure, credit to invest in opportunities, technical and business skills, and active social networks. For example, having access to credit through self-help group savings may enable a member to either scale up an existing livelihood or start a new one. Or being part of active social networks may lead to collective buying when prices are low and selling when they are high: sharing the risk with other people.

Sustainable natural resource management describes the use and care of natural resources that results in their long-term flourishing for the good of all.

The success of natural resource-based livelihoods relies not only on access to assets and resources but also on how they are used. Having skills and abilities alone is not enough; the rules – both formal and informal – governing access to environmental resources and how they are implemented must also be favourable. For example, a pastoralist may know of traditional, communal dry season pasture for animals but not be able to use it due to fencing off of that land by recently arrived wealthy people who are able to pay to privatize the land. Conversely, people may cut down trees to sell as firewood knowing they are damaging the environment but, in times of acute shock or stress, lacking alternative means to buy food.

Adaptive capacity describes the ability of people and communities to make changes in their lives and livelihoods. Key factors that may help or hinder the ability to adapt are critical reflection and problem-solving, awareness of risks, ability to appropriately use early warning (especially climate) information to reduce risk, knowing what external support (e.g. government entitlement) is available and being able to access it, experimentation, and innovation.

Health and relationships describes the physical, mental, and social well-being that enables active engagement. It is underpinned by social connectedness, seen in healthy meaningful relationships, and access to services – such as health care and education – that are themselves resilient to shocks and stresses.

Hope describes the personal belief that despite current problems things will improve, that in the long run good will win and justice will prevail (e.g. Isa 40:31; Jer. 29:11; 1 Cor 15). This is often based on a faith worldview that there is more than can be seen. In adversity, hope helps people recover more quickly from personal trauma, being thankful that they have survived.

Lessons Learned So Far

Tearfund seeks to create learning opportunities around this CCT resilience approach. This has been with colleagues and peer agencies in a number of countries, including Zimbabwe, Haiti, Uganda, Indonesia, Bangladesh, and Nepal.

The Role of the Local Church

As described in the introduction, Tearfund believes the church has an important role to play in communities, in bringing transformation and working with communities to achieve this. In our trialling of this approach and others over the years, the use of Scripture has been important in increasing the engagement of churches as it has showed people that this isn't something separate from church life but rather enables them to work for God's kingdom. It moves resilience from being a development term to a practical outworking of their faith. Faith plays an important part in the lives of many people in the countries in which we are working, so when we seek to engage communities, it is important that we are able to communicate in this language.

Another key aspect is using the Bible to unpack how churches and communities view disasters, and to uncover any unhelpful beliefs around hazards and disasters that hinder or prevent action. This process needs to be embedded within an existing understanding of integral mission[2] and a belief that the church is called to work in partnership with the community and those who are most vulnerable in working towards transformation. Therefore it is important to ensure that this fits within an existing strategy and journey of local churches and is not seen as a one-off NGO exercise. This must also be done recognizing the churches' own biases and barriers to working with others. Those supporting churches must be continually walking with them to assess who is engaging in the process and who might be being missed.

One of Tearfund's main CCT approaches is CCM – a process that seeks to mobilize churches and communities to work together to bring transformation. While this has been impactful it doesn't explicitly seek to identify hazards. Therefore, in particularly vulnerable contexts, integrating this CCT resilience approach could bring even greater change for resilience outcomes. As explained above, in Zimbabwe this process was introduced by training three communities that had already been through the whole of CCM. A recent review of CCM work in Zimbabwe indicated that while CCM has had an impact, in areas that had been hit hard by drought and other slow-onset disasters engagement with CCM decreased. This suggests that we need to be making sure at the planning stage that people's interests and immediate needs are met in order for them to be able to engage in this approach. This echoes another piece of research in Tanzania that found that while CCM brought significant gains for those within CCM, often those who were most marginalized and vulnerable were not able to participate and were therefore left behind. This exclusion created a greater gap between the vulnerable and others in the community. Therefore we need to be more intentional in the design of the CCM and CCT resilience approach so that it includes those who are most vulnerable and addresses people's needs.

---

2. "Integral mission" is defined as the work of the church in contributing to the positive physical, spiritual, economic, psychological, and social transformation of people.

Stanley Enock, a CCM trainer in Zimbabwe, suggests this process could be used with CCM at the "church and community description" stage of CCM, as at this stage the church and the community (including business community, NGOs, etc.) would have begun establishing organic relationships which are critical for resilience work. Social capital is a key factor in the sustainability of resilience work. At the church and description stage the community is answering these questions: "Where are we coming from?" and "Where are we?" Communities use ten tools such as seasonal calendars, a community resource map, and historical trends analysis to answer the two questions. The hazard, capacity, and vulnerability assessment basically asks the same questions as those asked at the church and community description stage. In addition, the same tools are used; for instance, when profiling a hazard one needs to look at historical trends.

What Does the CCT Resilience Approach Add to the CCM Process?

- It promotes "a culture of preparedness" which ensures that the development gains brought through various CCM initiatives can be protected in the event of disasters like drought and floods in Zimbabwe. Communities become disaster-conscious when planning and developing infrastructure; for example, in thinking where to locate a school, and what materials to use.
- It further strengthens the concepts of use of locally available resources. Capacity assessment in this process, although it also looks at external resources, helps the community to identify the local resources the community can harness to reduce vulnerability to a hazard. In this regard it can help to significantly reduce dependency on food aid as a drought risk management strategy.
- It builds the capacity of the community in initiatives that they have embarked on through CCM. For instance, in Zimbabwe, the communities have embraced conservation farming as a strategy for enhancing food security. It has helped communities approach farming as a business so as to ensure they gain an income in addition to being food secure.

Recommendations to Others

- There is need to ensure that resilience is not introduced as a different subject but flows with the CCM work. The Bible study "God's Purpose for Humanity" is a good start for introducing resilience issues. If the community has been implementing projects it will be good to discuss resilience issues in the context of sustainability of development initiatives.
- It is paramount to train facilitators in both theory and practical facilitation skills. The theory will focus on helping them understand disaster preparedness. The practical aspect of this training that focuses on facilitating and participation will help the facilitators gain skills and confidence in facilitating the tools in a community.
- There needs to be a good pool of community-based facilitators who are able to train this CCT resilience approach. The contexts (hazards, vulnerabilities, and capacity) differ and community-based facilitators will be better placed than external trainers to deliver training in their context.

Working with Networks

In Haiti, resilience training was delivered to a network of Christian NGOs comprised of organizations that have different models for mobilizing churches and communities. Some had a focus on education, some on self-help groups (SHGs), others on church mobilization, and so on, but they were united under a commitment to increase resilience. This network was convened by Tearfund Haiti but now exists as a separate entity. Training for the CCT resilience approach was introduced with the aim of developing church-level contingency plans that would be simple and practical, encouraging ownership. Since the training each organization has adapted the CCT resilience approach to its own ways of working and context. Training within a network is helpful as some organizations have greater experience of certain aspects of the CCT resilience approach and are able to share and encourage others on that step. A challenge for Tearfund is not just to run training without any follow-up, and this network has built in peer support and therefore ongoing engagement.

Importance of Facilitators and Participation

This CCT resilience approach emphasizes the role of facilitators and the participation of vulnerable groups. This is not because it is seen to be good practice, but because we believe that unless we listen to, involve, learn from and act together with all groups, we will not see resilience and transformation. The quality of facilitation is consistently identified in our evaluations as key in CCT and influencing good practice. In the recent review of CCM in Zimbabwe, the facilitators' peer review showed that there is a direct link between facilitators scoring high and the impact of CCM in communities. When introducing this CCT resilience approach in Zimbabwe and Haiti, a key emphasis was that this shouldn't be seen merely as training in theory and tools, but that there should also be practice and reflection on engagement and participation. This was done by using peer assessment, asking those who had been trained to grade each other on different aspects of facilitation. Emphasizing the importance of constant reflection on facilitation and participation, and including fieldwork in the training, also assisted in this.

Valuing the Abilities People Have

A key part of our work is that we don't want to create dependency. Rather, we want to encourage individuals and communities to realize their potential and ability to act. We also want to identify where there might be gaps or needs, and to creatively work with the partner and other national actors to meet those needs. The capabilities aspect of this process encourages communities to feel enabled to act. It was found in Zimbabwe that while CCM communities where this CCT resilience approach was introduced were better at using the resources they had more efficiently, this could be done more sustainably. The environment is obviously an important aspect of resilience and therefore this aspect of the process needs to emphasize the sustainable utilization of resources. In a review of our historic work using a resource called "Disasters and the Local Church," it was seen that the church has a significant role and capacity to play around peace-building, psychosocial support, and addressing taboos.

Next Steps

Going forward, Tearfund will be evolving this CCT resilience approach as we work collaboratively with our partners to fill gaps and strengthen opportunities that exist in this area. We have identified focus countries and strategic networks to learn with and build capacity. Through these we will pilot this approach to make adaptations and collate learning. As part of this phase, we will be seeking learning opportunities to review and research the impact and relevance of this CCT approach in building resilience. We will be considering how we will engage with the wider aspects of resilience and make appropriate linkages.

In order to understand how resilience is being built we will develop indicators based upon the resilience framework to feed into pilot CCT projects and for ongoing monitoring approaches and other CCT approaches.

Inclusion continues to be a challenge, as often those most vulnerable to hazards and disasters are either stigmatized or invisible and therefore excluded. Or, at times, their needs are so extreme that they are not reached by these types of interventions. Therefore we need to find a balance in how we can truly engage with those most affected by hazards and disasters.

The structures that exist around this approach are as important as the approach itself. Examples of these structures are the wider church denomination, local community actors, and networks that already exist. Being conscious and strategic in these linkages, to challenge unjust ones and utilize potential, is an ongoing priority. This is twofold in that these structures encourage ownership, follow-up, and peer support, and also hold capacity and resources beyond those which exist in the community.

We recognize there is a need to understand how we link to other areas, and that this approach might reveal the need for technical support in areas such as livelihoods, advocacy, peace-building, urbanization, and the environment. This follows on from our appreciation of resilience being much wider than just DRR, as expressed in our resilience framework. It is of huge importance to us that we are not imposing outside expertise on churches and communities, or turning local actors into NGOs, but working in partnership to agree relevant actions and support, following the lead of the church and community. Our observation is that this approach can reveal such gaps and opportunities. We will therefore be continuing to assess how this approach will be adapted within our partners' work, and existing CCT approaches, so that it can enhance resilience.

23

Church and Community Mobilization in Cooperation to Build Resilient Communities in South East Asia

Fennelien Stal, Debora Suparni, Arshinta Soemarsono, and Norman Franklin C. Agustin

To build the resilience of communities to disasters in Indonesia and the Philippines, Yayasan Sion, Lingap Pangkabataan Incorporated (LPI), YAKKUM, and Tear Netherlands have partnered to establish a network and a community of practice (CoP). By presenting these two cases we show in this chapter how resilience can be built through church and community mobilization processes that are owned and resourced by communities themselves. Churches have a valuable position for initiating these processes, and these processes encourage an integrated approach which is essential to resilience-building. Furthermore, forming networks or CoPs supports and equips member churches and organizations to bring change in their communities, and it enables churches and organizations to cooperate on multi-stakeholder platforms, which increases their ability to influence social, political, and economic systems in such a way that communities in Indonesia and the Philippines will become more resilient to shocks and stresses.

The Asia-Pacific region is the region of the world that is most affected by natural disasters. The frequency and intensity of natural disasters such as floods, tropical cyclones, and droughts are increasing due to climate change. Vulnerable communities and countries with little capacity to prepare for or respond to disasters are hit hardest by disasters. Disasters destroy their livelihoods and assets, trapping people in poverty and leading to increasing inequality. Moreover, natural disasters can create unstable social and economic situations which can form the basis for conflicts. At the same time, conflicts undermine the capacity of communities and countries to prevent and respond to natural disasters and crises.[1]

To reduce the vulnerability of communities in South East Asia to disasters, starting in Indonesia and the Philippines, Yayasan Sion, Lingap Pangkabataan Incorporated (LPI), YAKKUM, and Tear Netherlands work in partnership with churches and organizations to build resilience in an effective and sustainable way. In this chapter, we share our experience and argue that building resilient communities can best be done in processes that are owned and resourced by local communities. These processes are initiated by churches which are supported and equipped by cooperation in networks and communities of practice (CoPs) to bring change in their community.

Rationale

A large number of international aid organizations provide humanitarian assistance to vulnerable countries and communities in South East Asia after they are hit by disasters.

However, the challenge we face is that the risk and scale of natural disasters are increasing much faster than the degree to which the communities and countries are becoming resilient to these disasters. We define resilience as "the ability to cope with shocks or stresses without crisis and recover quickly."[2] We see resilience-building as a call to move from responding to the needs of those impacted by shocks and stresses after a disaster or conflict, to reducing the likelihood and severity of a disaster or conflict before it happens. Building resilience is therefore not about helping people rebuild their lives in the same way, through which they remain vulnerable to the same disaster or conflict striking them; resilience-building is about helping people and communities to reduce their vulnerability so that they are not so badly impacted in the first

---

1. United Nations ESCAP, Leave No One Behind: Disaster Resilience for Sustainable Development; Asia-Pacific Disaster Report 2017 (Bangkok: United Nations ESCAP, 2018), accessed 5 October 2019, http://www.unescap.org/publications/asia-pacific-disaster-report-2017-leave-no-one-behind.

2. C. McDonald, "From Disasters to Resilience: When Disasters Strike What Makes the Difference between Those Who Cope Well and Those Who Don't?," 1, Micah Global: 7th Global Consultation, Philippines, 2018, accessed 5 October 2019, https://www.micahglobal.org/sites/default/files/doc/page/chris_mcdonald_tearfund_from_disasters_to_resilience_for_micah_trienniel.pdf.

place.³ In the context of a development project we often use the term "disaster risk reduction," which we see as an important component of resilience-building.⁴

As partners we work on building resilient communities because disasters and conflicts pose a serious threat to their sustainable development. We believe that building resilience can best be done in cooperation and through transformational processes.

Church and Transformation

As Christian organizations our natural network through which we can access vulnerable communities is the global church. We work through local churches worldwide on the basis of our shared faith and values. We believe that the global church is called by God to fight poverty and injustice and to work towards creating flourishing and resilient communities. Working with churches brings three key advantages to our resilience-building work, in that local churches are integral, inspirational, and influential (see box).⁵

> **Why We Work with the Church**
>
> *Integral*: The situation of the church in local communities affords the benefits of
> • Access
> • Immediacy
> • Sustainability
>
> *Inspirational*: The Christian identity of the church acts as an asset in
> • A whole-person approach
> • A biblical mandate to help those in need
> • The influence of church leaders
>
> *Influential*: The reach of the church at all levels, from local communities to international organizations, gives it
> • The influence to shape attitudes and the ability to speak up on behalf of the poor and oppressed.

---

3. McDonald, "From Disasters to Resilience," 1.

4. The definition of DRR by the United Nations International Strategy for Disaster Reduction (UNISDR) is "the concept and practice of reducing disaster risks through systematic efforts to analyse and manage the causal factors of disasters," including "reducing exposure to hazards, lessening vulnerability of people and property, wise management of land and the environment, and improving preparedness for adverse events." "What Is Disaster Risk Reduction?," UNISDR, 2018, accessed 5 October 2019, https://eird.org/esp/acerca-eird/liderazgo/perfil/what-is-drr.html.

5. L. Wooly, "Integral, Inspirational and Influential: The Role of Churches in Humanitarian and Development Responses," 2017, https://www.tearfund.org/~/media/files/tilz/churches/integral_mission/2017-tearfund-integral-inspirational-and-influential-en.pdf.

We believe resilience can best be built by working with churches through transformational processes (which we refer to as church and community mobilization [CCM] processes). CCM starts with envisioning and equipping churches with the use of Bible studies, exercises, and training on the biblical calling of integral mission. This unlocks people's God-given potential and transforms their mindsets about their calling, their abilities and possibilities, using local resources, caring for their environment, and valuing relationships and cooperation with everyone, including the poorest and most marginalized.

Churches then build relationships with the wider community and together form a vision for the community. To reach this vision, the needs, vulnerabilities, solutions, and local resources of the community are identified. The churches and communities work together to start projects that address their needs and vulnerabilities. They do this in cooperation with different actors and structures in the community and by using local resources. These projects will eventually lead to resilient villages in which vulnerabilities are reduced and needs are met.

Cooperation

In these CCM processes we work with churches and local Christian organizations. To empower, connect, and train these different churches and organizations in their work, we stimulate them to cooperate in organizational forms such as networks or communities of practice (CoP).

We believe cooperation stimulates mutual understanding and learning among the stakeholders. Through the exchange of resources between the members, the limited resources of each member are multiplied into a wealth of knowledge, skills, and experiences. This reduces the need to acquire external resources. Lastly, the formation of networks or CoPs unites the voices of churches and organizations and increases their ability to influence and shift political, legal, and economic systems.

Approach

Before we start this work of cooperation of churches and organizations in CCM and resilience-building we choose to have an explorative approach to ensure that the processes are locally decided, owned, and resourced:

- We start with a context analysis and consult different relevant organizations in our network to share experiences and to discuss the idea of cooperation on CCM.

- Then we approach churches and organizations to get insight into their work and consult them on their opinions about joining a network or CoP to work on resilience-building through CCM. (When churches and organizations have already cooperated and have voiced interest in starting work on CCM, this step is not needed.)
- The churches and organizations that are interested are then invited to a consultation to discuss the general plan for a network or CoP and to decide together about its formation.
- Once the network or CoP has been formed it is important to ensure that the members keep ownership of it; that they, rather than an external donor or partner, take the decisions and plan for action.

In the following two sections we share how this approach has worked in practice in the network in Indonesia and the CoP in the Philippines.

JAKOMKRIS PBI: Church and Community-Based Disaster Risk Reduction Network in Indonesia

Because of its geographical location along a seismic strip called the "Ring of Fire," Indonesia has to cope with the risk of volcanic eruptions, earthquakes, and tsunamis. The extreme wet and dry seasons in Indonesia, which are linked to the monsoons, can cause floods and landslides, and ruin harvests. Furthermore, Indonesia is heavily affected by tropical cyclones which cause heavy rainfall, flash floods, and mudslides. Due to climate change such extreme hydro-meteorological events are predicted to increase.

Natural disasters can also be exacerbated by human action. For instance, during heavy rains, floods and landslides occur more often due to deforestation and poor water management in Indonesia. Furthermore, conflicts between groups of different ethnicities and religions in Indonesia have increased since the fall of the Suharto regime in 1998.

Challenges and Opportunities for Churches Working on Resilience

For many years various churches and church-based organizations in Indonesia have taken active roles in responding to disasters and conflicts. Since the devastating tsunami that struck Aceh and Nias in 2004, churches have become increasingly active in responding to the needs of internally displaced people and disaster survivors throughout Indonesia. But from the monitoring visits and evaluations of ACT International it became clear that capacity-building was needed to improve the capacity of churches in disaster management and project management.[6]

Furthermore, the tsunami brought an understanding to many humanitarian actors that prevention and DRR needed to be prioritized. After the tsunami, the Indonesian government learned that DRR and effective multi-stakeholder coordination was key. The government therefore restructured the national disaster mechanisms and founded coordination agencies on the regional and national level.[7] Churches were often left out of such coordination platforms due to the lack of capacity mentioned above.

However, in a government programme, Desa Tangguh Bencana (Resilient Village), the national agency for disaster management invited all faith-based organizations (FBOs) including churches to help the Indonesian government meet the target of five thousand resilient villages by 2020.[8] This invitation signified a renewed interest and appreciation of the government in the engagement of FBOs in humanitarian response, mirroring growing attention on the unique role of faith-based action in the public sphere.

Network Development

Yayasan Sion and Tear wanted to take action to address this lack of capacity of churches to respond to and prepare for disasters and conflicts in their communities, and to increase the unique role of churches in communities in order to be better able to cooperate in multi-stakeholder platforms. However, they did not want to just start a new regional DRR project; they intended to build on and learn from the experiences of other NGOs active in Indonesia or in DRR and resilience-building.

Therefore, in 2016 a research initiative was launched to analyse the context, possibilities, and relevance of initiating a DRR network. Interviews with seventeen international NGOs were conducted to discuss the network and possible connections with other organizations in Indonesia. Additionally, interviews were conducted with twenty-four churches and (non-)Christian NGOs in Indonesia to get insight into their work in the field of DRR and church

---

6. J. Eriksson and J. Borton, *Unlocking the Potential Within: Evaluation of the Act Alliance in the International Response to Crises* (Geneva: ACT International, 2004), 17.

7. The BPBD are Regional Agencies for Disaster Management and the BNPB is the National Agency for Disaster Management.

8. BNPB, *524 Desa Tangguh Bencana* (Jakarta Timur: Badan Nasional Penanggulangan Bencana [BNPB], 2017), accessed 5 October 2019, https://bnpb.go.id/berita/524-desa-tangguh-bencana.

involvement, to explain the idea of the network, and to ask their opinions about it.⁹

At the end of this period a three-day consultation meeting was organized with twenty interested churches and Christian organizations to discuss a general plan for the network and to decide about its formation. During the consultation meeting the following vision for network outcomes was developed:

> The network contributes to:
>
> (1) Resilient communities in Indonesia, in which churches work according to a church-based DRR model together with the communities to
>
> (2) proactively reduce the risk of natural disasters.
>
> To increase the capacity of the network members in church and community-based Emergency Response (ER) and Disaster Risk Reduction (DRR), the network should have the following concrete outcomes:
>
> (1) A model for church and community-based DRR
>
> (2) Training on ER, DRR and church involvement
>
> (3) A database of network agencies and their capacity
>
> (4) Advocacy on synod level to increase access to local churches.¹⁰

The participants discussed which stakeholders should be involved in the network and what they should contribute to the network in order to achieve the vision for network outcomes, and this formed a plan of action for the first two years. A working group was formed with one chosen representative from each stakeholder group, whose main task was to set up the coordination and structure of the network.¹¹

A year after the consultation, in August 2017, a members' conference was held in Jakarta. During this conference several other stakeholders were invited, including Muhammadiyah Disaster Management Center and Nahdlatul Ulama Disaster Prevention and Climate Adaptation Centre, two of the largest Muslim organizations in the country. The goal was to discuss the opportunities for faith-based organizations to contribute to DRR in Indonesia and to cooperate

---

9. F. Stal, *Final Report: Network Development for Church and Community Based Disaster Risk Reduction* (London: Tearfund, 2016), 3–6.

10. Stal, *Final Report*, 11–12.

11. Stal, 12–13.

with other disaster management and DRR institutions. During this conference, the network was officially founded as JAKOMKRIS PBI (an abbreviation for the Christian Community Network for DDR in Indonesia). The nationwide network received warm responses from different churches, faith-based organizations (FBOs), and disaster management organizations. The network is led by a steering committee that was elected and appointed during the conference. The network is legally part of the justice and peace department of the Indonesian Council of Churches (PGI), but operates independently in terms of funding and coordination.

Progress

In the past year, the network has achieved significant progress. It has finalized the organizational governance structure and bylaws and gained strong buy-in from several large church denominations that are active in disaster management.

More than thirty churches have already received disaster preparedness training from the network, facilitated by experienced organizations that are part of the network. One of these organizations is YAKKUM, one of the most experienced organizations in Indonesia when it comes to disaster response and DRR. In addition to training, the JAKOMKRIS PBI network and its members have mobilized funding and response teams for several disasters, such as a flood caused by a cyclone in Yogyakarta in 2017 and an eruption of the Sinabung volcano on Sumatra in April 2018.

On 29 July 2018 an earthquake struck the island of Lombok in Indonesia: at least fourteen people died and at least 160 people were injured. The network coordinated its response together with PGI and two Muslim organizations and organized an emergency response team to go to the affected area. This was an important milestone for the JAKOMKRIS PBI network, as it was the first time the member organizations and churches responded by using the name of the network instead of their own names.

Challenges

Despite the great progress that has been made, the network faces several challenges. Because of the sheer size of Indonesia it is very costly to travel for committee meetings and capacity-building training. The intention is therefore to work more regionally instead of organizing the network at a national level.

Furthermore, it has been a challenge for the network to train local churches in DRR and resilience-building because most local churches prioritize response after a disaster has happened. The network is striving to make local churches aware of the relevance of training in resilience-building before a disaster happens.

The network has also had trouble filling the full-time position of network coordinator because of a lack of funding. A staff member from YEU has now been hired as a part-time coordinator for the network to temporarily fill the position.

Lastly, clarity is needed on the roles and responsibilities among member organizations, the steering committee, and PGI, since almost all members of JAKOMKRIS PBI are also part of other networks which sometimes overlap. It has therefore also been difficult to mobilize funding through membership fees because churches already pay membership fees to PGI and organizations already pay fees to multiple networks. These issues are still to be resolved.

Way Forward

The priorities of the network are to work on effective public communication so that the contributions of churches and church-based organizations in disaster risk reduction and resilience-building are recognized. They hope this will contribute to the interfaith dialogue in Indonesia and eventually to a more inclusive and tolerant society.

The network also wants to increase the trust of and coordination with the government so that the network can increase its influence on government policy and the achievements of the network will become part of national progress reports on the Sendai Framework for DRR as well as the Sustainable Development Goals.

Community of Practice on Church and Community Mobilization to Build Resilient Communities in the Philippines

Typhoon Haiyan (known as typhoon Yolanda in the Philippines) was one of the strongest tropical cyclones ever recorded. It made landfall in the Philippines on 7 November 2013. A total of 16 million people were affected, the most affected area being the Eastern Visayas, especially Samar and Leyte. More than six thousand people were killed, 1,061 people were reported missing, 28,689 people were injured, and around six hundred thousand people were homeless and displaced. The typhoon also caused widespread damage to property. This typhoon is now considered as the benchmark of the "new normal" as such super typhoons are predicted to happen more often in the future due to climate change.

Lingap Pangkabataan Incorporated (LPI) and Tear cooperated in the Restore Eastern Samar Together (REST) consortium with five other organizations to respond to the immense scale of damage caused by the typhoon.[12] Based on the expertise of the members of each consortium, the collaboration resulted in houses and day care centres being (re)built, child-friendly spaces established, psychosocial interventions conducted, and food packs distributed.

LPI in partnership with its member churches[13] implemented a community-based livelihood and DRR project for five hundred households affected by Typhoon Haiyan in Leyte and Samar. The main project activities included learning sessions among the member churches; participatory needs assessments of the affected communities, churches, local governments, and schools; capacity-building training on DRR; and natural farming training for church and community members.

From Disaster Response to Community Development

In the Haiyan response, local churches played a powerful role as local implementers of emergency aid. As funding for the emergency response came to an end in December 2016, and aware that another natural disaster could happen at any time, Tear Netherlands, Tearfund UK, and its partner organizations in the Philippines asked the question of how "we move forward in a way that builds on this learning, this experience and this energy?"[14]

As a result, in November 2016 a consultation assessment "to explore the possibilities and appreciation for Church and Community Mobilization (CCM) in the Philippines with focus on DRR" was prepared and carried out by a team of local and international NGO staff and a lead consultant. The assessment brought together different people from the government, communities, CSOs, NGOs, and churches to explore the question together, and to make the

---

12. Consortium members were ZOA, Center for Community Transformation (CCT), Philippine Children's Ministries Network (PCMN), Ang Mananampalatayang Gumagawa (AMG), Lingap Pangkabataan, Incorporated (LPI), Tearfund UK, and Tear the Netherlands.

13. The Wesleyan Church of the Philippines (WCP) in Tacloban City; Jesus Christ the Strong Foundation Community Church Inc. (JCSFCCI) in Balangiga, Eastern Samar; The United Church of Christ in the Philippines (UCCP) in Lawaan, Eastern Samar; The Roman Catholic Church through the Diocese of Borongan.

14. B. Langeler, "Consultation to Assess Possibilities and Appreciation for CCM in the Philippines with Focus on DRR," October 2020, 8, https://live-micah-global.pantheonsite.io/wp-content/uploads/2020/10/integral_mission_declaration_en.pdf.

assessment itself an experience of the possibilities of CCM.[15] The assessment team concluded that "there is significant evidence that important criteria and circumstances for a potentially successful CCM programme are in place: (1) developing understanding of Missio Dei amongst influential church leaders; (2) organisational capacity within the church (registered CSOs); (3) recognition by the population, the government, and other CSOs of the church as having a role to play in DRR; and, (4) awareness of the need for ongoing development of DRR amongst the population and government."[16]

As a result of this assessment, LPI and Tear continued their cooperation in 2017 with the start of a three-year CCM programme. The goal of the programme was to enhance the capacity of churches to transform communities in such a way that communities become resilient to disasters and children and vulnerable adults are able to flourish.

Community of Practice

LPI is convinced that in addition to being first responders in cases of disaster, churches can play a significant role in building resilience because they are an influential structure in communities. Churches can be catalysts of change, especially if they collaborate with one another and learn together. Therefore, as part of the CCM and resilience-building programme, a network in the form of a community of practice (CoP) was formed and launched during a Learning Conference in January 2018. This learning conference was co-organized by LPI and the Asian School of Development and Cross-Cultural Studies (ASDECS) for church leaders and community workers on community transformation and resilience-building through CCM.

The CoP now consists of four local churches that were active in the Haiyan response and had decided together to collaborate to continue their DRR capacity-building and livelihood projects, even though the REST consortium has ceased to exist. Through the CoP, the churches will be able to build each other's knowledge, experience, motivation, and resources to strengthen the resilience of their community through CCM processes.

In addition to bringing churches together on the local level, in May 2018 LPI organized a consultation for church leaders and programme coordinators at national and diocese level to discuss the CCM approach, to get their buy-in, and to stimulate them to support their local churches that practise CCM

---

15. Langeler, "Consultation," 2.
16. Langeler, 2.

to build resilience. While the CoP is still very new, its members have already formulated the vision to have annual consultations in which the pilot villages participate as well.

LPI mainly acted as a facilitator in establishing the CoP by providing a space for the churches to listen and learn from one another. Rather than LPI making plans and decisions for the CoP, the churches as owners of the CoP decide on matters affecting them.

In addition to establishing a community of learning, the goal of the CoP is also to increase the ability of churches and Christian organizations to cooperate with different stakeholders such as government agencies, academics, the business sector, and civil society organizations. Because of their experience in the Haiyan response, the local churches in Eastern Samar have learned that they can appeal to local governments to develop DRR and climate adaptation plans. The CoP unites the voices of these local churches and makes them a more influential stakeholder in resilience-building.

Progress

Since the start of the programme, five pilot villages were identified in Eastern Samar to start CCM processes to build their resilience to disasters. The four churches that had previously been active in the Haiyan response and continued their project after the REST consortium had stopped are part of the pilot villages. These churches have made a start with CCM processes in their communities, and they will organize meetings and training to introduce CCM to the church and community members. Because the CCM and resilience-building programme has just started, LPI is now mainly focusing on the capacity-building of members' churches, staff, and other stakeholders:

- LPI continuously equips church workers and community leaders with various workshops, learning sessions, and resources on appreciative inquiry, integral mission, transformational development, project management, and monitoring and evaluation.
- LPI staff and partners have participated in learning visits to Cambodia and Indonesia to get a better grasp on resilience-building through CCM processes. Learning from the experiences and best practices of practitioners in the region has widened their perspective and deepened their appreciation of CCM.

Challenges

The progress of the CCM and resilience-building programme is challenged by multiple factors. One is the change in leadership, both in churches and in villages. After pastors and priests are trained in CCM and resilience-building they can be reassigned to new churches by the diocese or conference. The same is true for local government officials. Following the May 2018 local elections there are new officials who need to be equipped in CCM and resilience-building; those with whom LPI had worked and coordinated the programme in previous months are no longer in position and can no longer make significant decisions for the community.

Another challenge is that the member churches in the CoP are diverse in their teachings. Some emphasize the need to share the gospel, while others are more focused on helping the poor in the community. But amid this diversity there is unity among the churches as they aspire and collaborate to see transformation in all aspects of people's lives.

Way Forward

In addition to working on resilience-building through CCM with churches in Eastern Samar, LPI would like to start CCM processes in local churches in Metro Manila. However, LPI first wants to finish the pilot processes with the churches in Eastern Samar, and gain experience and learn from these pilots, before expanding the programme to a new geographic area.

LPI is also working towards expanding the CoP; its vision is to not only include local churches and organizations that work on CCM, but to also have government agencies, businesses, and academics as partners to make the CoP a multi-stakeholder platform. Communities can become resilient only when all stakeholders are involved to work towards reducing people's vulnerability to shocks and stresses. The involvement of government representatives will enable the CoP to influence policy or political decisions; academics can bring knowledge and research; and the involvement of businesses enables the CoP to ensure fair and safe working conditions for workers and to challenge child labour.

Lessons Learned and Recommendations

Since 2016 Yayasan Sion, YAKKUM, LPI, and Tear have gained rich experience in establishing a network and a CoP to support and equip churches to build resilient communities through CCM processes. This experience has taught them the following valuable lessons:

1. An Integrated and Multi-Stakeholder Approach Is Needed to Build Resilience

Vulnerability to shocks and stresses can be created by natural, social–cultural, economic, and political factors. Therefore DRR should not be a stand-alone project; rather, an integrated and multi-stakeholder approach is needed to build resilience. The formation of networks or CoPs enables churches and organizations to cooperate on multi-stakeholder platforms with governments, civil society organizations, businesses, and academics, and increase their influence. Furthermore, working in communities through the CCM approach encourages an integrated approach to resilience-building. In an open-ended CCM process, churches and communities identify together what their needs and vulnerabilities are and by what different factors these are caused. Then they decide together what action they can take with their own resources.

2. Expectations Must Be Managed

It is important to have clear agreement from the start of a network or CoP about what is expected of the coordinators and members and what their responsibilities are. It is therefore important to first identify the existing capacity and resources of the coordinators and members so that mutual expectations, for instance in terms of time, funding, input, and output, are in line with the available capacity and resources of the members and coordinators. When the expectations of both the members and the coordinators are not managed well, action may be prohibited because of a lack of involvement, funding, or time.

3. Local Ownership Is Essential

The network and CoP were formed via an open and participative process in which the experiences, opinions, and decisions of the different churches and organizations drove the design of the programme and the formation of the network and CoP. Because the churches and organizations themselves decided to form a network and CoP, they own, drive, lead, and support it. A network or CoP that is driven and led entirely by its members is more likely to be compatible with their needs, desires, and abilities. This high degree of local ownership contributes to the sustainability of the network and CoP and prevents it from being a donor-driven project that stops as soon as the involvement of the donor ends.

4. It Is Important to Reflect on Your Role as an International Donor Agency

Tear strives to stimulate local ownership but realizes it played a considerable role in the establishment of the JAKOMKRIS PBI network in Indonesia and the programme and CoP in the Philippines. Tear has tried to minimize its influence on the outcome of the processes through open discussion with Yayasan Sion and LPI to ensure the local perceived need, welcoming feedback and having processes in which all the stakeholders can participate and decide. Ongoing reflection on your own role and influence is key, because it can be difficult for donor agencies such as Tear to sustain local ownership, to leave the ownership of a network or CoP with its members, and to not exercise too much influence on its progress, especially when progress seems to be slow or when reporting procedures require concrete outputs.

As we witness the increasing risk and scale of natural disasters, we continue our work to build resilient communities. By providing two case studies, we have argued that resilience can best be built through church and community mobilization processes that are owned and resourced by the communities themselves. Churches have a valuable position from which to initiate these processes which encourage an integrated approach to resilience-building. Forming networks or CoPs supports and equips member churches and organizations to bring change in their communities, and enables churches and organizations to cooperate on multi-stakeholder platforms, which increases their ability to influence social, political, and economic systems in such a way that extreme weather conditions, natural events, and stresses will no longer become disasters and conflicts that strike communities worldwide.

24

Lessons from the Frontline of Global Movement-Building

Reflections from Three Years of Tearfund's Restorative Economy Approach

Naomi Foxwood, Richard Gower, Helen Heather, and Sue Willsher

Over the past forty years, millions of people have escaped poverty, hunger, and disease. However, the paradox of our time is that the same economic model responsible for our success could now be responsible for our failure: casting millions of people back into poverty by driving climate change and other environmental hazards. We need to adapt our model, creating a truly "restorative economy" that addresses the triple challenges of poverty, inequality, and environmental sustainability.

This requires systemic change. However, as activists we have been frustrated to find that there is rarely the political space to achieve the reforms required.

Tearfund has spent the last three years innovating around a model designed to help create the political space needed to challenge the broken governance systems, vested interests, and ultimately prevailing social values that are preventing the bold actions necessary for this change.

This chapter outlines our approach – including our focus on three key components of movement-building (mobilizing, organizing, and connecting) – and finishes with key lessons from our work so far.

Introduction: A Restorative Economy

In 2012, Tearfund took a brave decision: we took a step back from our advocacy work in order to reflect on the systemic challenges of our time, and to consider how we should adapt our approach in order to respond to them adequately. We recognized that over the past forty years, we had seen huge progress in tackling global poverty. However, this progress was now being threatened by human-driven changes in our natural environment which undermine the planet's capacity to support life.

We recognized the choice that lay ahead for this generation: continue with our unsustainable economic model or lay the groundwork for a green and fair global economy. However, we also recognized that change on this scale does not come about easily. Neither does it arise from traditional NGO advocacy techniques. Historically, systemic change often depends on grassroots social movements: civil rights, abolition of the slave trade, anti-apartheid, and so on.

From this was born our *Restorative Economy* vision (published in 2015), designed to challenge Christians to respond to the triple challenges of poverty, inequality, and environmental sustainability. We believe Christians around the world can play a key role in catalysing movements for environmental and economic transformation. This is part of our call as God's co-workers here on earth.

The *Restorative Economy* report contained four key arguments:

- We must address the earth's growing environmental problems, otherwise they will undo all our recent progress on reducing poverty;
- We can't address them without a movement of people making changes themselves and helping to create more political space so governments act too;
- This mission is part of our role in extending God's kingdom on earth and anticipating the "renewal of all things," and the Jubilee laws provide particular inspiration;
- Christians are ideally placed to give a lead.

It also suggested five personal changes and ten big policy ideas to start creating a "restorative economy."

Shifting the narrative away from excessive individualistic and unchecked consumerist narratives towards narratives that reflect the theology of restored relationships (with God, with each other, and with creation) is fundamental to achieving our vision.

Tearfund has spent the last three years innovating around a model designed to help create the political space needed for these changes. Historically, moments of systemic change are often bound up with the emergence of a movement that challenges prevailing values and norms in society. We want to help incubate and strengthen these movements, and this is what our approach is designed to achieve.

We have seen notable successes at local level in Nigeria, Brazil, and elsewhere, as well as at major global moments, but we are still at an early stage, and learning all the time.

What follows is a discussion of what we mean by movement-building as a theory of change – how we think change happens – followed by an outline of work we've done. We finish by sharing what we have learned so far.

Theory of Change: Movement-Building

The traditional campaigning techniques international NGOs have used for the last twenty or thirty years work well in contexts where there is already political space for progress in an area. However, political actors will not move much beyond the social norms and values common in society at large; therefore in order to achieve systemic change it is necessary to influence a society's norms and values – to change the story and the way people think. We now seek to combine "traditional" NGO advocacy and campaigning with a movement-building approach. This helps foster a groundswell of public opinion that becomes a force for change on institutions that wield power, particularly political power. Figure 24.1 provides a diagram of our theory of change.

We understand movement-building as follows:

> *Movement-Building = Community Organzing + Campaigning + Connecting*

Research shows that in order to build a movement a number of things need to happen:

- Strong committed leadership needs to be built at the grassroots through community organizing;
- Large numbers of people, including influential figures, need to be mobilized to take supportive action (most traditional NGO campaigning falls into this category);
- Those engaged in building the movement need to be connected in order to magnify their voices.

This is how we understand and define our movement-building work.

280 Relentless Love

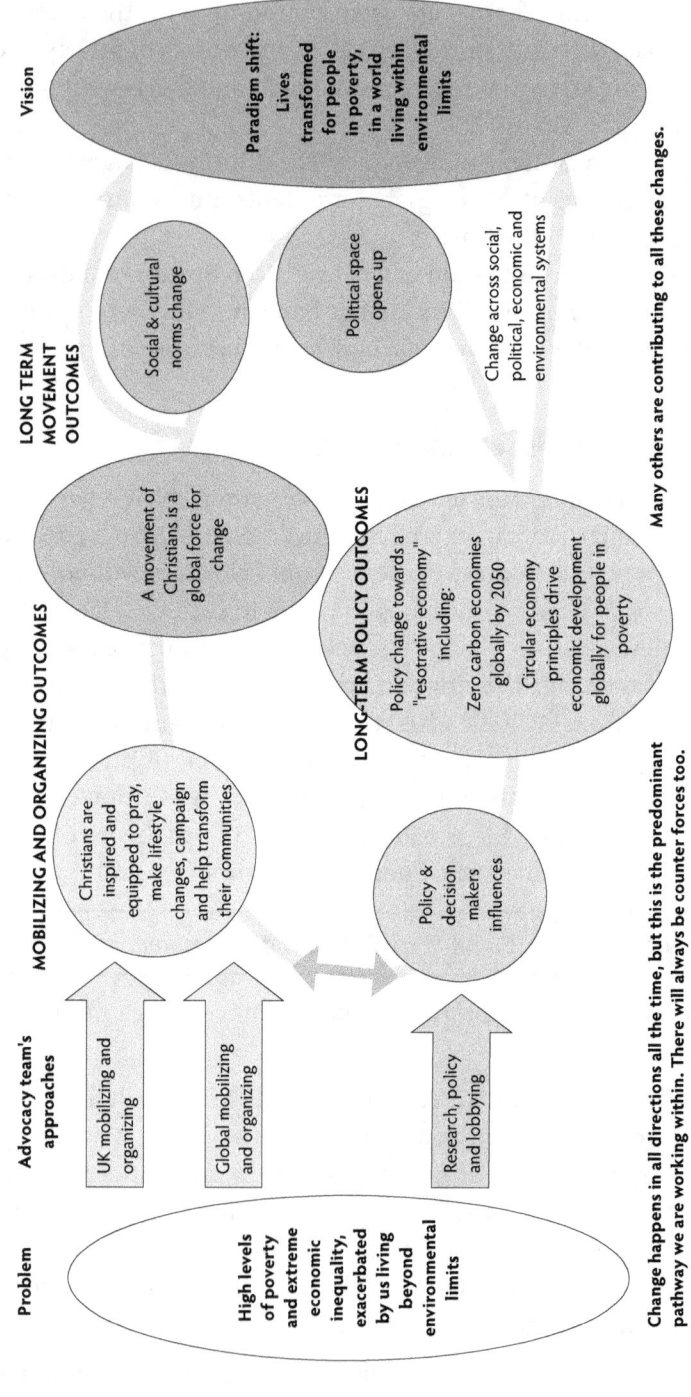

Figure 24.1: Theory of change

What's Happened So Far?

Since the launch of *Restorative Economy*, Tearfund's Global Advocacy team has been busy outworking our vision, focusing on three areas:

- *Community organizing* to develop a strong body of grassroots and institutional leaders who are driving a movement for change among Christians.
- *Mobilizing* through campaigns to equip and inspire Christians to be disciples who pray, live, and act on these issues in their day-to-day lives.
- *Continuing to develop* policy expertise and carry out high-level advocacy towards a "restorative economy."

We have frequently and deliberately chosen to act in partnership with other organizations and individuals in pursuit of these aims where possible, recognizing that we ourselves are part of a wider movement that includes other evangelicals, other Christians, and groups of other faiths and no faith.

Tearfund has also adopted a new corporate priority of economic and environmental sustainability, extending beyond advocacy to include our country programming.

Community Organizing and Grassroots Leadership

> Movement-Building = Community Organzing + Campaigning + Connecting

Community organizing is integral to our new theory of change. In 2017/18, organizers nurtured by Tearfund took 700 actions which mobilized 29,000 people. This number is ever-growing as they replicate. To explain what organizing means for us, here are four examples.

In Middle Belt and North East Nigeria, Tearfund has been working with groups of young people since 2015. Tearfund's vision is to build leadership and capacity among Christian young people to tackle environmental and justice issues at community and national level. The young people are recommended by local youth pastors of churches for their leadership qualities and their commitment to their Christian faith. Our pilot group, which now call themselves the Jos Green Centre, have been working as a cohesive unit for two years, independently initiating a wide variety of practical and advocacy work. Among their activities are research on plastic waste; starting a social enterprise developing fashion products out of waste; hosting a green jobs conference attended by two hundred other young people and government policy staff; and awareness-raising in multiple schools and colleges. They have taken the lead in organizing other groups of young people using the same methodology, resulting in the mobilization of over 250 young people, and the establishment of a number of other new cohesive and active groups.

In Brazil, Tearfund supports the work of the Instituto Solidare set up by Iglesia Batista Coquerial, particularly the School of Faith and Politics. The School brings together pastors, leaders, and active members of evangelical churches to reflect on the social and political ramifications of their faith, and to deliver training on the ways in which they can make an impact. They take 120 students in the north-east of Brazil, balancing the numbers between the rural semi-arid region inland and the coastal city of Recife. In tracking the 2016 cohort, Instituto Solidare have seen six locally initiated practical projects in their communities led by former students. They have also seen the establishment of four public policy monitoring groups and around 40 percent of the students engaging directly with advocacy actions. The most high-profile of these is the "Clean River, Healthy City" campaign focused on Tejepio river in Recife. This river has been clogged annually with waste and floods, causing great suffering to local poor communities living on its banks. The campaign has brought together churches, community groups, local politicians, schools, and the university in Recife, seeing 13,000 local community members signing a petition for local government action and hundreds attending a campaign march covered by local TV and newspapers. These activities have resulted in numerous meetings with the municipality, taking steady steps towards seeing government, as well as community, action.

In southern Africa, Tearfund has worked closely with the Anglican Communion Environmental Network (informally known as Green Anglicans) to particularly focus on young change-makers identified by their churches as active on environmental issues. In April 2016, seventy-two young people from nine countries attended a Young Green Anglicans Intentional Discipleship Climate Change Conference in Lusaka, Zambia, where they received theological input and technical equipping on environmental issues and movement-building. Since the gathering they have received ongoing mentoring and support from Green Anglicans and the Church hierarchy. Research has shown that thirty-six of forty respondents have visited other churches to inform them on how to be eco-friendlier, while twenty-eight have organized events for their families, friends, and communities to participate in being eco-friendly. Thirty-two have also developed action plans which they presented to their bishop or priest for official approval. External evaluation of the impact of the "Lusaka" group concluded: "Results show that within the Anglican Church in Central and Southern Africa an eco-friendly change is occurring, and it is building momentum. Hence it can indeed be said that an eco-friendly social movement has begun. A major catalyst of the movement is the Young Green Anglicans."[1]

In the UK, we've started towards more of an organizing approach, and have trialled two small (approx. twenty-five people) "communities" of organizers for two years, the first year collaborating with other organizations, and the second running our own community. We've experimented with community-organizing approaches and are currently encouraging activists to use some of the community-organizing tools alongside more traditional mobilizing. Our aims are to build the capacity of grassroots campaigners/leaders within churches and communities around the UK, and to strengthen them by giving them a sense of belonging to a community of like-minded people, so that they are able to mobilize others to action. We've found that putting good theology into the training has motivated people. We've also learned that relationships and community help people feel supported, and giving people good resources to use to mobilize others is important.

Campaigning and Connecting: The "Renew Our World" Campaign

How does this new focus on organizing connect to national and international campaigning? Tearfund has continued to run campaigns in the UK to mobilize Christians to act, pray, and make lifestyle changes. In addition, we initiated and now help to run the international "Renew Our World" campaign.

"Renew Our World" is a global campaign seeking a restorative economy and life within environmental limits. We are committed to a movement-building theory of change so at national and global level there are actions to mobilize Christians to act and support for organizing grassroots and institutional leaders. "Renew Our World" is conceived as a bridge that can connect different communities, and a megaphone amplifying their voices onto the national and international stage with national campaigns and global moments where we campaign together.

The campaign is seeking to bring together Christians passionate about responding to this vision in prayer, lifestyle change, and speaking out to people in power. We have started with a focus on climate change, recognizing its

---

1. R. Marandu-Kareithi, *Review of Green Anglicans: What Is Working and Why?* (Cape Town: DAS Associates, 2017).

impacts across the world and the urgent need for action to reduce emissions and support adaptation, particularly for the most vulnerable communities.

There are ten national campaign expressions running so far, including in Australia, Brazil, Peru, the UK, the USA, and Zambia. Many of these had not undertaken campaigning on environmental issues or used a movement-building approach before. Twice a year we join together in global moments when we prophetically speak out for justice and pray together. This happens at strategic times like the COP climate summits.

Key achievements so far:

- The campaign has connected organizations from the global north and south, and regional and global networks, to campaign together under the restorative economy vision. This has provided a space for us to share ideas and learning at national, regional, and global levels, and to bring together our expertise from many different contexts, resulting in strong strategies, activities, and impacts.
- Tens of thousands of people from over sixty countries have been mobilized to take action and pray.
- We have engaged over fifty Christian influencers, many with international reach to speak out on climate change, encouraging other Christians and political leaders to respond.
- As well as mobilizing Christians in their countries, the "Renew Our World" national campaign expressions have also started to train organizers who can organize and promote actions to other individuals and churches.

In the UK, we've seen significant growth in mobilizing people for Tearfund's centralized campaigns. A rebrand and clearer messaging as part of a greater movement for change with "Renew Our World" have contributed to this. We worked in coalition with many others to get the Paris Agreement on climate in 2015, and led campaigns for the Department for International Development (DFID) and the World Bank to fund clean energy so poor communities can have access to electricity. Since the launch of *Restorative Economy* we've also included lifestyle change actions alongside policy change, and used the number of Christians pledging to live differently in our influencing of businesses and other decision-makers, and to demonstrate a growing movement in the UK.

In 2018 we launched "Restoration Story" in the UK; an attempt to communicate restorative economy through a series of personal testimonies, helping people to identify themselves as part of a greater movement for change as they live differently, engage their churches, and speak out to MPs and businesses. We produced a film and a small-group Bible study guide, and launched a Tearfund Campaigners Facebook group. We hope all of these resources will encourage those who feel as if they are the lone voice on climate and justice in their churches, and will inspire people who are currently lukewarm.

Policy Change Towards a "Restorative Economy"

We view policy change as a crucial part of systemic change – putting laws and policies in place, legislating for what society is calling for in order to achieve a restored economy. We aim to amplify the voices we help join together through our movement-building work, to help open up political space for wider change. We currently have two focus areas for our policy work at UK and global level.

Climate: Zero Emissions

Climate change is the gravest environmental threat of our age, and we have maintained a policy focus on reaching zero emissions through the Paris Climate Agreement. Within this, we have developed expertise on increasing access to renewable energy for people living in poverty.

One billion people still have no access to electricity.[2] The majority of these people live in rural areas and half live in sub-Saharan Africa. Off-grid renewable electricity, particularly solar, now offers a wider range of modern solutions, such as solar lamps and stand-alone solar panels, that are often cheaper, faster, more reliable, safer, and cleaner than extending a centralized electricity grid or using kerosene lanterns and diesel generators. This technology is a game-changer to power people in rural areas and challenges the historic centralized grid approach, like mobile phones and landline phone networks. Faster progress is needed. Under a business-as-usual scenario, almost 700 million people will still be without access to electricity in 2030, mostly in sub-Saharan Africa.

Circular Economy

Parallel to our focus on climate change, we have developed expertise in another vital area of environmental and economic transformation: the circular economy. This concept "holds out the promise of an alternative growth model that reduces the tension between lifting people out of poverty and protecting

---

2. World Bank, "Global Tracking Framework 2017: Progress toward Sustainable Energy," 2017, https://www.worldbank.org/en/topic/energy/publication/global-tracking-framework-2017.

the planet, dramatically increasing the scope for meeting the SDGs."[3] However, three years ago, the concept of the circular economy was almost entirely absent from the development discourse, with less than 0.3 percent of aid money spent on waste management globally (for example), despite the fact that two billion people lack access to any form of waste collection or management.

> What Is a Circular Economy?
> Currently, we have a primarily linear economy. We make a product – for example, a toaster or a mobile phone – we use it, and, when it breaks or there's a better model available, we throw it away. At this point, all of the resources (energy, metals, water) used to make that phone are lost. In Europe, an average of 95 percent of a product's material and energy value is wasted in this way.
>
> A circular economy would address these issues by eliminating waste and inefficiency at each stage of the product life cycle. It's about repairability, waste minimization, and resource efficiency. The concept has its roots in biomimicry: in the natural world, there is no waste; instead, when an organism reaches the end of its life, it provides nutrients for another part of the system.[4]

Circular economy principles can offer a triple win to those in poverty: creating livelihoods, improving health, and reducing pollution. For example, one community-based approach to waste management and recycling in Pakistan was recently found to offer ten dollars in benefits for every dollar invested in establishing it.[5] These benefits include reducing premature deaths associated with burning waste, reducing diarrhoeal diseases, mitigating climate change, and creating jobs. In addition, circular approaches often allow value to be created from waste. In this case, the waste management centre became self-financing in its third year (through a mix of user fees and selling recyclables).[6]

---

3. R. Gower and P. Schroeder, *Virtuous Circle: How the Circular Economy Can Create Jobs and Save Lives in Low and Middle-Income Countries* (Brighton: Institute of Development Studies [IDS], 2016).

4. Based on R. Gower and P. Schroeder, *Cost-Benefit Assessment of Community-Based Recycling and Waste Management in Pakistan* (Brighton: Institute of Development Studies [IDS], 2018).

5. Gower and Schroeder, *Cost-Benefit Assessment*.

6. Gower and Schroeder.

What Have We Learned?

Tearfund has learned, perhaps unsurprisingly, that *speaking to theological belief and spiritual values* is a key first step in the process of catalysing and sustaining action among Christian believers. We begin our work by engaging participants with group biblical study and reflection, something that is particularly critical for working with evangelical Christians. Our material looks at biblical elements such as Jubilee laws or the creation story, and asks people to discuss applications for their own contexts. This process enriches and deepens the group's understanding of Christian identity, practice, and culture, and provides unity in giving the group a shared sense of values. Often this biblical study is described as "mind blowing" and providing participants with an entirely new sense of godly purpose and an understanding of integral mission. A good example of this comes from one of our Anglican organizers from southern Africa who commented, "People are really embracing an eco-spirituality. It is almost like people are re-embracing their spiritual roots of what it means to be a believer on African soil – I think that the dominion/individualist theology is one of the legacies of colonialism." *Live Justly* (see below) has been a key tool for us in this area.

Great power exists in developing a *hope-filled narrative*. In Christ we have the good news of personal redemption but also of the renewal and restoration of all things: and that includes our communities, our economies, and our environment. Through "restorative economy" we have been telling a story of a sustainable future and flourishing communities and nations, alongside a call for Christians to be engaged in building this future. We have found this hope-filled narrative to catalyse action, and to sustain that action through long-term struggle, in a way that anger cannot. One of our most successful experiences in movement-building has occurred in north-east Nigeria. As Jimmy, part of our Yola group of organizers, said, "Some of us had lost hope, we were seriously broken by the insurgency. But after Tearfund's engagement we realized we had all we need and we said, how do we start?"

Small actions early on can help to create greater unity in a group of activists and provide momentum and great motivation. This has been true both at a grassroots level, with community organizers, and at a macro level through launching the international "Renew Our World" campaign.

The *modelling of the change that you would like to see – prefiguration –* is a very powerful testimony. This early move to action and prefiguration is nicely encapsulated in the testimony of Pastor Renilson from Brazil, who said, "I never got involved [in local politics], but after I started attending the School [of Faith and Politics] I heard about the irregularities practised in some councils. It filled me with a holy indignation; my blood boiled. So I decided to participate in the election of civil society councillors to the Municipal Health Council. I was elected. I act on the council today and I do not let wrong things get past me."

Tearfund has found that there is considerable appetite for *practical equipping* in advocacy on restorative economy issues, and that the desire for it flows naturally from the theological input which catalyses a desire into action. In many contexts we've found it helpful to give this training intensively over a few days in the form of a "bootcamp" covering all that is needed to start movement-building, from policy cycles, to alliance building, to communications and framing. In order to maintain momentum and create peer accountability, we've found it most successful to encourage the participants, before they leave the event, to prayerfully draw up plans for changes that they wish to make. "Renew Our World" has also provided opportunities for equipping as the organizations running the campaign learn from each other to sharpen strategies and tactics.

Resources for Movement-Building

Live Justly Global is a resource that speaks to theological belief and spiritual values, and then urges a practical response. Micah Challenge USA produced *Live Justly* for a US audience. Tearfund collaborated with them to produce a global version which we have used widely. From Brazil to Haiti, from the Mekong Delta to the City of London, it has proved an effective way to start people on their journey to activism. The book is a series of scriptural and practical studies that help people live justly in six key areas of life: advocacy, prayer, consumption, generosity, creation care, and relationships. It is designed to be used in a group over ten weeks, and we have found that the groups often remain unified after the study is finished and go on to take action together over the longer term.

"It is a resource that unleashes the power of immersion into the life of the individual studying it. By this I mean that, at the end of it, you cannot help but have an immersive relationship with your neighbours, your community, the environment, and the world at large – a relationship that seeks to correct injustice and leads to the flourishing of all." These are the words of a young campaigner in Jos, Nigeria.

Movement-building bootcamps can be used to build the capacity of people who are convinced of the need to do something but are not confident of exactly what – perhaps those who have just finished a *Live Justly* course. We have developed a model three-day bootcamp. The bootcamp provides a thorough understanding of restorative economy issues such as climate change, as well as technical equipping on a movement-building and advocacy response (media, coalition-building, policy work, etc). In February 2018, a group of young people from the UK travelled to Haiti for one such bootcamp, and the participants found the experience extremely rich. A UK participant said, "I was inspired by the way the Haitians talk about their country. I truly believe that change can start with the church. It inspired me to do the same thing when I go back home."

The *"Renew Our World"* campaign has produced a number of prayer and campaign resources for individuals and organizations which can be found at www.renewourworld.net.

Young evangelicals represent a particular opportunity. It seems that the evangelical space is changing so that young evangelicals can be environmental and justice activists as a core part of their theology and practice, in contrast to previous generations who may view this as a more secular activity undertaken by some Christians. In some contexts Tearfund has seen a real rejection of what are seen as the values of older generations of Christian leaders, and an attempt to define a new way of being evangelical. In evangelical churches it is often young people who most effectively (1) accept justice issues as part and parcel of their faith, (2) organize committed groups of their peers, (3) mobilize large numbers of their peers, and (4) connect among their other networks, both in person and through various media. As one US activist said to a researcher contracted by Tearfund to assess our movement work, "There has been a shift for those aged below thirty or forty who feel social justice is part of their faith."[7]

Connecting is an underappreciated part of movement-building. Connecting doesn't just involve introducing people to each other; rather, it demands the ability to see the whole picture of what you are trying to achieve on a systemic level, and the reach to pull in the necessary threads to link up the sum of the parts to create a greater whole. These links may be between people or institutions that can be linked in order to increase the impact of their work. Certainly it's in Tearfund's DNA to build relationships. We have found ways to use technology to keep activists engaged with us and each other in order to sustain their work. "Renew Our World" works on the basis of creating coalitions at the national and global level, with some powerful results as

---

7. O. Wilkinson, *Tearfund and a Movement Building Approach to Advocacy* (Washington, DC: Joint Learning Initiative on Faith and Local Communities [JLI], 2019).

organizations with similar missions and values come together with a magnified voice. Connecting also means linking up organizing and mobilizing work; it means linking up the grassroots community work with the ability to speak into large systemic issues through policy work.

In our high-level advocacy work, we have also found connecting and convening to work well. Rather than launching our research at large events with a presentation from the front, we have instead frequently found that smaller private roundtables are much more effective. They allow policymakers to develop relationships with practitioners and experts, and permit honest discussion in a way that larger events cannot. For both climate change and the circular economy, this has proved fruitful.

As we look to the future, we are exploring new ways of telling the Restoration Story, rolling out new campaigns on waste, and seeking to increase our scale and reach through the "Renew Our World" campaign and other initiatives. If you are on a similar journey, we hope these reflections are useful for you, and we would love to hear what you are learning too.

What's Next?
Restorative Economy Contextualizations

The *Restorative Economy* report was globally applicable but written from a Western point of view. We are now going to develop a contextualized version for Africa that draws from contemporary thought-leadership within the continent to inform the theology, transformative policy ideas, lifestyle, and social change.

Many countries in Africa are entering a phase of rapid economic growth and are searching for successful economic models. The leaders and people of Africa have the opportunity to forge a new African way that takes into account the needs and culture of its people and relatively unspoiled environment. It is uniquely placed to become the first region of the world to build an environmentally sustainable economy whilst pulling its citizens out of poverty. If reaching this paradigm shift was possible, it could become a "city on a hill" ready to teach the world a new way of doing economics.

This contextualized version of *Restorative Economy* will be undertaken through a partnership approach to enable it to be written and owned by many Christian networks, denominations, and organizations across the continent. If you'd like to be involved with this, please get in touch.

Waste

Having developed policy expertise and grassroots work on waste and the circular economy, we are now poised to take advantage of growing interest in plastic pollution by launching a public campaign on this topic in the UK, and hopefully also internationally. This will build on our existing grassroots work and hopefully provide a framework for connecting organizing, campaigning, and policy work on this issue.

Renew Our World

It is encouraging to see action and prayer locally, nationally, and globally calling for the church and governments to tackle environmental issues like climate change, particularly focusing on the poorest and most vulnerable people who are impacted first and most. The "Renew Our World" campaign brings together the actions of many to tackle these problems together. We would love to see many more people joining us! The number of national campaigns is growing monthly, with new Campaign Members joining regularly too.

Scale Up?

With our first three years of operating under our new model complete, we are now reflecting on how we could scale up to increase our impact. Watch this space . . .

25

North and South

Boureima Diallo

My name is Boureima Diallo and I come from Burkina Faso in West Africa. And I stand here as a Fulani, one of forty million Fulani in Africa. Statistically this is insignificant. But I am here to voice the gratitude of the Fulani people to you who have been praying for us. We are thankful to those who have sent their children among the Fulani people, so that the Fulani may hear the good news of Jesus Christ. Thank you.

Many Westerners – if you allow me to use the term – who came among the Fulani people laboured faithfully, yet they didn't see any Fulani come to Christ. Some died in the field, and some went back home to retire. I am the fruit of the prayers and the investment of so many, and I'm so grateful to you. Thank you very much. In Fulani we say, "May God honour you as you enter his presence."

And also, as I stand here, I would like to say, please depart from the guilt mentality. Let go of guilt that your great-grandfathers have done wrong. That was them and that was their thinking at the time. I believe they did what they could, with their best efforts.

To say thank you, I would like to let you listen to part of a Fulani song that says thank you to God. Please take this song as gratitude from many Fulani people. *[Fulani song plays.]*

The song means, "God I thank you." "Allah" is the word for God that we've adopted from Arabic. Fulani have got their own name for God as well: *Geno*. I think that many tribes, including Western tribes, have borrowed their names for God from somewhere else.

I want to share with you a bit of my story. I was born as a Fulani among the Muslims in West Africa, in Burkina Faso. All my family are Muslims, and my village is a Muslim village. It's a small village that you won't find on the map.

My father used to be a forestry engineer, working for the government. He was the first forestry engineer in Burkina Faso and at one point he was a government minister. He had studied in Europe, especially in France, and whilst he was in France he had met Christians. And he bought himself a Bible and read it. He brought that Bible home but no one knew. I never knew that my father had a Bible until one day when one of my father's employees visited me and told me about Jesus.

This employee challenged me, saying, "Boureima, what would happen to you if, before God, your good deeds and your bad deeds are equal?"

I knew that this was written in the Quran. In Sura 101 of the Quran it is written that Allah has a pair of scales to weigh our good deeds and our bad deeds. If our good deeds are heavier, we will go to heaven, to paradise, to be with Allah. If our bad deeds are heavier, we will go to hell.

I was rattled by this question, to say the least. And I did not know the answer. I had never been challenged about where I was going. And it was my searching to discover where I would go that led me to decide to follow Jesus.

All of this happened in secret. My father's employee kept telling me more: that Jesus has the power to heal. I had had polio when I was little. I don't remember it as I was three. And yes, I wanted to walk just as other children walk. This employee convinced me that Jesus is the one who can heal me – and that really encouraged me. At one point, he said to me: "Boureima, if you are really serious about following Jesus, then I invite you to come to church with me."

In his understanding, church was a place to go. I discovered that church is where you are, not where you go. But he said to me, "You need to ask your father first, for permission to come to church with me." That was a challenge; I knew it was a dangerous path to go down. There has never been a Christian in my village or in my family. So I postponed it.

For a few months he kept telling me about Jesus, and I desired God. I wanted to connect with Christians, so I found the courage to go and ask my father: "Father, I would like to go to church with my friend."

My father said to me, "Why do you want to go to church?"

I was silenced; I didn't know what to say. But my father said to me, "I'll allow you to go to church, but I would like you to be a good Christian." It was like a dream – I didn't expect that!

My father encouraged me. Once, I came back from church with my friend, and my father asked me, "Boureima, what did you learn?" My father was like that. In fact, we were taught as much at home as at school. And I was among the first from my primary school to go to university. I scored highly in order to get to university, because my father made sure that he had time for us, so that we might succeed.

So when my father asked me "What did you learn?" I explained it to him. The same afternoon, my father gave me the Bible in French. He told me he had bought it in France. When I took it, I saw that the Bible had some underlining and notes – my father had been reading the Bible.

My story didn't stop there; it is an ongoing story. But I would like to pause here to say that my father had contacts with believers in France, he got himself a Bible, and that Bible became my Bible. And my father encouraged me and protected me. Not only that, but my father paid for me to do Bible studies by correspondence. And he made sure that I went. Two years later, he died.

Then my uncle became the father figure for our family. It was hard. He has been to Mecca twice. By then I had led three of my siblings to Christ, but he prevented us from going to church. But at school there was a Christian union, and that became my church. That was how I kept hanging on to Christ. That's why I am affiliated with the Christian unions at schools and universities, and I would encourage you to pray for them and encourage them.

And by the grace of God – to jump ahead – here are now two churches that we have started in my village. Not only that, but by the grace of God we have started a training centre in my village. We Fulani are focused Christians, and we are the fruit of the labours of so many: of the African church, and of Westerners who have been among the Fulani people for many years. We are the fruit of your labour, and we carry that holy burden to pass on this message to our people.

I did two long rides in 2006, including one around the perimeter of Great Britain. Why did I do it? When I was working for HSBC, a bank in the UK, I was inspired by one of their customers. I hadn't seen him for a few days when suddenly he turned up, looking tanned. I asked him, "Where have you been?"

He said he had been cycling for charity, so I started encouraging him. And he encouraged me. He said, "You can do it too."

I said, "I can't, I'm disabled."

He said, "No, don't look at it that way; you can do it."

So I challenged myself to do it. And I did it by the grace of God – 4,500 miles. It is still on the BBC. I remember the BBC asking me, "How did you do it with one leg?"

I recited this verse to them: "I lift up my eyes to the mountains – where does my help come from? My help comes from the LORD, the Maker of heaven and earth."

"But how? How did you do it with one leg?"

I said to them, "Listen to this: one leg composes, and one leg sings. That's a team." That's what I said – but they didn't put that on their website!

I was asked to explain how we do ministry among the Muslims.

I believe that there is value in people. And culture is not utterly wrong; I believe that culture is a gift of God for humanity. We believers need to discover the values that God has placed in culture, and to connect with cultures as we make disciples. And note that our Lord Jesus spoke about his kingdom: he didn't speak about my kingdom or your kingdom, or about NGOs. So let's discover what our Lord Jesus meant by his kingdom and connect with that.

As we minister among Muslims, the first thing I have discovered is in Genesis 1:27–28: they are created in the image of God. Unless we rediscover that the "other" is made in the image of God, that the other is a mirror of God to me, we will never be able to express the love of God to him or her. You can't. No matter what programme you offer in order to help or better a person, you will not be able to help him or her unless you first see that person as made in the image of God – and that God loves that person.

We Fulani are appreciative of your prayers and your support. Now, the relationship between the West and the Fulani is ongoing. I am a nomad; the Fulani are nomadic. And God is the nomadic God who is inviting us to journey with him. It is not for us to settle down; we are discovering and moving with God.

You can learn about *generosity* from nomads. Learn to receive the widow's offering. Enjoy the hospitality. There are some important values here. Please discover these values.

There are several elements that constitute the culture of the Fulani. First it is *strength*, strength of character. The Fulani need to discover that you have strength of character in order to listen to you. They will test you on that before they connect with you – no matter what programme you come with.

Shame is also important. How much do you protect yourself from shameful situations? How much do you care for others, so that they will not fall into shameful situations? When I read the story of the first miracle of Jesus I ask, "What did he do?" He transformed water into wine. But when you examine the story from a Fulani understanding, you see that Jesus was protecting that young couple from falling into shame. Imagine holding your wedding, or holding the wedding of your daughter or your son, and the food runs out. That is shameful! And, in certain cultures, that isn't just the end of the celebration, that's divorce.

There is also *patience*. Fulani people are patient. Discover patience. *Hospitality* is another element. Please discover hospitality. The Fulani people show hospitality, and God can redeem hospitality. There are several things you can talk about when serving the Fulani and Muslims.

Now, as we train the Fulani in Burkina Faso, we make sure that we *make disciples* in our training – maybe you have heard of our disciple-making movement. We focus on disciple-making and church planting. This is the model we have adopted for the Fulani.

By the grace of God, the Fulani who are coming to us to be trained are being trained in *self-reliance*. Self-reliance includes things like tailoring, carpentry, shop-keeping, restaurant work, hair-braiding, and more. In this way, when they go into their local communities, be they towns or rural areas, they arrive as merchants, not as pastors, missionaries, and teachers. And then, as they engage with the community, they intentionally look for the *person of peace* to connect with.

If you arrive among the Fulani people, or among Muslims, and say something like, "Here I am, Father John, to tell you about Jesus. And here is my Bible," often you may be kicked out. But if you arrive as a merchant and *add value* to the community, I believe that you can have meaningful relations with them.

Another thing that we do is get involved in *community health*.

I have lived, studied, and worked in the UK. When I go back to my home country of Burkina Faso, I see so many needs. So I am mobilizing what God has given us. When I think about the two loaves and the five fish, I hear Jesus ask, "What have you got?"

God has given me *relations*. I have so many students I studied with at university who are doctors and nurses. So I *mobilize them* once every three months to come to a designated village and provide health care for free. This is working; we are making relationships through that.

Part 5

Summaries from the Six Consultation Tracks

26

"Church and Community Resilience" Consultation Track

The Church at the Heart of the Resilient Community

David Boan

The Community Resilience track at the 8th Micah Global Triennial Consultation focused on the intersection of community resilience with each of the daily themes and integral mission. A range of speakers discussed their work and local experience, with an emphasis on disasters, conflict zones, disadvantaged people, and people in extreme need. The track aims included showing that resilience is as much about community as it is about individuals, that the church is central to carrying out God's plan for communities, and that the work of creating resilience is in keeping with integral mission.

Overview
Resilience and Trust

Our first panel session focused on conflict zones and reducing conflict by restoring trust. This included trust in leaders and institutions, as well as in people different from ourselves. The presentations used DRC as a case example to show trust as fundamental to resilience. Panel members included the following:

- Rev Israel Ngirababo (Evangelical Alliance of DRC)

- Wissam al-Saliby (Advocacy Officer, World Evangelical Alliance)
- Albert Baliesima Kadukima (Executive Director of the ESADER (Ensemble pour la santé et le développement holistique en milieu rural et périurbain)

Resilience and Compassion

Compassion depends on bringing down barriers between groups and developing the ability to see how and when people are in need. This requires being open to relationships with people different from ourselves. Likewise, working across faiths and cultures to bring down barriers and become prepared to serve is basic to creating resilient communities. Panel members included the following:

- Socrates Evangelista (PhilRADS)
- Joseph Nyamutera (Regional Director at Le Rucher Great Lakes Aka Mercy Ministries)

Resilience and Crisis Response

This panel explored lessons from disaster response that can help us build more resilient communities. It explored whether the way we respond to a crisis builds a more resilient community, or, conversely, diminishes resilience. Participants explored some challenging questions, such as the following: Is there a preferred way to represent the gospel? How do NGOs best engage the local church? How do we balance urgency with attention to long-term development? The panel on community engagement includes participants from the Philippines and Nepal. Panel members included the following:

- Chris McDonald (Tearfund)
- Socrates Evangelista (PhilRADS)
- Thir Koirala (Micah Nepal)

Outcomes

Following the panel presentations, participants worked in small groups to list the key lessons brought by the panels, and what they would recommend to local churches. The list of lessons included the following:

- The church should be equipped in both awareness and preparedness to respond to disasters/crises.

- Churches should build relationships and be recognized as responders.
- There is a need for more deliberate discipleship in the church about the meaning of loving others.
- The church should preach and teach our identity as citizens of heaven more than national identity.
- There is a need for a more unified and coordinated disaster response between churches.
- Aid and evangelism should be kept separate so there is no appearance of manipulation.
- The Christian witness should be kept, but we must trust in the authenticity of that witness.
- Disasters create opportunities [for a demonstration of] the gospel, but we must be wise in how we conduct ourselves.
- Networking is important, especially before disasters happen.
- Follow-up is very important, including counselling, sharing the gospel, and psychosocial support.
- Basic services can be overlooked in a disaster, such as garbage disposal and recycling.
- We need a better definition of what a church is – namely, a local group of believers.
- The Christian church has an important role to play in resilience because the church itself is a model of discipleship and resilience.
- We need capacity-building resources for churches, and they need to be accessible not just online, for those who cannot access in that way.
- Churches should be encouraged to develop local, regional, and national networks to develop synergy and reduce waste and duplication.
- Churches need to see other organizations as potential partners, not competitors or threats.
- Churches need to bring awareness to the church, help families to be prepared, be integrated with a village plan, and be known and supported by various stakeholders, NGOs, and government.
- Churches need to advocate for their inclusion in government planning.
- Donor organizations should promote church planning that is aligned with government disaster planning, not just at the individual local church level but across the community.

Based on these lessons, the participants said they would recommend the following actions for their local churches:

- Avoid situations where separate churches work on individual and uncoordinated disaster resilience programmes.
- Develop shared understanding of the role and benefits of churches working together.
- Generate more awareness of people in need and the responsibility of the local church beyond mission offerings.
- Emphasize the importance of partnership in intervention; the local church does not need to do everything.
- Encourage Christians to open their homes to people in need.
- Recognize non-Christian neighbours not as enemies or objects of evangelism, but as neighbours to be loved and served.
- Understand disasters and the context for disasters (i.e. vulnerability).
- Get education on disaster response and preparedness.
- (And more broadly:) Provide data on resources and church networks that can be made available in a crisis.

Conclusion

The overlap between integral mission and community resilience was clear and compelling to the participants. The presentation of disaster cases, conflict, and community engagement programmes evoked much discussion of issues around being open to others, the need to be connected to all groups in a community, and the need to use discretion in presenting one's faith. Not only do relationships lead to all groups' ability to access resources, but those relationships themselves are a resource for the support and compassion that are critical during extreme events.

Justice is seen as one of the main roots of the overlap between resilience and integral mission. It is the lack of justice that puts people at risk and reduces resilience, and it is establishing justice that is at the core of integral mission. Thus, integral mission is more than simply helpful for understanding resilience; it is a method for the church to understand the role it plays in fostering community resilience. In a reciprocal way, resilience opens up resources in the form of research, case studies, and programme reports that can expand and add depth to our understanding of integral mission.

27

"Church and Corruption" Consultation Track

Martin Allaby

When those entrusted with power use it for personal gain instead of to serve the common good, they undermine human resilience. God's Word reveals his desire for leaders to show integrity in public office, business, and church life. He is calling Christians to respond to his Word and end their silence about corruption.

Rationale for Theme

Corruption undermines justice and human flourishing. The Bible and secular development agencies have a lot to say about corruption, but the church has been almost silent on the matter.

Key Learning and Issues Raised

Christians can draw on their spiritual resources to be effective in fighting corruption, but first we need to face and address problems within the body of Christ.

Resolutions

After discussing the issues, we made the following resolutions:

- To humbly acknowledge corruption within us and the body of Christ.

- To read the Bible afresh through local eyes – it contains more than instructions to "obey the rulers" (Rom 13).
- To fight corruption with simple, well-researched messages, courage, solidarity, and organization.
- To support public leaders who show integrity.

Outcomes and Way Forward

The Faith and Public Integrity Network is taking this agenda forward.[1] It is a learning community of Christians striving to counter corruption in their local communities, and it welcomes applications for membership from Christians who support the following four goals:[2]

- To build up and sustain Christians already involved in public integrity and anti-corruption work.
- To catalyse collaboration and outreach to Christians who want to get involved in public integrity and anti-corruption work.
- To raise awareness about faith and public integrity within the body of Christ.
- To raise awareness about faith and public integrity in the public square.

Conclusion

Whatever aspect of integral mission you care about, corruption will undermine the change you want to see. History shows that Christians have helped to reduce corruption in the past, and there are some inspiring examples of Christians who are fighting corruption in the present. So we invite you to visit the Faith and Public Integrity Network (FPIN) website, https://fpinetwork.wordpress.com/, where you can see how Christians are fighting corruption in different parts of the world and connect with them. As we work together, God can use us to make his desire for integrity in public office, business, and church life more of a reality.

---

1. Faith and Public Integrity Network, https://fpinetwork.wordpress.com.
2. Applications for membership can be sent to benji@fides-intl.org.

28

"Formation for Integral Mission (Discipleship)" Consultation Track

Tori Greaves and Ruth Padilla DeBorst, INFEMIT

This consultation track and workshop was facilitated by the International Fellowship for Mission as Transformation (INFEMIT). INFEMIT's workshop on "Formation for Integral Mission (Discipleship)" stems from our commitment for Christian formation to contribute to whole-life discipleship and mission by responding to the question: what difference does our Christian faith make in our family and church life, in our work, in our community, and in society at large? This consultation track took the form of a workshop in order to allow people to wrestle with the design and implementation of modes of theological education that further those objectives.

Our workshop had four objectives. The first objective was to exchange experiences in theological formation for integral mission and evaluate their potential beyond their original context. The second was to arrive at consensus among participants regarding key theological, missiological, and pedagogical commitments necessary for full-orbed formation. The third was to familiarize participants with "Faith and Life," a formation process generated in Latin America and being used as a basis for contextually designed programmes in other places. The fourth was to agree on practical next steps as partners in Micah and INFEMIT committed to integral mission formation.

We express our most sincere gratitude to the diverse and enthusiastic group of participants who worked with us to consider the questions we brought to the table. Together, we reflected on the issues we face in our contexts and globally, comparing these with the theological tools and formation processes aimed at addressing them. Recognizing that theology is often treated as a package to be exported and imposed, a subject only for the elite and the educated, we appreciate recent efforts to refocus the "doing of theology" to the centre of daily life in community. These efforts emerged mostly out of the Majority World, among communities who understood that their resistance to colonization and oppression were intimately linked to their faith in Christ.

We examined one such effort, the "Faith and Life" programme that emerged out of Latin America, and we used this programme to explore questions of how we learn, the purpose of theological formation, and the missiological end of all Christian discipleship.

We organized into groups depending on our current involvement in theological formation, whether in formal educational institutions, in informal programmes, or by our interest in initiating such programmes. Within our groups, we talked about the sorts of tools available in our contexts, along with the opportunities for collaboration that exist. Finally, we made recommendations for the consideration of INFEMIT, Micah, and its members about how to proceed in the months and years ahead.

The recommendations presented during the workshop for INFEMIT, Micah, and its members are listed below. As INFEMIT, we are committed to following-up on these conversations and recommendations as well as to involving Micah Global leadership in the process.

Some Highlights
Issues in Our Contexts

We discussed the major issues in our contexts. These include materialism, injustice, indifference, violence, colonization, rejection, tension, dehumanization, ethnicity, greed, white male supremacy, money, power (political/religious), poverty, marginalization, detachment, theory without life, bad theology, pluralism, HIV, identity crisis, diversity, corruption, fear, despair, disconnection, patriarchy, dysfunctional families, individualism, loss, self-absorption, shifting blame, and suppression of women.

Collaborations and Recommendations

Participants discussed the questions "What are our opportunities for collaboration? And what recommendations would you have for Micah Global and INFEMIT?" We list the responses and recommendations in the rest of this chapter.

Opportunities for Collaboration

1. Curriculum Development and Training
- Develop grassroots training
- Translate Tearfund's Light Wheel to measure transformational impact in campus settings
- Collaborate with INFEMIT for training
- Prioritize young people and youth development

2. Consultations
- Invite a group of influential speakers (such as CB Samuel, Bishop Zac, and Ruth Padilla DeBorst) to an open forum discussion with all top church leaders, theological experts, and so on, in the country to debate what the gospel is – to arrive at some consensus about the role of the church, and so on.
- Ask several members for consulting assistance
- Assemble writers for designing a "theology of life"
- Start whole-of-life discipleship consultations with churches

3. Contextual and Cross-Contextual Reflection
- Engage with INFEMIT regarding making theology relevant to the context
- Develop "Micah Young People" and offer support and theological reflections in light of contexts
- Continue to dialogue among seminaries to do contextual theological education in the seminary
- Start video conference calls between leaders in different countries and contexts
- Facilitate church responses to the LGBTQI issue – including sharing of experiences in different countries and regions

4. Awareness and Consciousness-Raising
- Listen more carefully to others
- Start exposure programmes
- Facilitate urban poor–urban rich exchanges

5. Networking
- Connect with other organizations and groups for knowledge and sharing (e.g. "Renew Our World")
- Network with government

- Connect with Lebanese Christians who work with migrants in France and Lebanon
- Network with Bible and theological school leaders
- Make the most of the significant involvement of Micah Philippines

Recommendations for Micah Global and INFEMIT

1. Connect Key Partners
- Connect regional Micah groups
- Connect with seminaries
- Create webinar opportunities
- Create dialogue spaces between key groups (e.g. Bible schools, denominations, faith-based organizations) about integral mission
- Connect the Angolan Bible School Association to Micah-INFEMIT
- Ensure Micah and INFEMIT collaborate with denominations (at national level)
- Bring educators and people in spiritual formation together
- Build networks and platforms to share resources
- Strengthen Micah regional meetings, for sharing new learning and planning together

2. Curriculum and Training
- Share materials on integral mission or similar
- Develop training (at national level)
- Train church leaders in Angola
- Create a list or directory to link all non-formal and formal programmes, especially those online
- Facilitate materials in different languages
- When facilitating a discussion about theological education, it would be helpful not to be so attached to one specific approach

3. Recommendations for Micah Triennial Meetings
- Have fewer presentations – make the time more about interactive learning or even serving together in the location where the event is held
- Create more discussion times, including Bible studies in relatively small but diverse groups where we read in light of the different contexts represented

- Facilitate collective art that evolves over the week as people participate – geared towards shared theological formation
- Condense topics and presentations in main plenary sessions
- Allow more time for people to collaborate and network
- Allow more break time

4. Organizational Structure and Programmes
- See INFEMIT as the theological arm of Micah
- Work towards less institutionalization of Micah – make Micah more of a movement
- Include more theological reflection in Micah structure and programmes
- Micah Global needs to develop a mechanism to hold its members accountable to the values and commitments of integral mission. Find out if these organizations work together in their countries, and whether their operations are ethical and are setting the example of Christ in their communities.

Conclusion

It is critical to do theology with and for the whole people of God in the midst of their daily lives and in light of the issues in their societies. Some examples of theological formation in this vein have emerged from the Majority World, and we are invited to learn from, share, and build upon these models as we seek to serve the church in our contexts. This type of theological formation equips the people of God to live out the whole gospel in every aspect of life and to reflect on and respond critically and faithfully to the issues that arise in our world.[1]

---

1. Material for further reading and reflection can be found at "2018 Micah Global Triennial: Formation for Integral Mission," INFEMIT, www.infemit.org/micah-workshop/.

29

"Urban Shalom" Consultation Track

Joel Kelling and Fiona Kelling

Shalom and the City

More than half the world's population live in urban areas, yet as a community of faith the church has not been active in engaging with the shift towards a more urban environment and how this relates to the outworking of God's mission in the world. Cities are often seen as places to save people from: places that suffer from over-crowding, poverty, epidemic loneliness, violent crime, poor planning, and massive inequality. Yet cities are also places of diversity, vibrancy, creativity, and opportunity – including the opportunity to be seedbeds for peace and a greater expression of the kingdom of God in the world.

The Christian community has largely been silent on systemic city issues such as urban development, social infrastructure, land use, the environment, policy frameworks, and poverty alleviation, despite growing focus on these topics in humanitarian response, development, and academia. The Urban Shalom Society is made up of practitioners, leaders, and academics passionate about working with others to create cities where people can flourish or experience God's dream of shalom. The purpose of this consultation track at the Micah conference was to explore what peace or shalom looks like in an urban context – how as people of faith we can be key facilitators of pathways towards it, and who we might partner with in achieving this.

Three different sessions aimed to unpack the concept of shalom in cities and discover where God is at work. The first session discussed how we experience the city through the built environment and how we can be part of advocating for people-centred design as a part of working towards shalom in our cities. The second session took a more theological approach, looking at the way in which the theology which has been developed thus far may have been influenced by a predominantly rural worldview, and what it may look like when adapted to an urbanizing world. The third session unpacked what flourishing looks like and some of the core principles required to partner with others in order to be more effective in accomplishing the huge task before us.

Working within the Built Environment

Led by Chris Elisara, the first session looked at how our experience of the city can be affected by the way in which it has been designed. Good design can positively affect our physical, social, and mental well-being. Chris reflected on place as a fundamental part of our ontology and on the spatial implications of rebellion (displacement) and salvation (being brought back in place) to highlight the importance of place to human existence, before delving into some key principles for good urban design including walkable cities and mixed-use developments. The notion of tactical urbanism was brought up as a way of instigating and building support for change, as well as the challenges and potential of engaging with city governments or authorities. The importance of fostering unity between churches in order to have a united front was noted as a key to influencing local law-makers, as well as inviting local authorities in to see what the church is doing.

A number of tools were shared including the "Urban Planning Toolkit" developed by the Prince's Foundation to support the ongoing work of participants and encourage further engagement in planning for the future growth of cities. This toolkit can be used by churches and in your neighbourhood to develop a vision for what is needed and how to accomplish it. This session highlighted how there is space for churches to advocate for and on behalf of local communities, use neglected or abandoned spaces, and meet key neighbourhood needs. By getting involved in the built environment, in the things that get built, you can have an influence beyond your own lifetime, and leave a legacy for future generations.

Key learning from this session included the encouragement that each of us is an expert in our own context. However, we would be wise to add some learning and skills to be able to engage better with professionals involved in city design and planning. Engaging in these issues is a way of caring for creation and an important way in which the church has a contribution to make.

Theology and the City

In the second session, facilitated by Bryan McCabe and Dwight Friesen, participants grappled with the differences between rural and urban contexts and the influence these may have had on theology developed over the past decades and centuries. While a hundred years ago 80 percent of the world's Christians were in Europe and the global north, now close to 80 percent are in the global south – these Majority World Christians were well represented in the group present for the discussion. There has been a slower shift in theology away from theologians and the predominant theologies of the global north. Likewise, there has not really been such a thing as the development of an urban theology.

In this conversation, theology was framed as an ongoing act of creation, a search for the least inadequate words to describe God. It was recognized that Christians can be scared of cities, as they are intimidating, messy places with systemic brokenness we don't know how to interact with. Yet there are over 1,200 verses in the Bible related to cities, and having a healthy and developed theological perspective on them can help us with how to engage with cities and the people in them. This session aimed to step up to this time in history and contribute to that growing conversation.

The premise was that the way that theology has developed is based on the predominant worldview we have, which up until this point has been that of a largely rural society. This was contested somewhat as theology has often come from centres of power, which are often urban in nature. Nevertheless, there is a need to think about what changes may be required when looking from a specifically urban perspective – to develop an urban theology. After identifying key features of both rural and urban contexts, participants discussed how they saw the rural being reflected in our ecclesiastical practices, as well as how these might change or what spiritual/worship practices may emerge from the urban environment. Feedback included that urban environments offer greater exchange and more inclusivity, narratives may need to be emphasized more, and our parables or terminology could change in order to be more recognizable and relevant in a digital age. Urban environments also increase the potential for transcultural theology, crossing the globe in all directions, but require more flexibility, adaptation, and experimentation.

The key learning points from this session were around our need to critically examine how our theology has been developed and how this has shaped our view of God. The discussion highlighted how questions of this nature and the quest to develop an urban theology lead us to take a step back and reflect on larger questions: about who God is, what the church is, what it means to thrive as a human being, what rhythms matter most in how God created us, how we gather, and so on. It also revealed how the city can be a place that we can learn from, that can actually teach us, rather than just challenging us. It also highlighted how a strong urban theology can help us partner with other people/groups working in cities in order to create shalom.

Strength-Based Approaches to the Creation of Shalom

Andre van Eymeren and Grace Dyrness led the final discussion focusing more on the "how," with practical examples from participants on the work they were doing and approaches they used, particularly to engage with other organizations and city officials.

The session opened with a brainstorming on what flourishing looks like in the city, using Isaiah 61 as a basis to paint a picture of a city full of shalom. The word "shalom" was explored to draw out the holistic nature of its meaning regarding the well-being of the individual in the context of community and the well-being of the individual being dependent on the well-being of the community. All the various aspects identified in the brainstorming exercise could be identified in the flourishing framework, which was developed in order to provide a framework that related to urban contexts that would capture urban shalom and lead to cities that flourish.

The six elements are the following:

- Basic needs are met (food, shelter, safety, security, education, health, etc.).
- A sense of belonging to land and to others.
- Contributions are valued as well as valuing the contributions of others.
- A growing sense of purpose: being able to live out interests and skills.
- Celebration: of achievements as well as culturally significant events.
- A growing spirituality: a growing sense of something bigger than ourselves.

Participants were invited to share stories of how they have worked in their cities to help people flourish. Based on the four stories shared, key principles were drawn out regarding what is required in order to work in urban environments to create shalom, as well as to partner with others working towards the same goal. These principles were consultation, cooperation, creativity, coordination, relationships, incorporating children, starting small, and being willing to take risks.

A key learning point, highlighted from the stories shared, was that God is at work in cities, and that it is our privilege to partner with him in this, remembering that this work is not ours to complete, but that does not take away our responsibility to be active.

Continuing the Conversation

Participants were invited to continue these conversations through further engagement with the Urban Shalom Society. Their website, http://urbanshalomsociety.org, contains a number of resources that can support and encourage people in their efforts and work in the city. Participants were also invited to contribute to the Urban Shalom Society by telling their stories of the work they are doing through the journal, newsletter, or website articles.

Most of all, participants were encouraged to keep up the good work or to get involved, and to learn more about what can be done, who it can be done with, what this can achieve, and how this can reveal God's ideal for people and creation.

Topics were also discussed further at the Urban Shalom Society Summit, a summary of which can be found at http://urbanshalomsociety.org/report-uss-summit-2018/.

30

"Reconciliation as the Mission of the Church" Consultation Track

Johannes Reimer

The theme of this consultation track was "Reconciliation as the Mission of the Church." Around a hundred people participated, and workshop leaders included Dr Oksana Gritzuita (Ukraine), Joseph Nyamutera (Rwanda), Dr Vladimir Ubeivolc (Moldova), and Dr Johannes Reimer (Germany). The workshop developed in three basic directions:

1. We described and discussed the basic theological foundation of our ministry of reconciliation.
2. We named and debated the process a given church will have to accomplish in order to start a community-driven reconciliation ministry.
3. We discussed methods of interhuman reconciliation.

Theology of Reconciliation and Peace-Building

A basic theological concept of reconciliation, as present in the writings of the New Testament, was presented by Dr Reimer. According to 2 Corinthians 5:18–21, Jesus was sent by the Father to reconcile the world with God the Father. He has brought peace to those near and those far off. He is the promised Prince of Peace, the Son of a God of peace. His message, the good news, is a gospel of peace.

The church is sent as the Father sent Jesus (John 20:21). He determines the church's mission and gives it the word of reconciliation (2 Cor 5:19–20). Reconciliation is at the heart of what Christians are called to do. Our mission is a mission of reconciliation, and this mission includes reconciliation with God, oneself, our neighbour, and even the world around us. It is motivated by the fact that Jesus Christ has already reconciled to God the world in which we live. We are invited to join him in his reconciling work as his church, which he calls *ecclesia*: those called out of the world in order to accept responsibility for the world. The church is God's major instrument of mediation, of peace-building, and reconciliation. The question is, how does the church practically become this agent of peace?

The Missionary Praxis Cycle

The mission of reconciliation, as given by God to the church, is in every way a holistic, integral mission. It must encompass all strata of personal and communal life.

Such a praxis is best described by a *missional praxis cycle* as developed by the University of South Africa. According to this cycle, the reconciliatory praxis of the church starts with *involvement in a concrete community* – the neighbouring community surrounding the church. Effective mediation starts when the church accepts the community as its primary missionary target, and accepts community development as the core mission. Involvement in this opens the door to an effective praxis.

The second step is *potential analysis*. The church must discover its reconciliatory potential in order to become effective. Mission is done by gifted people. And it is the Spirit of God who provides the needed competence in his gifts.

Equally important is the next step – *context analysis*. Reconciliation only makes sense where it serves real needs, transforms real conflicts, and brings peace into a broken community. To know the crying heart, it is important to understand the conflict zones of a community. Jesus says that only when we know the truth will we experience deliverance (John 8:32).

Finally, knowing the community we are sent to as God's church (aware of our potential and competence, and having understood the felt needs of the people), we may undertake the next steps of the cycle: *develop a context-relevant vision and name the first hands-on projects of reconciliation*. The mission of reconciliation may begin.

Sharing Methods of Healing

Reconciliation is a process in which the reconciling parties

1. Discover and name their perspectives on what has created tension and conflict.
2. Agree on the corrupted sides in their perspectives and name jointly the sin and wrong in what happened.
3. Ask for forgiveness and forgive each other.
4. Determine new ways of living together in peace.

Different methods from both a pastoral-counselling and psychological standpoint were presented and discussed in depth in our consultation track. Participants shared their own experiences and the results they have witnessed. Especially valuable were the reports on approaches being developed in various countries:

- *Healing of Ethnic Wounds:* Rwandan approach.
- *Healing of Memories Approach:* Developed in South Africa and redefined in Ireland and Romania.
- *Psychological Treatments of Victims of Violence:* A Ukrainian approach dealing with post-war trauma.

The practice of such approaches in real-life contexts was reported and the results described. In all settings healing and reconciliation is happening.

We concluded that reconciliation methodologies are important, but other factors determine positive results – such as the experience of love and grace, God's presence, and efforts towards concretely expressed forgiveness. In Rwanda, for example, victims and perpetrators are reconciling and starting to work together for peace. In Ukraine, deeply traumatized people are turning to God and experiencing full healing, recovering their own dignity. Participants from the Philippines, Indonesia, and the Middle East report healing stories as a result of the reconciliation praxis. All of us express thanks and joy to God and to one another.

31

"Integral Mission and Community Health" Consultation Track

James Pender, Jim Oehrig, and Sara Kandiah

Dedicated to Mr Faustino Paulo Mandavela, presenter in the "Integral Mission and Community Health" track, who passed away on 28 January 2019 in his home country of Angola

Overview

Community health is central to the gospel. Well-being comes through gospel-connected healthy practices and interventions, miraculous healing, and treating our bodies as "temples of the Holy Spirit." In his earthly ministry, Jesus prioritized health restoration, strengthened the profiles of different people and groups, and addressed a wide variety of health conditions. The Gospels highlight healings of diseases and marginalizing conditions including neglected tropical diseases (leprosy and other skin conditions), physical disability, and mental ill health. Jesus's healing work also served to restore healthy community dynamics – connection, access, and participation – for stigmatized, exploited peoples.

Today millions of people remain highly stigmatized by neglected tropical diseases (NTDs), disability, and other conditions. Throughout history, the poorest and most marginalized communities have suffered the greatest ill health and face the greatest health challenges.

The "Integral Mission and Community Health" track treated several themes:

- sustainability

- service access
- neglected tropical diseases (NTDs)
- self-care
- faith-healing
- awareness-raising, advocacy, and stigma reduction
- churches' responses to marginalized peoples

This consultation track included lively debate, case studies, breakout sessions, and a diverse group of presenters and facilitators from Angola, Australia, Bangladesh, Côte d'Ivoire, Ghana, Kenya, Mozambique, Myanmar, Nepal, South Africa, Sri Lanka, the United Kingdom, and the United States of America.[1] The goal was for participants to gain a more complete understanding of integral mission in the community health context, and to take away tangible lessons from the successes and failures shared by practitioners from the Majority World and other parts of the world. This was the first time a consultation track at Micah focused on health, with participants being challenged to include in their work people affected by leprosy, NTDs, and disability.

Local Ownership and Sustainability in Community Health

Session 1 (pre-consultation) looked at integral mission, marginalizing health conditions, and sustainability: identifying challenges and exploring alternative approaches.

Interventions in health provision need to be sustainable, locally owned and managed, and without "start and stop" inputs. The pattern of outsiders/Westerners arriving to solve community problems was often the historical norm, but it led to unhealthy dependency. At the same time, many of the best-known integral mission approaches – Umoja and Disciple the Nations Alliance – mobilize the community with zero input. However, this is difficult where people need medicine, clinical support, or ongoing self-care support to prevent ulcers or other complications for people affected by neglected tropical diseases such as leprosy, lymphatic filariasis, trachoma, Buruli ulcer,

---

1. These included Faustino Paulo Mandavela (RIP) of SOLE Angola, Phil Wilkerson of TEAR Australia, Salomon Sumon Halder of The Leprosy Mission International Bangladesh, Aubin Yao of MAP, Josue Tchimou of Sustainable Mission Aid, Florence Muindi of Life in Abundance, Manuel Luis Maliquito of ALEMO, Zaw Moe Aung of The Leprosy Mission Myanmar, Chiranjivi Sharma of The Leprosy Mission Nepal, Flip Buys of World Reformed Fellowship, Raghu Balachandra of Alliance Development Trust, James Pender of The Leprosy Mission England and Wales, Sara Kandiah of The Leprosy Mission International, Mike Soderling of Health in Mission, and Jim Oehrig of American Leprosy Missions.

and leishmaniasis, or diabetes and other conditions causing limitation of movement or nerve damage. Self-care also uses a participatory methodology, but marginalized peoples are likely to be excluded and their needs not addressed by the wider community, who may in fact be stigmatizing them.

It was mentioned in the session that sometimes double standards are followed with an expectation that in the Majority World hospitals should be fully financially sustainable while in Western countries they are usually not. However, it was agreed that sustainability is desirable, with it being observed that Jesus came for three years then was able to exit his "intervention" and leave it in such a way that it was able to multiply. This included leaving the Holy Spirit. It was argued that the most sustainable way is to work with local churches, making them the hero of the work. When the Christian development agency eventually withdraws, nobody will realize, as the churches are at the forefront and beneficiaries will never know that the agency was there in the first place.

A case study from the Advocacy for Empowerment Project in Bangladesh showcased how instead of using direct health service provision, the health of communities could be more sustainably improved by working in partnership with civil society, including local community-based organizations. We need the media to advocate for better government services and to include health activities alongside existing intervention. We must partner with government health institutions through training and technical support. It was also noted that this project partnered with non-Christian organizations and individuals to achieve sustainability.

It was concluded in discussion that "Whoever discards working with non-believers as partners underestimates the common grace of God; we should work on partnerships from a kingdom perspective, not only from a church perspective; partnerships work well when partners don't have a hidden agenda, which applies to believers and non-believers (believers need to model this); we pursue mutual transformation, including transformation of partners, not only the transformation of beneficiaries; but we need to set values for partnership; and apply a good theology for partnerships."[2]

A presentation on a photovoice study on barriers and enablers for people with lived experience of psychosocial disability, in which beneficiaries took photos of aspects of their lives and then used them as an aid to talk about some of their struggles, widened the discussion to include mental health and well-being. It highlighted that in order to make changes facilitated by project

---

2. Luis Noda, Vice President for Transformational Engagement at Food for the Hungry.

interventions sustainable in the longer term (in beneficiaries' lives), these must also address their inner well-being needs. Participants were inspired towards the need for increased sensitivity and inclusion within churches and development projects, and decided that mental health is not a distinct issue; it's integrated, and communities must own the problem from a holistic, whole-person perspective.

The Holy Spirit, Modern Medicine, and Traditional Healers

Session 2 explored the tension between modern medicine, traditional approaches, faith, prayer, and miraculous healing.

Jesus described his ministry in Matthew 11 saying, "The blind receive sight, the lame walk, those who have leprosy are cleansed, the deaf hear, the dead are raised, and the good news is proclaimed to the poor." Health and healing were central. Although his healings were miraculous, he did not negate the value of medicine, saying that healthy people don't need a doctor, but sick people do (Matt 9). The disciples performed miracles but also included Luke, a physician, on their team. Medical missions rely on medicine and treatments; some community-based programmes include traditional healers/herbalists; and some faith missions focus exclusively on miracles.

While Western groups do not usually integrate miraculous healing, modern medicine, and traditional medicine in the Majority World (where people have more holistic worldviews), participants shared how communities in the Majority World typically make use of all kinds of medicine from Western, herbal, and traditional systems. Traditional medicine providers, even witch doctors, are recognized and even regulated alongside conventional doctors (by national governments in parts of Asia, Oceania, and Africa). The two African presenters highlighted the positive role of traditional medicine, but also the negative impact of some traditional practices, such as the burying of a person affected by leprosy in sand up to his or her neck for the healing of ulcers. The need for integration was highlighted by a story of a person affected by leprosy who had been told to stay with a witchdoctor for a year for healing. Upon discovery by Christian project field staff the person was removed and treated with multi-drug therapy; however, that person died the following year, and the community supposed it was because the person had been removed from the witchdoctor. This obviously hindered the leprosy work of the Christian organization, showing that even though we might disagree with or disbelieve in certain practices, we cannot ignore and must address them. It was also emphasized that biblical discernment is needed in identifying beneficial traditional remedies that could assist us or traditional practitioners that we can work with. However, remedies that may give harmful physical or spiritual results must be refuted and rejected.

All participants agreed that prayer and medicine could be used side by side, with examples shared from Nepal of how, when prayer had not "healed" someone affected by leprosy, the pastor referred the person to Anandaban Hospital for successful treatment; and, conversely, of a person who had not been cured by modern medicine but was instead healed through "deliverance prayer." Participants believed that prayer for healing should accompany Christian health interventions using modern medicine more often, and that it can also complete the healing process by covering associated inner well-being needs. Ultimately it was recognized that all healing, whether herbal, miraculous, or from modern medicine, needs to be attributed to God the Healer!

A Billion People Neglected

Session 3 looked at how Jesus prioritized neglected people, including people with disability and people affected by the neglected tropical disease of leprosy. Participants examined how the church and parachurch organizations can raise awareness of NTDs that cause disability and marginalization, assist in case detection and referrals, reduce stigma, and provide appropriate support alongside their existing interventions.

Neglected tropical diseases (NTDs) are endemic in over a hundred countries and impact more than one billion people. Leprosy alone totals 200,000 new cases a year. One of the main challenges is early detection. People affected must be treated quickly to avoid developing permanent disability. Even after they have been treated, NTD-affected people are often in need of medical, socio-emotional, livelihood, spiritual, and advocacy support. Many are scattered geographically, typically in remote areas. While there may not be institutions present, there are usually churches, and often faith-based NGOs, nearby.

The Gospels talk about Jesus healing the sick, but a few of these miracles are singled out. These include healings of fever, leprosy, paralysis, a withered hand, a bent back, haemorrhage, deafness and dumbness, and blindness. It is significant that all but the first of these were stigmatizing and marginalizing conditions. This connects with the bias toward those at the bottom (those marginalized) shown by Jesus's ministry on earth, as he deliberately sought out those most in need. Out of around thirty specific healings recorded in the

Gospels, seven concerned leprosy, with sixteen people healed. Blindness (also often caused by NTDs) is the next most mentioned, with six healed.

The focus Jesus gives to leprosy, a neglected disease, really is remarkable. Healing from leprosy is mentioned as a "sign of the kingdom" three times (e.g. Luke 7:22). Jesus heals somebody with leprosy after his debut and most important teaching in the Sermon on the Mount (Matt 8:1–4). The first miracle the disciples see is someone healed of leprosy (Luke 5:12–15). Jesus broke the law to heal a man who was probably afflicted by leprosy with a clawed hand (Matt 12:10–14; Mark 3:1–6; Luke 6:6–11), leading to the plot to kill him. Jesus ate in the house of Simon, a person affected by leprosy who was healed by Jesus just before he died (Matt 26:6; Mark 14:3). People affected by leprosy were and still are considered "untouchable," yet Jesus deliberately touched them to heal them (Mark 1:40–45; Luke 5:12–15). Jesus instructed people affected by leprosy, so they could be restored within the community (Mark 1:44). A Samaritan healed of leprosy was one of the few people Jesus praised for their faith (Luke 17:11–19).[3] The reason why leprosy was given such a focus by Jesus is that he wanted to focus on the most marginalized people and the most neglected of diseases. As he sent his disciples to heal people affected by leprosy (as in Matt 10:8), neglected tropical diseases (NTDs) should still be on our agenda.

Examples of local church involvement in supporting people affected by leprosy were shared from Sri Lanka and Mozambique. In Sri Lanka, evangelical pastors have partnered with the Government Anti-Leprosy Campaign and district interfaith committees, facilitated by a parachurch organization, the Alliance Development Trust, to raise awareness of leprosy, to reduce stigma, and to detect new cases that can be treated. Their collaborative approach has wider implications for practitioners, as it demonstrates how integral mission projects involving churches in their communities are possible even in countries where Christians are a small minority and suffer persecution. It also shows that working alongside government officers and religious leaders from multiple faiths can prove very effective in raising awareness. Furthermore, it has contributed greatly towards peace-building and increased understanding in a fragile context. The churches have also learned how to engage with other faiths in positive ways, without compromising their message, around a "neutral issue" and have learned the value of being "salt and light" in their communities. These churches are reaping the benefits of improved relations with their neighbours, as well as increasing their status in the eyes of government authorities.

---

3. James Pender, The Leprosy Mission England and Wales.

The Leprosy People's Association (ALEMO) are mobilizing the local church in Mozambique using the Umoja tool.[4] This tool helps local congregations make improvements to their communities using their own resources. This includes equipping them to support people affected by leprosy and another NTD (lymphatic filariasis)[5] to meet their basic needs, as well as to advocate to local authorities on their behalf to ensure they receive their rights and entitlements. Participants in the session shared that they believed the church could do more on NTDs. As well as helping directly, churches could also involve seminaries and the wider community. It was also felt that their involvement should include psycho-spiritual support and services.

Pulling the Roof Off the Church

Just as in Luke 5:17–26 the friends of a person with a disability made a hole in the roof to allow him to meet with Jesus, so we also should remove the metaphorical "roof" of the church. In other words, we should remove barriers to people with disabilities, so they can be involved and included within churches. Therefore session 4 looked at how to break down barriers that affect people with disabilities, and the church's role as a champion of this issue.

Jesus came to break the chains of injustice and the barriers people with disabilities face in all areas of life: employment, services, rights, education, and even worship. People affected by NTDs and people with disability are also stigmatized – they face prejudice in addition to physical barriers – and their situations are further exacerbated. Unfortunately, the same barriers faced in wider society are often present in the church. They are both attitudinal and physical.

Romans 8:19 states, "For the creation waits in eager expectation for the children of God to be revealed." But often the church is not revealing the light of Christ through supporting or including marginalized people such as those with disabilities. The church has an important role to play as true transformation can happen only by challenging the lies in the lives of individuals and communities with what God says and facilitating holistic change that includes improved health outcomes and spiritual and socio-economic transformation.[6]

---

4. "Umoja," Tearfund Learn, accessed 26 September 2019, https://learn.tearfund.org/en/themes/church/umoja/.

5. Lymphatic filariasis is also known as elephantiasis.

6. Aubin Yao of MAP Côte d'Ivoire.

An example of how the church is supporting people with disabilities was shared from Myanmar, where a Baptist church in Chaungsone in the south of the country has constructed a building on its own land to use as a Disability Resource Centre. Church members staff the centre and provide various services to people with disabilities, including counselling, physiotherapy, provision of assistive devices, special education to children with learning difficulties, and assisting them to obtain their rights and entitlements. As well as giving support to this congregation, The Leprosy Mission Myanmar has been working with churches, denominations, and theological colleges to assist them in becoming more inclusive and accepting of people affected by leprosy and/or disabilities.[7] The need for greater disability inclusion within churches as well as within Micah Global was considered to be an issue that needs prioritization.

Inclusion is an issue not only in regard to disability or leprosy; it concerns other issues, such as the role of the church in overcoming HIV/AIDS stigma in South Africa. Traditional African worldviews can often create and maintain stigma. Therefore, some participants of this consultation talked about how they use biblical themes that relate to local worldviews in order to tailor materials to their local contexts. These are successfully used in advocacy and in addressing negative attitudes.[8]

Conclusions

In summary, our consultation reached the following conclusions:[9]

- The church is a sleeping giant waiting to be awakened for the health of the nations [this was presented in the plenary by Aubin Yao of Côte d'Ivoire].
- Community health is central to the gospel.
- Health is bigger than just physical needs; it includes social and spiritual well-being – it's integral.
- There is a role for prayer, miraculous healing, modern medicine, and herbal medicine; but all healing should be attributed to God.
- Jesus prioritized people with disabilities and with neglected tropical diseases; so we should too!

---

7. Dr Zaw Moe Aung, National Director of The Leprosy Mission Myanmar.
8. Flip Buys, Professor in Theology at Northwest University, South Africa.
9. Presented in the plenary by Aubin Yao of Côte d'Ivoire.

- The church has a crucial role in raising health awareness, fighting stigma, and combating discrimination.
- Inclusivity is contagious!
- Micah Global needs to (1) involve people with disabilities in the planning of national, regional, and global Micah gatherings, and commit to using fully accessible venues; (2) spearhead the development of a biblical rights-based approach for a theology of neglected tropical diseases, disability, and mental health.

Lessons Learned and Action Points – Participant Quotes
Role of the Local Church and Integral Mission

"We probably need to see the role of the church in a different way. The local church can take a vital role in reaching out to people, as per our mandate. There is scope to work with churches. In our organizational culture and practice we need to be more intentional to evidence the integral mission concept. We need more direct approaches, including dialogue with churches for partnership, and we need to take further steps with stakeholders and beneficiaries for the sake of resilient communities." — *Salomon Sumon Halder, TLM Bangladesh*

"Improving the health and life of marginalized people and their integration at various levels of society is of great concern for Christian organizations in many countries. The great role of churches is not only their presence in communities but also their knowledge and practice of the Word of God – they promote love of neighbour, they help to combat stigma and discrimination, and they lead marginalized people to integration at various levels of society. For this the church must wake up from its comfort, from its deep sleep, so it can fulfil the holistic ministry of Jesus."[10] — *Pastor Malaquito, ALEMO, Mozambique*

"Communities, groups, and individuals we are supporting and helping should be at the centre of our actions. So the well-being of families and individuals in a community should be the main purpose of our programmes. Our actions should not be systematic but driven by a holistic approach. We need each other to make things happen: funding agencies, partners, churches, faith-based organizations, NGOs, and health systems." — *Josue Tchimou, Sustainable Mission Aid, Ghana*

---

10. ALEMO = Association for People Affected by Leprosy.

"Integral mission in community health should not be considered a project (i.e. output- and outcome-driven), because people are unique and have unique needs. Jesus did not run a project – he had unique relationships with people in need. We should move away from output-/outcome-driven approaches to lively relationship-building approaches in community health. This will enable us to achieve integral mission." *Aubin Yao, MAP International, Côte d'Ivoire*

"The main consultation presentations underlined the importance of working with churches as well as facilitating the spiritual growth of the staff of The Leprosy Mission (TLM) as mentioned in the new TLM Global Strategy. I was struck by the 'Life in Abundance' approach of 'making local church the hero not us; we decrease our role in order for Christ to increase'. Our consultation track inspired participants towards the need for increased sensitivity and inclusion within churches and development projects around issues of mental health. We discussed that mental health is not a distinct issue; it's integrated, and communities must own the problem from a holistic, whole-person perspective." — *James Pender, TLMEW*

"The Micah Global meetings served as the impetus for greater integral mission intentionality with our partners and projects. We hope to add integral mission advisers to our staff, one for Africa and one for Asia, by 2020. This will ensure a better balance of gospel demonstration and proclamation in our programmes, support local and national efforts to build integral mission awareness and capacity, inform project development processes, and build links to local churches and the Christian community. Partner ministries in Ghana and Côte d'Ivoire will grow capacity via the provision of specific integral mission-related inputs during the project design process." — *Jim Oehrig, ALM*

Collaborative Approaches

"Compared with work-related workshops and conferences, this is a wider platform from which I could learn and hear a lot more about what others are doing. It really benefits me and is also a way of being revived spiritually. Getting involved in discussions like the Micah partnership agreement review helped me have the chance to share what The Leprosy Mission is doing, and gain from positive partnerships." — *Dr Zaw Moe Aung, TLM Myanmar*

"As a Christian institution, organization, or church, we should be aware of how God can use the different local community resources available to bring healing and transformation. We can work with other faith groups and members in the Spirit of Christ, where the gospel seems invisible." — *Chiranjivi Sharma, TLM Nepal*

32

Final Remarks

Integral Mission and Community Resilience

Sheryl Haw

I had the privilege to live and work in South Sudan from 1995 to 2000. It was a turbulent period as the civil war raged on and the Sudanese people resiliently struggled from crisis to crisis. There was always so much to do: health care, clean water provision, food security, education, and essential household items to distribute. We built a clinic and it would be bombed. We would distribute seeds; but people would have to run before harvest from a pending attack. Then we would all gather again and start rebuilding.

Living with the community, weeping together when a young boy died from a venomous snake bite, celebrating when a new baby was born after a difficult delivery by torchlight, we started to discover friendship and solidarity. Every Friday afternoon, I would invite anyone who wanted to study the Bible to gather together under a big shady tree. To my surprise and joy people would walk sometimes for as long as eight hours just to share two hours under the tree together.

I remember being accosted in the village one evening by some women who argued that they felt left out of the study because they were illiterate. So we started to gather in one of their homes and developed a pictorial study plan. The round mud and thatched house (*Tukul*) was crammed full of eager women hungry to know about God. Sitting next to me was the traditional healer, asking probing questions, in awe that Jesus would carry their burdens, pain, and sin (especially remarkable for them in a culture where the women carry all the heavy loads).

In one area which had been historically a Catholic mission station, a number of men asked if I would do their training. On my next trip out to Kenya I made an appointment to meet the Catholic Father responsible for this region and asked for his permission and blessing, which he freely gave, and we started the training. It wasn't long before one of the men asked to be baptized! I must confess I was hesitant, as looking into the Nile River with its large crocodiles was off-putting – I suggested we might need to simply use a bucket!

I had not heard about the raging debate over what was primary: proclamation or social action. Nor had I sat in on a denominational argument about whose church and interpretation of the truth was better. I had yet to learn of the aid organization debate around the topic of evangelism and good works.

Towards the end of my five years in South Sudan I had grown to realize that without the pursuit of justice and reconciliation, without a new way of thinking about relief and development, the transformation we longed for would not come.

As I have continued to learn and grow in my understanding, I am now able to use terms such as "integral mission" to help in our rethinking about the changes that need to be considered as we respond to our world in need. However, I recognize that we have some way to go as our approach is still very dualistic.

The Great Commission commanded us to teach all nations all the things Jesus had commanded. We are still cherry-picking from this. We are choosing our audiences; we are selecting our themes; and the result is an incomplete gospel. Integral mission is not just evangelism and good works; it is the pursuit of justice, the persistence towards peace and reconciliation, the care of creation, and the liberation, healing, and restoration of all things in heaven and earth in Jesus Christ (Col 1:20). Integral mission is obedience to Jesus and following his way of love. This means incarnational living, solidarity with those who are in need, changed lifestyles that reflect God's kingdom, and a resilience to set our mission towards his agenda.

What Does This Mean for Micah? What Are Our Next Steps?

The "Micah Declaration on Integral Mission" (September 2001) has been an inspirational document and we were thrilled to see the use of its definition of "integral mission" in the Lausanne "Cape Town Commitment." We have come to realize that we need to write an evolved explanation of integral mission together, so as to ensure we avoid the dualistic dangers and include our growing understanding and recognition of the paradigm shifts occurring in our pursuit of mission as transformation.

We have further recognized that in order for our members and the wider Christian community to be effective witnesses, servants, and ambassadors for God's kingdom, we need to ensure that together we provide platforms for ongoing reflection and shared learning. Provision of networking spaces that enable both transnational and grassroot conversations and cooperation remains at the heart of Micah. We long to see a greater transgenerational engagement and we are intentionally pursuing ways to engage the younger up-and-coming leaders.

One of the hallmarks of Micah Global Triennial Consultations is our commitment to not allow language to be a barrier, and we are grateful for the committed individuals and members around the world who use their gifts to translate and enable translingual engagement.

The growing concerns of environmental degradation and the need to be restorative and protective of creation will require us increasingly to draw on technology to enrich fellowship and learning on virtual platforms. We are committed to respond with ecological integrity and witness in and through all we do.

The context of our times also prompts us to prioritize the important distinctives of Micah. In an increasingly prejudiced society (racially, ethnically, nationally, lingually, sexually, economically, religiously, socially, and around ability), unity in our diversity is a demonstration of love and kingdom dynamics. We follow the Prince of Peace and therefore need to be people of peace, recognizing that the gospel message is one of reconciliation.

Resilience

We are amazed at the resilience we have seen in individuals and communities that have faced and are facing unimaginable challenges. We long to see every church in every community enable greater resilience towards flourishing, free from poverty, injustice, and conflict.

It is a privilege to walk alongside our members who touch the lives of those in need, daily and compassionately, who raise their voices against the travesties of injustice, and who risk their lives to work towards reconciliation in place of conflict. Our resilience is strengthened because of the cries of pain of those in need and the testimonies of all who choose to respond.

After all, what does God require of us? To act justly, love mercy, and walk humbly with him (Mic 6:8).

Bibliography

Amresh, S., M. Johnston, M. Thakar, S. Shrivastava, G. Sarkhel, I. Sunita, and S. Parkar. "Impact and Origin of Stigma and Discrimination in Schizophrenia: Patient Perceptions." *Research and Action* 1, no. 1 (2011): 67–72.

Anderson, B. W. *Contours of Old Testament Theology.* Minneapolis, MN: Fortress, 2011.

Aten, J. D. "Disaster Spiritual and Emotional Care in Professional Psychology: A Christian Integrative Approach." *Journal of Psychology and Theology* 40, no. 2 (2012): 131–135.

Balmaceda, V., and C. Zimmer. "Our Calling to Pursue Peace and Justice." *Journal of Latin American Theology* 12, no. 1 (2017): 101–116.

Barclay, J. M. G. *Paul and the Gift.* Grand Rapids, MI: Eerdmans, 2015.

Barnette, H. H. *Introduction to Christian Ethics.* Nashville: Broadman, 1961.

Bartholomew, C. G. *Where Mortals Dwell: A Christian View of Place for Today.* Grand Rapids, MI: Baker Academic, 2011.

Bass, B. M., and B. J. Avolio. "Shatter the Glass Ceiling: Women May Make Better Managers." *Human Resource Management* 33, no. 4 (Winter 1994): 549–560.

Bassler, J. "The Theology of Romans 1:18 – 4:25." Theology of Paul's Letter Group at the Society of Biblical Literature (SBL) Annual Meeting, Washington, DC, 1993.

Beesley, A. "National Debt and Its Servicing Still Weigh Heavily on State." *The Irish Times,* 16 October 2014. Accessed 19 September 2019. http://www.irishtimes.com/news/politics/national-debt-and-its-servicing-still-weigh-heavily-on-state-1.1965128.

Beker, J. C. *Paul the Apostle: The Triumph of God in Life and Thought.* Philadelphia: Fortress, 1980.

Benner, D. G. *Healing Emotional Wounds.* Grand Rapids, MI: Baker, 1990.

Berkes, F., and H. Ross. "Community Resilience: Toward an Integrated Approach." *Society and Natural Resources* 26, no. 1 (2013): 5–20.

Bevans, S. B., R. Schroeder, and L. J. Luzbetak. "Missiology after Bosch: Reverencing a Classic by Moving Beyond." *International Bulletin of Missionary Research* 29, no. 2 (2005): 69–72.

Blomberg, C. L. *Neither Poverty Nor Riches.* Grand Rapids, MI: Eerdmans, 1999.

BNPB. *524 Desa Tangguh Bencana.* Jakarta Timur: Badan Nasional Penanggulangan Bencana (BNPB), 2017.

Boan, D., and J. Ayers. *Faith and Community: Creating Shared Resilience.* Carlisle: Langham Global Library, 2020.

Bowen, D. *The Protestant Crusade in Ireland, 1800–70: A Study of Protestant-Catholic Relations between the Act of Union and Disestablishment.* Dublin: Gill & Macmillan, 1978.

———. *Souperism: Myth or Reality? A Study in Souperism*. Dublin: Mercier, 1970.

Broyles, C. C. "Psalms of Lament." In *Dictionary of the Old Testament: Wisdom, Poetry and Writings*, edited by Tremper Longman III and Peter Enns, 384–399. Nottingham: Inter-Varsity Press, 2008.

Brueggemann, W. *The Message of the Psalms: A Theological Commentary*. Minneapolis, MN: Augsburg, 1984.

———. *The Psalms and the Life of Faith*. Minneapolis, MN: Fortress, 1995.

Burgess, R., and K. Mathias. "Community Mental Health Competencies: A New Vision for Global Mental Health." In *The Palgrave Handbook of Sociocultural Perspectives on Global Mental Health*, 2nd edition, edited by R. G. White, S. Jain, D. Orr, U. Read, 211–235. London: Palgrave Macmillan, 2017.

Burnett, D. *The Healing of the Nations: The Biblical Basis of the Mission of God*. Carlisle: Paternoster, 1996.

Calvin, J. *Commentaries*. Bellingham, WA: Logos Bible Software, 2010.

Campbell, D. A. *The Deliverance of God: An Apocalyptic Rereading of Justification in Paul*. Grand Rapids, MI: Eerdmans, 2009.

Carroll, A., B. Davar, J. Eaton, R. Catherine, J. Cambri, A. Devine, and C. Vaughan. "Promoting the Rights of People with Psychosocial Disability in Development Research and Programming." *Development Bulletin* 77 (2016): 25–30.

Center for the Study of Global Christianity. *Christianity in Its Global Context, 1970–2020: Society, Religion, and Mission*. South Hamilton, MA: Center for the Study of Global Christianity, 2013. Accessed 6 August 2018. https://archive.gordonconwell.edu/ockenga/research/documents/ChristianityinitsGlobalContext.pdf.

Chambers, R. *Rural Development: Putting the Last First*. Harlow: Longman, 1983.

Chester, T. *Good News to the Poor: Social Involvement and the Gospel*. Leicester: Inter-Varsity Press, 2004.

———, ed. *Justice, Mercy and Humility: Integral Mission and the Poor*. Carlisle: Paternoster, 2002.

Cohen, D. J. *Why O Lord?* Milton Keynes: Paternoster, 2013.

Collins, J. *Good to Great: Why Some Companies Make the Leap . . . And Others Don't*. New York: HarperCollins, 2011.

Cooke, A., L. Friedli, T. Coggins, et al. *Mental Well-Being Impact Assessment: A Toolkit for Well-Being*. London: National MWIA Collaborative, 2011.

Costas, O. E. *Christ outside the Gate: Mission beyond Christendom*. Maryknoll, NY: Orbis, 1982.

———. *The Integrity of Mission: The Inner Life and Outreach of the Church*. 1st ed. San Francisco: Harper & Row, 1979.

Cromie, S., et al. *Psycho-Social Outcomes and Mechanisms of Self-Help Groups in Ethiopia*. Dublin: TEARFund Ireland, 2017.

Cui, K., and Z. Han. "Resilience of an Earthquake-Stricken Rural Community in Southwest China: Correlation with Disaster Risk Reduction Efforts." *International Journal of Emergency Response and Public Health* 15, no. 3 (2018): 407.

Curry, J., and A. Reynolds. *Missional Effectiveness: Achieving Institutional Goals and Mission*. Wrentham, MA: Gordon College, 2016.

Curtin, G. "Religion and Social Conflict during the Protestant Crusade in West Limerick 1822–49." *The Old Limerick Journal* (Winter 2003): 43–54.

Daugherty, K. "*Missio Dei*: The Trinity and Christian Missions." *Evangelical Review of Theology* 31, no. 2 (2007): 151–168.

DeGroat, C. R. "The New Exodus: A Narrative Paradigm for Understanding Soul Care." *Journal of Psychology and Theology* 37, no. 3 (2009): 186–193.

De Menil, V., and A. Glassman. *Making Room for Mental Health: Recommendations for Improving Mental Health Care in Low- and Middle-Income Countries*. Washington, DC: Center for Global Development, 2016. https://www.cgdev.org/publication/ft/making-room-mental-health-recommendations-improving-mental-health-care-low-and-middle.

"Disruptive Innovation in Higher Education." City Vision University, 2018. Accessed 30 August 2019. https://www.udemy.com/course/disruptive-innovation-in-higher-education/.

Donnelly, J. S. *Captain Rock: The Irish Agrarian Rebellion of 1821–1824*. Cork: Collins, 2009.

Dube, M. W. "Who Do You Say That I Am?" *Feminist Theology: The Journal of the Britain & Ireland School of Feminist Theology* 15, no. 3 (2007): 346–367.

Dunn, J. D. G. *The Theology of Paul's Letter to the Galatians*. New Testament Theology. Cambridge: Cambridge University Press, 1993.

Eaton, J., M. DeSilva, M. Regan, J. Lamichhane, and G. Thornicroft. "There Is No Wealth without Mental Health." *The Lancet Psychiatry* 1, no. 4 (2014): 252–253.

Eaton, J., O. Gureje, M. De Silva, et al. "A Structured Approach to Integrating Mental Health Services into Primary Care: Development of the Mental Health Scale Up Nigeria Intervention (MHSUN)." *International Journal of Mental Health Systems* 12 (2018): 11.

"Economic Discipleship." Urban Leadership Foundation. 2018. Accessed 30 August 2019. http://www.economicdisciple.org.

Ensor, G. *Letters Showing the Inutility, and Exhibiting the Absurdity, of What Is Rather Fantastically Termed "the New Reformation."* Dublin: R. Coyne, 1828.

Eriksson, J., and J. Borton. *Unlocking the Potential Within: Evaluation of the ACT Alliance in the International Response to Crises*. Geneva: ACT International, 2004.

Escobar, S. *A Time for Mission: The Challenge for Global Christianity*. Leicester: Inter-Varsity Press, 2003.

Exline, J. J., and J. B. Grubbs. "'If I Tell Others about My Anger toward God, How Will They Respond?' Predictors, Associated Behaviours, and Outcomes in an Adult Sample." *Journal of Psychology and Theology* 39, no. 4 (2011): 304–315.

Fahey, T. "The Catholic Church and Social Policy." In *Values, Catholic Social Thought and Public Policy*, edited by B. Reynolds and S. Healy, 143–163. Dublin: Conference of Religious of Ireland, 2007.

Ferguson, D. S. *Biblical Hermeneutics: An Introduction*. Atlanta: John Knox, 1986.

Fernandes, H., S. Cantrill, R. Kamal, and R. L. Shrestha. "Inclusion of People with Psychosocial Disability in Low- and Middle-Income Contexts: A Practice Review." *Christian Journal for Global Health* 4, no. 3 (2017): 72–81.

Fileta, Jason, ed. *Live Justly: Global Edition*. Portland, OR: Micah Challenge / Tearfund, 2017.

Fisher, J., M. Cabral de Mello, V. Patel, A. Rahman, T. Tran, S. Holton, and W. Holmes. "Prevalence and Determinants of Common Perinatal Mental Disorders in Women in Low- and Lower-Middle-Income Countries: A Systematic Review." *Bulletin of the World Health Organization* 90, no. 2 (1 Feb. 2012): 139–149.

Freire, P. *Pedagogy of the Oppressed*. New York: Herder & Herder, 1968.

Funk, M., et al. *Mental Health and Development: Targeting People with Mental Health Conditions as a Vulnerable Group*. Geneva: World Health Organization, 2010. Accessed 2 October 2019. https://www.who.int/mental_health/policy/mhtargeting/en/.

Furness, S., and P. Gilligan. "Faith-Based Organisations and UK Welfare Services: Exploring Some Ongoing Dilemmas." *Social Policy and Society* 11, no. 4 (Oct. 2012): 601–612.

Gaventa, B. R., ed. *Apocalyptic Paul: Cosmos and Anthropos in Romans 5–8*. Waco: Baylor University Press, 2013.

Gill, A. *Life on the Road: The Gospel Basis for a Messianic Lifestyle*. Scottdale, PA: Herald, 1992.

"Global Surgery Map." College of Surgeons of East, Central and Southern Africa (COSECSA). 2018. Accessed 29 May 2018. http://www.cosecsa.org/global-surgery-map.

Gorman, M. J. *Apostle of the Crucified Lord*. Grand Rapids, MI: Eerdmans, 2017.

———. *Becoming the Gospel*. Grand Rapids, MI: Eerdmans, 2015.

Gower, R., and P. Schroeder. *Cost-Benefit Assessment of Community-Based Recycling and Waste Management in Pakistan*. Brighton: Institute of Development Studies, 2018.

———. *Virtuous Circle: How the Circular Economy Can Create Jobs and Save Lives in Low and Middle-Income Countries*. Brighton: Institute of Development Studies, 2016.

Grant, J. A., and D. A. Hughes, eds. *Transforming the World? The Gospel and Social Responsibility*. Nottingham: Inter-Varsity Press, 2009.

Griffith, R. *Old Testament Survey*. Vol. 1. Singapore: Singapore Bible College, 2006.

Grigg, V. *Slum Dwellers' Theology: Pedagogy in the Slums*. Slum Dwellers' Pedagogy 1. Auckland: Urban Leadership Foundation, 2018.

Guder, D. L. "Missional Hermeneutics." *Mission Focus: Annual Review* 15 (2007): 106–124.

Hankle, D. D. "The Therapeutic Implications of the Imprecatory Psalms in the Christian Counselling Setting." *Journal of Psychology and Theology* 38, no. 4 (2010): 275–280.

Hanlon, C., et al. "Challenges and Opportunities for Implementing Integrated Mental Health Care: A District Level Situation Analysis from Five Low- and Middle-Income Countries." *PLoS One* 9, no. 2 (2014): e88437.

Hay, R. *Worth Keeping: Global Perspectives on Best Practice in Missionary Retention.* Pasadena, CA: William Carey Library, 2007.

Hayes, L., G. Hawthorne, J. Farhall, B. O'Hanlon, and C. Harvey. "Quality of Life and Social Isolation among Caregivers of Adults with Schizophrenia: Policy and Outcomes." *Community Mental Health Journal* 51, no. 5 (2015): 591–597.

Herrman, H., S. Saxena, R. Moodie, and L. Walker. "Introduction: Promoting Mental Health as a Public Health Priority." In *Promoting Mental Health: Concepts, Emerging Evidence, Practice: A Report of the World Health Organization*, edited by H. Herrman, S. Saxena, and R. Moodie, 2–17. Melbourne: Department of Mental Health and Substance Abuse; The Victorian Health Promotion Foundation; The University of Melbourne, 2005.

Hicks, R. *Failure to Scream.* Nashville: Thomas Nelson, 1993.

Hill, G. J. *Global Church: Reshaping Our Conversations, Renewing Our Mission, Revitalizing Our Churches.* Downers Grove, IL: IVP Academic, 2016.

———. *Salt, Light, and a City: Ecclesiology for the Global Missional Community.* Vol. 2, Majority World Voices. Eugene, OR: Cascade, 2019.

Hoek, M., and J. Thacker, eds. *Micah's Challenge: The Church's Responsibility to the Global Poor.* Milton Keynes: Paternoster, 2008.

Hoffmann, R., and R. Muttarak. "Learn from the Past, Prepare for the Future: Impacts of Education and Experience on Disaster Preparedness in the Philippines and Thailand." *World Development* 96 (2017): 32–51.

Hoggett, P., M. Mayo, and C. Miller. *The Dilemmas of Development Work: Ethical Challenges in Regeneration.* Portland, OR: Policy, 2009.

Hughes, D. A. *Power and Poverty: Divine and Human Rule in a World of Need.* Downers Grove, IL: IVP Academic, 2008.

———. "Theology of Integral Mission." Accessed 5 June 2020. https://arkaidawareness.weebly.com/the-social-gospel.html.

Hughes, D., and M. Bennett. *God of the Poor: A Biblical Vision of God's Present Rule.* Carlisle: Authentic, 2007.

Ife, J. *Community Development in an Uncertain World: Vision, Analysis, and Practice.* Cambridge: Cambridge University Press, 2013.

Ife, J., and F. Tesoriero. *Community Development: Community-Based Alternatives in an Age of Globalisation.* Frenchs Forest: Pearson, 2006.

Imperiale, A. J., and F. Vanclay. "Experiencing Local Community Resilience in Action: Learning from Post-Disaster Communities." *Journal of Rural Studies* 47 (2016): 204–219.

Izutsu, T., A. Tsutsumi, H. Minas, G. Thornicroft, V. Patel, and A. Ito. "Mental Health and Wellbeing in the Sustainable Development Goals." *Lancet Psychiatry* 2, no. 12 (Dec. 2015): 1052–1054.

Jenkins, P. *The Next Christendom: The Coming of Global Christianity*. 3rd ed. Oxford: Oxford University Press, 2011.

Jones, B. D. *Dwell: Life with God for the World*. Downers Grove, IL: InterVarsity Press, 2014.

Käsemann, E. *Primitive Christian Apocalyptic*. London: SCM, 1969.

Katongole, E. *The Sacrifice of Africa: A Political Theology for Africa*. Grand Rapids, MI: Eerdmans, 2011.

Kelley, T. J. "'Come Lord Jesus, Quickly Come!': The Writing and Thought of Edward Nangle, 1828–1862." In *Protestant Millennialism, Evangelicalism and Irish Society, 1790–2005*, edited by C. Gribben and A. Holmes, 99–118. Basingstoke: Palgrave Macmillan, 2006.

Kemeny, P. C., ed. *Church, State and Public Justice*. Andhra Pradesh: Authentic, 2007.

Kinoti, H. "Evangelical Women and Politics in Africa." *Transformation: An International Journal of Holistic Mission Studies* 11, no. 4 (1994): 7.

Klein, N. *The Shock Doctrine: The Rise of Disaster Capitalism*. 1st edition. New York: Metropolitan, 2007.

Kobau, R., M. E. Seligman, C. Peterson, E. Diener, M. M. Zack, D. Chapman, and W. Thompson. "Mental Health Promotion in Public Health: Perspectives and Strategies from Positive Psychology." *American Journal of Public Health* 101, no. 8 (Aug. 2011): e1–9.

Konig, A., A. Eonta, and S. R. Dyal. "Enhancing the Benefits of Written Emotional Disclosure through Response Training." *Behavior Therapy* 45, no. 3 (2014): 344–357.

Koschorke, M., et al. "Experiences of Stigma and Discrimination of People with Schizophrenia in India." *Social Science and Medicine* 123 (Dec. 2014): 149–159.

Kretzschmar, L. "An Ethical Analysis of the Implementation of Poverty Reduction Policies in South Africa and Chile and Their Implications for the Church." *HTS Theological Studies* 70, no. 1 (2014): 1–11. Accessed 10 September 2019. http://www.scielo.org.za/scielo.php?script=sci_arttext&pid=S0259-94222014000100044.

Langeler, B. "Consultation to Assess Possibilities and Appreciation for CCM in the Philippines with Focus on DRR." November 2016. https://www.micahnetwork.org/sites/default/files/doc/page/161228_final_report_assessment_ccm_-_drr_philippines_2016.pdf.

La Sor, W. S., D. A. Hubbard, F. W. Bush, and L. C. Allen. *Old Testament Survey: The Message, Form, and Background of the Old Testament*. 2nd ed. Grand Rapids, MI: Eerdmans, 1996.

Lauber, C., and W. Rossler. "Stigma towards People with Mental Illness in Developing Countries in Asia." *International Review of Psychiatry* 19, no. 2 (Apr. 2007): 157–178.

The Lausanne Movement. "The Cape Town Commitment: A Confession of Faith and a Call to Action." 2010. http://www.lausanne.org/en/documents/ctcommitment.html.

Lehtinen, V., A. Ozamiz, L. Underwood, and M. Weiss. "The Intrinsic Value of Mental Health." In *Promoting Mental Health: Concepts, Emerging Evidence, Practice: A Report of the World Health Organization*, edited by H. Herrman, S. Saxena, and R. Moodie, 46–58. Melbourne: Department of Mental Health and Substance Abuse; The Victorian Health Promotion Foundation; The University of Melbourne, 2005.

Lepore, S. J., P. Fernandez-Berrocal, J. Ragan, and N. Ramos. "It's Not That Bad: Social Challenges to Emotional Disclosure Enhance Adjustment to Stress." *Anxiety, Stress and Coping* 17, no. 4 (2004): 341–361.

Lerner, M. *The Belief in a Just World: A Fundamental Delusion.* New York: Plenum, 1980.

Lester, W., and M. Nguyen. "The Economic Integration of Immigrants and Regional Resilience." *Journal of Urban Affairs* 38, no. 1 (2016): 42–60.

Liechty, J., and C. Clegg. *Moving beyond Sectarianism: Religion, Conflict, and Reconciliation in Northern Ireland.* Dublin: Columba, 2001.

Locke, J. *An Essay Concerning Human Understanding.* Oxford: Clarendon, 1894.

Lockyer, H. *Nelson's Illustrated Bible Dictionary: An Authoritative One-Volume Reference Work on the Bible, with Full-Colour Illustrations.* Nashville: T. Nelson, 1986.

Luitel, N. P., M. J. Jordans, A. Adhikari, N. Upadhaya, C. Hanlon, C. Lund, and I. H. Komproe. "Mental Health Care in Nepal: Current Situation and Challenges for Development of a District Mental Health Care Plan." *Conflict and Health* 9 (2015): 3.

Lund, C., A. Breen, A. J. Flisher, R. Kakuma, J. Corrigall, J. A. Joska, L. Swartz, and V. Patel. "Poverty and Common Mental Disorders in Low and Middle Income Countries: A Systematic Review." *Social Science and Medicine* 71, no. 3 (Aug. 2010): 517–528.

Lund, C., M. Waruguru, J. Kingori, S. Kippen-Wood, E. Breuer, S. Mannarath, and S. Raja. "Outcomes of the Mental Health and Development Model in Rural Kenya: A 2-Year Prospective Cohort Intervention Study." *International Health* 5, no. 1 (Mar. 2013): 43–50.

Luther, M. *Luther's Works.* Vol. 4. American ed. St. Louis, MO: Concordia, 1955.

Ma, J. C. "The Role of Christian Women in the Global South." *Transformation: An International Journal of Holistic Mission Studies* 31, no. 3 (2014): 203.

Ma, W., and B. Woolnough, eds. *Holistic Mission: God's Plan for God's People.* Eugene, OR: Regnum, 2010.

Marandu-Kareithi, R. *Review of Green Anglicans: What Is Working and Why?* Cape Town: DAS Associates, 2017.

Marshall, C. D. *The Little Book of Biblical Justice: A Fresh Approach to the Bible's Teachings on Justice.* Intercourse, PA: Good Books, 1989.

Mascayano, F., J. E. Armijo, and L. H. Yang. "Addressing Stigma Relating to Mental Illness in Low- and Middle-Income Countries." *Front Psychiatry* 6 (2015): 38.

Mathias, K., M. Kermode, M. San Sebastian, M. Koschorke, and I. Goicolea. "Under the Banyan Tree: Exclusion and Inclusion of People with Mental Disorders in Rural North India." *BMC Public Health* 15 (1 May 2015): 446.

Mattner, S., C. Ehrlich, P. Chester, D. Crompton, and E. Kendall. "Self-Determination: What Do People Who Experience Severe Mental Illness Want from Public Mental Health Services?" *International Journal of Integrated Care* 17, no. 3 (2017): 50.

McDonald, C. "From Disasters to Resilience: When Disasters Strike What Makes the Difference between Those Who Cope Well and Those Who Don't?" Micah Global: 7th Global Consultation, Philippines. 2018. https://www.micahglobal.org/sites/default/files/doc/page/chris_mcdonald_tearfund_from_disasters_to_resilience_for_micah_trienniel.pdf.

McKay, E. A. "Mothers with Mental Illness: An Occupation Interrupted." In *Mothering Occupations: Challenge, Agency, and Participation*, edited by S. A. Esdaile and J. A. Olson, 238–258. Philadelphia: FA Davis, 2004.

McKenzie, K., and T. Harpham. *Social Capital and Mental Health*. London: Jessica Kingsley, 2006.

McKnight, S. *Embracing Grace: A Gospel for All of Us*. Brewster, MA: Paraclete, 2005.

McNair, J., "A Christian Model of Disability." *Disabled Christianity*. 20 September 2017. http://disabledchristianity.blogspot.com/2017/09/a-christian-model-of-disability.html.

———. "Disability and Human Supports." *Christian Journal for Global Health* 2, no. 2 (2015): 10–15.

Meehan, É. "Faith in Action: Trócaire and the Future of the Church in Ireland." iCatholic Player, 5 October 2014. Accessed 19 September 2019. http://www.icatholic.ie/irish-catholic-eamonn-meehan/.

Mehta, N., et al. "Evidence for Effective Interventions to Reduce Mental Health-Related Stigma and Discrimination in the Medium and Long Term: Systematic Review." *British Journal of Psychiatry* 207, no. 5 (Nov. 2015): 377–384.

Metzger, B. M., and M. D. Coogan. *The Oxford Companion to the Bible*. New York: Oxford University Press, 1993.

Mills, C. "The Psychiatrisation of Poverty: Rethinking the Mental Health–Poverty Nexus." *Social and Personality Psychology Compass* 9, no. 5 (2015): 213–222.

Miranda-Feliciano, E. "Women in Revolution: The Philippine Version." *Transformation: An International Journal of Holistic Mission Studies* 6, no. 2 (1989): 10.

Mitchel, P. *Evangelicalism and National Identity in Ulster, 1921–1998*. Oxford: Oxford University Press, 2003.

———. "Evangelicals and Irish Identity in Independent Ireland: A Case Study." In *Irish Protestant Identities*, edited by M. A. Busteed, F. Neal, and J. Tonge, 155–170. Manchester: Manchester University Press, 2012.

———. "God's Preference for the Poor: The Bible and Social Justice in Ireland." In *Ireland and the Reception of the Bible: Social and Cultural Perspectives*, edited by B. A. Anderson and J. F. Kearney, 193–210. New York: T&T Clark, 2018.

———. "Sex, Truth and Tolerance: Some Theological Reflections on the Irish Civil Partnership Bill 2010 and Challenges Facing Christians in a Post-Christendom Culture." *Evangelical Quarterly* 84, no. 2 (2012): 155–173.

Mnookin, S. *Out of the Shadows: Making Mental Health a Global Development Priority.* Washington, DC: World Bank Group and World Health Organization, 2016. Accessed 27 September 2019. http://documents.worldbank.org/curated/en/270131468187759113/Out-of-the-shadows-making-mental-health-a-global-development-priority.

Moffitt, M. *The Society for Irish Church Missions to the Roman Catholics, 1849–1950.* Manchester: Manchester University Press, 2010.

———. *Soupers and Jumpers: The Protestant Missions in Connemara, 1848–1937.* Dublin: Nonsuch, 2008.

Morgan, A., and C. Swann, eds. *Social Capital for Health: Issues of Definition, Measurement and Links to Health.* London: Health Development Agency, 2004.

Mother Teresa and B. Kolodiejchuk. *Mother Teresa: Come Be My Light; The Private Writings of the "Saint of Calcutta."* New York: Doubleday, 2007.

Mugambi, J. "Christianity in Africa, 1910–2010." In *Atlas of Global Christianity, 1910–2010*, edited by T. M. Johnson and K. R. Ross, 110–111. Edinburgh: Edinburgh University Press, 2009.

Murali, V., and F. Oyebode. "Poverty, Social Inequality and Mental Health." *Advances in Psychiatric Treatment* 10, no. 3 (2004): 216–224.

Muralidharan, A., A. Lucksted, D. Medoff, L. J. Fang, and L. Dixon. "Stigma: A Unique Source of Distress for Family Members of Individuals with Mental Illness." *Journal of Behavioral Health Services and Research* 43, no. 3 (Jul. 2016): 484–493.

Murray, S. "Post-Christendom, Post-Constantinian, Post-Christian . . . Does the Label Matter?" Accessed 19 September 2019. https://amnetwork.uk/wp-content/uploads/2019/07/After-Christendom-Does-the-label-matter.pdf.

Myers, B. L. *Walking with the Poor: Principles and Practices of Transformational Development.* Maryknoll, NY: Orbis, 1999.

Newbigin, Lesslie. *The Open Secret: An Introduction to the Theology of Mission.* Grand Rapids, MI: Eerdmans, 1995.

Nkansah-Obrempong, J. "Evangelical Theology in Africa." *Evangelical Review of Theology* 34, no. 4 (2010): 293–299.

Oades, L. *Building Community Resilience and Wellbeing Report.* Wollongong: Mental Health Commission of NSW, 2014.

O'Donnell, K. *Global Member Care.* Vol. 1, *The Pearls and Perils of Good Practice.* Pasadena, CA: William Carey Library, 2011.

Office of the Deputy Prime Minister. *Mental Health and Social Exclusion: Social Exclusion Unit Report Summary.* London: Office of the Deputy Prime Minister, 2004. http://www.nfao.org/Useful_Websites/MH_Social_Exclusion_report_summary.pdf.

Ögtem-Young, O. "Faith Resilience: Everyday Experiences." *Societies* 8, no. 1 (2018): 10.

Olarinmoye, O. O. "Faith-Based Organizations and Development: Prospects and Constraints." *Transformation: An International Journal of Holistic Mission Studies* 29, no. 1 (Jan. 2012): 1–14.

Olubunmi-Smith, P. "Feminism in Cross-Cultural Perspective: Women in Africa." *Transformation: An International Journal of Holistic Mission Studies* 6, no. 2 (1989): 11.

Padilla, C. R. *Mission between the Times: Essays on the Kingdom*. Grand Rapids, MI: Eerdmans, 1985.

———. "What Is Integral Mission?" http://www.dmr.org/images/pdf%20 dokumenter/C._René_Padilla_-_What_is_integral_mission.pdf.

Padilla, C. R., and T. Yamamori, eds. *The Local Church, Agent of Transformation: An Ecclesiology for Integral Mission*. Buenos Aires: Ediciones Kairos, 2004.

Patel, V. "Mental Health in Low- and Middle-Income Countries." *British Medical Bulletin* 81 (2007): 81–96.

Patel, V., and C. Lund. "Mental Disorders: Equity and Social Determinants." In *Equity, Social Determinants and Public Health Programmes*, edited by E. Blas and K. A. Sivasankara, 115–134. Geneva: WHO, 2010.

Pennebaker, J. W., and S. K. Beall. "Confronting a Traumatic Event: Toward an Understanding of Inhibition and Disease." *Journal of Abnormal Psychology* 95, no. 3 (Aug. 1986): 274–281.

Pevalin, D., and D. Rose, Institute for Economic and Social Research, University of Essex. *Social Capital for Health*. NHS Health Development Agency, 2003. Accessed 27 September 2019. http://repository.essex.ac.uk/9143/1/socialcapital_BHP_survey.pdf.

Pieterse, H. "A Grounded Theory Approach to the Analysis of Sermons on Poverty: Congregational Projects as Social Capital." *Verbum et Ecclesia* 33, no. 1 (2012): 1–7.

Pinfold, V., G. Thornicroft, P. Huxley, and P. Farmer. "Active Ingredients in Anti-Stigma Programmes in Mental Health." *International Review of Psychiatry* 17, no. 2 (Apr. 2005): 123–131.

Porsdam Mann, S., V. J. Bradley, and B. J. Sahakian. "Human Rights-Based Approaches to Mental Health: A Review of Programs." *Health and Human Rights* 18, no. 1 (Jun. 2016): 263–276.

Prince, M., V. Patel, S. Saxena, M. Maj, J. Maselko, M. Phillips, and A. Rahman. "No Health without Mental Health." *The Lancet* 370 (2007): 859–877.

Prunty, J. "Battle Plans and Battlegrounds: Protestant Mission Activity in the Dublin Slums, 1840s–1880s." In *Protestant Millennialism, Evangelicalism, and Irish Society, 1790–2005*, edited by C. Gribben and A. R. Holmes, 119–143. Basingstoke: Palgrave Macmillan, 2006.

Putti, J. *The Fair Deal*. Bangalore: Kristu Jyoti College, 1993.

Rahman, A., P. J. Surkan, C. E. Cayetano, P. Rwagatare, and K. E. Dickson. "Grand Challenges: Integrating Maternal Mental Health into Maternal and Child Health Programmes." *PLOS Medicine* 10, no. 5 (2013): e1001442.

Ramachandra, V. "Integral Mission: Exploring a Concept." In *Integral Mission: The Way Forward*, edited by C. V. Mathew, 44–59. Kerala: Christava Sahitya Samithy, 2006.

Reid, J. *Faith Expressing Itself through Love: An Applied Theology of Evangelical Social Action for Today's Ireland*. Saarbrücken: Lap Lambert Academic, 2012.
Reimer, J. *Missio Politica: The Mission of Church and Politics*. Carlisle: Langham, 2017.
Reynolds, A. "Evangelical Feminism in Brazil and the USA." In *Brazilian Evangelicalism in the Twenty-First Century: An Inside and Outside Look*, edited by E. Miller and R. J. Morgan, 177–199. Cham: Palgrave Macmillan, 2019.
Reynolds, A., and J. Curry. "Best Practices for Attracting, Promoting, and Retaining Female Leadership in Christian Organizations." Gordon College, Wrentham, MA, January 2017. https://gordonedu.sharepoint.com/WebLinks/Shared%20 Documents/Provost/WILNS_PhaseIIIFinal_Jan2017.pdf?&originalPath=aHR0cHM6Ly9nb3Jkb25lZHUuc2hhcmVwb2ludC5jb20vOmI6L2cvV2ViTGlua3M3M vRWNCYTNhTVd3ODFHaGRRKSEI4UHZMck1CenVSZGsxengyb0JtaXItZTE1Qkg5Zz9ydGltZT1wYUQ2VjQzcjEwZw.
Richards, L. O. *The Believer's Guidebook*. Grand Rapids, MI: Zondervan, 1983.
Ries, E. *The Lean Startup: How Today's Entrepreneurs Use Continuous Innovation to Create Radically Successful Businesses*. 1st ed. New York: Crown Business, 2011.
Ringma, C. *The Seeking Heart: A Journey with Henri Nouwen*. Brewster, MA: Paraclete, 2006.
Rosenfield, S. "Triple Jeopardy? Mental Health at the Intersection of Gender, Race, and Class." *Social Science and Medicine* 74, no. 11 (Jun. 2012): 1791–1801.
Salzer, M., and R. Baron. *Well Together: A Blueprint for Community Inclusion; Fundamental Concepts, Theoretical Frameworks and Evidence*. Melbourne: Wellways, 2016.
Samuel, V., and A. Hauser. *Proclaiming Christ in Christ's Way: Studies in Integral Evangelism*. Oxford: Regnum, 1989.
Samuel, V., and C. Sugden, eds. *The Church in Response to Human Need*. Grand Rapids, MI: Eerdmans, 1987.
———, eds. *Mission as Transformation: A Theology of the Whole Gospel*. Oxford: Regnum, 1999.
Saraceno, B., M. van Ommeren, R. Batniji, A. Cohen, O. Gureje, J. Mahoney, D. Sridhar, and C. Underhill. "Barriers to Improvement of Mental Health Services in Low-Income and Middle-Income Countries." *Lancet* 370, no. 9593 (29 Sep. 2007): 1164–1174.
Sayed, G. D. *Mental Health in Afghanistan: Burden, Challenges and the Way Forward; Health, Nutrition and Population (HNP) Discussion Paper*. Washington, DC: World Bank, 2011.
Schwartz, G. *When Charity Destroys Dignity: Overcoming Unhealthy Dependency in the Christian Movement*. Bloomington, IN: AuthorHouse, 2007.
Semrau, M., S. Evans-Lacko, M. Koschorke, L. Ashenafi, and G. Thornicroft. "Stigma and Discrimination Related to Mental Illness in Low- and Middle-Income Countries." *Epidemiology and Psychiatric Sciences* 24, no. 5 (Oct. 2015): 382–394.

Seng, J. S., W. D. Lopez, M. Sperlich, L. Hamama, and C. D. Reed Meldrum. "Marginalized Identities, Discrimination Burden, and Mental Health: Empirical Exploration of an Interpersonal-Level Approach to Modeling Intersectionality." *Social Science and Medicine* 75, no. 12 (Dec. 2012): 2437–2445.

Sider, R. J. *Rich Christians in an Age of Hunger: Moving from Affluence to Generosity*. 20th anniversary revision ed. Dallas: Word, 1997.

Snow, K. N., M. R. McMinn, R. K. Bufford, and I. A. Brendlinger. "Resolving Anger toward God: Lament as an Avenue toward Attachment." *Journal of Psychology and Theology* 39, no. 2 (2011): 130–142.

Solantaus, T., A. Reupert, and D. Maybery. "Working with Parents Who Have a Psychiatric Disorder." In *Parental Psychiatric Disorder: Distressed Parents and Their Families*, edited by A. Reupert, D. Maybery, J. Nicholson, M. Gopfert, and M. Seeman, 238–247. 3rd ed. New York: Cambridge University Press, 2015.

Stal, F. *Final Report: Network Development for Church and Community Based Disaster Risk Reduction*. London: Tearfund, 2016.

Stassen, G. H., and D. P. Gushee. *Kingdom Ethics: Following Jesus in Contemporary Context*. Downers Grove, IL: InterVarsity Press, 2003.

Stendahl, K. "The Apostle Paul and the Introspective Conscience of the West." *Harvard Theological Review* 56, no. 3 (1963): 199–215.

Stott, J. R. W. *The Lausanne Covenant: Complete Text with Study Guide*. Peabody, MA: Hendrickson, 2012.

Sturgeon, S., and J. Orley. "Concepts of Mental Health across the World." In *Promoting Mental Health: Concepts, Emerging Evidence, Practice; A Report of the World Health Organization*, edited by H. Herrman, S. Saxena, and R. Moodie. Melbourne: Department of Mental Health and Substance Abuse; The Victorian Health Promotion Foundation; The University of Melbourne, 2005.

Surkan, P. J., C. E. Kennedy, K. M. Hurley, and M. M. Black. "Maternal Depression and Early Childhood Growth in Developing Countries: Systematic Review and Meta-Analysis." *Bulletin of the World Health Organization* 89, no. 8 (1 Aug. 2011): 607–615.

Sweetland, A. C., M. A. Oquendo, M. Sidat, P. F. Santos, S. H. Vermund, C. S. Duarte, M. Arbuckle, and M. L. Wainberg. "Closing the Mental Health Gap in Low-Income Settings by Building Research Capacity: Perspectives from Mozambique." *Annals of Global Health* 80, no. 2 (Mar.–Apr. 2014): 126–133.

Thornicroft, G., et al. "Evidence for Effective Interventions to Reduce Mental-Health-Related Stigma and Discrimination." *Lancet* 387, no. 10023 (12 Mar. 2016): 1123–1132.

Thornicroft, G., and V. Patel. "Including Mental Health among the New Sustainable Development Goals." *British Medical Journal* (20 Aug. 2014): 349.

Thorogood, B. *A Guide to the Book of Amos*. London: Hollen Street, 1977.

Tomlin, G. *Philippians, Colossians*. Reformation Commentary on Scripture, New Testament. Downers Grove, IL: InterVarsity Press, 2013.

Toyama-Szeto, N., and T. Gee. *More Than Serving Tea*. Westmont, IL: IVP, 2007.
Trani, J. F., P. Bakhshi, J. Kuhlberg, S. S. Narayanan, H. Venkataraman, N. N. Mishra, N. E. Groce, S. Jadhav, and S. Deshpande. "Mental Illness, Poverty and Stigma in India: A Case-Control Study." *BMJ Open* 5, no. 2 (23 Feb. 2015): e006355.
Trócaire. *My Rights Beyond 2015: Making the Post-2015 Framework Accountable to the World's Poor*. Dublin: Dublin City Resource Centre, 2013.
Trudgen, R. *Why Warriors Lie Down and Die: Towards an Understanding of Why the Aboriginal People of Arnhem Land Face the Greatest Crisis in Health and Education since European Contact*. Darwin: Aboriginal Resource and Development Services, 2000.
UNISDR. "What Is Disaster Risk Reduction?" 2018. https://eird.org/esp/acerca-eird/liderazgo/perfil/what-is-drr.html.
United Nations ESCAP. *Leave No One Behind: Disaster Resilience for Sustainable Development; Asia-Pacific Disaster Report 2017*. Bangkok: United Nations ESCAP, 2018. https://www.unescap.org/sites/default/files/publications/0_Disaster%20Report%202017%20High%20res.pdf.
Van Ness, D., and K. Heetderks Strong. *Restoring Justice*. London: Routledge, 2015.
Van Opstal, S. *The Mission of Worship*. Downers Grove, IL: InterVarsity Press, 2012.
———. *The Next Worship: Glorifying God in a Diverse World*. Downers Grove, IL: InterVarsity Press, 2016.
Ventevogel, P. "Integration of Mental Health into Primary Healthcare in Low-Income Countries: Avoiding Medicalization." *International Review of Psychiatry* 26, no. 6 (2014): 669–679.
Votruba, N., J. Eaton, M. Prince, and G. Thornicroft. "The Importance of Global Mental Health for the Sustainable Development Goals." *Journal of Mental Health* 23, no. 6 (Dec. 2014): 283–286.
WEA Missions Commission. *Remap II: Worldwide Missionary Retention Study and Best Practices*. Deerfield, IL: World Evangelical Alliance, 2010.
Westen, D., L. Burton, and R. M. Kowalski. *Psychology*. 4th edition. Milton, Queensland: John Wiley, 2006.
Westermann, C. *Praise and Lament in the Psalms*. Atlanta: J. Knox, 1981.
Whelan, I. *The Bible War in Ireland: The "Second Reformation" and the Polarization of Protestant–Catholic Relations, 1800–1840*. Madison, WI: University of Wisconsin Press, 2005.
Wilkinson, O. *Tearfund and a Movement Building Approach to Advocacy*. Washington, DC: Joint Learning Initiative on Faith and Local Communities (JLI), 2019.
Wolffe, J. *The Expansion of Evangelicalism: The Age of Wilberforce, More, Chalmers and Finney*. Nottingham: Inter-Varsity Press, 2006.
Wolterstorff, N. *Justice in Love*. Grand Rapids, MI: Eerdmans, 2011.
———. *Justice: Rights and Wrongs*. Princeton: Princeton University Press, 2008.
Wooly, L. "Integral, Inspirational and Influential: The Role of Local Churches in Humanitarian and Development Responses." 2017. https://www.tearfund.org/~/

media/files/tilz/churches/integral_mission/2017-tearfund-integral-inspirational-and-influential-en.pdf.

Worden, J. W. *Grief Counselling and Grief Therapy*. Hove: Brunner-Routledge, 2001.

The World Bank. "Global Tracking Framework 2017: Progress toward Sustainable Energy." 2017. https://www.worldbank.org/en/topic/energy/publication/global-tracking-framework-2017.

———. "Mortality Rate, under-5 (per 1,000 Live Births)." 2016. Accessed 29 May 2018. https://data.worldbank.org/indicator/SH.DYN.MORT.

World Health Organization. "Gender Disparities in Mental Health: WHO Fact Sheet." Accessed 27 September 2019. http://www.who.int/mental_health/prevention/genderwomen/en/.

Wright, C. J. H. *The Mission of God: Unlocking the Bible's Grand Narrative*. Downers Grove, IL: IVP Academic, 2006.

———. *Old Testament Ethics for the People of God*. Downers Grove, IL: InterVarsity Press, 2004.

———. "Reaffirming Holistic Mission: A Cross Centered Approach in All Areas of Life." Accessed 5 June 2020. http://www.lausanneworldpulse.com/themedarticles-php/61/10-2005.

Wright, N. T. *Paul: A Biography*. San Francisco: HarperOne, 2018.

———. *Paul and the Faithfulness of God*. Christian Origins and the Question of God. London: SPCK, 2013.

About Micah Global

Micah is a global network and movement of Christian ministries and individuals committed to integral mission expressed through their shared vision to see communities living life in all its fullness, free from poverty, injustice, and conflict.

Micah Network was established in 2001 and launched its Micah Challenge Campaign in 2004. The campaign sought to raise awareness of the travesty of poverty and to hold leaders to account for their commitments made to reduce poverty through the Millennium Development Goals. In 2015, as the campaign drew to an end, Micah Network and Micah Challenge merged to form Micah Global.

Micah seeks to answer three pressing questions of Christian ministries:

- How can we effectively respond to the travesty of poverty, injustice, and conflict in such a way that God's shalom is evident in word, deed, and sign?
- How can we together discern, theologically and practically, how to speak and act with prophetic authority so as to disciple our nations and hold leaders to account for their responsibilities for the flourishing of humanity and all of creation?
- How can we walk together in humility, serving one another, as we seek to enable the local church to be the agent of change in each community?

Every three years Micah facilitates a Global Consultation which draws members from around the world to gather and discuss, learn, and reflect on issues of concern.

The 2018 Global Consultation was held in Tagaytay, Philippines, on the theme of "Integral Mission and Community Resilience." This book captures our shared learning from this amazing week together.

To explore further resources and learning, see our website, www.micahglobal.org.

Micah Global Publications – M Series

Corruption and the Church: A Brief Introduction, by Martin Allaby
The Five Marks of Mission: Making God's Mission Ours, by Christopher Wright

Integral Mission: Biblical Foundations, by Melba Padilla Maggay
Living in God's Story: Understanding the Bible's Grand Narrative, by Mark Galpin
Rethinking Church: Community Called Out to Take Responsibility, by Johannes Reimer
Rethinking Shame and Honour, by Arley Loewen

List of Contributors

Norman Franklin C. Agustin

Norman Franklin C. Agustin is the current Executive Director of Lingap Pangkabataan, Incorporated (LPI) or "Care for Children," a non-profit faith-based social development organization established in the Philippines in 1981. Agustin has more than twenty years of experience in community development work. He started as a youth volunteer of the National Council of Churches in the Philippines (NCCP) during his college days where he facilitated the organizing of ecumenical student ministry groups in four colleges and universities in Metro Manila. He graduated with a BA in Political Science and completed his Master's degree in Public Management at the Ateneo School of Government.

Martin Allaby

Martin Allaby is a British doctor and researcher who worked for ten years in South Asia and conducted field research in Laos, Cambodia, Myanmar, Vietnam, the Philippines, Kenya, Zambia, and Peru. In Nepal he worked for the UK Department for International Development on health sector reform. His experiences have convinced him that corruption is a potent cause of poverty, and that the church needs to do more about it. He currently chairs the steering group of the Faith and Public Integrity Network and works as a consultant clinical adviser at the National Institute of Health and Care Excellence in London.

Becca Allchin

Becca Allchin is a population-focused occupational therapist with experience in mental health services and international development. She works locally supporting families where a parent has a mental illness (FaPMI service development coordinator) in the Eastern Region of Melbourne, regionally as a PhD candidate researching sustainability of family-focused practice in adult mental health services, and globally supporting mental health work in low- and middle-income countries. Becca has a long association with TEAR Australia as church representative, field worker in India, TEAR group coordinator, international programme allocation committee convenor, and occasional programme evaluator.

Vilma "Nina" Balmaceda

Dr Vilma "Nina" Balmaceda is a scholar-practitioner whose work focuses on civic leadership formation and the promotion and defence of the fundamental rights of vulnerable populations in Latin America. Nina earned her PhD in political science from the University of Notre Dame du Lac. In addition to serving as CETIContinental's Dean of Graduate Studies, Nina is the President and CEO of Peace and Hope International (PHI). Through its sister organizations in Latin America, PHI supports efforts to prevent violence and other forms of injustice, mobilizing individuals and communities to foster systemic change for peace and democratic civic engagement.

Clinton Bergsma

Clinton Bergsma manages a small development organization called Amos Australia and is a facilitator of the Masters of Transformation programme at Eastern College of Australia. He enjoys exploring the intersection between theology and practice for community development approaches.

David Boan

Dr David Boan is a 1978 graduate of the Rosemead Graduate School of Psychology at Biola University. His early career was practising clinical psychology in California, USA. In 1996 he became the Vice President of Research for the Delmarva Foundation for Medical Care in Maryland, working on the quality and safety of health care. In 2010 Dr Boan joined the Humanitarian Disaster Institute at Wheaton College (Wheaton, IL, USA) as co-director and associate professor of psychology in the graduate school of psychology. His work focused on church-based community resilience and risk reduction. In January 2016 Dr Boan moved into his current role as the Director of Humanitarian Advocacy for the World Evangelical Alliance, helping national evangelical alliances respond to humanitarian crises.

Stephanie Cantrill

Steph Cantrill is an occupational therapist by background. After completing a Master's in Public Health, she spent four years in India, working with a community development team in Old Delhi. She has volunteered with two TEAR projects, both related to the inclusion of people with disability. Steph now works with Polio Australia, a small organization that supports people living with disability related to polio and its late effects.

Ruth Padilla DeBorst

A wife of one and mother of many, theologian, missiologist, educator, and storyteller, Ruth Padilla DeBorst has been involved in theological formation for integral mission in her native Latin America and beyond for several decades. She serves with Resonate Global Mission, leading the Comunidad de Estudios Teológicos Interdisciplinarios (CETI), the International Fellowship for Mission as Transformation, and leadership development initiatives of the Christian Reformed Church. Along with her husband, James, she lives in Costa Rica as a member of Casa Adobe, an intentional Christian community with deep concern for right living in relation to the whole of creation. Her studies include a Bachelor's in Education (Argentina), an MA in Interdisciplinary Studies (Wheaton College), and a PhD in Theology (Boston University).

Boureima Diallo

Boureima Diallo is a Fulani from Burkina Faso. He grew up as a Muslim, like all Fulani in Africa. One of his father's employees told him about the good news when he was in his teens, and with the permission of his Muslim father he decided to follow Jesus. In following in the footsteps of Jesus he has faced persecution, but by God's grace he has clung on to him. Boureima Diallo is currently the lead facilitator of FULNET (Fulani Network), comprising several missions and ministries that are making disciples and planting churches among the Fulani in several countries in the Sahel in Africa.

Emily Edwards

Emily Edwards, BS, is on the MEd in Counselling Psychology programme at the University of Louisville. A graduate research assistant and student clinician, Emily has overlapping research and clinical interests in the areas of building resilient communities, empowering helping professionals to combat adversity, and supporting and preserving families. At the University of Louisville, Emily does research with the Resilience, Adaptation, and Well-Being lab and the Human Trafficking Research Initiative. Additionally, Emily is on the founding and planning team for the Emerging Care Summit, an annual gathering focused on building the future of global worker care (for more information, see www.emergingcaresummit.org).

Stanley Enock

Stanley Enock Hanya works with the Evangelical Fellowship of Zimbabwe as the Church and Community Mobilization Process Coordinator. He is committed to the engagement of church leaders as well as the empowerment of the local church and community to champion holistic transformation. Over the last few years he has overseen the integration of resilience, self-help groups, as well as social inclusion in church, and community mobilization work. He has a strong interest in the building up of local churches and communities with skills and knowledge to anticipate, prepare for, respond to, and recover from disasters.

Helen Fernandes

Helen Fernandes is an occupational therapist and a public health and development specialist with TEAR Australia. Helen has experience in health, community-based rehabilitation, and social inclusion projects in Africa (Niger, Nigeria), South Asia (Nepal and India), and South East Asia and the Pacific (Timor-Leste, Papua New Guinea). Her current roles include working with TEAR's partners on organizational development and heading up TEAR's work and learning in mental health.

Naomi Foxwood

Naomi Foxwood works for Tearfund leading their support for movement-building in a number of different countries. She is particularly engaged in developing, learning from, and sharing their impactful movement-building work. Naomi has over fifteen years' experience in NGOs and policy organizations, in advocacy and research roles, all of which have centred on her passion for seeing change to systems of injustice and poverty.

Thandi Gamedze

Living in Cape Town, South Africa, Thandi works in communications and resource development for an organization called The Warehouse. She has recently completed a Master's in Public Administration with a focus on education. Some of the things that take up space in her heart are writing poetry, live jazz, the Jesus that is good news to the poor, family, friends that are like family, radical education, conversations about decolonizing theology, laughing, and dreaming about and working towards a world that is just and kind.

Richard Gower

Richard Gower is a former UK government economist who escaped from the civil service (via Oxfam) and now leads some of Tearfund's policy and advocacy work. He co-authored Tearfund's seminal "Restorative Economy" vision paper in 2015 and is passionate about social movements for justice and restoration, having spent several years working at the grassroots in both inner-city Bradford and Zimbabwe. Alongside his work at Tearfund, he leads the Praxis Centre for Hope and Activism.

Tori Greaves

A lover of stories and adventure, baking and hiking, learning and culture; a spouse, daughter, and sister, Victoria (Tori) Greaves was raised in California (USA) and received her BA in Anthropology from Wheaton College with a certificate in Human Needs and Global Resources. She is now completing an MA in Interdisciplinary Theological Studies for Integral Mission through CETI (Comunidad de Estudios Teológicos Interdisciplinarios). Tori lives in Peru with her husband, where she seeks to live out values of hospitality, justice, and simplicity locally. She works as the Director of Operations for INFEMIT (International Fellowship for Mission as Transformation) and as the Administrative Assistant for CETI.

Viv Grigg

Viv Grigg is a New Zealander and a prophetic voice among the poor of the slums, focused on multiplying poor people's churches and community organizations in Manila, Kolkata, São Paulo, and Los Angeles. He has catalysed networks of communities of workers (apostolic orders) in the slums of over forty emerging mega-cities, creating a plethora of organizations that transform poverty. Viv Grigg is the author of *Companion to the Poor*, *Spirit of Christ and the Postmodern City*, *Slumdwellers' Pedagogy*, among others. These have been seminal for new paradigms of incarnational mission among the urban poor, the new Western apostolic orders, transformative city-wide revival, and economic discipleship. Viv Grigg is Professor of Urban Leadership at William Carey International University, multiplying the MA in Transformational Urban Leadership in universities globally (www.matul.org).

Sheryl Haw

Sheryl Haw is the former International Director of Micah Global (www.micahglobal.org). She has spent over twenty-eight years working with communities around the world to address relief, development, and justice concerns. Her career has included Operations Director for Medair, Accountability Development Manager for HAP International, lecturer at All Nations Christian College, and, for the last nine years, International Director of Micah Global (representing a merger between Micah Network and Micah Challenge). Sheryl was privileged to grow up in Zimbabwe surrounded by examples of amazing resilience that have inspired a persistent pursuit of justice for all.

Helen Heather

Up until June 2019, Helen Heather worked at Tearfund leading an international campaign, working with many organizations across the world. She also helped to lead climate change campaigning for over a decade. She is now taking a break from paid work to spend time with her children.

Graham Joseph Hill

Graham Joseph Hill is Interim Principal and Director of Research at Stirling Theological College (University of Divinity) in Melbourne, Australia. He has planted and pastored churches, and been in theological education for twenty years. Graham is the author or editor of nine books including *Global Church* (IVP, 2016), *Healing Our Broken Humanity* (IVP, 2018, with Grace Ji-Sun Kim), *Salt, Light and a City* (Cascade, 2017 and 2020), *Hide This in Your Heart* (NavPress, 2020, with Michael Frost), and *Hold Up Half the Sky* (Cascade, 2020). He also directs the Global Church Project (www.theglobalchurchproject.com).

Sara Kandiah

Sara Kandiah has worked within the faith-based international development sector with organizations such as Tearfund, Coventry Cathedral, The Leprosy Mission International (TLMI), and A Rocha UK. Sara has recently focused on climate justice in recognition of the drastic impact climate change is having today on people and planet. As a keen champion of the church, Sara spends her time connecting with churches around the UK to address climate injustice and mobilizing them to share a message of hope in uncertain times.

Fiona Kelling and Joel Kelling

As a result of regional conflict, the indigenous and migrant Christian populations of the Middle East are in need of support. A third of Jordan's population are refugees from Syria, Iraq, and Palestine, and Jordan has become a regional hub for the response to ongoing humanitarian crises. Joel Kelling works with the Anglican Alliance and the Anglican Province of Jerusalem and the Middle East, covering the dioceses of Cyprus and the Gulf, Egypt and North Africa, Iran, and Jerusalem. He is building the capacity of churches within the region and facilitating the educational, health, and youth development activities across the province. He is also strengthening relationships between the diverse Christian communities. Fiona Kelling is hoping to use her experience in humanitarian response to support refugee and marginalized populations currently residing in Jordan. She is currently volunteering with the Urban Shalom Society in an administrative role.

Jané Mackenzie

Jané Mackenzie is Tearfund's Resilience Programme Manager. She started in Tearfund's advocacy team working with networks in the UK to mobilize faith communities to campaign. From there she moved to coordinate research and learning around Tearfund's international work with churches and communities, focusing on Asia, inclusion, and resilience. She has a passion to see those most marginalized and invisible to church and society be brought to the centre, both in her own community in London and in the global work she does at Tearfund.

Melba Padilla Maggay

A writer and a social anthropologist, Melba Padilla Maggay holds a doctorate in Philippine studies, a Master's degree in English literature, and a first degree in mass communication. A specialist in intercultural communication, she was research fellow on the subject at the University of Cambridge under the auspices of Tyndale House, applying it to the question of culture and theology. She has lectured on this and other cross-cultural issues worldwide, including a stint as Northrup Visiting Professor at Hope College, Michigan, and Visiting Lecturer at All Nations Christian College in England. As founder and long-time director of the Institute for Studies in Asian Church and Culture, she was cited for her outstanding leadership in organizing the evangelical Protestant presence at the EDSA barricades during the February People Power Uprising in 1986. As a social anthropologist, Dr Maggay is resource speaker and consultant on culture, social change, and development issues. A frequent speaker and participant-expert in international conferences, Dr Maggay travels widely and has had cross-cultural experience in over forty countries on all five continents.

Chris McDonald

Chris McDonald is Tearfund's Resilience Adviser and, as Resilience and Livelihoods Unit lead, manages a small team of technical specialists. He has worked in non-profit international development for twenty years, in Africa, Asia, and the UK, working with World Vision, Medair, and The Leprosy Mission International, as well as several short consultancies. He is passionate about exploring ways to help build people's ability to thrive despite disaster hazards, and to adapt to the effects of climate change.

Peter McVerry

While working as a priest in the inner city in Dublin, Fr Peter McVerry SJ encountered some homeless children and opened a hostel for them in 1979. The organization he started is now called Peter McVerry Trust. It has twenty-five hostels with a thousand homeless people staying every night, four hundred apartments where homeless people or families can have a home for life, four drug treatment centres, and a drop-in centre. He has written about his experience in the book *The Meaning Is in the Shadows*. Subsequent publications were *Jesus: Social Revolutionary?* and *The God of Mercy, the God of the Gospels*.

Jocabed Reina Solano Miselis

Jocabed Reina Solano Miselis is from the Gunadule nation, an indigenous people which is one of seven original ethnic groups in Panama. She works as co-director of Indigenous Memory – http://www.memoriaindigena.org. Jocabed is currently studying a Master's degree in the Community of Interdisciplinary Theological Studies, and she is part of the team called "Identity, Indigeneity, and Interculturality" within the Latin American Theological Fraternity. Her mother is Reina Miselis and her father is Guillermo Solano. She has three sisters (Yamileth, Yaneth, and Miriam), two brothers-in-law, Jonathan and John, and two nieces, Zoe and Giah. One of her dreams is to continue serving among the church of Abya Yala, recognizing that we need to dialogue and listen to these diverse and important voices. Learn more about Jocabed and support her work at http://uwm.org/missionaries/31569/.

Patrick Mitchel

Dr Patrick Mitchel is Director of Learning at the Irish Bible Institute in Dublin where he teaches theology. He has been involved in theological education and church development in the Republic of Ireland for nearly thirty years. He blogs at Faith in Ireland and is author of a new volume in the Bible Speaks Today: Bible Themes series, *The Message of Love*. He is married to Ines and they have two grown-up daughters.

Florence Muindi

Dr Florence Muindi is considered the industry leader in community development work. A native of Kenya, Dr Florence is the founder and president of Life In Abundance International, a non-profit organization committed to bringing health to the poor through the local church in Africa and the Caribbean. She is a trained medical doctor, specializing in public health interventions, and has a diploma in Urban Poor Theology. She regularly speaks and writes about empowerment of the vulnerable and sustainable transformation. After serving as a missionary in Ethiopia, she now lives with her family in Kenya.

D. Zac Niringiye

David Zac Niringiye (PhD) is a bishop in the Church of Uganda (Anglican tradition). He is social-justice activist and Senior Fellow with the Institute for Religion, Faith, and Culture in Public Life (INTERFACE) in Uganda, and a Visiting Fellow at Fuller Theological Seminary, Pasadena, California. He previously served as the Assistant Bishop of Kampala Diocese in the Church of Uganda. He is the author of *The Church: God's Pilgrim People*.

Jim Oehrig

Jim Oehrig is Vice President of Integral Mission at American Leprosy Missions. He develops partnerships and collaborations with Christian organizations and churches in communities where American Leprosy Missions works, and ensures the organization implements programmes in ways that honour God and uphold people's dignity. Enabling others' success inspires and delights him. Jim's expertise includes community health development, capacity cultivation, NGOs, member care, and inter-organizational collaboration. He has lived in six different countries on three continents, and has hands-on operational experience in seventy-five countries across Central and South America, sub-Saharan Africa, and South Asia.

James Pender

James Pender works with The Leprosy Mission England and Wales where he has had responsibility for supporting projects in Bangladesh, Nepal, Mozambique, India, Myanmar, and Sri Lanka. He is also The Leprosy Mission Global Fellowship's lead on integral mission and church engagement across the twenty-nine member countries in Europe, Oceania, Africa, and Asia. Previously he was a mission partner for ten years, working with the Church of Bangladesh Social Development Programme with foci on safe water provision, anti-human trafficking, and climate change adaptation. He also worked on Creation Care with A Rocha, including assisting in the foundation of A Rocha, Ghana.

Johannes Reimer

Johannes Reimer was born in 1955 in the former Soviet Union and became a believer during adolescence. In 1976, he moved to Germany with his family. Johannes studied theology in Wiedenest, Hamburg (Germany), and Fresno (USA), and became a pastor in 1985. In 1986, he founded the missions organization LOGOS International with a focus on Eastern Europe. In 1995, he gained his doctor of theology and was called to be Professor of Missiology in 1997 at the UNISA (South Africa). Johannes has a big heart for church planting and reformation. He is involved as counsellor and international speaker and has written more than twenty books and a variety of articles. He chairs the

Network for Education and Research in Europe (GBFE). Johannes is on the Micah Global Panel of Reference.

Manavala Reuben

Manavala Reuben is an Indian Christian leader who worked as a pharmacist at Christian Medical College and Hospital, Vellore, Tamil Nadu, South India, from 1974 to 1984 and served as a mission worker in Northern India from 1984 to 1997 for the mission organization called Navjeevan Seva Mandal, a sister concern of Friends Missionary Prayer Band. Reuben moved to Singapore to do theological studies at Discipleship Training Centre from 1997 to 1999, and from 2000 to 2001 at Theological College for Asia, obtaining an MA in Intercultural Studies. Since 2002, Reuben has been serving among grassroots international workers as a ministry staff worker.

Amy Reynolds

Amy Reynolds is an associate professor of sociology at Wheaton College (IL, USA). Her research focuses primarily on the intersections of the global church, economic globalization, development, and gender inequality. She is the author of *Free Trade and Faithful Globalization* (Cambridge, 2014), which examines how Christian communities in the Americas have engaged in trade policy debates. She coordinates the Wheaton Network Initiative on Gender, Development, and Christianity, which aims to advance the work of holistic development that promotes gender justice.

CB Samuel

CB Samuel is an itinerant Bible teacher focusing on spiritual, missional, and leadership formation. CB and his wife Selina live in Delhi and minister among university students, young adults, and families. While CB has developed a global ministry, teaching frequently in Asia, the USA, and Australia, he and his wife Selina remain strongly engaged in integral mission in India. They have a particular passion for building and strengthening younger leaders in their spiritual formation and their mission engagement. CB serves as a Theological Adviser for both EFICOR and Micah Global.

Anna Savelle

Anna Savelle is Special Projects Coordinator at Jennings County Economic Development Commission. Prior to that she served in the ESJ School of World Mission and Evangelism at Asbury Theological Seminary.

Arshinta Soemarsono

Arshinta Soemarsono is the Director of YAKKUM Outreach Units (called Extramural) in Indonesia. She has twenty years of experience working on development and humanitarian issues. She has worked in organizations responding to small as well as major disasters across Indonesia. Arshinta has worked in various roles in the ACT Alliance, including on the governing board from 2010 to 2018, as a former member of the Rapid Support Team, and as a current member of the Membership and Nomination Committee. Holding a Master's in Public Health from the Gadjah Mada University, Arshinta does research into community resilience during disasters (including the Merapi volcanic eruption and the Mentawai tsunami). She has also been involved in scoping studies for persons with psychosocial disability in Yogyakarta, and disability studies in Nias. Arshinta currently serves on the executive board of JAKOMKRIS, the Christian community network in Indonesia for disaster management.

Fennelien Stal

Fennelien Stal is Impact and Learning Coordinator and country lead for Indonesia and the Philippines at Tear Netherlands. In this role, she manages church and community mobilization (CCM) and disaster risk reduction (DRR) in Indonesia and the Philippines as well as humanitarian response projects when disaster strikes. In 2016, Fennelien worked together with Yayasan Sion on the research initiative to analyse the context, possibilities, and relevance of starting a DRR network. This resulted in the foundation of JAKOMKRIS in 2017. Fennelien has a Bachelor's and a Master's degree in Cultural Anthropology from the VU University Amsterdam.

Andrew Steere

Andrew is a management and engineering adviser supporting individuals and organizations working in resource-limited contexts. Projects and leadership teams he supports have won multiple industry awards for innovation and successful project delivery. Andrew and his family have lived in Kijabe, Kenya, since 2011, where his wife, Mardi, is a paediatric emergency physician at Kijabe Hospital. He is a PhD candidate at the London School of Theology in Biblical Studies and Contextual Theology, and holds degrees in civil engineering (BSc, George Washington University), physics (MSc, Michigan State University), and theology (MDiv, University of Divinity).

Debora Suparni

Debora Suparni is the Director of Yayasan Sion in Salatiga, Central Java, Indonesia, for the period 2015–2020. She has a Master's in International Diaconic Management from Protestant University in Wuppertal, Bethel, Germany. Formerly, she was the head of Community Development Division from 2010 to 2015, with the unit of Disaster Management Response as her responsibility. She has experience working in the area of disasters, such as the earthquake of Yogyakarta in May 2006, the Merapi eruption in 2010, and the tsunami in Mentawai on October 2011. She was appointed to the board of JAKOMKRIS (Christian community network in Indonesia for disaster management) from 2016 to 2019, then elected to the executive board for the period 2019–2022.

Nikki Toyama-Szeto

As Executive Director of Evangelicals for Social Action (ESA), Nikki Toyama-Szeto guides the execution of ESA's mission and vision. Nikki came to ESA with a long history of working with leaders of faith communities to help ignite a passion for biblical justice among the global church. As an educator and advocate, she is passionate about gender issues, racial justice, refugees/displaced peoples, and fighting poverty. She speaks and trains leaders globally. Past engagements include speaking for Tearfund (Nepal) and Centro Esdras (Guatemala), CCDA (USA), and Billy Graham Center (USA). She writes and speaks from her experiences as a leader in organizations like International Justice Mission, the Urbana Conference, and InterVarsity Christian Fellowship. She served on the Third Lausanne Congress (2010), helping to develop the plenary programme. Nikki Toyama-Szeto was a co-editor of the book *More Than Serving Tea* (IVP, 2006), a collection of essays, stories, and poems looking at the intersection of race, gender, and faith for Asian American women. She also co-wrote *Partnering with the Global Church* (IVP, 2012) with Femi Adeleye and edited the *Urbana Onward* series. Additionally, she is a co-author of *The God of Justice: IJM Institute's Global Church Curriculum* (IVP, 2015).

Sandra Maria Van Opstal

Sandra Maria Van Opstal, a second-generation Latina, pastors at Grace and Peace Community on the West Side of Chicago. She is a preacher, liturgist, and activist who is reimagining the intersection of worship and justice. In her fifteen years with InterVarsity Christian Fellowship, Sandra has mobilized thousands of college students for God's mission of reconciliation and justice in the world. Sandra served as Director of Worship for the Urbana Missions Conference, Chicago Urban Program Director, Latino National Leadership Team (LaFe), and Northwestern University Team leader (multi-ethnic fellowship). Sandra's influence has also reached many others through her leadership and preaching on topics such as worship and formation, justice, racial identity and reconciliation, and global mission. Sandra Maria Van Opstal has been published in multiple journals and has authored *God's Graffiti Devotional*, *Still Evangelical*, *The Mission of Worship*, and *The Next Worship*.

Geoff Whiteman and Kristina Whiteman

Geoff Whiteman, MA, ThM, is an Orthodox Christian, couple's counsellor, and resiliency researcher who is passionate about God's mission in the world. Kristina Whiteman, MA, is a PhD candidate at Asbury Theological Seminary, focusing on resiliency research. Married since 2003, they encourage global workers to be united in marriage and resilient in ministry. They began serving in vocational ministry in 2000 and have been supporting global workers since 2007. They currently serve as the Mission Specialists in Missionary Care and Training for the Orthodox Christian Mission Center (OCMC) and as the founders of ResilientMissionary.org and ResilientGlobalWorker.org which disseminate the results of the Resilient Global Worker Study through innovative solutions to support global workers and those concerned with enhancing global worker resiliency. Download the results of the study and connect with Geoff at linktr.ee/geoffwhiteman.

Mari Williams

Mari Williams is a freelance researcher and writer. She has worked in international development for more than fifteen years and is passionate about producing resources that seek to equip communities and challenge decision-makers on issues related to climate change, environmental sustainability, poverty, and justice.

Sue Willsher

Sue Willsher is the Senior Policy Adviser at Tearfund, where she has worked for eleven years. She has done research and lobbying on a range of issues including clean energy and water and sanitation. She led on the publication of Tearfund's "Restorative Economy" paper, which set out a vision for Tearfund's global advocacy today.

He has shown you, O man, what is good. And what does the Lord require of you? To act justly and to love mcery and to walk humbly with your God. Micah 6:8

Micah's Vision
Communities living life in all its fullness, free from poverty, injustice and conflict.

Micah's Mission
Rooted in the Gospel we become agents of change in our communities by being:

- **Catalysts** for transforming mission by promoting and living out **integral mission**
- A **movement** that advocates for poverty reduction, justice, equality, reconciliation and safety and wellbeing for all
- A **network** providing a platform for shared learning, collective reflection and action, inspiration and mobilisation of the Church, and the demonstration of Integral Mission.

Why Does Micah Exist?
Micah exists to be a catalyst, a movement and a network for **transforming mission**, with a special focus on enabling a united response to reducing poverty, addressing injustice and enabling reconciliation and conflict resolution.

We believe that Jesus came to give life in all its fullness (John 10:10). We believe that God has called out his church (*ecclesia*) to be his body, his representatives, his servants and demonstrate the new Kingdom in word and deed. We call this **integral mission**.

To learn more about Micah Global see: www.micahglobal.org
Find us on Facebook: www.facebook.com/MicahNetwork
Follow us on Twitter: @MicahGlobal
Enjoy our Instagram: www.instagram.com/micahglobal

Micah Global Secretariat
Email: info@micahglobal.org

Langham Literature and its imprints are a ministry of Langham Partnership.

Langham Partnership is a global fellowship working in pursuit of the vision God entrusted to its founder John Stott –

> *to facilitate the growth of the church in maturity and Christ-likeness through raising the standards of biblical preaching and teaching.*

Our vision is to see churches in the Majority World equipped for mission and growing to maturity in Christ through the ministry of pastors and leaders who believe, teach and live by the word of God.

Our mission is to strengthen the ministry of the word of God through:
- nurturing national movements for biblical preaching
- fostering the creation and distribution of evangelical literature
- enhancing evangelical theological education

especially in countries where churches are under-resourced.

Our ministry

Langham Preaching partners with national leaders to nurture indigenous biblical preaching movements for pastors and lay preachers all around the world. With the support of a team of trainers from many countries, a multi-level programme of seminars provides practical training, and is followed by a programme for training local facilitators. Local preachers' groups and national and regional networks ensure continuity and ongoing development, seeking to build vigorous movements committed to Bible exposition.

Langham Literature provides Majority World preachers, scholars and seminary libraries with evangelical books and electronic resources through publishing and distribution, grants and discounts. The programme also fosters the creation of indigenous evangelical books in many languages, through writer's grants, strengthening local evangelical publishing houses, and investment in major regional literature projects, such as one volume Bible commentaries like *The Africa Bible Commentary* and *The South Asia Bible Commentary*.

Langham Scholars provides financial support for evangelical doctoral students from the Majority World so that, when they return home, they may train pastors and other Christian leaders with sound, biblical and theological teaching. This programme equips those who equip others. Langham Scholars also works in partnership with Majority World seminaries in strengthening evangelical theological education. A growing number of Langham Scholars study in high quality doctoral programmes in the Majority World itself. As well as teaching the next generation of pastors, graduated Langham Scholars exercise significant influence through their writing and leadership.

To learn more about Langham Partnership and the work we do visit **langham.org**

www.ingramcontent.com/pod-product-compliance
Lightning Source LLC
Chambersburg PA
CBHW050428240426
43661CB00055B/2304